William Retlaw Williams

The parliamentary history of the county of Oxford, including the city and university of Oxford

William Retlaw Williams

The parliamentary history of the county of Oxford, including the city and university of Oxford

ISBN/EAN: 9783337152574

Printed in Europe, USA, Canada, Australia, Japan

Cover: Foto ©ninafisch / pixelio.de

More available books at **www.hansebooks.com**

THE

PARLIAMENTARY HISTORY

OF THE

COUNTY OF OXFORD,

INCLUDING THE

CITY AND UNIVERSITY OF OXFORD,

AND THE

BOROUGHS OF BANBURY, BURFORD, CHIPPING
NORTON, DADINGTON, WITNEY, AND WOODSTOCK,

From the EARLIEST TIMES to the PRESENT DAY

1213—1899,

WITH BIOGRAPHICAL AND GENEALOGICAL
NOTICES OF THE MEMBERS.

———

By W. R. WILLIAMS,

AUTHOR OF

"WORCESTERSHIRE MEMBERS," AND "GLOUCESTER-
SHIRE MEMBERS."

———

BRECKNOCK

Privately Printed for the Author by EDWIN DAVIES.

———

1899.

TO THE PRESENT

REPRESENTATIVES IN PARLIAMENT

OF

OXFORDSHIRE,

THIS RECORD OF THE SERVICES

OF THEIR

Predecessors during SIX CENTURIES is most
respectfully

DEDICATED.

.

186

INTRODUCTION

THIS Work being the fifth of the series of Parliamentary Histories, little fresh need be said in the way of introduction, otherwise than to point out a few salient features especially relating to the record of Members for the County of Oxford, which important shire, so rich in historical interests, still remains with its County History yet unwritten, as if the abundance of Books describing the history and antiquities of the University and its Colleges had overshadowed all else in the county besides. And yet one branch of the subject alone—its Members of Parliament—cannot but possess for the historian and antiquarian alike objects of the greatest interest, for among its Representatives during the last six centuries Oxfordshire has elected to Parliament members of such ancient families as those of Williamescote, Elsefield, Nowers, Abberbury, Wace, Barentyne, Quatermayns, and Feteplace, now long extinct, Harcourt, Stonor, and' Norreys, Fiennes and Knollys which still exist, and among more modern names those of Doyly, Cope, Wenman, Jenkinson, Dashwood, Spencer, Churchill, Herbert, Stapleton, Lee, Parker, North, Annesley, and Fane.

The earlier Knights of the Shire were often literally " belted Knights " for prowess on many a hard fought field or expedition in France or Scotland ; they held their lands by actual tenure of Knight-service, and so doing were granted " Protection when abroad on the King's service," and by their valorous deeds obtained the King's pardon for their slayings and robberies; and at home acted as Sheriffs, Escheators, or Coroners or were placed in Commissions of the Peace, of Oyer and Terminer, of Subsidy, or of Array. Several of them were the " King's Servants," as ' Esquires ' or ' Yeomen,' and as such shewed themselves thorough courtiers by the grants of forfeited lands or annuities which they obtained from successive Monarchs. William le Marescbal was a Purveyor of the King's Stables. Thomas Chaucer was the King's Chief Butler, as well as an Ambassador, and Speaker of the House. Danvers (a contemporary of Jack Cade), was Chief Justice of the Common Pleas. During those rough and stormy times it is not surprising to find that Ralph Chastiloun died from the effects of a violent affray with another Member, Sir Ralph de Nowers, while Sir Robert Harcourt was slain by the Staffords.

In later times it was Sir John Williams of Thame who proclaimed Queen Mary at Oxford in 1553, and afterwards took a prominent part in Archbishop Cranmer's martyrdom. His colleague Sir John Pollard was Speaker in the House. George Owen was Physician to three of the Tudors. Of Courtiers there were Sir Francis Knollys, and his son the Earl of Banbury, Lord Norreys, Edward Wraye, and the Earls of Godolphin and Lichfield. Of Soldiers and Sailors there were Sir John Norris, Sir Andrew Dudley, and Major Weyland, a hero of Waterloo. Lord Charles Spencer was Vice Treasurer of Ireland, and Joseph Warner Henley was President of the Board of Trade. Sir Lawrence Tanfield was made Lord Chief Baron of the Exchequer. Sir Francis Maclean is the present Chief Justice of Bengal.

Sir Anthony Cope suffered imprisonment in the Tower in 1587 for making an unwelcome motion in the House. James Fiennes and Viscount Wenman were secluded by Col. Pride's Purge in 1648, the latter being also imprisoned for some time. More advanced in their opinions were the Commonwealth Members, Sir Charles Wolseley, one of the Major Generals, Dr. Goddard, physician to Cromwell's army, William Lenthall the Speaker of the famous Long Parliament, Lieut. Gen. Charles Fleetwood, Lord Deputy of Ireland and Cromwell's son-in-law, and Nathaniel Fiennes, a Commissioner of the Great Seal. William Knollys and Thomas Horde the Royalists were among those who compounded and were fined for delinquency, and Sir William Walter had to pay an assessment to the Parliament's coffers.

The most noted of the Oxfordshire elections was that of 1754, when each side is said to have expended £40000, upon the contest and petition which followed. The political opinions of the various Members during the eighteenth century are the result of the special researches of the Rev. A. B. Beavan, M.A., who has also very kindly revised the portion relating to Woodstock. Due mention must be made of the assistance derived from the various parochial histories, and from such standard works as the *Dictionary of National Biography*, and the *Alumni Oxonienses* of *Wood*, and *Foster*, and the *Patent Rolls*, *Close Rolls*, and *Calendars of State Papers*.

My friend Mr W. Duncombe Pink has again been kind enough to place at my disposal the results of his many years researches into the subject, and I am very greatly indebted to him for the very great assistance he has rendered me. And in conclusion I desire to return my most grateful acknowledgments to those Noblemen and Gentlemen, who have so kindly comprised the list of Subscribers to this Work, and to express a hope that it may prove worthy of their support.

W. R. WILLIAMS,

Talybont, Brecknock.

1st June 1899.

MEMBERS FOR OXFORDSHIRE.

1213, 1226, 1254, 1261, 1265, 1275, Jan. and Sept. 1283. No Returns found. The Parliament of 1265 appears to have been the first complete Parliament consisting of elected Knights, Citizens, and Burgesses, but even in later years, as in 1290, 1294, 1297, 1300, and 1316, the original custom was again adverted to of summoning only Knights of the Shire to form the Parliament.

1290. Johannes fil' Gwydon'.

Ricardus de Wyllamescot'.

The Returns were generally filled in in Latin until the reign of Queen Elizabeth commenced. Sir Robert fil' Guidon was M.P. co.Warwick 1307, as was this Johannes filuis Gwydonis in 1298. Sir Richard de Williamscote of Kiddington, son of Thomas de W., was lord of the manors and advowsons of Kiddington and Asterley, and m. Joan dau. of Robert Foliot, lord of Birckmarsh, co. Warwick. He presented to Asterley 1288, was Sheriff of Oxon and Berks for the first half of the year 19 Edw. I. (1291), but died during his Shrievalty. The following references to him appear in the *Patent Rolls* :—23 Jan. 1282, Licence for Rd. de Wyliamescote to hold during the minority of the heir, the custody of the lands and of the heir of Thomas de Langele, deceased, tenant in chief, together with the custody of the forest of Wicchewod, in the form in which it was granted to Thomas de Maydenhaith, king's yeoman, who has demised it to the said Richard. 1285, Commission to Rd. de Wylliamescote and three others to deliver the gaol of Oxford of Robert Bone, put in exigent after the last eyre in the county of Oxford for receiving stolen goods, who has since surrendered. Another Commission to him and three others 24 April 1285 to deliver Oxford gaol of Thomas de Rothewell who was put in exigent etc. for harbouring felons: another one 23 Nov. 1285 to deliver the gaol of the castle of Walingeford of William Fowel for larceny ; and Commission 10 Jan. 1287 to R. W. and three others to enforce the articles of the statute made at Winchester (13 Edw. I.) for the preservation of the peace in co. Oxford.

1294. (Four members). Return lost.

1295. Robert Pogeys.

John de Elsefeld.

Robert Pogeys of Stoke Pogeys was again M.P. Oxon 1302, and for Bucks March 1300, 1301, 1312, (but in 1301 Gerard de Braybrok was elected in his stead, because " Robertus Pogeys, miles, qui ad parliamentum ultimo praeteritum venit infirmus est.") He was made a Commr. of the Peace for Bucks 24 Dec. 1307, and 17 March 1308, and was one of those appointed to hold an enquiry touching forestalling and other offences in Bucks, 17 March, 1 Edw. 2. (1308), and to hear the cases in Beds and Bucks of forestallers and transgressors 16 Dec. 1310. As Sir R. Pugey Knt. he witnessed in Aug. 1285 the *inspeximus* and confirmation of a charter of Eleanor, the king's mother, granting to Edmund, the king's brother, houses and land in London, and as Sir R. Pogeys witnessed another grant 14 April 1292. His dau. and co-heir Margaret m. John Mauditt of Somerford. Pardon dated Woodstock 14 May 1310 to John Brun of Rollondrith for the death of Adam de Sutton, as it appears by the record of John Randolf and Robert Pugeys, justices of gaol delivery of the late King for Oxford, that he killed him in self-defence.

John de Elsefeld again sat for Oxon 1301, 1302, 1309, 1311, and was app. a Commr. of the Peace for the county (as Elsefeud) 24 Dec. 1307, one of those app. to hold an enquiry touching forestalling and other offences in Oxon 17ᵗ March 1308, and to hear the cases in Northants, Oxon, and Berks of forestallers and transgressors 16 Dec. 1310. Appointment 4 Dec. 1295 of John de Elsefeld Knt. and another to assess and collect in co. Oxford the eleventh and seventh on moveables recently graciously granted in aid of the present war. J. de E. and two others were app. 10 May 1300 in co. Oxford to hear and determine complaints of transgressions against Magna Carta and the Forest Charter of Hen. 3, and to punish offenders by imprisonment ransom or amercement. On 14 April 1308, Commission of oyer and terminer issued to him and Roger de Bella Fago concerning an assault at Abyndon, Berks, and on 18 Dec. 1309 he and Gilbert Wace and another were app. to enquire touching all prises taken in co. Oxford for the King's use or for the use of other persons, contrary to the statute made in Parliament at Stamford. *(Patent Rolls).* On 14 May 1308 John and Gilbert de Elsefeld, Knights, were among the witnesses to the Enrolment of a grant by Peter de Gavaston, Earl of Cornwall, to the King, of his manors of Crokham and Leychamsted, Berks. *(Close Rolls)* 10 March 1312, Grant to J. de E. of 100 marks a year, to be received by him at the Exchequer, until the King shall provide him with lands and rents to the value of 100 marks a year. 18 Oct. 1312, Grant to J. E. for life in satisfaction of the last grant of the manor of Idenne, Sussex, which is extended at £7 2 11½, and 2½ lbs of pepper, with 1½ lb of cumin, and several other lands in Totenham, Middlesex and elsewhere extended at £54 and 8 marks a year. 1 May 1313, Licence at the request of J. E. for the prior and convent of Great Massingham to acquire in mortmain lands and rents to the value of £10 a year.

1296. Return lost.

1297. Henry de Bruyli.

John de Prewes.

Henry de Bruilly was made a Commr, of the Peace for Oxon 20 Jan. 1287, and was again M.P. 1298, as was his colleague 1301.

1298. William de Scalebrok'.

Henry de Bruly.

On 28 June 1301 William de Scalebrok, Thomas Parco, and Henry de Brully, Knights, were witnesses of Morpeth to the *Inspeximus* of a Charter dated 5 June, 29 Edw. I. whereby Ralph Pippard granted and confirmed to Sir Hugh le Despencer his whole manor of Great Haselee, co. Oxford. W. de S. was one of the three app. 1 Nov. 1301 to assess and levy in Oxon the fifteenth lately granted to the King. He again sat for the county 1306, 1307, 1309, 1311, and 1312. Pardon, dated Woodstock 14 May 1310, to William Hert of Hervynton for the death of John Basely as it appears by the record of John de Foxle and Wliliam de Scalebroke, justices of gaol delivery for Oxford, that he killed him in self-defence. (*Patent Rolls*). 7 Jan. 1317, Order to the Sheriff of Oxford to cause a Coroner for that county to be elected in the place of William de Scalebrok deceased. (*Close Rolls.*)

1300. March. ⎫
1300. May. ⎬ No Returns found.

1301. John de Elsefeld.

John de Pratell.

The latter is given as John de Prewes in the Enrolment of the Writ de Expensis. (See 1297).

1302. John de Elseffeld.

Robert Pogeis.

1305. Sir Roger de Burghefeld.

Sir Giles de Insula.

Sir Roger was M.P. Berks 1301, and Oxon 1305, 1306, and probably derived his name from his property at Burfield, Berks. 9 March 1327, Order to Wm. Trussel, escheator, this side Trent not to intermeddle further with the lands of Roger de Burghefeld and to restore the issues thereof, as it appears by inquisition that Roger held no lands in chief on the day of his death of the late King, but that he held divers lands of other lords by various services. (*Close Rolls.*)

Many of the de Insula family are mentioned in the *Patent Rolls* 1281-1301, and Sir John de Insula was made a Baron of the Exchequer 1295. Several of them were in the Church, one of them being Archdeacon of Exeter and Wells. On 28 Nov. 1307 Giles de Insula and Roger de Englefeld were app., together with a clerk to be app. by them, and for whom they were responsible, to assess and collect the twentieth and fifteenth for the county of Oxford granted to the King

1306.   Sir Roger de Burghfeld.

             Sir William de Scalebrok.

1307. Jan.   John de Hynton.

             William de Skelbrok

The Sheriff of Oxford and Berks made no Return, but these two came for the county of Oxford. Hugh de Hynton going with Adam de Nortoft to Wales on the King's service, received Protection 24 June 1287. Grant to John de Hynton, King's yeoman, 23 Jan. 1310, of the reversion of the forestership in the forest of Hunts granted for life by the late King to John Pycard, or as soon as for any reasonable cause it falls into the King's hands. Grant to J. de H. of that office 24 Oct. 1310 upon the surrender of J.P. (*Patent Rolls.*) He was apparently dead before 1 Oct. 1311, when the *Close Rolls* makes mention of Margaret late the wife of J. de H. Probably father of John de Hynton, lord of Hynton, who presented Geoffrey Norton to the Church in the manor of Hynton, 5 April 1339

1307. Oct.   William de Scalebrok.

             John de Hynton.

1308.   Return lost.

1309.   John de Elsefeld.

             William de Scalebrok.

1311. Aug.   Sir W. de Scalebrok, miles.

             John de Elseteud, or Ellesfeld.

1211. Nov.   Sir W. de Scalebrok, miles.

             Sir John de Elsefeld, miles.

1312. July. William de Scalebrok.

             John de Croxford.

The latter was son of John de C., and was again M.P. 1316, 1318, 1320, 1321, 1324, 1345. He was a defendant in a suit, the King *versus* Croxford and others, in which the King recovered the presentations of the Church of Blechesdon, calends of May 1311. On 1 Dec. 1319 the *Close Rolls* refers to him as late escheator in co. Oxford. 28 Feb. 1320, Enrolment of obligation of J. de Croxford, sub-escheator in cos. Oxford and Berks, to Sir

Richard de Rodneye, escheator this side Trent, for £50, to be paid in St. Paul's, London, at Michaelmas and the Purification next.

    1313. March. John Bardolf.

                       John le Myrie.

5 May 1317, Order to the Sheriff of Oxford to cause a coroner for that county to be elected in place of John Bardolf, lately elected, who cannot conveniently attend to the duties of the office, as he resides in the counties ef Norfolk and Leicester for the greater part of the year. (*Close Rolls*)

    1313. July. John Bardolf.

                      Ralph Chasteloun.

28 Oct. 1319, Order to the Sheriff of Oxford to cause a coroner for that county to be elected in place of Ralph de Chastiloun who cannot attend to the duties of the office as he is continually occupied in the office of verderer in the forest of Wuchewode. (*Close Rolls*). 1 Oct. 1337, Appointment of Wm. de Eyte, King's Serjeant at Arms, to take to the King's gaol of Oxford Castle, and there deliver into the custody of the sheriff of the county, Roger de Nowers Knt. (see 1320), and John his son, now imprisoned in the prison of the Marshalsea of the Household for the death of Ralph de Chasteleyn, late one of the King's coroners for the county of Oxford, at Keyngham. Malcolm Chastiloun was M.P. for Bucks 1327, *et sequitur*.

    1313. Sept. John Bardolf.

                      Ralph de Chastillon, or Chastyllon.

    1314. April. Return lost.

    1314. Sept. Robert de Arderne.

                      John de Chaumpaigne.

Licence 3 Dec. 1311 (by fine of 60s.) for Robert son of Adam de Dounhalle to grant a messuage and one carucate of land in Hanebergh held in chief to John de Chaumpagne and Nicholaa his wife for their lives with remainder over to the grantor and his heirs. On 8 Feb. 1323 John Chaumpagne acknowledged that he owed 10 marks to John de Moleyns, to be levied in default of payment of his lands and chattels in Hants and Oxon.

Robert de Arderne lived at Wickham, and owned Drayton where he had a charter of free warren in 1317, and much other property thereabouts. In 1322 he was app. Commr. to array the forces of Oxon and Berks raised against the confederated nobles who opposed the King in the North under the Earl of Lancaster, and the next year was directed to enforce the general array in the county of Oxford, and was also re-app. Commr. of Array with special powers in 1324. The Bishop of Lincoln's Castle of Banbury was given by the King into the keeping of Robert de Arderne 3 Jan. 1322. In 1329 he had a fair at Drayton and view of frankpledge and other liberties there and the same year received, as Sir R. de Arderne Knt., the King's Pardon for all murders etc. He obtained license to fortify his mansion at Wickham 2 May 1330, and died the next year seised of a very fair estate. 11 May 1315, Order to Robert de Kendale, Constable of Dover Castle and Keeper of the Cinque Ports, to permit Robert de Arderne and John le Leyre whom Bartholomew de Badelesmere is sending to parts beyond sea to buy horses for his use, to pass the sea in the port of Dover. Sir Robert de Ardern was Constable of Northampton Castle on 1 Nov. 1317 when he was ordered to put 30 fencible men in that Castle at the King's wages which the King had ordered the Sheriff to pay him by Indenture ; and as such he was ordered to repair the houses and gate and other buildings of the Castle 4 May 1318. On 29 May 1318 he acknowledged that he owed Isabella Bardolf (see 1313) £400 ; to be levied in default of payment of his land and chattels in Northants. This however was cancelled on payment. (*Close Rolls.*)

1315. Sir Richard de Bere.

Thomas Golafre.

The former was app. 26 Aug. 1309 to assess and levy in Oxon the twenty-fifth upon all movable goods for the war in Scotland. Licence 18 Nov. 1312 for the alienation in mortmain to the abbot and convent of St. Augustine's, Canterbury, by Rich. de Bere of 46 acres of land and 4 acres of meadow in Liteburne ; and a further similar licence 18 Nov. 1312 of 70 acres and a moiety of a messuage in Gerneweye, which are extended at 30s. a year. (*Patent Rolls.*) On 13 Sept. 1312 Wm. West acknowledged at Westminister that he owed to Rd. de Bere 40 marks, to be levied etc of his lands and chattels in Middlesex. Order 24 April 1316 to Wm. Merre, keeper of the Abbey of Westminster, void, and in the King's hands, to cause the £10 from the manor of Todenham granted by the abbot and convent by virtue of the late King's letters patent dated 3 Aug. in the 27th year of his reign, to Wm. de Derneford and Cicely his wife for their lives, to be paid to Rd. de Bere, who married the said Cicely. (*Close Rolls.*) He again sat for Oxon 1316, 1324, 1325, and for Beds 1330.

Thomas Golafre was also M.P. for Northampton town Sept. 1313, and 1318, and on 6 April 1322 he and another were app. to levy £100 in co. Oxford to bring it into the King's chamber before the Parliament summoned at York in three weeks from Easter next which they ought to have paid before the Purification last. 6 May 1327, Order to Wm. Trussel, escheator this side Trent, not to distrain Thomas Golafre of Cerleden for homage for the lands that he holds of the King, as the King has granted him respite until Easter next. 12 July 1329, Order to the Sheriff of Oxford to cause a verderer for the forest of Whucchewod to be elected in place of Thomas Golofre who is incapacitated by infirmity and age. (*Close Rolls.*)

1316.	Jan.	John de Croxford.
		John de Chaumpaigne.
1316.	April.	John de Croxford.
		Richard de la Bere.
1316.	July.	(One member only). John de Croxford.
1318.		John de Croxford.
		Adam de la Fenne.

30 Jan. 1318, Order to the Treasurer and Barons of the Exchequer to acquit Wm. de Monte Acuto of certain monies, his father's debts, including 100s. for an unjust detinue against Adam de la Fenne. (*Close Rolls.*)

    1319. John de Bloxham.

           Thomas Blaket.

30 Dec. 1308, Protection during pleasure for John de Bloxham, King's yeoman. Commission of oyer and terminer to certain justices 16 Aug. 1309 on complaint that J. de B. and others by night burned the houses and goods of John de Paskedene at Aylesbury. 10 Nov. 1311, Order to J. de B. to deliver to Robert de Harwedon the manor of Rokerle, Wilts, belonging to the Templars, and the issues of the same received by him, whose lands in that county the King committed to the said John. In Dec. 1311 he was keeper of the lands of the Templars in Oxon and Berks, and of Walter de Langeton in Northants and Oxon; and also keeper of the lands of W. Bishop of Coventry and Lichfield in Oxon, Berks, Northants, and Wilts, until ordered to restore them to the Bishop 20 Jan. 1312. On 13 Sept. 1312 Walter, son of Walter le Ran 'of Agmundesham, acknowledged that he owed John de Bloxham £10, to be levied etc. of his lands in Bucks. He received the honour of Knighthood. 15 Oct. 1337, Protection will clause *volumus* for Thomas Blaket, going with John de Monte Gomeri beyond seas with the King. John Blaket was M.P. for Bucks 1315, 1318, 1327, 1328, as was Thomas Blaket 1332, 1334.

    1320. Roger de Nowers.

           John de Croxford.

Roger de Nowers was M.P. Oxon 1320, 1327, 1328, 1330, and Beds 1328, and on 20 Feb. 1327 acknowledged that he owed 12 marks and 7 shillings to John, Bishop of Ely, to be levied etc.

of his lands and chattels in Oxon : this was however cancelled on payment.   He was keeper of the hundred of Chadelyngton until 22 April 1328 when he was ordered to deliver it to Eleanor late the wife of Hugh le Despencer the younger.   27 Sept. 1334. Pardon in consideration of a fine of 40s. made before Geoffrey le Scrope and Robert de Tanton, to Roger de Nowers for the rescue of cattle and goods of his, which had been seized at Churchill, co. Oxford, for money due to the King, whereof he is impeached before John de Stonore and his fellows, justices of oyer and terminer.   20 Aug. 1336, Appointment of John de Broghton and Gilbert de Chasteleyn to take the following suspected persons and imprison them in the Tower of London, namely Roger de Nowers Knt., and Richard and Roger his sons.

> 1321.   John de Croxford.
> Richard de Burncestr.

The latter is mentioned in *Kennet's Antiquities* as a witness to a deed concerning rents and lands in Burcester 1318, and was of kin to Wm. de Burncestre (Bicester) Mayor of Oxford 4 Oct. 1311, and (as W. de Burcestre) 1317, 1325, 1329-30, 1331, 1332, 1333, 26 Sept. 1334, and (as W. Burchestree) 1339.

> 1322.   May.   John de Bloxham.
> Robert de Trillawe.

The latter acknowledged 22 April 1317 that he owed Simon de Welles 20 marks, to be levied etc. in Oxon.   3 May 1330, Pardon to Thomas de Beaufou and Robert de Trillowe of a recognisance of 100 marks made to Hugh de Despencer, late Earl of Winchester. on their petition, confirmed by Roger de Mortuo Mari, whereby it appears that they made the same to save their lives when imprisoned in the late reign by reason of the quarrel of Thomas then Earl of Lancaster.

> 1322.   Nov.   John de Harecourt.
> John de la Pole, de Sidenham.

John son of Richard de Harecurt was app. a Commr. of the Peace for Oxon 24 Dec. 1307.   Order on 15 Aug. 1314 to him who supplies the place of the Treasurer, and to the Barons of the Exchequer to acquit John de Harecourt, lord of Boseworth, of the service of one Knight's fee for the King's army of Scotland in the seventh year of his reign, as Wm. de Monte Acuto has testified before the King that he had his service in the said army by the King's order.   Sir John de Harcourt of Stanton Harcourt, was the son of Sir Richard of that place (who d. 1293), and was Knighted, with Edward, Prince of Wales, at Whitsuntide 1306, and d. 1330.

> 1324.   Jan.   Gilbert de Ellesfeld.
> William le Mareschal.

Sir Gilbert was brother to the M.P. 1295, (see *Close Rolls* 1313,) and again sat for Oxon 1328. On 21 April 1308 he and Warin de Insula were made Conservators of the Peace for the town of Oxford, and on 1 May writs of aid issued to the Mayor Bailiffs and good men of Oxford, and to the Chancellor of Oxford University, to assist them in that duty. 25 Feb. 1327, License at the request of Roger de Surimerton, for Gilbert de Ellesfeld to impark his wood at Ellesfeld, co. Oxford. 4 May 1327, Writ of aid for G. de E. and Miles de Bello Camfo, app. to arrest Stephen Dunheved and bring him to the castle of Walyngford to be there imprisoned. 24 May 1327, Commission of oyer etc. to G. de E. and others, on complaint that large numbers of malefactors in the counties of Oxford and Berks, confederating together, lately attacked the town and abbey of Abingdon, entered and burnt houses, assaulted and beat the monks and servants of the abbey as well as others, killing some and detaining others in prison until they paid fines for their release, and carried away chalices, vestments, and ornaments of the Church, with other goods.

William le Mareschal was of Crowemersh, and he and Alan le Mareschal (his father,) were mentioned in a Commission dated 11 Nov. 1308 as being charged with others by Edmund de Chauncy with having assaulted him at Wald, Neuton, Lincolnshire, and carried away his goods. (*Patent Rolls.*) On 7 June 1309 Herbert de Marisco and William, son of Richard of Ireland, acknowledged that they owed Wm. Le Mareschal 40 marks, to be levied etc. on their lands in Somerset and in Ireland. (Cancelled on payment). On 17 June 1309, Order to Irish officials to deliver to W. de M. the bailiwick of the Marshalsea of Ireland of his inheritance. Order 20 July 1311 to Nicholas de Segrave and also to W. le M. forbidding them to come to the Parliament with an armed force or otherwise than they were wont to do in the late King's time, as the King understands that they are coming armed on account of dissensions between them. His name also appears in the *Close Rolls* for 1310, as a Knight, as a witness to a release and enrolment; he was placed in a commission of oyer and terminer 18 Sept. 1327; and the *Close Rolls* refer to him in June 1329 as "late Sheriff of Berks." On 24 February 1328, Writ of aid for one year for W. le M. app. a purveyor for the King's Household; on 25 Feb. 1329, Writ of aid for W. le M. app. a purveyor for the royal stables : and on 26 Oct. 1329, a commission of oyer etc. issued on his complaint that John de Urtiaco, Knt., and others carried away £30 of the King's money delivered to him for the purchase of provisions for the King's horses, at the parish of St. Clement without the bar of the New Temple, co. Middlesex. His wife was named Elizabeth.

1324. Oct. Sir Richard de Bere.

1324.   Oct.   John le Croxford, senior.

1325.   Richard de la Bere.

John de Croxford, senior.

1327.   Roger de Nouwers

John de Whitefeld.

23 Sept. 1327, Writ to the Sheriff of Oxford for payment to Richard Nowers (see 1320) and John de Whitefield of £6 16 0 for their expenses for attending the treaty at Lincoln, to wit for 17 days at 4/- a day. On 3 May 1313 J. de W. who with Aymer de Valence, Earl of Pembroke, is going beyond seas, has letters of protection until St. Peter ad Vincula. It appears from the *Close Rolls* of 1321 that J. de W. then held a quarter of a Knight's fee in Loneford, Dorset. He was again M.P. (as a Knight) 1330, 1331.

1328.   Feb.   Roger de Nowers.

James de Wodestoke.

The latter acknowledged on 24 March 1327 that he owed Reginald de Evesham, clerk, £60; to be levied etc. on his lands in Oxon. (Cancelled on payment). On 23 May 1329 Richard Talbot going beyond seas with the King has letters nominating William de Holynes clerk, and James de Wodestoke his attorneys until a fortnight after midsummer. Commission of oyer and terminer to try certain cases issued to the same J. de Wodestoke on 28 Sept. 1334, and 1 June 1337 and on 24 July 1337, he and Rd. Kary of Oxford (see that city 1320) were made Commrs. of oyer on information that Reginald Colt and others broke the sluices of the pond of the King's mills in the suburb of Oxford, and his weir there carried away the timber of the sluices and the earth and stones placed there for the safety of the pond, with the hurdles and palings of the weir. He was again M.P. 1332.

1328.   April.   John le Brumpton.

William le Mareschal.

The former was Sheriff of Oxon (the last part of) 1318,1319, 1320 (the first part of) 1321, 1327, 1328, 1333. On 13 March 1327 a commission of oyer and terminer issued on the complaint of Richard de Louches and John his son (see 1331) that J. de Brumpton and others had carried away their goods at Chiselhampton, Baldindon, St Lawrence, Whatele, and Milton, co. Oxford. In a suit between the Prior of St. Frideswide and Sir John Handlo of Borstall (see 1337) for the manor of Pidington, in Easter term 7 and 8 Edw. 3, the Sheriff returned the names of Sir Wm. Harcourt, Sir John de Brumpton, Sir Richard de Beaufo, and Sir John Miry, who attended in Court and upon their oath elected 13 other Knights (of whom Sir Richard de Abberbury, see

Oct. 1328, was one,) to attend at York at Michaelmas ; but no determination was given in the case, and so Handlo kept the manor. Sir J. de B. seems to have died before 24 July 1337, when Isabella, " late the wife of J. de B. Knt." is mentioned.

1328. July. John de Chancy.

Roger de Nowers.

1328. Oct. Gilbert de Elsefeld.

Richard de Abberbury.

On 7 June 1318 Richard de Wyndesore acknowledged that he owed Rd. de Abberbury 50 marks ; to be levied etc. of his lands in Berks. 12 March 1327, Commission of oyer etc. to R. de. A. and three others on complaint of the Abbot of Eynesham and Brother Nicholas de Stanlake of the same Abbey that Thomas le Gay and others assaulted the said Nicholas at Hampton Pule, co. Oxford, and maltreated him. 14 July 1327, Commission of the Peace for co. Oxford to Drew de Barentyn, Richard de Abberburye, and John de Whitefeld (see 1327). The said R. de A. and John de Meriet were app. 12 Oct. 1327 collectors in co. Oxford of the twentieth of movables granted to the King by Parliament for the defence of the kingdom against the Scots.

1330. March. Sir Roger de Nouwers.

Sir John de Witefelde.

1330. Nov. William de Leghe.

Robert de Morby.

William de la Legh on 18 July 1316 acknowledged that he owed £100 to Master Rd. de Clare ; to be levied etc. on his lands in Surrey. 24 May 1327, General Pardon to W. de Legh (? son of Thomas). Protection with clause *volumus* until Michaelmas for W. de Leghe who is going with the King.

Robert de Morby was app. Keeper or Constable of the Castle town and land of Breghennogh (Brecknock) in 1322, and on 18 Feb. 1322 was ordered to inform himself of the names of those who lately adhered to the King's contrariants, and of the names of their hostages by whom the King may best be secured, and to certify the King of the same without delay. On 24 Nov. 1322 William Byset acknowledged that he owed Robert de Morby Knt. £10 ; to be levied etc. in Yorkshire. 8 June 1328, Writ of aid until Michaelmas for R. de Moreby Knt. and three others Purveyors for Queen Isabella's Household, sent to Berwick upon Tweed.

1331. John de Whitefelde.

John de Louches.

20 July 1322, Order to the Sheriff of York to receive John de Louches, John de Whitefeld and others as prisoners to be kept

in York Castle. Pardon 3 Jan 1330 to John de Louches (son and heir of Richard de L.,) an adherent of Thomas Earl of Lancaster in the late· quarrel with Hugh le Despencer the elder—since adjudged by Parliament to have been·a good and just quarrel— of the £100 for the payment of which the said Richard was by duress induced to enter into a recognisance with the said Hugh to save his life, and which by reason ·of the said Hugh's for-feiture, is now demanded by the said John by the Exchequer; upon testimony of several of the Council to the truth of the premises.—Mandate in pursuance to the treasurer and Barons of the Exchequer.

1332.   March.   Richard de Williamescote.

John de Leukenore.

The former was son of the M.P. 1290, and was again Member 1334, 1336, 1339, 1346. The family ceased to be con-nected with Kiddington about 1373. On 3 Feb 1327 Isabella de Clare late the wife of Maurice de Berhele acknowledged that she owed £80 to R. de W., to be leyied etc. in Oxon. Rd Damory, John de Whitfield (see 1329) and Rd. de Williamescote were made the Commrs. of the Peace in Oxon 18 May 1329.

The latter was again · M.P. 1336, 1337, 1338, 1343. John de Leukenore and James de Wodestok (see 1328) were placed in a Commission of a Oyer 19 July 1337, and on 24 May 1337 another Commission of Oyer issued to Wm. de Shareshull, J. de Leukenore, Thomas de la Mire, John Golafre. and J. de Wodestok, on complaint by Ralph Chastiloun (see 1313,) that Roger de Nowers Knt. (see 1320) Burga his wife, Richard, John, Robert. and Roger his sons, and others assaulted him at Keyngham. Ralph died the same year from the violence received in this affray.

1332.   Sept.   John de Alveton, or de Aveton.

Robert de Barton.

John de Alveton was Sheriff of Oxon 1335, 1337, 1343, 1344' 1345, 1346, 1347, and Joint Sheriff 1354 or the first part of that year, and again M.P. 1334, 1335, 1337, 1338, and placed in a commission of oyer (as John de Adveton) 14 Oct. 1335. A commission issued 12 July 1335 to Wm. de Shareshull, J. de Alveton, T. de Langele (see 1335,) and Hugh de Berewyk to make an acquisition in Bucks touching the dispute of the Abbess of Burnham and Geoffrey de Bulstrode. On 28 Sept. 1338 James le Botiller, Earl of Ormond, staying in Ireland has letters nominating Thomas de Evesham clerk and John de Adveton his attorneys in England.

There are several references in the *Close Rolls.* for 1318 to Robert de Barton the King's clerk as Keeper or Receiver of the King's victuals in the parts of Carlisle, but on 26 June 1320 he is mentioned as the "late Receiver." On 9 **Feb.** 1328 he is styled "lately receiver of the issues of the Bishopric of Durham," and on 3 Aug. 1328 as "late keeper of the Bishopric of Carlisle" He was app. 28 Nov. 1334 Receiver and Keeper of the King's victuals of corn wine and other things in the town of Carlisle, and in those parts, during pleasure, and was placed in a commission of oyer with John Giffard de Twyford, and J. de Wodestok 6 Nov. 1334, and in a similar commission with Thomas de Langele 28 Nov. 1334.

> 1332. Dec. James de Wodestoke.
>
> Hugh de Berewyk.

20 Aug. 1337, Grant to Hugh de Berewyk, King's yeoman, and Isabella his wife, tenants in fee, of a messuage, 71½ acres of land, 2 acres of meadow, and 3 acres of pasture, in Croumersh and Newenham, of the lands of Wm. de Mareschal, (see 1324,) sometime Constable of the Castle of Walyngford, who at his death owed divers debts to the King. On 3 Oct. 1337, John Tybbetot going beyond the seas with the King on his service had letters nominating John de Sancto Paulo and Hugh de Berewyk his attorneys in Ireland until Easter.

> 1334. Feb. John Golaffre.
>
> James de Wodestoke.

John Golafre of Golafers in Nafford, son of the M.P. 1315, was placed in commissions of oyer and terminer 24 May 1337, and 10 Sept. 1338, and was M.P. co. Worcester 1337, 1338, co. Gloucester 1337, and co. Oxford 1334 and 1340. He was one of those app. 21 March 1332 Keepers of co. Oxford to arrest all disturbers of the Peace therein and to hear and determine the trespasses whereof they were indicted.

> 1334. Sept. Richard de Williamescote.
>
> John de Alveton.
>
> 1335. May. Thomas de Langele.
>
> John de Alveton.

8 Feb. 1327, License for Thomas West to grant to Thomas de Langele in fee the bailiwick of the forestry of Whichewood Forest, held in chief. It was evidently on account of this transaction that the same T. de L. acknowledged two days later that he owed Thomas West 100 marks; to be levied in default of payment on his lands in Oxon. He was styled Keeper of the Forest in 1330. On 18 Aug. 1327, Commission of oyer etc. on complaint by Robert de Wilughwys, parson of the Church of Wolfamcote, co. Warwick, that Robert de Langele, Thomas de Langele, and others broke his close at Wolfamcote, burned his houses, and carried away his goods. 24 June 1335, Appointment of James de Wodestoke Rd. de Williamescote, and Thomas de

Langele to assess and levy in co. Oxford (the city of Oxford excepted) 240 marks which certain men of the county have granted before the King and Council in the last Parliament at York for themselves and other men of the county for his services against the Scots, and for relief from 80 hobelers requisitioned from them for the said service. The money is to be paid at the King's receipt at York by St. Peter ad Vincula.

1336. March. John de Leukenore.

Richard de Williamescote.

1336. Sept. Richard de Alveton.

Richard de Williamescote,

1337. Jan. John de Leukenore.

John de Alvetone.

1337. Sept. John de Alveton.

Thomas de Langele.

By Writ dated at Westminster 18 Aug. 1837, the following persons were summoned to *attend* this Parliament, for the purpose of giving their advice, namely, for the county of Oxford, John de Handlo, John Giffard of Twyford, and Thomas de Langele. They were of course not regular Members of Parliament. Sir John de Handlo, son of Richard de H. was lord of the manor of Borstal and Muswell, and died 1346. He was sole tenant of the manor of Pydyngton, Oxon, on 20 Sept. 1329, (see *Close Rolls*), and his wife was named Matilda. On 11 Aug. 1329 John de Handlo Knt. acknowledged that he owed 1006 marks to John de Sancto Amando Knt., for which he pledged his lands in Oxon, 1 Feb. 1327, Grant to John Giffard, King's Yeoman, for service to Queen Isabella, of the custody of the bailiwick of Gotesle and Dersle in Rokyngham Forest, during good behaviour.

1338. Feb. John de Leukenore.

Thomas atte More.

1338. July. Thomos atte More.

John de Alveton.

1339. Jan. Richard de Williamescote.

Richard de Hattecoumbe.

The latter was a witness to the enrolment of an indenture in London on 5 Nov. 1327, (see *Close Rolls.*)

1339. Oct. Richard de Hattecombe.

John le Peyntour.

1340. Jan. John Golafre.

Thomas de la More.

The latter was probably the same as the M.P. 1338, and again sat for the county 1343, 1351. He was granted by the King exemption from Knighthood 29 June 1336, and on 3 May 1337 was app. (in the place of Thomas de Langele) to act with John de Handlo, Gilbert de Ellesfield, Thomas Coudray, Robert Achard, and James de Wodestok, lately app. to arrest persons openly suspected in cos. Oxford and Berks, and to hear and determine the charges brought against them, as for certain causes the King does not wish T. de Langele to take any further part in the matter.

1340.	March.	John Golafre.
		Thomas de la More.
1341.		Richard de Beaufo.
		John Frelond.

Beaufo seems to have been a contraction of Bellafago.

1343.		John de Leukenore.
		Thomas de la More.
1344.		Thomas Huscarl.
		John de Herdwyk.

Commission of oyer etc. 8 March 1337 on complaint by the prior of Daventre that whereas he and his predecessors time out of mind have used to have the grinding of all malt for brewing within the town of Daventre and to find a man and horse to carry the malt to and from their mill, John de Herdewyk. Geoffrey de Herdewyk and several others have by force prevented him and his men and servants from the exercise of his right of grinding. John de Heredwyk was made J.P. for Coventry 8 Sept. 1377.

| 1346. | | Richard de Williamescote. |
| | | John Laundeles. |

The latter was Sheriff of Oxon 1348, 1349, 1350, 1331, 1352, 1353, 1356, 1357, 1358, 1359, and was made a Commr. of the Peace for Oxon with John Golafre and Gilbert Wace 2 July 1377, but on 9 April 1378 Edmund de Stonore was app. in the room of John Laundels deceased.

1348.	Jan.	Richard de Williamescotc.
		John Laundels.
1348.	March.	Richard de Williamescote.
		Richard de Hattecombe.
1351.		Thomas de la More.
		Thomas de Langeley.
1352.	Jan.	John de Trillowe.
		John de Alveton.

Sir John de Trillowe witnessed in 1367 a deed relating to the manors of Borstal and Musewell. (*Kennet*).

1352. Aug. (One Member only). John de Whitefeld.

1353. (One Member only). Thomas de Langeleye.

1354.· John de Leukenore.

Thomas de Langeley.

1355. Thomas de Langele.

Adam de Shareshull.

Sir Adam de Shareshull who was also M.P. Gloucester-shire 1360, was probably brother or son of William de Shareshull, Lord Chief Justice of England 1351-8. License 12 May 1337 for the alienation in mortmain by A. de S. Knt. to the master and brethren of the hospital of St. John without the east gate of Oxford of a messuage in the suburb of Oxford, towards the sup-port of the poor and sick in the hospital. Appointment 21 June 1337 of A. de Shareshull, John de Whitefeld, and Wm. Was (Wace) to arrest and imprison in the Castle of Oxford certain suspected persons. 20 April 1346, Power to Ivo de Clynton and Sir A. de S. to recover the inheritance of Queen Philippa, come to her by the death of the Count of Holland.

1357. Thomas de Langeleye.

John Laundels.

1358. John de Nowers.

Thomas de Langeleye.

John de Nowers, son of the M.P. 1320, was made a Commr. of Array for Oxon with John Golafre and Gilbert Wace 1 July 1377, a Commr. of the Peace there with G. Wace and H. Poure 28 June 1378, and a Commr. of the Peace for Bucks 14 Dec. 1381 and 9 March 1382. Commission 26 May 1378 to J. de N. and Hugh Poure and three others to enquire touching divers forestallings, re-gratings of wool and other merchandise, con-cealments false weights and measures, and withdrawals of presentments therefor before the late King's ministers at Bureford and other merchant towns adjacent to the marches of Codeswold in cos. Oxford and Gloucester.

1360. Thomas de Langelegh.

Nicholas Poure.

A member of the family of Power of Blechington, Wilcot, and Shipton.

1361. Roger de Elmerugg.

Nicholas Dammory.

The former was Sheriff of Oxon 1361, 1362, 1366, 1367, 1368, 1373, and was of the same family as the Members for

Worcestershire 1302, and Herefordshire 1318.

The latter was probably son of Sir Richard Damary of Goddington, Oxon, King's yeoman in 1337. *Rymer* states that on 27 May 1357 the King desires Simon de Sudbury, Chancellor of Salisbury, to assist Sir Nicholas Damory and Sir Thomas de Fulnetby, whom he sends to the Pope.

1362. Roger de Elmerugg.

   John de Nowers.

1365. Roger de Elmerugg.

   Roger de Cotesforde.

The latter was Sheriff of Oxon 1363, 1364, 1365, 1369.

1365. Roger de Elmerugge.

   Nicholas Dammory.

1366. Nicholas Dammory.

   John de Tryllowe.

1368. Nicholas Dammory.

   Roger de Elmerugg.

1369. Roger de Elmerugg.

   Roger de Cotesford.

1371. Feb. The same.

1371. June (One Member). Roger de Cotesford.

1372. Sir Gilbert Wace.

   Sir Thomas de Broughton.

Both styled chivaler. Sir Gilbert Wace of Ewelme, was Escheator and Sheriff in Oxon and Berks in Dec. 1377, Sheriff of Oxon 1372, 1375, 1379, 1387, and a Commr. of the Peace for Oxon (as G. Was) with John James and Edmund Stonore 14 Dec. 1381. Pardon 7 Feb. 1381 to G. W. late Sheriff of Oxford and Berks for all escapes of felons before Nov. 4, excepting those previously adjudged. 20 Jan. 1383, Commission of oyer to Reginald Malyns, G. Wace and three others touching the erection of certain wears mills mill-ponds stakes and kiddles in the Thames between Walyngford and Goryng in cos. Oxford and Berks contrary to the statute of 25 Edw. 3, and another similar commission to them, J. Nowers and E. Gifford 11 July 1383. On 24 Nov. 1383 Rd. Abburbury, Reg. Malyns, T. Harcourt, Thomas Poile, G. Wace, T. Barentyn, and E. Gifford were made Commrs. of the Peace in Oxon. One of the manors of Ewelwe was called Wace's Court. Sir Gilbert made his will in 1407, but was still living in May 1408.

Thomas Broghton's name appears as one of the King's Clerks in Chancery in 1382.

1373.   Reginald de Malyns.

Richard de Adderbury.

Sir Reginald de Malyns of Chinnor, Sheriff of Oxon 1376, was made a Commr. of the Peace for Oxon 1 July 1377, and 22 March 1378, and was placed in several commissions in 1379. He was granted 40 marks yearly at the Exchequer of Chester 18 Nov. 1367, and had this grant confirmed 24 Feb. 1377, and 22 March 1378. On 24 Feb. 1380 the King granted him exemption for life from being put on assizes juries attaints inquisitions or recognisances, from being trier of the same, and from being made mayor, sheriff escheator coroner collector of tenths, fifteenths, or other tax or subsidy, or other officer or minister of the King against his will. A Commission of Array in Oxon issued to him, Rd. Adderbury, G. Wace, and J. de Nowers 20 March 1380.

Grant 1 Sept. 1377 to Rd de Abburbury, the King's Knight (son of the M.P. 1328, and lord of Gatehampton, 1393) of the custody of the forest of Dertemore, (Dartmoor) for life, with the profits of the herbage, without rendering aught therefor to the King, saving to John Sully, the King's Knight, the yearly rent of £20, granted to him by Edward, late Prince of Wales. Commission 17 Feb. 1378 to R. de A. to view the jewels and other goods which belonged to the late King on the day of his death, and to make a true inventory and appraisement of them, swearing all persons to make discovery of the same and of the persons in whose hands they are.   17 March 1378, Grant to Rd. Abberbury Knt of the ship *La Alice.*   22 March 1378, Exemplification and confirmation in favour ot R. de A. of letters patent of the King when Prince of Wales 29 Feb, 51 Edw. 3, and 6 Nov. 41 Edw. 3, granting him £40 out of the issues and profits of the lordship of Chester, for what annuity the said Richard is to serve the Prince when summoned in time of war with two squires, without other fees.—Also of a grant dated 18 May 51 Edw. 3, for life, as he was the first master of the Prince, of the manors of Helleston in Trig, and Southteng, in Cornwall and Devon.   8 July 1382, Commission of the Peace and of Oyer and terminer in Oxon to Rd. Adderbury, John Nowers, Reg. Malynes, T. Harecourte, G.Waas, T. de la Puylle, John de Herle, Thomas Barantyn, John Haroudon, and Edmund Giffard. R. de A. was the head of a wealthy family at Steeple Aston.

1376.   Sir Thomas Harecourte.

Robert Symeon.

Sir Thomas Harcourt of Stanton Harecourt, second but only surving son of Sir Wm de H. who d. 1349, by Jane dau. of Richard Lord Grey, of Codnor, and grandson of the M.P. 1322, was Knighted 1366, Sheriff of Oxon 1407, a Commr. of the Peace there 8 March 1382, and 24 Nov 1383, and a Commr. of the Peace and of oyer and terminer 8 July and 21 Dec. 1382. He m. Maud (or Alice, or Eleanor,) dau. of Robert Lord Grey, of Rotherfield, and widow of Sir John Botetourt of Woody, Lord Botetourt, and died 12 April 1417.

Sir Robert Symeon was again Member 1377, 1378, 1379.

1377. Jan. Gilbert Wace.

John James.

John James of Wallingford was Sheriff of Oxon 1374, 1380, J.P. Berks 1 July and 6 Nov. 1377, 1 Feb. 1378, 14 Dec. 1381, a Commr. of Array for Berks 20 March 1380, Escheator of Somerset in 1378, J.P. Oxon 14 Dec. 1381, a Commr. of the Peace and of oyer for Berks 8 March and 20 Dec. 1382, and on 5 Aug. 1382 obtained exemption for life, at the supplication of the King's mother, from being put on inquisitions juries assizes attaints or recognisances, and from being being made trier of them, knight, mayor sheriff escheator, coroner justice of assizes, the peace, or labourers or other justice steward constable, collector of tenths fifteenths or other subsidy, arrayer leader or trier of men at arms hobelers or archers, or other minister of the King against his will.

1377. Oct. Reginald de Malyns.

Robert Symeon.

1378. Sir John Herlee.

Sir Robert Symeon.

Sir John Herle was made Commr. of the Peace for Berks 14 Dec. 1381, and for Oxon 26 May 1380, (as John de Herle) 8 March, and 21 Dec. 1382, and 12 July 1383, and a Commr. of the Peace and of oyer for Berks and Oxon 8 March 1382, and also again for Oxon 8 July 1382. On the Nov. 1384, Revocation of appointment by letters patent dated 3 Sept. last of Wm Beyvill to the custody of the possessions in Cornwall late of John Trevarthean the elder, because by letters patent long before that date viz. 10 May last John Herle esq. was app. thereto. On 11 May 1402 the King order Sir John Herle and ten others to contradict the reports that the King does not intend to observe the laws, and to prevent the circulation of such a report. *(Rymer.)*

1379. John Herle.

Robert Symeon.

1380. Jan. Reginald de Malyns.

Edmund de Stonore.

The latter was the son of Sir John S. of Stonor (who d. 1361,) and was made Sheriff of Oxon and Berks 1377, a Commr. of the Peace for Oxon 26 May 1380, a Commr. of the Peace and of oyer there 8 March 1382.   On 8 May 1380 he received a license of alienation in mortmain to the Prioress and Convent of Merlawe of the advowson of the Church of Duddecot (Didcot), held in chief as of the honour of Walyngford.   He was Knighted, m. a dau. of — Beville of Ulton, and died (before 27 Oct.) 1382 leaving his son and heir John a minor.

> 1380.   Nov.   John Herle.
>
> John Harowedon.

John Harwedon was made J.P. Northants 17 May and 6 Nov. 1377, a Commr. of oyer there 4 Sept. 1377, and in Hunts 16 Feb. and 3 June 1378, and a Commr. to assess Staunford town 6 April 1378.   On 29 April 1385 John Harewedon, R. de Adderbury, Edm. Malyns, T. Barentyn, Thomas Louches, and Edm. Gyffard, were made Commrs. of Array in Oxon in view of imminent invasion by the French.

> 1381.   John Herle.
>
> Thomas Blount.

It is doubtful if the latter was the same as T. B. made a Commr. of Array in Dorset 1 July 1377 and 20 March 1380, or T. B. senior or junior commissioned 19 Aug. 1382 to arrest those who lately rose in insurroction at Lynhurst, Hants.

> 1382.   May.   The same.
>
> 1382.   Oct.   Gilbert Wace.
>
> Roger Cheyne.

Inspeximus and confirmation 6 may 1378 in favour of Roger Cheyne, Yeoman of the late King, of (1) letters patent dated 20 March 27 Edw. 3, being a grant to him for life of a messuage and virgate of land called " Wappenhamplace " in Wodestok, within the lordship of Wotton, and (2) of letters patent dated 4 Jan. 41 Edw. 3, being an exemplification of others dated 11 Jan. 38 Edw. 3, being a grant to him for life of £10 yearly from the issues of counties Oxford and Berks, and a robe yearly of the suit of esquires of the King's Household.   Appointment 22 March 1384 of Roger Cheyne the King's esquire, and two others until All Saints to take artificers labourers and carriage for the works in progress at the Queen's manor of Wodestok to be paid out of her moneys.

> 1383.   Feb.   Gilbert Wace.
>
> John Harowedon.
>
> 1383.   Oct.   The same.
>
> 1384.   Apl.   Gilbert Wace.
>
> Edmund Giffard.

Edmund Giffard of Thame, was app. 22 Nov. 1377 collector in Berks and Oxon of the subsidy on cloth, a Commr. of the Peace (with John Herle) in Oxon 26 May 1380, a Commr. of the Peace and of oyer there 8 July 1382, and a Commr. of Array there 29 April 1385 with R. de Adderbury, Reg. Malynes, T. Barentyn, J. Haroweden, and T. Louches. He was escheator of Oxon and Berks in 1381, and having been granted for life 6d daily out of the issues of those counties 3 Jan. 43 Edw. 3, had those letters patent confirmed 6 May 1378.

1384. Nov. Gilbert Wace.
Roger Cheyne.

1385. Sir Gilbert Wace.
William Wylcotes.

William Wilcote of Wilcote was made Sheriff of Berks and Oxon 1391, 1399, had license in 1397 to purchase the manor of Willicotes, co. Gloucester, of the abbey of St. Elnuef, Normandy, and was granted in 1399 Hedington manor, Bullington Hundred, and Northgate Hundred at Oxford, for which he paid £40 yearly to the King. He m. Elizabeth " called Blaket " dau. and heir of John Tryllowe of Castleton, co. Warwick, (see 1352,). She re-m. to Sir John Blaket of Northleigh. He had the custody of the royal park of Cornbury in 1409, was granted jointly with John Norbury and Philip la Vache, by Queen Joanna of Navarre, the farm of Woodstock Manor and Wootton Hundred, and died 1411 (M.I. Wilcote Chapel in North Leigh Church.) Inquisition p.m. 1410.

1386. Richard Abberbury.
Gilbert Wace.

1388. Feb. Thomas Barentyne.
William Welycote.

Thomas Barentyne of Little Haseley, was sheriff of Oxon 1378, 1382, 1386, 1394, made a Commr. of the Peace there 26 May 1380, and was granted exemption for life 20 June 1380 from being put on assizes juries inquisitions attaints or recognizances, and from being made mayor sheriff escheator collector of subsidy or aid, arrayer or leader of men at arms hobelers or archers, or other minister of the King against his will.

1388. Sept. Thomas de la Poyle.
John Rede.

Sir Thomas de la Poyle of Hampton Poyle, eldest son of Henry de la P. by Elizabeth dau of Sir Wm. Shareshull, presented to Hampton 27 Nov. 1387, was Sheriff of Oxon 1388, and m. Catherine————, but died s.p.

John Rede was Escheator of Norfolk and Suffolk in 1381 and 1383, made J.P. Bucks 14 Dec. 1381, and a Commr. of the

Peace and of oyer for Bucks 9 March and 21 Dec. 1382. On 24 June 1384 Reg. Malyns, Thomas Sakevyll, Edm. Malyns, T. Barentyn, and John Reede were app. to arrest and bring before the King and Council the persons found to have entered with an armed force the manor of the King's clerk, Edm. Brudenell, at Wodemondesle, co. Oxford, assaulted his servants and threatened to kill them and burn the manor. On 25 Oct. 1420 Peter Huet, John Rede and others were app. to provide victuals for the King's Household. His wife Cecily gave Gathampton manor to their son Edmund Rede (see 1450).

1390.	Jan.	Thomas Barentyn.
		William Wilycotes.
1390.	Nov.	Thomas de la Poill.
		Thomas Barantyn.
1391.		William Wyllycote.
		John Rede.
1393.		Sir Thomas Paynell.
		Thomas Barentyn.

The former was made with T. de la Puyle a Commr. of the Peace and of oyer in Oxon 8 March, 8 July, and 21 Dec. 1382.

1394.		William Wilycotes.
		John Adderbury.
1395.		William Wilycotes.
		William Bruly.

Eldest son of Sir Henry Bruly, presented to Waterstock 30 Jan. 1411, and released to Robert James of Boarstall all his right in Oakle manor, Bucks, 12 June 1417.

1397.	Jan.	Thomas Barentyne.
		John Adderbury.
1397.	Sept.	William Wilcotes.
		Janyn Golafre.

Sir John Golafre of Fyfield, (son of Sir John and Isabella G., and grandson of the M.P. 1334,) was Sheriff of Oxon 1397, 1398, 1414, 1424, and died 1442, (M. I. Fyfield.)

1399.		Thomas Barentyne.
		John Wilcotes.
1401.		John Wylcotes.
		Thomas Chaucer.

"Some say that this Chaucer was a merchant man and had about £1000 by the year." (Leland.) Thomas Chaucer of Ewelme, "Chief Butler of England," Sheriff of Oxon and Berks, 1400, 1403, who was born 1367, was not the son and heir of the famous poet Geoffrey Chaucer (the King's esquire and yeoman in 1278, and Comptroller of the Customs and Subsidies in the port of London in 1385.) He m. Maud 2nd dau. and a great co-heir of Sir John Burghersh, held lands in Ewelme, and dying " very rich" 18 Nov. 1434, or 28 April 1436, was buried in Ewelme Church (M.I.) His only dau. Alice m. Wm. de la Pole, Duke of Suffolk, and founder of Ewelme Hospital. *Rymer* mentions that on 4 June 1414 Henry Lord de la Scrop, Thomas, Chaucer and three others were empowered to treat with Ralph Major and the other Ambassadors of the Duke of Burgundy concerning the marriage of the King with the French King's daughter Catherine; and that on 28 Jan. 1417 the King addressed Thomas Chaucer, "the King's Chief Butler," to deliver 100 tuns of wine, imported for the Duke of Bourbon to the Duke's servants. He was Speaker (Prolucutor) of the House of Commons in the Parliaments of 1407, 1410, 1411, and 1415, and app. Constable of Wallingford Castle 1400, Ambassador to France 1404, was granted the farm of the manor of Woodstock by Queen Johanna 23 Feb. 1411, and again after her death, by the King for life 15 March 1411, and continued Chief Butler by Hen. 6 in 1422.

      1402. Thomas Chaucer.

           Thomas Wykham.

The latter was of Broughton, Sheriff of Oxon 1413, and next heir to the famous William of Wykham, Bishop of Winchester, and Founder of New College, Oxford. On 12 Oct. 1383, Grant for life to Thomas Wykham, servitor of the King in his pantry, of the lands late of Walter Moigne of co. Cambridge, forfeited by his share in the late insurrection, not exceeding the value of 47s. 4d yearly. On 3 May 1384, Grant for life, to T. W. groom of the pantry, of the lands and tenements in Sneyleseswelle, co. Cambridge, forfeited by John Goseberkirke for his insurrection against the King, and extended at 19s 3d yearly. *(Patent Rolls)*. 6 Nov. 1414, Pardon to John de Wykham of Swalcliffe, co. Oxford, adherent Sir John Oldcastell, who had conspired to kill the King and make himself Regent. *(Rymer.)*

      1403. William Makkenny.

           Sir Peter Besyles.

The former was perhaps brother or son of Robert de Makeny, "Yeoman of the Poultry and chief buyer of victuals of the late King" who was retained in that post by Richard II. in 1377. He was otherwise styled Serjeant, and on 8 Aug. 1377 a writ of aid issued, until Easter, for R. M. "one of the buyers for the Household," which post he still held in 1384.

Sir Peter Besyles of Bessels Leigh, younger son of Sir Thomas B., was Sheriff of Oxon 1408, made his will 23 Oct. 1424, whereby he bequeathed lands for the maintenance and repairs of Burford and Culham bridges, near Abingdon, to the building of which he had been a principal contributor, and dying that year

was buried in Dantesbourne Church, of which he had been a
great patron, having built the south wing and left £120 for
making six windows therein.   20 May 1384, Pardon, by main-
prise of Ralph Waleys of co. Gloucester, and Rd. Brouns of
Berks, and by five of 50 marks which Peter de Besils kinsman
and heir of John son of John son and heir of Thomas de Besils
Knt. deceased, tenant in chief, and Thomas Catewy (Hathewy
M.P. co. Gloucester 1373) have made with the Council, (whereof
10 marks are to be paid at once, the rest in four years,) to the
said Peter, a minor in the King's custody, for marrying Joan,
dau. of the said Thomas Catewy without licence.

> 1403.   Sir John Drayton.
>
> John Wilycotes.

Sir John Drayton of Bensington was app. 24 July 1377 to
the custody, during pleasure of the King's swans on the Thames,
its affluents, and all other waters in the counties of Kent, Surrey,
Sussex, Middlesex, Essex, Herts, Southampton, Wilts, Oxford,
Berks, Bucks, Lincoln, Somerset, Dorset, and Gloucester.   19
March 1378, *Inspeximus* and confirmation in favour of John
Drayton, "Yeoman of the late King, retained" of (1) letters
patent dated 7 April 40 Edw. 3, being a grant to him for life of
100s. yearly at the Exchequer, and (2) of letters patent dated 14
Aug. 43 Edw. 3, being a like grant to him of 43s 4d. yearly from
the issues of the March of Bray in lieu of the office granted to
him by Queen Philippa of hayward and warrener of that manor, in
room of Roger de Yerdle.   30 Oct. 1378, Pardon to the said J. D. for
the death of Nicholas Doyngton, killed before Michaelmas 1377.
Inspeximus etc. in favour of J. D. for life of letters patent of the
King's brother Thomas de Holand, Marshal of England, dated
23 Feb. 3 Richard II, granting to the said John, his esquire, the
offices of serjeant-marshal and clerk-marshal of Marshalsea of
the King's Household. Commission to J. D. 28 July 1382 to seize
and bring before the King and Council, Joan and Margaret
kinswomen and heiresses of Edmund de Clyvedon, tenant-in-
chief, minors, whose marriages belong to the King—(Vacated by
surrender, and nothing was done therein.) Commission of
Array in Oxon 29 April 1385 to John Drayton Knt. and Wm.
Drayton Knt.

John Wilcote of Great Tewe, (? son of the M.P. 1385,) was
Sheriff of Oxon 1401, 1406, 1415, 1419.

> 1406.   Thomas Chaucer.
>
> John Willicotes.
>
> 1407.   Oct. 5.   Thomas Chaucer.
>
> John Wilcotes.
>
> 1410.   Jan.   William Willicotes.
>
> Thomas Chaucer.

The former was son of the M.P. 1404, and was granted by the King the manor Hedington in fee for £40 a year rent in 1400.

1411. Oct. }
1413. Jan. } Returns lost.

Thomas Chaucer's name however appears as Speaker and Member for Oxfordshire 1412, and he probably was also elected M.P. in Jan. 1413.

1413. April 27. Thomas Chaucers.
              John Willicotes.

1414. Feb. 1. William Lyle.
             John Wilycotes.

Sir Wm Lisle was Sheriff of Oxon 1410, 1420, 1421, 1422. Commission 1 May 1380 to Thomas Sayvill and W. Lylie, serjeants at arms, and three others to arrest and deliver to the Marshalsea prison John Trevarthian and three others indicted for certain misprisions against the King. 8 Sept. 1384, Commission of the Peace and of Oyer in Beds to Wm Lile.

1414. Nov. 8. Thomas Chaucer.
             John Wilycotes.

1415. Oct. Return lost.

Thomas Chaucer was however again Speaker and M.P. for Oxon in this Parliament.

1416. April 27. Sir Thomas Wykeham.
              Thomas Stonore.

Thomas Stonor of Stonor, Sheriff of Oxon 1423, and 1427, was son of Sir Ralph, and grandson of the M.P. 1380. He m. Alice dau of Sir John Kirkley of Kent, was M.P. for Oxon 1416, 1419, 1425, 1427, 1429, and d. 3 May 1440.

1416. Oct. Return lost.

1417. Oct. William Lisle.
          John Willicotes.

1419. Oct. 5. John Wylcotes.
            Thomas de Stonore.

1420. Nov. 28. John Danvers.
             Richard Gryvell.

John Danvers of Cokethorpe presented to Waterstock 16 March 1422, and m. (1) Alice dau of Wm. Verney of Byfield, and (2) Joan dau. of Wm. Bruly of Waterstock, (see 1395.)

1421. April 17. Thomas Chaucer.
              John Wilcotes.

1421. Nov. 27. John Daumvers.
                Peter Feteplace.

John Daumvers was of Bannebury, and again sat 1423. His colleagues was of North Denchworth, and Sheriff of Berks and Oxon 1441. A Baronetcy existed at one time in the Fetiplace family, which was of ancient standing in Oxon and Berks.

1422. Oct. 29. Sir Thomas Wykeham.
                Thomas Chaucer.

1423. Sept 30. Peter Feteplace.
                John Daumvers.

1425. April 12. Sir Thomas Wykeham.
                Thomas Stonore.

1426. Feb. 14. Thomas Chaucer.
                William Lyle.

1427. Sept. 25. Thomas Chaucers.
                Thomas Stonore.

1429. Aug. 25. Thomas Chaucer.
                Thomas Stonore.

1431. Jan. 11. The same.

1432. May 1. Thomas Feteplace.
                Richard Quatermayns.

Sir Thomas Feteplace of Childrey, Sheriff of Berks and Oxon 1435, "received a great addition of blood and honour" by his marriage with Beatrix daughter of the King of Portugal.

The Quatermayns were seated and located at the noble domains of Ricot and Thame, in the 14th century, and were possessed of great estates in Oxon, having seats at North Weston and Shirburn Castle. Sir Richard (? son of Thomas who d. 1399,) possessed them in 1424, was Sheriff 1436, 1454, and was succeeded by Richard in 1460 Commission 23 April 1463 to Robert Harecourte Knt., Rd. Quatermayns, Edmund Rede, Rd. Danvers, and others to enquire into the breaches in Oxon of the statute of 13 Richard II. enacting that no man shall buy or sell wools at a higher weight than 14lbs. for the stone, etc. Commission of oyer and terminer 19 April 1464 to the King's kinsman John, duke of Suffolk, John Lovell of Lovell Knt., Robert Danvers, Robert Harecourt Knt., Rd. Harecourt, Rd. Quatermayns, and Edm. Rede within Oxon and Berks. "Through great mortality all the lands descended to Richard the youngest son, a merchant of London," who m. Sybil——, and dying s.p. 1460, (M.I. Thame Church,) adopted his Godson Sir Richard Fowler as his heir.

1435. June 25. Stephen Haytfeld.
              Richard Quatermayns.
Stephen was Sheriff of Oxon 1434.
1435. Sept. 15. Peter Feteplace.
              John Daunvers.
1437. Jan. 3. Richard Drayton.
            Robert Daunvers.

Rd. Drayton of Oxon, was son of the M.P. 1404, and received protection 28 Jan. 1435 in the Duke of Bedford's retinue. He sat again 1453. He sold the manor of Rotherfield Peppard to Mr. Stonor. Commission 27 May 1463 to R.D. and the Sheriff of Kent and three others to enquire what lands and tenements Richard late Duke of York held there on the day of his death.

Robert Danvers was eldest son of the M.P. 1420, and became a Governor of Lincolns Inn 1428, Common Serjeant of London 1422-42, Recorder of London 1442-50, Serjeant at law 14 Feb. 1443, King's Serjeant 1444, M.P. for the City of London 1445, and in July 1450 was forced by Jack Cade to be the head (as the Recorder) of a Commission of oyer and terminer under which several noblemen and gentlemen were tried for "high treason," some of whom were executed. He had the satisfaction however, when the rebellion was put down, of being made 1 August a Commr. in Kent for the trial of Cade's adherents. He m. Agnes dau. of Rd. Quatermayns of Rycot, (see 1433,) though *Stow* calls her Sir Rd. Delaber's daughter. Danvers was a Justice of the Common Pleas 14 Aug. 1450-70. and Chief Justice thereof 9 Oct. 1470, until May 1471, when his death probably took place, being made K.B. at the coronation of Elizabeth, Queen of Edw. 4, on 26 May 1464. His brother Richard was ancester of the Earl of Danby.

1441. Jan. 28· John Noreys.
            William Wykeham.

John Norreys of Ockholt, lord of that manor, was Sheriff 1437, 1442 and (as Knt.) 1457, and an Esquire of the body to Hen. 6. He m. Milicent dau. and heir of —— Ravenscroft of Cotton-end, Hardingstone, Northants. As John Nores he was made J.P. Berks 28 Feb. 1463, and 1 Oct. 1464.

Wm Wykeham was of Broughton Castle, and Sheriff 1449.

1447. Jan. 12. Sir Robert Harecowrte.
            Thomas Stonore.

Sir Robert was of Stanton Harcourt, grandson of the M.P. 1376, and son of Sir Thomas Harcourt. He m. Margaret dau of Sir John Byron of Clayton, Lancashire, was made High Steward of

Oxford Univ. 1446, K.G. 1463 Sheriff of cos. Leicester and
Warwick 1445, and of Berks and Oxon 1455, J.P. Oxon 17 July
1461, 28 Oct. 1462, and 18 Aug. 1466, J.P. Berks 28 Feb. 1463,
1 Oct. 1464, and 18 Feb. 1467, and on 6 May 1467 was empowered
with Richard the great Earl of Warwick and three others to treat
for peace or a truce with France. He fought in the wars of
Hen. 6 and Edward 4, and lost his life in the service of the latter,
being slain by the Staffords 14 Nov. 1470, and buried in Stanton
Harcourt Church (M. I.) The Harcourts have been settled in
Oxon for over seven centuries. Commission 1 April 1463 to
Robert Harecourt Knt., Rd. Harcourt, and Thomas Walrond to
arrest and imprison one Edw. Bray and others who wander about
making confederacies in divers parts of Berks. Pardon 15 Oct.
1465 to Robert Harcourt Knt. of Stanton Harcourt, of all offences
committed by him before Oct. 5, contrary to the statute of
liveries, and all fines issues amercements reliefs scutages debts
accounts and arrears due from him to the King. Commission 3
May 1464 to R. H. Knt. and three others to array the King's able-
bodied subjects of Oxon, Berks, Beds, and Herts for the resistance
of the King's enemies.

Thomas Stonor, son of the M.P. 1416, m. the Duke of
Suffolk's daughter Johanna, or Jane, was Sheriff 1455, J.P. 18
Aug. 1466, app. to inquire into certain grants of lands in Calais
11 July 1449, commissioned with Rd. Harecourte Esq., John
Stokes, and Humphray Foster, 13 Dec. 1464 to enquire into John
Mervyn's petition, was granted 100 marks from the issues of Oxon
and Berks 20 Nov. 1465, and d. 23 April 1474.

>   1449. Jan. 16. Edmund Hampden.

>   John Pury, or Pery.

Hampden again sat 1453, 1459, but shared in the downfall
of Hen. 6, for on 15 March 1462 Sir John Wenlok of Wenlok was
app. "for such time as her husband is alive," keeper and
governor of Anne wife of Sir Edm. Hampden attainted of high
treason by authority of Parliament at Westminster 4 Nov. 1461,
and the castles lordships manors lands and possessions which they
hold in her right. He is to levy and expend rents to sustain her
and four servants in her company and other reasonable expenses,
to appoint and remove all servants, and account to the King for
the surplus. On 2 Jan. 1462, Grant to the King's servants Rd.
Croft. jun. and Thomas Croft and the heirs of their bodies of all
reversions when they fall in late of Edmund Hampden Knt. in
Oxon and Berks to the value of £50 yearly.

John Pury of Camberbouse, Oxon, (son of Thomas Pury,
"servant to Hen. 4," m. (1) Elizabeth sister to Sir John Sylsey,
and (2) Isabell Wayne of Beverley. 23 July 1461, General Pardon
to John Pury of Chamberhous, Berks, of all offences committed
by him before 20 June last. His dau. and heir Anna m. Wm.

Danvers, Justice of the Common Pleas 1488, half-brother to the M.P. 1437.

> 1449. Oct. 23. Sir Edmund Hampden.
> Thomas Stonor.
> 1450 Oct. 21. Sir Robert Harecourt.
> Edmnnd Rede.

Sir Edmund Rede of Borstall, son of Edm. Rede, Sheriff 1438, son of the M.P. 1388, by Christiana, only dau. of Robert James of Chakenden and Boarstall, son and heir of the M.P. 1377, and who gave £20 to the Abbot and Convent of Dorchester to pray for him 19 Feb. 1438,) was Sheriff of Oxon (as Edward) 1450, J.P. Bucks 19 March 1463, and 13 May 1466, app. Sheriff of Beds and Bucks during pleasure 13 May 1461, and was commissioned with three others 28 Sept. 1462 to arrest Robert Bunkle, John Dalahowe, Rd. Harreys, and Edmund Warde, and bring them before the King in Chancery. *Kennet* has much to say about him. He m. (1) Agnes dau. of Sir John Cottesmore, Chief Justice of the Common Pleas, and (2) Katherine widow of Sir John Gaynesford, (see 1491) and died 1487.

> 1453. March 8. Sir Edmund Hampden.
> Richard Drayton.
> 1455. June Return lost.
> 1459. Nov. 8. Slr Edmund Hampden.
> William Lovell.

Licence by the King 8 Jan. 1463 for £100 paid in the Hanaper for Alice late the wife of Sir Wm. Lovell of Lovell to marry Sir Ralph Boteler of Sudeley. (*Patent Rolls*).

> 1460. Sept. 11. Richard Harcourte.
> John Stokes.

Sir Richard Harcourt of Combe, m. Emily ———— —, and inherited Wytham manor Berks, on the death of Alice Denton widow in 1479 as her next of kin aad heir. He was 2nd son of Sir Thomas H., and brother to the M.P., 1447, and m. (1) Edith one of the three daughters and co-heirs of Thomas St. Claire of Wethersfull, Suffolk, (2) Eleanor dau. of Sir Roger Lewknor of Raunton, co. Stafford, and (3) Katherine dau. and heir of Sir Thomas de la Pole, son of Michael, Earl of Suffolk, and built Wytham manor house, and by his will made 15 Sept. and proved 25 Oct. 1486 he bequeathed £20 to Wytham Church, and directed his body to be buried in Abingdon Abbey. He was app. Sheriff of Oxon and Berks during pleasure 13 May 1461, and 1466, J.P. Oxon 28 Oct. 1462, and 18 Aug. 1466, granted for life 14 May 1461 the Parkership of the King's park of Cornbury, with the accustomed fees, and because this proved to be invalid received a fresh grant thereof 10 Nov. 1464,receiving 3d daily. Sir Rd. H. Knt. and John Eyres were commissioned 13 Nov. 1466 to arrest Robert Stokes and bring him before the King in Chancery.

John Stokes was made a Commr. of the Peace for Oxon 17 July 1461, 28 Oct. 1462, and 18 Aug. 1466. (He was probably son of John Stokes, Sheriff of Oxon and Berks 1440, who with three others was empowered 8 Dec. 1439 to' treat with the Ambassadors of Holland and Zealand for the redress of injuries, had been an Ambassador to the Pope in 1428, and been often employed as an Envoy between 1410 and 1439.) Grant for life 13 March 1461 to John Stokys esq. of the office of Parker or the custody of the park of Bekkeley, Oxon, which he had of the grant of the King's father Richard, Duke of York, with the accustomed fees. (Fresh grant of this office, on surrender of the last, to J. S. and Wm. Staveley 20 June 1465). Appointment of John Stokes and John Aldey 5 July 1461 to provide all kinds of victuals for an expedition by sea against the King's enemies. *Inspeximus* and confirmation 2 July 1463 (—for 6s. 8d. paid in the Hanaper—) in favour of J. S. and Alice his wife the present tenants of the manor of Bigenhull in Burcestre, of a charter dated Westminster 20 Oct. 1377 granting to John de Worthe Knt. that he and his heirs shall have a market weekly on Monday, and a fair yearly for 3 days at St James the Apostle, at the said manor. Pardon 28 Aug. 1464 to J. S. of Biginhill, co. Oxford, esq. late Escheator in the counties of Oxford and Berks, of all fines amercements issues reliefs debts accounts and arrears due to the King and all actions for the same.—By the King.

    1467. April 16. Humphrey Foster.

                     John Barantyne.

    Sir Humphrey Foster of Harpenden, Oxon, and Alder-maston, Berks, m. Alice 4th and yst. dau. of Thomas Stonor (see 1447) was Sheriff of Oxon and Berks 1475, and dying 18 Sept. 1500, was buried in St. Martin's in the Fields, London (M. I.) H. F. was made J.P. Berks 1 Oct. 1464, and 18 Feb. 1467, and with three others was commissioned to enquire by the oath of good men of Kent, Herts, Essex, Surrey, Middlesex, Berks, Bucks, Oxon, and Gloucester into the capture of swans and cygnets on the river Thames, and its tributaries from Cirencester to its mouth, by hooks, nets, 'lymestrynges,' and other engines, and the taking of swans' eggs, and to arrest and imprison the offenders.

    John Barantyne of Little Haseley, was Sheriff of Oxon and Berks 1464, 1484. His family was of long standing and repute in Oxon.

    1472. Sept. 24. Richard Quatermayns.

                     Richard Crost, junior.

Richard Croft jun. of Chipping Norton, son of R. C. senior, was " the King's servant," on 9 Aug. 1461 when he was granted during pleasure the office of Receiver of all manors lands and other possessions late of John, Earl of Shrewsbury in cos. Gloucester and Hereford, receiving the accustomed fees and also ten marks yearly from the issues of the same. The next day he was granted for life the whole office of the Parkership of the King's park of Wodestock, with fees as in the times of Edw. 3, from the issues of the manor. He was made 27 Nov. 1461 for life Supervisor of the King's manor of Wodestocke and had the custody of the King's garden and the meadows there, and on surrendering this grant received a fresh patent of the same office to him and his brother Thomas Croft " the King's servitor " in survivorship 8 Feb. 1464, Thomas being made Steward or lieut. of the manor 7 July 1467, and confirmed as such 1485. The two brothers also obtained a grant of many manors and lands in Oxon and Bucks 22 April 1465, and were made J.P.s Oxon 1485.

1477. Dec. 11. Sir Richard Harecourt.

William Stonour.

Sir William Stonor of Stonor, eldest son of the M.P. 1447, was High Steward of Oxford in 1492, and m. Lady Anne Nevill, eldest dau. of John, Marquis of Montagu, and co-heir of her brother George Duke of Bedford, He and Edm. Hampden and two others were appointed Commrs. to examine archers etc. and take the musters in Oxon for the relief of Brittany 23 Dec. 1488.

1483, 1484, 1485, 1487. Returns lost.

1491. Oct. Robert Harcourt.

George Gaynsfield.

The discovery of the list of Members of this Parliament is entirely due to the private researches of *Mr W. Duncombe Pink.*

Sir Robert Harcourt of Stanton Harcourt, only son and heir of John H. the eldest son the M.P. 1470, m. Agnes dau. of Thomas Lymerick, and was Standard-bearer to Hen. 7 at the battle of Bosworth 1485, and made a Knight Banneret after the battle of Blackheath 1497.

His colleague and brother-in-law George Gaynsford of Hampton Poyle, 2nd son of Sir John G. of Chowhurst, Surrey, and Hampton Poyle, by Catherine (who re-m. as 2nd wife to Sir Edmund Rede of Borstall, see 1450,) married three times (1) 1471 Isabel (who d. before July 1513,) dau. and sole heir of Thomas Croxford of Kidlington-on-the-Green, (2) Anne dau. of Nicholas Warham of Malshanger, Hants, and widow of Sir Wm. Reade of Borestall, (who d. about 1525, son of Sir Edmund by his first wife,) and (3) Elizabeth dau. and co-heir of Sir Robert

Harcourt K.B. By her will dated 8 June 1489 his mother gave him "her grete salt," and to his wife "a crymson." By deed dated 3 May 1502 George Gaynesford sold Hampton Poyle manor and advowson for £316 6 8 to Rd. Hungerford.

1495, 1497, 1510, 1512, 1515, 1523. Returns lost.

1529. Oct. Sir John Dauntesey.

Sir William Barentyne.

Sir John Dauntsey, Daunce, or Dantsey, M.P. for Oxfordshire 1529-36, was Knighted 1513. There are many references to him in *Brewer's Letters and Papers of Hen.* 8, from which it appears that he was made a Commr. of the Peace for Oxfordshire 12 Feb. 1524 and 24 Jan. 1525, in Middlesex 26 Nov. 1524, and Berks and Bucks 24 Nov. 1530, a Commr. to collect the subsidy in Middlesex 1 Aug. 1524, and a Commr. for searches in London 12 Feb. 1525. He was one of the "King's servants," (and quære a Treasurer of War to Henry 8.) John Dauntsey, J. Barentyne, John Latton (see Oxford city 1529,) and Thomas Denton (see 1558,) were made Commrs. of Gaol Delivery for Oxford Castle in cos. Oxon and Berks.

Sir William Barentyne of Little Haseley, was Knighted 1513, M.P. Oxon 1529-36, and High Sheriff of Berks and Oxon 1511, 1525, and 1542. He was the son of John Barentyne (see 1467) by Mary dau. of Thomas Stonor, and married Anne Gray of Eton, widow, (who died 27 Dec. 1522.) In 1513 Barentyne was Captain of The Trinity Dytton of 100 tons, 259 men, and in June 1513 he went over with a retinue of 12 with the King to Calais. On 17 June 1513, Protection and writs of recoveries in Oxon, Southampton, and Wilts for W. Barentyne. squire of the body, appointed to serve in the war. He was made J.P. for Oxford city 22 Aug. 1516, and was one of the foremost and most active men of the county, of which he was made a Commissioner of the Peace 12 Feb. 1524, 24 Jan. 1525, and 11 Feb. 1526, and app. a Commr. to collect the subsidy 1 Aug. 1547. He was M.P. for Oxfordshire 1529-36, and in Dec. 1529 wrote from his house at Hasley to "his heartily beloved friend, Master Cromwell. Hoped to have seen him in those parts before Christmas. Will make him welcome if he will come to his house. Asks his favour in his suit for the ferme of the parsonage of Churchyll. Heard to-day that John Hacker has a new grant of it for 42 years from the Dean of my Lord Cardinal's College. Hears that the Indenture is engrossed, but hopes Cromwell will stop it being sealed. It is very commodious for Barantyne, as it is within his own manor." *(Brewer).* On 25 April 1539 Sir Wm. Barrentyne, Sir John Brome, John Wellsborne, and John Pollerd (see 1553,) as Commrs. in co. Oxon for taking the musters, certified the same. *(Cal. State Papers.)* He died 17 Nov. 1546, his will being proved 12 Feb. 1550, and ing. p.m. at Oxford 21 Feb. 1550.

1536. May. } Returns lost.
1539. April. }

1542. Jan.   Sir John Willyams Knt.
              Edward Bridges.

Sir John Williams of Thame, second son of Sir John
Williams Knt. of Burghfield, Berks, by Elizabeth dau. and co-
heir of Richard Moore of Burfeilde, was descended from a common
progenitor with Sir Robert Williams *alias* Cromwell, ancestor to
the Protector, and was a very powerful personage in the county.
He was "servant" to Hen. 8, had a patent of £10 per annum for
the keeping of a greyhound 18 Hen. 8, and was Clerk of the
King's Jewel Office in 1541, where on Christmas Eve a great fire
took place, and many of the royal jewels were burned or stolen.
He had a Patent for the office of Master or Treasurer of the Jewel
Office, and on surrendering that he afterwards had a joint Patent
of the same with Thomas Cromwell. On 10 May 1545 he was one
of the Commrs. app. to suppress St. Frideswide's College, (now
Ch. Ch. Oxford,) and the Cathedral Church of Osney, by receiving
the surrender of them into the King's hands. 20 May 1549
Warrant to Sir John Williams to send £3000 to the North. 26
June 1552, Conveyance by Sir J. W. (Treasurer of the Court of
Augmentations,) to Richard Warde of the lands called Woods
Grove in the parish of Hurst. Wilts. He was M.P. Oxon 1542-4,
1547-52, Feb. to 31 March 1553, and Sept. to Dec. 1553, was Knighted
18 Oct. 1537, H. S. Berks and Oxon 1538, 1544, 1533, High
Steward of Oxford (fee £5 a year) from 1554 until his death, and
as sucn received numerous presents from the city. Sir John
Williams was one of the foremost to support Queen Mary's claim
to the throne, and proclaimed her in Oxfordshire, and was by her
created Baron Williams of Thame 2 April 1554, and was Lord
Chamberlain of her Household 1553-7. In 1554 he and Sir Henry
Bedingfield were app. Keepers of the Princess Elizabeth. Lord
Williams was present at the martyrdom of Archbishop Cranmer
at Oxford on 21 March 1556, in which he took an active and prominent part. He purchased in 1539 the manors of Great and Little
Rycot, Oxon, and had a grant from the Crown in 1540 of the
manors of Wytham, and Botley, Berks, and Weston on the Green,
Oxon. He was soon afterwards made chief supervisor of all the
swans within the river Thames, and all other waters in England,
except those of the Duchy of Lancaster, and Treasurer of the
Court of Augmentations. He surrendered the latter office in 1554,
and received a grant of £320 a year from the Crown. On the
Queen's marriage he was made Lord Chamberlain of the House-
hold to King Philip, He m. (1) Elizabeth dau. and co-heir of
Thomas Bledlow of London, and widow of Andrew Edmunds of
Cressing Temple, Essex, and (2) about 1557 Margery dau. of
Baron Wentworth. "Item 28 May 1557, geven unto my Lady
Wyllyams for her welcome into the countre at her comming fyrst

after maryage, £5, and a pair of gloves," (*Turner*). In Feb. 1559 Queen Elizabeth app. him to be Lord President of Wales, an office much sought after, and on 17 March following, Lord Paget wrote to Sir William Cecil, stating " Lord Williams of Thame is very sick and not likely to recover. Solicits his office of Lord President of Wales." Lord Williams however recovered at the time, but died 14 Oct. 1559, and was buried in Thame Church. (M.I.) The Barony fell into abeyance between his two surviving daughters, (see 1571 and 1597.)

Edward Bridges M.P. for Oxon 1542-4, was probably uncle to the first Lord Chandos, and to the M.P. 1559, and in that case would be the son of Sir Gyles Brydges of Cuberley, co. Gloucester.

1545.   Jan.   Return lost.

1547.   Oct 4.   Sir John Willyams.

Richard Fener, (Fenys.)

Sir Richard Fenys or Fiennes, of Broughton, was the son of Edward Fiennes, *de jure* Baron Saye and Sele, and m. Ursula dau. of William Farmer.

1553.   Feb.   Sir Andrew Dudley.

Sir John Wylliams.

The former was the second son of Edmund Dudley, and brother to that powerful nobleman John Duke of Northumberland, who was beheaded for placing his daughter in law Lady Jane Grey upon the throne in 1553. He m. 1553 Margaret Clifford dau. of Earl Clifford.   27 Feb. 1547, Instructions by the Council to A. Duddeley esq. appointed to be Admiral of the Fleet to command the Pauncy, and to cruize in the North Seas off the coasts of England and Scotland.   He was speedily engaged with the enemy, for on 12 March he wrote from Harwich to Thomas Lord Seymour, Lord High Admiral, " sending letters taken in the late action, and desiring to know what to do with the prisoners.   Repairs necessary for the Pauncy."   He was knighted by the Duke of Somerset, Lord Protector, 18 Sept. 1547, and in 1549 was one of the four Knights in attendance on the young King, and Keeper of his Wardrobe.   In 1550 he was Keeper of the Palace of Westminster, and was soon afterwards made Captain of Guisnes.   He was granted a small pension 17 May 1551, and made a Knight of the Garter 24 April 1552.   On 8 Jan. 1552 John Duke of Northumberland wrote from Ely Place to Sir William Cecil, mentioning the dispute between the Lord Deputy of Calais and the Duke's brother Sir And. Duddeley.   The upshot was that Sir Andrew was recalled from Guisnes on 6 Oct. 1552, and on 28 Dec. following Northumberland wrote to Cecil, " Finds the King purposes to employ some ministers abroad. Suggests that his brother Sir A. D. should be sent to the French

King." The death of Edward 6, on 6 July 1653, put an effectual bar to Northumberland's power of advancing his brother, but Sir Andrew repaid the Duke's kindness by assisting him in his ambitious design of placing Lady Jane Grey upon the throne, and the two brothers were convicted of high treason. More fortunate than the Duke, Sir Andrew was respited, and eventually set at liberty 18 Jan. 1555. He made his will 1556, and died s.p. 1559.

1553. Sept. Sir John Willyams.

John Pollarde.

John Pollard who was Speaker of the House of Commons during this Parliament and that of Oct. to Dec. 1555, was the 2nd son of Walter P. of Plymouth, and entered the Middle Temple (? 3 June 1515,) where he was called to the bar, and served as Autumn Reader 1535. He became a Sergeant at law 1547, but was relieved by patent of that degree 21 Oct. 1550, in order to be app. Vice President of the Council of the Marches of Wales, and was Justice of the Great Sessions for counties Brecknock, Glamorgan, and Radnor Nov. 1550-7, and Justice of Chester 1557-58. He was Knighted 2 Oct. 1553, M.P. Oxon. Sept. to Dec. 1553, March to May 1554, and Oct. 1554 to Jan. 1555, Barnstaple March to May 1554, Chippenham Sept. to Dec. 1555 also Exeter Oct. 1555, (but preferred Chippenham,) and Grampound 1562-7, Recorder of Gloucester 1553-6, and Recorder of Oxford 15 April 1554 until his death, in which capacity he received several gifts from the city. Pollard received a grant of the manor of Nuneham Courtney after 1545 and made his residence there. He m. Mary dau. of Richard Gray of London, and was buried 25 Aug. 1577. (See *Williams' Welsh Judges.*)

1554. March. Sir Leonard Chamberlen.

John Pollard.

Sir Leonard Chamberlain of Shirburn Castle, H. S. Berks and Oxon 1546 and 1552, was the son of Sir Edward Chamberlain K.B., and m. Dorothy dau. of John Newdigate, serjeant at law. As Esquire he was in the procession bringing Ann of Cleves to London on 3 Jan. 1540. He was Knighted the day after the Queen's Coronation, on 2 Oct. 1553, was M.P. Oxon March to May 1554 and Oct. 1554 to Jan. 1555, and died 27 Aug. 1561. On 7 July 1557 the Queen wrote to the Council giving orders that Sir Hugh Paulet and Sir Leonard Chamberlain, Captains of Jersey and Guernsey, were to repair with all speed to their respective charges. Sir Leonard was still "a Captain at Guernsey," (that is the Governor thereof,) at the time of his death there in 1561. He had held the government since 1553, but in 1555 his son Francis Chamber was made Joint Governor with him. He attended the Princess Elizabeth during her captivity at Woodstock 1554-5.

1554.   Oct. 13.   Sir L. Chamberlyne.
· John Pollard.
1555.   Sept. 24. Sir Thomas Wenman.
Edmund Powell.

Sir Thomas Wenman was the eldest son of Richard
Wenman of Thame Park, and Caswell, H. S. 1562 and 1570, who
died 1572, by his wife Isabella dau. and co-heir of Lord Williams
of Thame, (see 1542.)   He married (? (1) Ursula dau. and heir of
of Thomas Giffard of Twyford, Bucks, and (2ndly) 9 June 1572
Hon. Jane West dau. of Wm. 8th. Lord de la Warr, was Knighted
in 1553, sat for Oxfordshire Sept. to Dec. 1555, and died 22 July
1577.

Edmund Powell of Sandford, elder son of Maurice
Appowel of Guernon, co. Cardigan, married Isabell Banester,
and was M.P. Ludgershall Sept. to Dec. 1553, and 16 to 31 March
1554, and Oxon Sept. to Dec. 1555.   He was the father of
Edmund Powell of Oxon, who matric. Hart Hall, Oxford,
(entry under date) 20 Dec. 1577, aged 11.   Edmund Powell
of Sandford received a grant from the King 15 Jan.
1542 of " the whole of the house and scite of the
Carmelite (White) Friars, commonly called " le white freers"
with a tenement and garden adjacent and a way called an 'entre'
(i.e. Friar's Entry,) and one close called le tymbre yarde etc."
On 20 Feb. 1572 Edmund Powell, prisoner in the Tower, in a
letter to Lord Treasurer Burghley " details the progress of the
design " made by him and Sir Henry Percy to effect the escape
of the Queen of Scots.   Requests to be liberated."   In 1573
appears a " Grant to Edmund Powell of pardon and remission of
the fine " of 3000 marks on condition of paying the sum of £20 a
year for his life.

1558.   Jan.   George Owen.
Thomas Denton.

George Owen of Godstowe, Oxon, was born in the diocese
of Worcester, and educ. at Oxford.   He became probationer
fellow of Merton College 1519, and took the degree of Doctor of
Medicine at Oxford 1527.   Soon after his gradation he was app.
Physician to Hen. 8, in which office he also served Edw. 6, and
Queen Mary.   He was adm. a Fellow of the College of Physicians
25 June 1545, an Elect 1552, and President 2 Oct. 1553, and 1554.
He was one of the subscribing witnesses to the will of Hen. 8,
who left him a legacy of £100.   He m. Letice dau. of ———— of
Suffolk, and was M.P. Oxon 1558, and Receiver General of the
Duchy of Lancaster until his death in October 1558.   On
22 Nov. 1541 the King granted to George Owen M.D.
for £1174 the manors of Walton and Wolvercote formerly
belonging to the dissolved monastery of Godstow.   On 7 Aug.

1552 the Privy Council wrote to the Mayor and Burgesses of Oxford to " withdrawe theyr sheape from ij pastures Crepley and Portmead and to cease theyre digging and rising of bancks in the sayd pastures until the matter in controversie between them and Mr. Owen for this purpose be had and determined." (*Cal. State Papers*). He presented to St. Giles' Church, Oxford, 9 Dec. 1553, and 2 Oct. 1554. He died 18 Oct. 1558, and was buried at St. Stephen's, Walbrook, London, 24 Oct. On 10 Nov. 1558 a Commission was given to Mr. Walgrave and the Auditor of the Duchy of Lancaster, to take the accompt of Dr. Owen late Rec. Gen. of the Duchy.

Thomas Denton of Sanderfield, Beselslee, and Hillersdon, Bucks, H.S. Berks and Oxon 1526, was elder son of Thomas D, of Caverfeild, Oxon, and m. Margaret dau. to the Lord Mordant. widow to —— Phetiplace. He was one of the chief means of obtainining for the town of Banbury the privilege of returning a Member of Parliament, and was its first Member March to May 1554, and probably again Oct. 1554 to Jan. 1555, and Sept. to Dec. 1555. Grant 15 Dec. 1540 to Thomas Denton, a sewer of the Chamber, to be under steward of the lands of the late abbey of Abingdon. (*Brewer*). He was a barrister of the Middle Temple, and M.P. for Berks 1547-52, Bucks Nov. 1554 to Jan. 1555, and Oxfordshire Jan. 1558 until his death 30 Oct. 1558, being Recorder of Oxford 14 Sept. 1557-8. " 1556, Payd to Mr. Denton for his hallfe yeare feyes—xxs. 1558, Pd. to Mr. Denton—xxs." (Corporation Accounts of Banbury).

1559. Jan. 10. Thomas Bridges.

Edmund Ashfilde.

Thomas Bridges of Corneburye, 2nd son to Sir Gyles Brydges of Cuberkley, co. Gloucester, and next brother to John 1st Lord Chandos. He m. Jane eldest dau. and co-heir of John Sydenham of Orchard, Somerset, and was H.S. Berks and Oxon 1556, and M.P. Oxon Jan. to May 1559. (The High Sheriff of Berks was also Sheriff of Oxon from 30 Henry 3 to 9 Elizabeth, when a separate Sheriff was appointed for each county). He was granted 10 March 31 Hen. 8, a lease for 21 years of the manor of Fulbroke and Westhall, Oxon, which the King purchased from George Lord Cobham, (*Brewer*), and died 14 Nov. 1559.

Edmund Ashfield or Ashefeld of Heythrop, Northants,and Ewelme, was the second son of John Ashfield, and m. Eleanor dau. of —— Humphrey of Mouston Park, Northants, and relict of William Stafford of Tottneshoo, Bucks. He was app. by the King to be keeper of the royal manor and park of Ewelme 9 June 1536, Bailiff for life of Whaddon manor, Bucks, 16 Feb. 1546, and Steward for life of Cuddesdon manor, Oxon, 1 Dec. 1551, all belonging to the King, and received 22 May 1554 a grant of the Priory and lands of Snellshall, Bucks, for ever, and was granted.

12 Sept. 1559 the office of Surveyor of all manors etc. belonging to the Crown in Bucks. Ashfield must have played his cards well to enjoy office for so long a period under four successive Monarchs, especially during the religious differences of that period. He was Knighted at Eythorpe 1570, H.S. of Berks and Oxon 1558, and of Bucks 1568, M.P. (as Asshefeld and Asschefyld) for Wallingford April to May 1554, and Nov. 1554 to Jan. 1555, and for Oxon Jan. to May 1559. As J.P. for Bucks he made his declaration to observe the Act of Uniformity 17 Nov. 1569, and on 25 Aug. 1571, the High Constable of Ewelme made to Sir Edmund Ashfield and other Justices of Oxon, his certificate of search for rogues and vagabonds in the Half Hundred of Ewelme. (*Cal. State Papers*). He presented to Wavendon, Bucks, in 1570, which manor he held *jure uxoris*, but both joined in selling it the same year. He died 24 Jan. 1577, and was buried at Shenley, Bucks, 15 Feb. His will was proved in the Prerogative Court of Canterbury 3 Feb. 1577.

> 1562. Dec. 8. Sir Francis Knolles.
>
> Sir Richard Blunt.

Sir Francis Knollys of Rotherfield Greys, elder son of Robert K. of that place, who died 1521, was born in or about 1514, and married Catherine dau. of William Carey, esquire of the body to Hen. 8, and sister to the 1st Lord Hunsdon. This lady was first cousin to Queen Elizabeth which partly accounts for the high position of her husband at Court during that Queen's reign. On 5 March 1547 Knollys writes to Paget, and " declares his long services, which had impaired his estate ; states the amount of his debts." He was Knighted 28 Sept. 1547, M.P. Horsham 1545-7, Camelford 1547-52, Arundel 1559. Oxon, 1362-7, 1571, 1572-83, 1584-5, 1586-7, 1588-9, and Jan to April 1593, created M.A. at Cambridge 10 Aug. 1564, and M.A. Oxford 6 Sept. 1566, being then Captain of the Halberdiers. and was made a Privy Councillor and Vice Chamberlain of the Queen's Household 1563, (Treasurer 1572,) Comptroller 1588-90, and Treasurer of the Household 1586-96, and also Captain of the Yeomen of the Guard 1569-78. On 23 Sept. 1560 the Queen gave orders to the Marquis of Winchester for a Warrant to make a grant to Sir Francis Knollys and the Lady Catherine his wife and to Robert K. one of their sons, of the manor of Taunton and Tandene, Somerset, for the term of their lives. On 17 Jan. 1569 Sir F. Knollys writing to the Queen, " Gives advice for the management of her Council. Is himself unfitted for a courtier," and on 8 Oct. following Her Majesty gave him directions to repair to the Duke of Norfolk, and to conduct him to the Tower. He was Constable of Wallingford Castle and Steward of the Honour of Ewelme, and Keeper of its Park 7 March 1551 till April 1578, when he was succeeded in these posts by his son Henry, (see 1572.) He was made High Steward of Oxford in succession to Lord Bedford 3

Feb. 1564, and he and his wife were the recipients of many gifts and presents from the city in return for their patronage and good offices. Knollys was made a Knight of the Garter 25 Jnne 1593, and died 19 July 1596.

Sir Richard Blount of Mapledurham Gurney was the 2nd but eldest surviving son of Richard Blount of Iver, Bucks, and Maple Durham, H. S. Bucks and Beds 1502, who died 1508, and grand-nephew to Walter 1st Baron Mountjoy, Lord High Treasurer of England, who died 1474. He m. Elizabeth dau. of Sir Richard Lister, Lord Chief Justice of England, was Knighted about 1550-52, and M.P. Oxon 1562-4. Blount was a Gentleman of the Chamber to Hen. 8, and of the Privy Chamber to Edw. 6, and served Queen Elizabeth in various offices, being finally Lieutenant of the Tower of London for a couple of years or so until his death 11 Aug. 1564, being buried in the Church of Peter in Vinculis in the Tower. On 6 April 1564 he wrote from Mapledurham to Cecill, "Perceives that the Queen has granted the Provost of Paris leave to come from Oxford to London. Cannot take upon him to leave the Provost at any place in London but the Tower." 5 March 1540, lease for 21 years to Ric. Blount, of the Household, of Hornesey rectory and manor, Yorkshire. (*Brewer*). He was father of Sir Michael Blount, H. S. Oxon 1586, 1596, who was also app. Lieut. of the Tower 1590, and who unsuccessfully laid claim to the Barony of Mountjoy before the House of Lords in 1596. His eldest son Richard Blount had livery of Bicester Priory 2 May 1592.

1564 ———— A Member (name unknown), *vice* Blount deceased.

1571. April. Sir Francis Knollys.
Sir Henry Norreys.

Sir Henry Norreys Knt. of Rycot, Oxon, and Wytham, Berks, was the son of Sir Henry Norreys who lost his head in the cause of Queen Anne Boleyn. He married Margery younger dau. and co-heir of Lord Williams of Thame, (see 1542,) by which he greatly increased his estate, and became one of the most powerful men of the county. He was Knighted at Rycot by the Queen 1566, H. S. Oxon 1561, M.P. 1571, and on his wife conveying to him the manor of Rycote he was summoned to Parliament as Baron Norreys of Rycote 8 May 1572. He was several times sent Ambassador to France, and on 18 Oct. 1564 wrote to Sir Wm. Cecill, requesting that he would allow him a reasonable time for despatch of his own affairs. On 8 March 1569 Lord Cobham informed Cecill, that the servants of the French Ambassador and of Sir Henry Norreys were gone to Dover on their way to Boulogne. On 22 Oct. 1570 Francis Walsingham (see Banbury 1562,) wrote to Cecill, hoping that the Queen had made choice of some other than himself to succeed

Sir Henry Norris in France. On 9 Feb. 1576, Request of Lord
Norreys to the Court of Parliament, to be restored in blood and
honours. This was on account of his father's execution and
attainder for high treason in the reign of Hen. 8, and was
doubtless granted. He died 27 June 1601, and was succeeded as
2nd Lord Norreys by his grandson Francis, who was created
Viscount Thame and Earl of Berkshire 28 Jan. 1621, but
committed suicide 29 Jan. 1623, when the Earldom became
extinct.

1572. April 15. Sir Francis Knolles.

Henry Knolles.

Father and son, Henry Knollys of Kingsbury, co. Warwick,
eldest son of Sir Francis K. (see 1562,) was educ. at Magdalen
College School, Oxford, and became an Esquire of the Body to
Queen Elizabeth. He m. before 11 April 1568 Margaret dau. of
Sir Ambrose Cave, and was M.P. Shoreham 1562-7, and Oxon
1572-82. He was Constable of Wallingford Castle, and Steward of
the Honour of Ewelme and Keeper of its Park, in succession to
his father, 4 April 1578, until his death v.p. Dec. 1582, His Will
was made 21 Dec. 1582, and proved 14 May 1583.

1584. Nov. 10. Sir Francis Knollys.

William Knollys.

Father and son again, a most unusual circumstance, and
one which shows the great influence of the family in the County.
William Knollys was the 2nd but eldest surviving son and heir
of the M.P. 1562, and was born 1547, and probably a commoner
of Magd. Coll. Oxford in and before 1564. He entered the
Middle Temple in 1565, and four year later was a Captain in the
army in the North. He was M.P. Stafford 1571, Tregony 1572-83,
and for Oxon 1584-5, Jan. to April 1593, Sept. 1597 to Feb. 1598,
and Sept. to Dec. 1601, and succeeded his brother Henry (see
1572) as Keeper of the manor of Ewelme and Constable of Wallingford Castle 20 June 1584, which posts he still enjoyed in 1609.
Knollys became a Captain of Horse in the Low Countries in 1585,
and was Knighted by the Earl of Leicester 7 Oct. 1586. He was
made Colonel of the Oxford and Gloucester regiments of Foot
1588, was a Dep. Lieut. of Oxon in 1591, created M.A. Oxford 27
Sept. 1592, and was sworn a Privy Councillor 30 Aug. 1596 on
being app. Comptroller of the Queen's Household, which position
at Court he held until 1602. He was made Joint Lieut. of Berks
and Oxon 4 Nov. 1596, sole Lieut. July 1601, Lord Lieut. 22
March 1613, Joint Commr. to treat with the Dutch Ambassadors
Aug. 1598, Constable of Wallingford Castle and High Steward
and Master of the Game in the honour of Wallingford (in
reversion) 8 Feb. 1601, Treasurer of the Household 22 Dec. 1602
to Dec. 1616, again sworn a Privy Councillor 10 May 1613, and

created Baron Knollys three days later. His Lordship was furthermore created Viscount Wallingford 7 Nov. 1616, and Earl of Banbury 18 Aug. 1626. He was also Cofferer of the Household to Henry Prince of Wales in 1606, a Commr. of the Treasury 24 Jan. to 11 July 1614, Master of the Court of Wards and Liveries 10 Oct. 1614 to Dec. 1618, Joint High Steward of Reading 1614, was High Steward of Oxford in 1620, made K.G. 24 April 1615, Joint Keeper of Alishott Forest and Chace 2 July 1625, Joint Lord Lieut. of Berks 7 March 1628. and J.P. Oxon and Berks. The Earl m. (1) after 1573 Dorothy (who died 31 Oct. 1605) widow of Edmund Lord Chandos, (see *Williams' Gloucestershire Members,*) and dau. of Edmund 1st Lord Braye, and (2) 23 Dec. 1605 Lady Elizabeth Howard dau. of Thomas Earl of Suffolk. He died 25 May 1632, aged 85, leaving two sons Edward and Nicholas. (See Banbury 1733.)

1586.   Oct. 11.   Sir Francis Knowles.

Richard Fynes.

Richard Fiennes of Broughton Castle, son of Sir Richard F. of that place, (see 1547,) matric. (entry under date) 1568 Hart Hall, Oxford, aged 13, and ent. Lincolns Inn (as Richard Fynes of Hants) 1 Dec. 1573. He was Knighted in 1592, M.P. Banbury 1584-5, Oxon 1586-7, Whitchurch 1588-9, (and quaere 1597-8,) H. S. Oxon 1582, and Berks 1593, J.P. Oxon, D. L. Oct. 1596, and was confirmed Lord Saye and Sele 9 Aug. 1603. His Lordship m. (1) before Sept. 1582 Constance dau. of Sir Wm. Kingsmill of Sydmanton, Hants, and (2) Elizabeth dau. and heir of Henry Codenham, Auditor of the Mint, and widow of Wm. Pawlett of Winchester. He was Lord Attendant on the Ambassador to Brussels 19 April to 20 May 1605, made Dept Lieut. of Oxon in 1608, and died in April 1613. In 1595 the Queen leased Banbury Castle to his three children, then minors. "He was a worthy gent. and bred fellow, (being the founder's kinsman,) of New College, Oxford." (*Wood*). On 11 Oct. 1603 he was Keeper of Banbury Castle, when the King app. him to preserve the game of venery and falconry, and to punish all offenders who transgressed the laws by shooting, taking of partridges, etc., in Banbury and Bloxham. 28 Feb. 1608, Letters to the Warden and Fellows of Oxford for Lord Say to have a grant, in reversion, of the farm of Woodmancot, Hants. On 24 Nov. 1609 his Lordship wrote from Broughton to Lord Salisbury respecting " the wilful destruction and robbery of the trees in Needwood Forest, near Tutbury. The Prince wishes to have a breed of horses at Tutbury." William 2nd. Lord Saye and Sele was app. Master of the Court of Wards 1641, and Lord Lieut. of Oxon for the Parliament 1642.

1588.   Oct.   Sir Francis Knowles..

Hon Sir John Norris.

The Hon. Sir John Norris, 2nd son of Henry 1st Lord Norreys (see 1571,) was born about 1547, or in 1559, matric. Hart Hall Oxford (entry under date) 17 Dec. 1576, aged 17, and perhaps Lord President of Munster July 1584, created M.A. 11 April 1588. He was Knighted by the Earl of Leicester in Holland 26 April 1586, and was M.P. co. Cork in the Irish Parliament April 1585 to May 1586, and Oxon Oct. 1588 to March 1589. He is said to have died in Ireland unmarried in 1597. He was one of the most distinguished generals of the age, and fought hard against the French and Spanish in the Low Countries, being Commander in chief of the English forces in the Low Countries 12 Aug. 1585, until superseded by the Earl of Leicester Dec. 1585. He fought at Zutphen 22 Sept. 1586, and was Marshal of the camp at Tilbury under Leicester in the year of the Armada 1588. He was sent to Ireland as Lord General in 1596, and being disappointed in his expectation of succeeding Lord Deputy Russell, retired to his government of Munster. He is said to have died broken-hearted, on 3 July 1597.

1593.   Jan.   Sir Francis Knowles.

Sir William Knowles.

1597.   Sept. 27.   Sir William Knollys.

Sir Richard Wayneman.

Sir Richard Wenman of Thame Park, was the eldest son of Sir Thomas Wenman, (see 1554,) and was born 1573, matric. Oxford Univ. (entry dated) 8 Dec. 1587, aged 14, ("Mr. Case's scholar,") and was Knighted for his bravery as a Volunteer at Cadiz in 1596. He m. Agnes (who was buried 4 July 1617,) eldest dau. of Sir George Fermor of Easton Neston, Northants. He was M.P. Oxon 1597-8, 1620-2, and 1625, H.S. (as of Wilcot) 1601 and 1627, was created Viscount Wenman in the Peerage of Ireland 30 July 1628, and died 3 April 1640, aged 67. He was an overseer of the will of Lord Norreys, (see 1571,) and was examined in connection with the Gunpowder Plot, on 3 Dec. 1605, when he stated his dislike to his wife's intercourse with Mrs Vaux, because the latter tried to pervert her. His brother Thomas left an only dau. Mary who m. Francis Wenman of Caswell, and had a son, the M.P. 1664.

1601.   Sept. 22.   Sir William Knolles.

Ralph Warcuppe.

Ralph Warcuppe of English, near Henley, eldest son of Cuthbert Warcup, was of kin to Sir Edmund Warcup the historian of Italy. Several of the family sat in Parliament for Westmoreland. Ralph was app. Dep. Lieut. Oxon Oct. 1596,

M.P. Sept. to Dec. 1601, m. Katherine dau. of Alderman Masey of London, but died s.p. On 13 Jan. 1584 Job Throckmorton wrote from Haseley to Ralph Warcuppe, stating that he had "apprehended William Skinner and searched his house, and examined witnesses, who were in great fear of the threats of the Papists." Chamberlain wrote to Carleton at Paris 8 July 1601,—"Mr. Warcup is thought of as Ambassador lieger for France," and Carleton replied Oct. 24—"We are still in doubt whether to expect Warcup or Parkins as ambassador from you." Cuthbert Warcup was an intended Knight of the Royal Oak for Oxfordshire 1660.

    1604. March 7. Laurence Tanfeild.

               John Doyleye.

    The former was the son of Francis Tanfield of Gayton, Northants, and having been called to the bar at the Inner Temple in due course, became Reader thereof Lent 1595, Serjeant at law Easter 1603, M.P. Woodstock 1584-5, 1586-7, 1588-9, 1593, 1597, 1601, and Oxon 1604 until made a Justice of the King's Bench 13 Jan. 1606. He was Knighted 14 March 1604, promoted to be Lord Chief Baron of the Exchequer 25 June 1607, and presided in that Court until his death. He m. Elizabeth Evans of Loddington, Northants, and resided at Burford Priory, Oxon, which estate, with the manor of Great Tew he had purchased. The Judge died 30 Aprll 1625. (M.I. Burford). Tanfield Court in the Temple was called after him. His only dau. and heiress Elizabeth m. Henry 1st Viscount Falkland, Lord Lieut. of Ireland, grandfather of the M.P. 1659.

    John Doyley of Chislehampton, 2nd son of Sir Robert D. of that place, matric. Univ. Coll. Oxford 1 Dec. 1592, aged 14, ent. Lincolns Inn 12 Feb. 1596, and migrated to Grays Inn 9 March 1606. He was heir to his elder brother Sir Robert and m. Ursula sister of Sir Anthony Cope Bart. (see 1606,) was M.P. Oxon 1604-11, and made Dep. Lieut. Oct. 1596.

    1606 (about Feb.) Sir Anthony Cope Knt. and Bart. *vice* Tanfield made a Judge.

    Sir Anthony Cope of Hanwell Castle, Hardwick, and Grimsbury, one of the foremost men of the county, was the elder son of Edward Cope, and grandson of Sir Anthony Cope who was H.S. 1548, and Vice Chamberlain to Queen Catherine Parr. He was of Oxford Univ. 1551, and m. (1) Frances dau. of Sir Rowland Lytton of Knebworth, Herts, and (2) Anne dau. of Sir William Paston of Norfolk. In 1584 he obtained a lease of two water-mills in Banbury from the Crown, and received a grant of the manor of Grimsbury. He had great influence at Banbury, of which he was Member 1571, 1572-83, 1586-7, 1588-9, 1593, 1597-8, and 1601, and he sat for the County 1606-11, and March to June 1614, being H.S. 1581, 1590, and 1603, and made a Dep. Lieut.

Oct. 1596. Cope was a leader of the early Puritans and was committed to the Tower on 27 Feb. 1587 for bringing forward a motion in the House of Commons, " That all laws then in force touching ecclesiastical government should be void." He remained a prisoner until Parliament was dissolved on 23 March following. This however did not prevent him being Knighted by the Queen 1591. Sir Anthony had the honour of entertaining James I at Hanwell on 20 Aug. 1606, for a day and night, and again on 27 Aug. 1612. He was made a J.P. for Banbury by the Charter 28 June 1608, created a Baronet 29 June 1611, and was buried in Hanwell Church in July 1614. On 12 Nov. 1588 he wrote from Hanwell to Lord Burghley, " desiring to have the wardship of the son of Mr. Ric. Hunston, who lies very dangerously sick at London, he being indebted to him." On 22 May . 1589 John Danvers of Cothropp, Sheriff of Oxon, wrote to the Lord Chancellor as follows,—" Has been obliged to acquaint the Archbishop of Canterbury with the bad proceedings of Ant. Cope and others of the town of Banbury who under the plea of religion were practising to abolish most pastimes used in the country, as May-poles, Morris dances, Whitsun-ales, and others to the great discontentment of Her Majesty's loving subjects. Desires that the matter may be considered by the Council." On 24 May the Council wrote to Lord Norris (see 1571,) that " They have been informed that there has been some disorder in the town of Banbury about the setting up of a May-pole, and like pastimes of recreation. They see no objection to such pastimes, so that they were not made an excuse for unlawful meetings."

1614.   March.   Sir Anthony Cope Knt. and Bart.

Sir John Crooke Knt.

Sir John Croke of Chilton, Bucks, was the elder son of Sir John Croke, Justice of the King's Bench 1608-20, by Catherine dau. of Sir Michael Blount of Mapledurham, Lieut. of the Tower, (see 1562,) and matric. Univ. Coll. Oxford 18 July 1600, aged 14, and entered the Inner Temple in 1601. He was Knighted 18 April 1609, m. (1) about 1616 Eleanor (who was only aged 14 at her marriage, and died in two years after it aged 15 years and 7 months, before 1618,) youngest dau. and co-heir of Jervas Gibon of Kent, and (2) Rachel dau. and heir of Sir Wm. Webb Knt. of Motcomb, Dorset. He was M.P. Oxfordshire March to June 1614, and Shaftesbury 1628-9, and died at Chilton 10 April 1640, aged 53. (M.I. Chilton).

1620.   Dec. 20.   Sir Richard Wenman Knt.

Hon. Sir William Pope Knt.

It is presumed that the former was the same as the M.P. 1597. His colleague was probably the elder son of William 1st Earl of Downe, who built a large mansion house near the site

and ruins of Witney Priory, and his family resided there a considerable time. James I paid a visit to Wroxton on one occasion.
Sir William was baptized 17 Oct. 1596, subscribed Oxford Univ.
1 July 1614, was Knighted 28 Aug. 1616, and m. Elizabeth only
child of Sir Thomas Watson of Halstead, Kent. He sat for Oxon
1620-2, and died v.p. 29 Aug. 1624, being buried at Wroxton.
" March 1611, Particulars of Sir Wm. Pope's lands in Whichwood
Forest." (*Cal. State Papers.*)

> 1624. Jan. 14.   Sir William Cope Knt. and Bart.   •
>   Sir Henry Poole Knt.

Sir William Cope of Hanwell Castle was the son of the
M.P. 1606, whom he succeeded as 2nd Bart. in July 1614. He
matric. Queen's Coll. Oxford 22 Feb. 1594, aged 17, and married
at Hanwell in 1602 Elizabeth dau. of (his father's second wife
Anne dau. of Sir William Paston, by her first husband) Sir
George Chaworth of Wiverton, Notts, whose sole heiress she was,
by which he acquired the manor of Marnham, Notts, and other
considerable property. He was Knighted at the Charterhouse
11 May 1603, M.P. Banbury 1604-11, 1614, 1620-2, and 1625 until
void, and Oxon 1624-5, and was H.S. 1619. He died 2 Aug. 1637.
Grant 26 July 1614, to Sir Wm. Cope on tenure of knight's
service, of purchase of certain lands, cos. Oxford and Gloucester,
late of the monastery of Brewerne, for the sum of £1347 6s 8d.
Grant to Sir Wm. Cope of the Office of keeping the armoury for
life 1 March 1615. " Winwood has bargained with Sir Phil.
Stanhope to pay £10000 to be made a Baron, Sir Wm. Cope
having dallied too long about it." (Chamberlain to Carleton,
12 Oct. 1616.

Sir Henry Poole of Okesey, Wilts, was the son of Edward
P. of that place, and matric. Trin. Coll. Oxford (entry under
date) 29 Jan. 1580, aged 16. He was Knighted 10 June 1603,
M.P. Cricklade 1604-11, Wilts 1614 and 1626, Malmesbury 1620-2,
and Oxon 1624-5, and died 3 Oct. 1632. On 17 Nov. 1625 Sec.
Conway wrote to Lord Keeper Conway,—I received your letters
and the three names submitted for Oxfordshire, viz. Sir Richard
Blunt, Sir Gyles Bray, and Sir Henry Poole, of whom His
Majesty has pricked Blunt.

> 1625. May.   Edward Wraye.
>   Sir Richard Wenman.

Edward Wraye of Rycote, was the third son of Sir Wm.
Wray Knt. and Bart. of Glentworth, co. Lincoln, and was
baptized at Louth in that county 9 Nov. 1589. Early in life he
formed the acquaintance of the celebrated George Villiers, afterwards Duke of Buckingham, who became his fast friend, and
with whom he was a great favourite. When Villiers acquired his
ascendancy over James I, he procured for Wray the appointment
of a Groom of the Bedchamber to the King in 1617, and the latter

was also in a fair way of becoming a great courtier, until his
romantic marriage in March 1622, brought about his downfall at
Court, and his dismissal from his office in attendance on the
King. Wray had been deeply attached for some time to his
future wife, and matters had prog.essed so favourably, that on 13
Jan. 1621 Chamberlain wrote to his friend Carleton,—"Lord
Norris is to be Earl of Thame, on marrying and assuring his
land to Edw. Wray of the Bedchamber." Norris was made Earl
of Berkshire but committed suicide two years afterwards leaving his
only daughter one of the richest heiresses at Court. A formidable
rival in the person of the Duke's brother Christopher Villiers,
had appeared as a suitor for the lady's hand, and the Favourite
using his influence over the King to back his brother's suit,there
is little doubt but that the heiress would have been forced into
the marriage, had not the lovers made a run-away match, in
defiance of the King's displeasure. " Mr Wray is put out of the
Bedchamber for marrying the Earl of Berkshire's daughter, who
was intended for Kit Villiers; the lady was very cunning and
resolute, more in order to be rid of the one than from love of the
other,"—wrote Chamberlain to Carleton on 30 March 1622, while
another correspondent, Thomas Locke, in a letter of the same
date gives Carleton a few more particulars of this little romance,
which furnished a good deal of gossip at the time:—"The Earl
of Berkshire's daughter, who was kept at the Earl of Montgomery's, got out of the house early, walked three miles on foot,
and was then met and taken to Aldermary Church, where she
married Mr Wray, of the Bedchamber ; they thence went to the
Earl of Oxford's house in Fleet Street, he being in the plot. Lord
Montgomery sent to fetch her away, but Oxford would not give
her up. His commission is taken from him, and Wray is put out
of the Bedchamber." Lord Oxford was on unfriendly terms with
Buckingham, and seems to have borne the brunt of his displeasure.
Wray was imprisoned for several months, for on 15 Feb. 1623
John Woodford wrote Sir Francis Nethersole that "Wray is set
at liberty." He was M.P. for Oxon May to Aug. 1625, and Secretary Conway wrote him on 30 Dec. 1625 stating that as there were
already more Knights than were necessary, the King was resolved
not to make any at his Coronation. A man of great charity and
piety, Wray lived thenceforth in retirement at Fritwell, Oxon,
until his death 21 March 1658, and was buried at Witham 29
March. By his wife Lady Elizabeth Norreys, only dau. and heir
of Francis 1st Earl of Berkshire (see 1571,) he left an only dau.
and heir Bridget who m. (2) Montagu 2nd Earl of Lindsey, and
their son James was created Earl of Abingdon 30 Nov. 1682, and
was father of the M.P. 1690.

1626. Jan. Hon. James Fynes.

Sir Thomas Wenman Knt.

The Hon. James Fiennes, Fenys, or Fynes, as his names was variously spelt in those days, was the eldest son of William 1st Viscount Saye and Sele, and grandson of the M.P. 1586. Born about 1603, he matric. Emmanuel College, Cambridge, and m. before Nov. 1638 Hon. Frances Cecil 4th dau. and co.-heir of Edward Viscount Wimbledon. He sat for Banbury 19 July to 12 Aug. 1625, and for Oxon Jan. to June 1626, 1628 to March 1629, March to May 1640, Oct. 1640 till secluded Dec. 1648, and April to Dec. 1660, presented to Weston under Edge, co. Gloucester, 1652, and succeeded his father as 2nd Viscount Saye and Sele 14 April 1662. His Lordship was seated at Broughton Castle, and was Lord Lieut. of Oxon 22 Feb. 1668 until his death s.p. 15 March 1674. He and his father sued out a Pardon in 1660. *Wood* said that "he had always been reputed an honest cavalier and a quiet man." On 13 Feb. 1660 the Declaration of the Gentlemen etc. of Oxon in favour of a free Parliament, and for the peace and settlement of the nation was presented to General Monk by Lord Falkland (see 1659,) Sir A. Cope (see 1661,) James Fiennes and others.

Sir Thomas Wenman of Thame Park, eldest son of the M.P. 1597, was born 1596, matric. Balliol Coll. Oxford (entry dated) 23 Nov. 1604 "aged 8," (subscribed as Waynman,) and entered the Inner Temple 1614. He was Knighted 10 Sept. 1617, m. Margaret dau. and heir of Edmund Hampden of Hart-well, Bucks, and succeeded his father (see 1597) as 2nd Viscount Wenman of Ireland 3 April 1640. He was M.P. Brackley 1620-2, 1624-5, 1625, 1628-9, and March to May 1640, and Oxon Jan. to June 1626, Oct. 1640 until secluded and imprisoned Dec. 1648, and again April to Dec. 1660. His Lordship died 25 Jan. 1664. He was one of the Adventurers in Ireland when that kingdom was reduced by the English Parliament. He was a Commr. to carry the Propositions for peace to the King at Oxford 1644, and for the Treaty at Uxbridge 1644, and at Newport 1648, and was app. by the Rump as Assessment Commr. for Oxon 2 March, 1660.

1628. March 5. Hon. James Fynes.
Sir Francis Wenman Knt.

Sir Francis Wenman of Caswell, son and heir of Francis W. (who d. in Ireland,) and nephew of the M.P. 1554, was Knighted 8 June 1618, and m. Anne third dau. of Sir Samuel Sandys of Ombersley, (see *Williams' Worcestershire Members*). He sat for Oxon 1628 to March 1629, and March to May 1640, and was cousin to the first Viscount Wenman (see 1597).

1640. March 18. The same.
1640. Oct. 28. Thomas Viscount Wenman.
Hon. James Fiennes.

This was the celebrated Long Parliament which lasted until it was expelled by Cromwell and his soldiers on 20 April 1653. Both of the Oxfordshire Members were however secluded from the House by Col. Pride's famous " Purge " in Dec. 1648.

1653. June. Sir Charles Worsley Knt.

William Draper. ·

Dr. Jonathan Goddard.

An Assembly, nominated by Oliver Cromwell and a Council of Officers, was summoned to meet at Westminster on 4 July 1653, by Letters under the hand of the Lord General Cromwell. This Assembly declared itself a Parliament on 6 July, and resigned its powers to the Lord General on 12 Dec. 1653. (*Commons Journals.*) It was called the "Little Parliament," or " Barebones' Parliament," from the name of its Speaker. Three Members were *appointed*, (not *elected*,) for Oxfordshire.

Sir Charles Wolseley of Wolseley, co. Stafford, was the eldest son of Sir Robert Wolseley, Clerk of the King's Letters Patent, whom he succ. as 2nd Bart. 21 Sept. 1646, and was born in or about 1630, being aged 16 in Oct. 1647, and m. 12 May 1648 the Hon. Anne Fiennes, sister of the M.P. 1626, and youngest dau. of William 1st Viscount Saye and Sele. He was an active military and civil supporter of Parliament, and being high· in favour with Cromwell, was made Major General of the counties of Chester, Lancaster, and Stafford, on the division of England into thirteen military districts Dec. 1654. He was M.P. Oxon July to Dec. 1653, and Staffordshire 1654-5, and 1656 until made one of Cromwell's Honse of·Lords as Lord Wolseley 10 Dec. 1657, and was added to the Sixth Council of State by Parliament April 1653, and also took the oath as a member of the Seventh Council of State on 1 Nov. 1653, which lasted till 10 Dec. 1653. On 30 June 1653 the Council ordered the Committee of Whitehall to provide lodgings there for Sir Charles Wolsely and Mr Draper, but this arrangement fell through, for on 18 July the Committee were again ordered to provide lodgings for Sir Charles. He was placed on numerous Committees. and took a leading part in Council matters. He was elected one of the Lord Protector's Council 16 Dec. 1653, and served as such until April 1658, and was also a member of his Privy Couucil (as it was then or previously called) from May until Sept. 1658, when Oliver Cromwell died. He was app. one of the Committee of Trade 12 July 1655, a Militia Commr. for co. Stafford 14 March 1655, and was one of the Privy Council to Richard Cromwell 1658 to April 1698. On 15 June 1660 the Attorney General wrote to Secretary Nicholas, " that the Earl of Bedford and Sir Charles Wolsher (*sic*) also desired Pardons." Wolseley made his peace with the King at the Restoration, and was M.P. for Stafford March to Dec. 1660. He died 2 or 9 Oct. 1714, aged 84.

From his fifth son Richard descended Garnet, Viscount Wolseley, the present Commander in Chief.

William Draper of Nether Warton, may have been the " William Draper (eldest son of Robert Draper,) who matric. Ch. Ch. Oxford 20 May 1636, aged 16." He was an active supporter of Parliament during the Commonwealth, and was a Sequestration Commissioner for Oxfordshire in March 1649 when he wrote to the Council of State concerning the " delinquents " at Oxford, (the Council replying 29 March, " Thanks for your letter manifesting care to preserve the peace of the Commonwealth,") and in Dec. 1649 when there is a reference to a conspiracy against him. Capt. Wm. Draper was app. by the Conncil to be Captain of the Horse Militia in Oxfordshire 2 April 1650, and as Governor of Oxford there are several references to his activity as such in the proceedings of the Council of State on 9 May 1651 and subsequent dates. He was made Captain of the Horse Volunteers of Oxford City and University 16 Aug. 1651, and on 17 Sept. following the Council wrote to Captain Draper, as follows:—" We ordered you to march with your company to Windsor Castle ; but since we have thought it necessary that your company should be appointed to the guard of Wallingford Castle. Therefore march to that Castle and remain there until you receive further order." On 30 June 1653 the Council of State, in their anxiety to house the Members of Barebones' Parliament, ordered " the Committee of Whitehall to provide lodgings there for Sir Charles Wolsely, and Mr Draper." On 5 Aug. following the same Committee was instructed " to assign to Mr. Draper a stable in the Mews," and furthermore on 22 Aug., " to put Mr Draper in possession of the lodgings in the Mews late Mr. Berry's, and the stable and coach-house late Mr Simpson's, unless Berry shew cause to the contrary." He was High Sheriff of Oxfotdshire in Jan. 1658.

Dr. Jonathan Goddard was the son of Henry Goddard, a wealthy ship carpenter, of Deptford, Kent, and was born at Greenwich, in or about 1617, and matric. Madg. Hall Oxford 11 May 1632, aged 15. He took the degrees of B.Med. from St. Catherine's Hall, Cambridge 1638, (aged 21,) and Doctor of Medicine 20 Jan. 1643, was incorporated at Oxford 14 Jan. 1652, and was adm. a candidate of the College of Physicians 22 Dec. 1643, of which he was elected a Fellow 4 Nov. 1646, read the Gulstonian Lectures in 1648, was Censor in 1660, 1661, 1664, 1665, 1666, 1668, 1670, 1672, and was named Elect 7 March 1672. Having practised physic in London for some time, Dr. Goddard became First Physician to the army and to Oliver Cromwell, whom he accompanied as his great confidant to Ireland in 1649, and to Scotland in 1650. He was app. Warden of Merton Coll. Oxon by the Parliamentary Visitors 9 Dec. 1651, but was removed by the King's letter 3 July 1660. Cromwell as Chancellor of Oxford

Univ. app. Goddard and four others to act as his delegates in all matters relating to grants or dispensations that required his assent, 16 Oct. 1652, during his absence in Scotland, He was M.P. Oxon July to Dec. 1653, added to the Hospitals Committee 17 May, and placed on several other Committees, took the oath as a member of the Seventh Council of State 1 Nov. to 10 Dec. 1653, and was placed 8 Nov. on the Committees for Lunaticks, and for · the Mint. He was made Professor of Physic at Gresham College 7 Nov. 1655, and was "an admirable chymist." (*Wood*). Goddard became a member of the First Council of the Royal Society on its establishment in 1663, and is said to have constructed the first telescope in this country. He died of an apoplexy 24 March 1675, seemingly unmarried.

1654. Aug. Robert Jenkinson.

Charles Fleetwood.

Col. James Whitlock.

Hon. Nathaniel Fienns.

William Lenthall.

(5 Members). Robert Jenkinson of Walcot, co. Oxon, and Hawkesbury, co. Gloucester, eldest son and heir of Sir Robert Jenkinson Knt. (High Sheriff 1643, who d. 1645,) by Anna Maria only dau. of Sir Robert Lee of Billeslee, co. Warwick, 2nd son of Sir Robert Lee, Lord Mayor of London. He was also descended from the celebrated Anthony Jenkinson who was Ambassador to Sultan Solyman the Grand Turk at Constantinople, to the Shah of Persia, Shah Tahmasp 1561, and to Abdullah Khan, King of Hircania 1563, and was the first Englishman to reach Bokhara and Khiva, where he opened up a trade route to Central Asia 1558-9, and was employed by Queen Elizabeth as Ambassador to Ivan the Terrible, Czar of Russia, in 1567, 1571, and April 1572, and opened up a trade route by the White Sea and Archangel. He was born in 1622, aged 12 at the Visitation of Oxon in 1634, and matric. Trin. Coll. Oxford 16 Dec. 1636, " aged 16," was adm. to the Inner Temple " at the request of Master Unton Croke " Nov. 1638, called to the bar 1649, and married Mary 2nd dau. of Sir John Bankes Knt. of Kingston Lacy and Corfe Castle, Dorset, Lord Chief Justice of the Common Pleas 1640-4, by Mary his wife only daughter of Ralph Hewtrey of Ruislip, Middlesex, the heroine of Corfe Castle. On 26 Jan. 1654 owing to his vigorous remonstrance, the committee for compounding allowed his title to houses in Fleet Street, London, (entailed on him by his father in 1642,) and forthwith discharged the sequestration thereon. He was H.S. Oxfordshire 1649, M.P. Aug. 1654 to Jan. 1655, Aug. 1656 to Feb. 1658, and Jan. to April 1659. He was created a Baronet 18 May 1661, and died 30 March 1677, being buried in the chancel of Charlbury Church, Oxon, (in which parish Walcot is situated,) on 10 April. (M.I. on chancel wall

and ledger stone on floor). He was the friend of the celebrated philosopher the Hon. Robert Boyle, and of Sir Matthew Hale. His widow died 13 June 1691, and was buried at Charlbury. On 12 June 1654, John Cary, Commissioner for co. Oxon, wrote to the Commissioners for Sequestions, as follows :—" I recommend Thos. Appletree of Deddington, late Commr. for Sequestrations, Rob. Jenkinson, of Walcot, Ald. Nixon, Mat. Langley, or ———— Berry of Oxford. all J.P.s., to assist me in examining witnesses, for though I should be faithful were the treasure of the nation committed to my trust, that cannot be known to you."—With note in reply 16 June, of a commission to Appletree or Nixon. On 29 March 1658 the Lord Protector's Council referred " the differences which have arisen touching the usages in Whichwood forest and the deer therein, in relation to Whitney Chase, to Miles Fleetwood (see 1656), Rob. Jenkinson and John Carey, to enquire what the ancient and latter customs have been, and what is expedient for preservation of the deer, to reconcile the differences if they can, and if not, certify their opinion." (*Cal. State Papers*).

The celebrated Lieut. Gen. Charles Fleetwood, was the third son of Sir Miles Fleetwood Knt. of Aldwinkle, Northants, who died 1641, (see Woodstock 1628,) but, unlike the rest of his family, who were staunch royalists, he was one of the leading supporters of Parliament and the Commonwealth. He ent. Grays Inn 30 Nov. 1638, and at the outbreak of the Great Civil War in 1642 entered the Life Guards of the Earl of Essex, and as Captain was wounded at the first battle of Newbury 20 Sept. 1643. In 1644 he was Colonel of a regiment in the Earl of Manchester's army, and fought at Naseby. He was made Governor of the Isle of Wight (with Col. Sydenham,) 14 Aug. 1649, and as Lieut. Gen. of Horse helped Cromwell to win the Battle of Dunbar 3 Sept. 1650. The next year he was recalled from Scotland and app. to command the forces retained in England, with which he defeated Charles II. at Worcester 3 Sept. 1651, and received the thanks of the House of Commons. Fleetwood was married three times, his first wife being Frances dau. of Thomas Smith of Winston, Norfolk. She was buried 24 Nov. 1651, and by his subsequent marriage in 1652 with Bridget, widow of the famous Lt. Gen. Henry Ireton, Lord Deputy of Ireland, and eldest dau. of Oliver Cromwell, he greatly increased his influence. He was M.P. Marlborough May 1646-53, Marlborough and Oxon 1654, when he preferred the latter till Jan. 1655, Norfolk, Oxon, and Marlborough 1656, when he preferred Oxon till made one of Cromwell's House of Lords as Lord Fleetwood 10 Dec. 1657. He was app. by Parliament to succeed his uncle Sir William Fleetwood (see Woodstock 1640,) as Receiver of the Court of Wards May 1644, was one of the third Council of State 13 Feb. to Nov. 1651, and of the fourth Council 1 Dec. 1651-2, app. one of

Cromwell's Council Dec. 1654, was one of the five Commissioners for the government of Ireland 24 Aug. 1652-4, Major General of the counties of Oxon, Norfolk, Suffolk, Essex, Cambridge, Huntingdon, and Bedford Dec. 1654, Commander-in-Chief in Ireland 10 July 1652 to Sept. 1655, and Lord Deputy of Ireland 27 Aug. 1654 (or earlier) to Nov. 1657. For some years previous to 1660 John Lambert, John Desborough, Robert Blake, and Charles Fleetwood were Commrs. to execute the offices of Constable of Dover Castle and Lord Warden of the Cinque Ports. He was chosen one of the Committee of Safety by the Army 7 May 1659, one of the Council of State by Parliament 13 May, one of the Committee for Dunkirk Sept. 1659, and Commander in Chief 9 June, but this last appointment was voided by Parliament Oct. 11, though he was made one of the seven Commissioners for managing the army. The army however again chose him Commander in Chief on Oct. 28, but on the Rump again getting the upper hand it once more deprived him of that post, and also of his regiment 26 Dec. 1659. He was made Col. of the Bucks Militia 1 Sept. 1659. In *The Mystery of the Good Old Cause, briefly unfolded*, a Restoration tract, dated 1660, the following character is given of Fleetwood:—" This pitiful Anabaptist was Oliver's son in law, and upon that score, advanced to be Lieut. Gen. of the Army; for merit he never had any. In the dividing of the murdered King's inheritance, Woodstock and other rich possessions fell to his share. About a year since he with some other officers ungratefully dethroned Protector Richard, restored the Rump for a while, and then unroofed them; after which during the space of near six weeks, he acted King at Wallingford House, (one of his Palaces,) but the Rump coming to sit again, the tender-hearted mock-prince melted into tears; and his hypocritical vizard of Religion being pulled off, he went off the stage ridiculously." He was excepted out of the Act. of General Pardon and Oblivion for penalties not extending to life 18 June 1660, but having taken no part in the King's trial, was not otherwise punished, though rendered incapable of ever holding any office of trust. Fleetwood buried Bridget his second wife, on 1 July 1662, and on 14 Jan. 1664 he married (3) Mary, dau. of Sir John Coke of Melborne, Derbyshire, and widow of Sir Edward Hartopp Bart. During the last years of his life he lived in retirement at Stoke Newington, Middlesex, where he died 4 Oct. 1692, his Will being made 10 Jan. 1690, and proved 2 Nov. 1692. (*Dict. Nat. Biog.*)

Col. James Whitlock of Trumpington, co. Cambridge, was the eldest son of Sir Bulstrode, Whitelocke, (see Oxford 1654,) being the only son by his first wife, and was baptized 28 July 1631, ent. the Middle Temple 1647, and was chosen a Fellow of All Souls College, Oxon, by the Parliamentary Visitors 22 Jan. 1649.

He was a Captain and afterwards a Colonel in the Army of the Parliament, was "Knighted" by Oliver Cromwell 6 Jan. 1656, and sat for Oxon 1654 to Jan. 1655, and for Aylesbury Jan. to April 1659. He m. (1) Feb. 1656 (morriage settlement dated 12 March 1658) Mary dau. of George Pyke of Trumpington, and widow of Thomas Pritchard, (2) Frances dau. of William Lord Willoughby of Parham, and (3) "the widow Wilson, (née Carleton.") He died in Oct. 1701, aged 69. On 8 April 1653 the Council of State ordered Col. Mordey to present to Parliament the petition of Miles Fleetwood, (see 1656,) James Whitelock, and two others, for a lease of the gold and silver mines in Ireland, as being a business of public concern.

Hon. Nathaniel Fiennes of Banbury, 2nd son of Williom 1st Viscount Saye and Sele, and brother to the M.P. 1626, was born at Broughton in 1608, educ. at Winchester, matric. New Coll. Oxford 19 Nov. 1624, aged 16, and was elected a Fellow (as founder's kin) 1624. He m. (1) Elizabeth eldest dau. of Sir John Eliot, and (2) Frances dau. of Richard Whitehead of Tuderley, Hants. He was M.P. Banbury March to May 1640, and Oct. 1640 until secluded by Col. Pride's Purge Dec. 1648, Oxfordshire 1654-5, and Oxford Univ. 1656 until made one of Cromwell's House of Lords as Lord Fiennes 10 Dec. 1657. He was also chosen Speaker of that Assembly. Fiennes was a very active supporter of Parliament in its rebellion against the King, and he was elected one of the Committee of Safety 4 July 1642. Taking up arms with the first, he commanded a troop of horse in the Earl of Essex's army, fought at Edgehill 23 Oct. 1642, and was Governor of Bristol from 1 May until 26 July 1643, when he surrendered the city to Prince Rupert. This act brought great odium upon Fiennes at the time, and he was brought to trial at St. Albans Dec. 14 to 23, and condemned to death 29 Dec. 1643. The sentence however was not carried into effect, and he received pardon, but his military career was at an end. Resuming his place in Parliament, he was added to the Committee of the Army 23 Sept. 1647, and made one of the Committee of Safety at Derby House 3 Jan. 1648, but was among the Puritan leaders secluded from the House and imprisoned in Dec. following. Fiennes was admitted a member of Cromwell's Council 26 April 1654, and continued as such until the Protector's death in Sept. 1658. He was a Commissioner of the Great Seal 15 Jan. 1656 to 14 May 1659, was called to the House of Lords as Lord Fiennes Jan. 1658, and was one of the Committee appointed to offer the Crown to Cromwell. Resolved 27 May 1647 "that Mr Nath. Fienis, a member of this House shall have leave to go into the country." (*Commons Journals.*) He escaped notice at the Restoration, and died at Newton Tony, Wilts, 16 Dec. 1669, aged 61. His son William became 3rd Viscount Saye and Sele in 1674.

William Lenthall the celebrated Speaker of the Long
Parliament 3 Nov. 1640 to 30 July 1647 and 6 Aug. 1647 to 20
April 1653, who was again Speaker July 1654 to Jan. 1655, and 7
May to 13 Oct. 1659, was the son of Wm. L. of Wilcot, Oxon, and
was born at Henley on Thames June 1591, matric. St. Alban
Hall, Oxford 23 Jan. 1607, aged 15, bar. at law Lincolns Inn 24
Oct. 1616, called to the Bench 14 and sat as such 23 May 1633,
and was Lent Reader thereof 1638. He m. Elizabeth dau. of
Ambrose Evans of Loddington, Northants, was M.P. Woodstock
1624-5, March to May 1640, Oct. 1640-53, was a candidate for
Gloucester Nov. 1640, but was refused a poll, and complained to
the House 2 Dec. 1640. He was returned for Gloucester and
Oxon 1654, when he preferred to sit for Oxon till Jan. 1655, and
again 1656 till created one of Cromwell's House of Lords as Lord
Lenthall 10 Dec. 1657, was a Rumper May 1659, and unsucc.
cont. Oxford Univ. 1660. Lenthall was Recorder of Woodstock,
in 1624 and 1637, Recorder of Gloucester 23 Jan. 1637 till
'amoved' Nov. 1660, app. one of the Committee on Ship Money
21 April 1640, a Commr. for Gloucester city for publishing scandalous Ministers etc. 10 March 1642, recommended by the House
of Commons to be added to the Dep. Lieuts. of Oxon 19 March
1642, and held the manor of Witney in 1651 and 1658. He was
also Chamberlain of Chester 1647-54, restored by Parl. to that
office 14 March 1660, Master of the Rolls 22 Nov. 1643-60, one of
the two Commrs. of the Great Seal Oct. 1646 to March 1648, and
sole Commr. thereof 14 May to 3 June 1659, and 13 to 17 Jan.
1660, Joint Chancellor of the Duchy of Lancaster Feb. 1644 to Aug.
1649, and Custos Rotulorum of Oxon and Berks 25 June 1659,
having previously held that post. He retired into private life at the
Restoration, and died at his seat, The Priory, Burford, 3 Sept.
1662. "William Lenthall of Lincoln's Inn had £6000 one time
given him by the House, and the rectory and demesne of Burford,
with a stately house belonging to the Lord Falkland, with £500
per annum. Oliver once made a spunge of him, and squeezed
him out of £15000, who turning him and his tribe out of doors,
he veered about to save himself and his great offices; and he that
had been so long bell-weather in the commons house was
thought for his compliance and his money to deserve to be one
of the herd of Lords in the other House." (*The Mystery of the
Good Old Cause briefly unfolded*, 1660.)

    1656. Aug. 20.   Charles Fleetwood.

                 William Lenthall.

                 Robert Jenkinson.

                 Miles Fleetwood.

                 Sir Francis Norreys Knt.

    (5 Members again). Miles Fleetwood of Aldwinkle, Nor-
thants, was the eldest son of Sir William F. the King's Cupbearer

(see Woodstock 1640,) and therefore half-brother to his colleague Lt. Gen. Charles Fleetwood. He was Knighted, and was app. an Assessment Commr. for Oxon by the Rump 2 March 1660, M.P. Oxon 1656-8, Woodstock 1659, and Northants Feb. 1678 to Jan. 1679. On 29 Nov. 1655 the Treasury Commissioners wrote to Wm. Lenthall, Master of the Rolls, Robert Jenkinson, Miles Fleetwood, and seven other persons of quality in Oxfordshire :— " We beg you to inform us from your knowledge of those parts and from your readiness to his Highness's service, of what he desires to know respecting Whichwood Forest," and a report thereon was accordingly made, and signed by Jenkinson, Miles Fleetwood, and two others.

Sir Francis Norreys, of Weston-on-the-Green, was the reputed son of Francis 1st Earl of Berkshire, (see 1571,) and was born about 1609, and on the death of his father, who committed suicide 29 Jan. 1623, succeeded to the manors of Weston on the Green, and Yaltendon. He m. Hester dau. of Sir John Rouse Bart. of Rouse Lench, (see *Williams' Worcestershire Members*,) was Knighted 27 Aug. 1633, H.S. Oxon 1635, and M.P. 1654 to Jan 1655, and in a Double Return 29 Jan. to 7 Feb. 1659, when unseated. He was app. by the Rump an Assessment Commr. for Oxon 15 Feb. 1660, nominated an intended Knight of the Royal Oak 1660, (his estate worth £1500 a year,) and died 5 of the ides of July 1669, aged 60.

1659. Jan. 29. Robert Jenkinson. ⎫
Viscount Falkland. ⎬

Robert Jenkinson. ⎫
Sir Francis Norris. ⎬

This was a double return of the three Candidates, but on 7 Feb. 1659, the latter Indenture, containing the names of Jenkinson and Norreys, was taken off the file by Order of the House, and Jenkinson and Falkland were declared duly elected.

Henry Cary 3rd Viscount Falkland, in the Peerage of Scotland, of Burford Priory and Great Tew, was the only son of Lucius 2nd Viscount Falkland, the gentle and patriotic Secretary of State to Charles I, who was killed at the first battle of Newbury 20 Sept. 1643, and who was the grandson of Sir Laurence Tanfield, (see 1604) He m. Margaret dau. of Anthony Hungerford, and on 12 Aug. 1659 was committed to the Tower upon suspicion of being concerned in Sir George Booth's Cheshire Rising. He was M.P. Oxfordshire Jan. to April 1659, Arundel and Oxford City April 1660, when he preferred the latter, until Dec. 1660, and Oxfordshire again 1661 until his death 2 April 1663, having been Lord Lieut. of Oxon from 11 Sept. 1660, when he was sworn into office. He was one of the Commrs. of both Houses ordered to set off on 18 May 1660 to meet and welcome the

King at the Restoration. Lord Chancellor Hyde wrote to Secretary Nicholas in July 1660, saying that Lord Falkland desired to be made a Lord of the Bedchamber to the King, and asking for a warrant for Lord F. as Lord of the Bedchamber "Extraordinary, if the number of those in ordinary is full." He was Col. of a regiment at Dunkirk in June 1661, which however was ordered on 4 Nov. to be disbanded before 17 Nov. 1662. Oa 5 Dec. 1661 a Warrant was issued to Lord F. to repair to the house of John Lenthall, son of the M.P. 1654, (see *Williams' Gloucestershire Members*,) to examine him on the late designs against the peace of the Kingdom, and he received a further warrant on 4 Feb. 1662 to deliver J.L. to Capt. Stuart Walker.

> 1660. April   Thomas Viscount Wenman (see 1626.)
>   Hon. James Fiennes.
> 1661. Mar. 10. Viscount Falkland.
>   Sir Anthony Cope Bart.

The latter was born 1632, educ. at Oriel Coll. Oxon, and succeeded his father Sir John Cope of Hanwell as 4th Bart. in 1638. He m. his first cousin Hon. Mary Gerard, dau. of Dutton Lord Gerard, of Gerard's Bromley, was an intended Knight of the Royal Oak for Oxon 1660, (his estate worth £4000 a year,) sat for Banbury April to Dec. 1660, and for the County 1661 until his death about Oct. 1675, aged 43. He received a commission as Captain of a company in the regiment of Lord Falkland (see 1659,) at Dunkirk, on 28 June 1661, and on 30 Dec. 1661 Secretary Nicholas wrote to him,—" The King wishes him and all other officers belonging to Dunkirk garrison to repair to their charge within 10 days, on pain of dismissal." On 27 July 1662 a commission was given to Wm. Gannock to be Captain of a foot company in Dunkirk in the place of Capt. A. Cope, who retired. He was grandson of the M.P. 1624.

> 1663. April. William Knollys. }
>   Sir William Walter. }

vice Viscount Falkland deceased. This was a Double Return of both Candidates, and on 14 April 1663 Walter presented a petition against Knollys, to whom however the seat was awarded.

William Knollys of Rotherfield Greys, eldest son of Sir Robert K. of Grayes, was born 1620, matric. St. Alban Hall, Oxon, 25 Nov. 1636, aged 16, and became a student of the Inner Temple 1639. He m. Mary dau. of John Saunders of Thame. On 27 Nov. 1645 he " Begs to compound for delinquency in absenting himself five weeks from his House, owing to the violence of the soldiers. Never acted to the disservice of Parliament. The Committee for co. Oxford have had £500 from him, and the Parliament's garrison at Henley have cut wood worth £2000, and

defaced his house by making it a garrison. 7 Feb. 1646, fined
£1100, £400 in hand; and the rest in 6 months, if Farringdon
and Wallingford garrisons be reduced. 30 Nov. 1648, on payment
of the fine, sequestration revoked." He was M.P. Oxon April
1663 until his death, being buried at Rotherfield Greys 4 Sept.
1664.

Sir William Walter of Sarsden, was the eldest son of Sir
John Walter Knt. Lord Chief Baron of the Exchequer 1625-31.
He matric. Ch. Ch. Oxford 16 March 1621, aged 17, created
D.C.L. 1 or 2 Nov. 1642, and was called to the bar at the Inner
Temple 1630. He was licensed 20 Dec. 1632 to marry Elizabeth
dau. of Thomas Lucas, and was created a Baronet 16 Aug. 1641.
Sir William was H.S. Oxon 1636 and 1644, M.P. Weobley 1628-9,
and Oxon in a Double Return April 1663 until void, and died 23
March 1674. He was one of those Noblemen and Gentlemen
who signed the Oxford Engagement to repay moneys lent thereon for the King's service, and he himself lent£421 1s 6d for that
purpose. On 28 Nov. 1645 he " Compounds by James Lloyd for
delinquency in assisting the King in whose quarters his whole
estate lay. For 2½ years has refused all employments in that
behalf and submits on the propositions of Parliament. His
estate was worth £800 a year, of which £100 a year is secured to
the Church, It is not now worth more than ¼ of that sum, and
he has 6 small children. 9 July 1646, Fine at one-tenth, £1430.
Aug. 18, Fine passed by the House. 20 Nov. 1650, Compounds
on the votes of 2 Oct. 1650 for undervaluations and concealments.
Dec. 3, Fine at one-tenth, £177. Dec. 11, Allowed his rents as he
compounds on his own discovery." He was also assessed at
£200 by the Committee for Advance of Money 21 Aug. 1646, but
on 23 Sept. following an order was made for his discharge on
payment of £50. On 22 June 1658 he petitioned the Protector as
follows: — " Being bound with sureties to keep the peace
according to the general order for compounders, I was summoned
by Major Crook to Oxford and made prisoner under the marshal's
custody. I went on Sunday 6 June to Carfax Church, and was
placed where the Mayor and Aldermen sit. After service Sir
Ant. Cope Bart. of Tangley (see 1661,) came up and said to me—
" Sir William Walter, if I were not a good Christian I would
cudgel you; you are an unworthy fellow."—I made no reply, but
appeal to you for relief." The Council then summoned Cope to
appear before them to answer the matter, and on his doing so,
they ordered on 13 July, that " Fiennes, Fleetwood and the Lord
Chamberlain try to compose the differences between him and Sir
W. Walter, and report ; also that they consider the information
against Cope in reference to Major Salway, (see *William's
Worcestershire Members*,) and others, reprove him, and admonish
him to prevent the like in future." To do them justice the
Commonwealth statesmen often attempted to play the part of
peacemakers, in settling local disputes.

1664 Dec. 21 Sir Francis Wenman Knt. and Bart. of Caswell, *vice* Knollys deceased. Only son and heir of the M.P. 1640, was Knighted, created a Baronet 29 Nov. 1662, and m. Hon. Mary Wenman 4th and youngest dau. of Thomas, 2nd Viscount Wenman, (see 1626,) and niece of the 1st and 3rd Viscounts Wenman. He was named a Knight of the Royal Oak for Oxon 1660, (estate £1500 a year,) and sat for the County Dec. 1664-79. On 11 Sept. 1661 Lord Falkland (see 1659) wrote the Secretary Nicholas recommending Wenman to be made a Dep. Lieut. of Oxon. He died about 1679-80. His son Richard became 4th Viscount Wenman on the death of his great uncle Philip in 1696, by virtue of a new entail dated 30 Jan. 1683.

1675 Nov. 10. Sir Edward Norreys Knt. of Weston on the Green, *vice* Cope deceased. Second but only surviving son of the M.P. 1656, he was born 1636, matric. Queen's Coll. Oxford 9 Dec. 1650, ent. Lincoln Inn 8 May 1654, and m. Jane dau. of Sir John Clerke Bart. of Shabington. He was Knighted 22 Nov. 1662, M.P. Oxon Nov. 1675 to July 1679, and 1701-8, (having failed 1681,) and Oxford city 1689-1700, app. Dep. Lieut. Oxon by warrant 30 May 1689, and died Oct. 1713, aged 77.

1679. Feb. 26. Sir Edward Norreys. ————

Sir Jone Cope. ————

Sir John D'Oyley. ————

John Clerke. ————

The poll at this contest was kept open for three days, when 3000 voted. John Clerk of Aston Rowant, bar. at law, was J.P. Oxon until left out of the commission 14 June 1685, as obnoxious to the Court. Sir John Cope of Hanwell, third son of Sir John the 3rd Bart., was born at Hanwell 1634, matric. Queen's Coll. Oxford 10 Nov. 1651, and afterwards travelled on the continent. He commanded a troop at Dunkirk in 1660, and married Ann Booth a lodging-house keeper at Dunkirk, dau. of Philip Booth, for which marriage Hanwell was willed away from their children. He succeeded his brother Sir Anthony (see 1661,) as 5th Bart. in 1675, was M.P. Oxon Feb. 1679-81, when defeated, and 1689-90, and Banbury Feb. 1699 to Dec. 1700. He was removed from being a J.P. for Oxon 14 June 1685, but was app. a Dep. Lieut. by warrant 30 May 1689. Sir John long resided at Chelsea, but in 1699 purchased Bramshill Park, Hants. He died 11 Jan. 1721, aged 87, and was buried at Eversley, Hants.

1679. **Aug. 13.** Thomas Horde.

Sir John Cope.

Sir Philip Harcourt "had the canvas," but did not take a poll.

Thomas Horde of Cote, eldest son of Sir Thomas H. of Aston, Oxon, married (1) Barbara (who d. 12 Aug. 1671, aged 44,) dau. of Charles Trinder, and (2) Susanna—(who d. 12 Aug. 1680, aged 37.) " Reasons for an Act to enable T. H. to provide for his younger children by letting leases of certain lands." *Cal. State Papers* 1 March 1670). *Wood* described him as " a most ill-natured man and of no religion," who might be compared to Brome Whorwood, (see Oxford 1679). By deed 15 Jan. 1712 he granted a perpetual benefaction for the criminal prisoners and debtors in the common ward of Oxford Castle, (the annual income of which amounted to £24 in 1868). He was M.P. Oxon Aug. 1679-81, but was defeated there 1685, 1689, and for the city 1690, and died 6 Nov. 1715, aged 92. (M. I. Bampton.) His dau. Juliana m. Peter Wentworth, brother of Lord Strafford. His son Allan Horde was H. S. Oxon 1724. On 13 April 1647 Thomas Hurd senior of Kingsdon, Somerset, compounded for delinquency in adhering to the King's party against Parliament, and on 13 May was fined at one-fifth, £80. On 11 May 1649 his son Thomas Hurd junior of the same place petitioned to compound for being sequestered for delinquency, and on 10 June was fined £106. Horde was J.P. Oxfordshire until left out of the commission 14 June 1685. On 21 June 1685 lord Abingdon wrote from Oxford to Lord Clarendon,—I am now sending out warrants to seize Hord, Blake and Bard," as persons suspected of favouring Monmouth's Rising. They were committed to Oxford Castle 22 June, and on 29 June,—" I told your lordship Messrs. Hord and Bard had sent for Habeas Corpus, which I hear is now coming."

1681.	Feb. 23.	Thomas Hord.	————
		Sir Philip Harcourt.	————
		Sir John Cope.	————
		Sir Edward Norreys.	————

The poll was kept open two days at this election.

Sir Philip Harcourt of Stanton Harcourt, was the son of Sir Simon Harcourt Knt., Governor of Dublin, (who was slain 26 March 1642 when beseiging Carrickmain, during the Irish Rebellion,) by Anne dau. of William Lord Paget. Sir Philip was Knighted 5 June 1660, m. (1) Anne (who d. 23 Aug. 1664) dau. of Sir Wm. Waller Knt. of Osterley Park, Middlesex, the Parliamentary General, and (2) the dau. of ——— Lee, Clerk of the Peace for London, sat for Boston Oct. 1665 to Jan. 1679, and for Oxon 23 Feb. to 28 March 1681, and was buried 12 April 1688. *Wood* called him "a gentle man but a Presbyterian." His son Simon Viscount Harcourt was Lord Chancellor 1713-14.

1685. March 18.   Viscount Falkland.   ———
                   Thomas Tipping.   ———
                   Thomas Beard.   ———
                   Thomas Hoord.   ———

" Thomas Beard of Fritwell, a phanatic, (son of Alderman Beard of London.) Hoord had many voices but gave no entertainment, and because he would not pay for their night's lodging, they went home and he lost it." (*Wood*).

Anthony Cary, Viscount Falkland, was the only son of the M.P. 1659, whom he succeeded as fourth Viscount in 1663. Born at Great Tew, he matric. Ch. Ch. Oxford 21 May 1672, aged 15, and m. Rebecca dau. of Sir Rowland Lytton Knt. of Knebworth, Herts. He was M.P. Oxon 1685-7, Great Marlow, 1689-90, and Great Bedwin 1690 until his death, and was Treasurer of the Navy June 1681 to April 1689, a Lord of the Bedchamber to Prince George of Denmark 168— to June 1690, a Lord of the Admiralty Jan. 1691 to April 1693, and First Lord of the Admiralty April 1693 until his death 24 May 1694. He was buried in Westminster Abbey. On 17 Jan. 1694, the House of Commons resolved, that Viscount Falkland, one of its Members, by begging and receiving £2000 from His Majesty, contrary to the ordinary method of issuing and bestowing the King's money, was guilty of a high misdemeanour and breach of trust, and that he be committed to the Tower. On 30 May 1689 a warrant issued to the Earl of Abingdon, Lord Lieut. of Oxon, to appoint Viscount Falkland, Viscount Wenman, Henry Bertie, (see Oxford 1685,) Sir William Walter, (son of the M.P. 1663,) Sir Robert Jenkinson (see 1669,) Sir John Doyley (see 1679,) Sir Wm. Glynne (see Oxford Univ. 1698,) Sir Robert Dashwood (see 1699,) Sir Thomas Tipping, Sir Wm. Whitelock (see Oxford Univ. 1703,) James Herbert, (father of the M.P. 1715,) and Thomas Tipping to be Deputy Lieutenants.

Thomas Tipping of Wheatfield, eldest son of Sir Thomas T. Knt. was born 1552, matric. Trin. Coll. Oxford, 16 Nov. 1669, aged 17, and ent. Lincolns Inn 1672. *Wood* in his *Life and Times* mentions the (false) " News (26 April 1665) that T. Tipping lately elected knight of the shire was killed." He was outlawed under James II, being excepted from the General Act of Pardon 1688, but his outlawry was reversed by William III. He was M.P. Oxon 1685-87, Wallingford 1689-90, and 1695-1700, made a Baronet 24 March 1698, and died 1 July 1718, the title expiring with his son in 1725.

1689. Jan. 14.   Sir Robert Jenkinson T ———
                  Sir John Cope   T ———
                  Thomas Hord.   ———

Sir Robert Jenkinson of Walcot and. Hawkesbury, was the only son of the M.P. 1654, whom he succeeded as 2nd Bart. 30 March 1677. Born in 1654, he matric. Bras. Coll. Oxford, 11 Nov. 1671, aged 17, and entered himself a student of the Inner Temple in 1672. He married Sarah dau. of Thomas Tomlins, of Bromley, Middlesex, (by Susanna dau. and (in her issue) co-heir of Wm. Cranmer and Susanna his wife, sister of Sir Edward Powell Bart., which Wm. Cranmer was grandson of Edmund Cranmer, Archdeacon of Canterbury, younger brother of Archbishop Cranmer,) and sister and heir to Thomas Tomlins of Bromley, Middlesex, who was murdered by his coachman, dying s.p. buried at St. Leonards, Bromley, 29 Nov. 1686. Sir Robert became D. L. Oxfordshire 30 May 1689, and was M.P. for the count in 9 Parliaments from 1689 until his death 30 Jan. 1710, being buried at Charlbury 4 Feb. His wife died 8 and was buried at Charlbury 15 Aug. 1709. (M.I. in chancel of Charlbury Church.)

1690.	March 5.	Lord Norreys	T
		Sir R. Jenkinson	T
		Sir John Cope	T

Montague Venables (Bertie), Lord Norreys, eldest son of James 1st Earl of Abingdon, (grandson of the M.P. 1625,) by Eleanor dau. and heiress of Sir Henry Lee Bart. of Ditchley, was born about 1668, and m. (1) 22 Sept. 1687 Anne (who died 28 April 1715) dau. and heir of Peter Venables, Baron of Kinderton, and (2) 13 Feb. 1717 Mary widow of General Charles Churchill, and dau. of James Gould of Dorchester. Lord Norreys became Captain of the Oxford Univ. Volunteers 1685, and was M.P. Berks 1689-90, and Oxon 1690 until he succeeded his father as 2nd Earl of Abingdon 22 May 1699. He was High Steward of Oxford July 1699-1743. and of Banbury, Lord Lieut. and Cus. Rot. of Berks 31 May 1701 to 11 June 1702, a Privy Councillor 21 April 1702 to Sept. 1705, Constable of the Tower 27 May 1702 to Sept. 1705, Lord Lieut. and Cus. Rot. of Oxon 21 June 1702 to Sept. 1705, and Lord Lieut. of the Tower Hamlets 29 June 1702 to Sept. 1705. He was again sworn a Privy Councillor 9 Feb. 1711, and 1 Oct. 1714, and was Warden and Chief Justice in Eyre of all the royal forests South of Trent 12 Jan. 1711 to 11 Nov 1715, Lord Lieut. and Cus. Rot. of Oxon 17 May 1712-15, and a Lord Justice of Great Britain during the King's absence in Hanover 1 August to 18 Sept. 1714. Lord Abingdon, who was " of a black complexion," (*Macky's Characters*), died 15 June 1743.

1695. Nov. 6. The same, re-el. 10 Aug. 1698.

1699. Nov. 29. Sir Robert Dashwood, Knt. and Bart of Wickham, and Northbrook, (Tory) *vice* Lord Norreys called to the Upper House. This Member was born in or about 1662, and was the son of Ald. George Dashwood, of London, a Commr. of Excise. He matric. Trin. Coll. Oxford 19 July 1679, aged 17, ent. the Inner Temple, 1679, and m. Penelope dau. and co-heir of Sir Thomas Chamberlayne Bart. of Wickham. He was Knighted at Windsor Castle 4 June 1682, created a Baronet 16 Sept. 1684, M.P. Banbury 1689-98, and Oxon Nov. 1699 to Dec. 1700, H.S. 1683, D.L. 30 May 1689, and died 14 July 1734.

1701.   Jan. 22.   Sir R. Jenkinson, (see 1689.)   T

           Sir Edward Norreys, (see 1675.) T

1701. Nov. 26. The same, re-el. 5 Aug. 1702, and 9 May 1705.

1708.   May 5.   Viscount Ryalton   W

           Sir R. Jenkinson   T

Francis Godolphin, Viscount Rialton, only surviving son of Sidney 1st Earl of Godolphin, (so created 29 Dec. 1706,) Lord High Treasurer 1702-10, was born 3 Sept. 1678, educ. at Eton, and King's College, Cambridge, and was M.P. East Looe Jan. to Nov. 1701, East Looe and Helston Dec. 1701, when he preferred to represent Helston, till 1708, became Viscount Rialton by courtesy 29 Dec. 1706, and sat for Oxon 1708-10, and for Tregony 1710 until he succeeded his father as 2nd Earl Godolphin 15 Sept. 1712. His Lordship m. March 1698 Lady Henrietta Churchill eldest dau. and co-heir of John the great Duke of Marlborough, which lady succeeded her father by special remainder as Duchess of Marlborough 16 June 1722. He was Joint Registrar of the Court of Chancery 29 June 1698 to 20 Jan. 1727, a Teller of the Exchequer 6 June 1699 to 1704. was a Dep. Lieut. for Cornwall in April 1701, Cofferer of the Queen's Household 1 April 1704 to June 1711, Lord Warden of the Stannaries in Cornwall 1705, High Steward of the Duchy of Cornwall, and Rider and Master Forester of Dartmoor 4 May 1705 to April 1708, Recorder of Helston, again Cofferer of the Royal Household 3 Oct. 1714 to 23 May 1723, Lord Lieut. and Cus. Rot. of Oxon (sworn in) 29 Nov. 1715 to Jan. 1735, a Lord of the Bedchamber to the King 12 Feb. 1716 to 1723, High Steward of Banbury 16 July 1718, Groom of the Stole and Firs, Lord of the Bedchamber to George I from 25 May 1723 to June 1727, and to George II. from 24 July 1727 to 8 Jan. 1735, a Privy Councillor 26 May 1723, a Lord Justice of Great Britain 10 June to 29 Dec. 1723, 9 June 1725 to 3 Jan. 1726, and 3 to 11 June 1727, a Commr. of Claims for the Coronation 12 Aug. 1727, High Steward of Woodstock 18 March 1728-66, Governor of the Scilly Islands 7 July 1733-66, a Commr. to inspect the Courts of Justice and inquire into fees in England and Wales 19 Feb. 1734, Lord Privy Seal 14 May 1735 to 25 April 1740, and a Governor of the

Foundling Hospital 7 Aug. 1739. The Earl was created Lord Godolphin of Helston 23 Jan. 1735, and died 17 Jan. 1766, aged 87, when the Earldom expired.

1710. Feb. 22. Sir Robert Jenkinson Bart. of Walcot, and Hawkesbury, *vice* his father deceased. Born in 1685, he was the eldest son of the M.P. 1689, whom he succeeded as 3rd Bart. 30 Jan. 1710. Having matric. Trin. Coll. Oxford 13 Feb. 1703, " aged 15," he became a student of Lincolns Inn 22 Oct. 1705, where he was called to the bar 1713. Sir Robert married (just before 7) Feb. 1712 Henrietta Maria, (who died 1760, buried at Horsham,) dau. of Charles Scarborough, Clerk of the Green Cloth to Queen Anne, and represented Oxfordshire from Feb. 1710 until his decease 29 Oct. 1717, aged 32, and was buried at Charlbury 5 Nov. His widow re-m. in Westminster Abbey 9 Aug. 1731 as 2nd wife to Charles Eversfield M.P. Dene. Sussex, who died 17 Jan. 1749.

1710. Oct. 10. Sir R. Jenkinson T.
Francis Clerke T

Francis Clerke of North Weston, was the son of Sir John Clerke Bart. (? the defeated candidate 1679,) and matric. Magd. Coll. Oxford 31 July 1671, aged 16, demy 1671-6, B.A. 22 April 1675, fellow 1676-82, and M.A. 17 Jan. 1678. He was app. Ensign of Capt. Henry Bertie's Troop of Independent Horse 18 June 1685, which was disbanded after Sedgemoor the same year. He. m. Catherine 3rd and youngest dau. of Hon. Henry Bertie (see Oxford 1685,) and sat for Oxon 1710 until death at Hillingdon, Middlesex, 2 May 1715.

1713. Aug. 29. The same, re-el. 2 Feb. 1715.

1715. May 25. James Herbert (Tory) *vice* Clarke deceased, Son of James Herbert of Tythorpe and Kingsey (who died 1709, by Lady Catherine Osborne 4th dau. of Thomas Duke of Leeds,) and grandson of Hon. James Herbert, 6th son of Phillip 4th Earl of Pembroke and Montgomery K.G. (see *Williams' Parl. Hist. of Wales.)* He m. the dau. of —— Hallet of Edgware, and sat for Oxon May 1715 untll his death, being drowned in a pond, 25 April 1721.

1717. Dec. 4. Sir Robert Bancks Jenkinson Bart. of Walcot, and Hawkesbury, (Tory) *vice* his brother deceased. This Member was the 2nd son of the M.P. 1869, and was baptized Charlbury 24 Jan. 1687, and m. Catherine 3rd dau. of Sir Robert Dashwood 1st Bart. (see 1699.) He succeeded his brother (see Feb. 1710) as 4th Bart. 29 Oct. 1717, sat for Oxon Nov. 1717-27, and died 2 July 1738, being buried at Charlbury 6 July. The title descended upon his two sons in succession, Sir Robert who died s.p. 8 Aug. 1766, aged 45, buried at Hawkesbury, and Sir Bankes who died unmarried at Headington 22 July 1790, aged 68, buried at Hawkesbury. The third and fourth sons died s.p. The subsequent history of the family is so interesting that it is given in detail :—

Charles Jenkinson, fifth son of the M.P. 1689, was born at Walcot 1693, bapt. at Charlbury 13 June 1693, and became Lt. Col. of the Horse Guards Blue 27 May 1745. He was Major of the Blues at the Battle of Fontenoy in 1745, and commanded the Regiment at Dettingen. He died at Burford Lawn Lodge in the Forest of Whichwood, in June 1750, aged 57, buried at Shipton under Whichwood 23 June, leaving by his wife, Amarantha eldest dau. and co-heir of Capt. Wolfran Cornewall, Royal Navy, a dau. Elizabeth, (who married her cousin Rt. Hon. Charles Wolfran Cornewall M.P., Speaker of the House of Commons 1780-9, see *Williams' Herefordshire Members*,) and two sons Charles and John. The latter was M.P. Corfe Castle 1768-80, a Genleman Usher Daily Waiter to the Queen 5 Sept. 1761-74, a Gentleman Usher of the Privy Chamber to Her Majesty 1774-1805, and Joint Secretary for Ireland, resident in Great Britain, (so in 1778) He married Frances dau. of Rear Admiral John Barker, and died 1 May 1805, aged 71. (M.I. Winchester Cathedral). His second son John Bankes Jenkinson was Bishop of St. Davids 1825-40, while Charles the eldest son became 10th Bart. in 1851.

Charles Jenkinson, the eldest son of the hero of Fontenoy, was born at Winchester 26 April and baptized 16 May 1727, matric. Univ. Coll. Oxford, 14 March 1746, B.A. 27 Oct. 1749, M.A. 24 Nov. 1752, created D.C.L. 7 July 1773, and ent. Lincolns Inn 6 July 1747. He married (1) at St. Marylebone 9 Feb. 1769 Amelia (who d. 12 July 1770, aged 19, buried at Hawkesbury, (M.I.) eldest dau. of William Watts, Governor of Fort William, in Bengal, and Frances his wife, and (2) at 26 Hertford St., Mayfair, by special license 22 June 1782 Catharine dau. of Sir Cecil Bisshopp, 6th Bart. and relict of Sir Charles Cope 2nd Bart. of Brewerne, Oxon, and Orton Longueville, Hunts, who was his first cousin. Jenkinson acquired some literary reputation through the active part he took in the famous election for Oxfordshire in 1754, which is alluded to in a letter from his son the 3rd Lord Liverpool to Mr. Croker which is printed in the Croker Correspondence and Diaries, Vol. III. 179-180, as follows :—" My father, Col. Jenkinson's eldest son, was bred for the Church. He was first at the Charterhouse and then at University College at Oxford where he took his M.A. degree. A living belonging to his uncle Sir Jonathan Cope of Brewern in Oxfordshire was destined for my father and was held in my recollection, by a clergyman of the name of Lockwood, to whom it was given to hold for my father ; but my father got connected when at Oxford with Charles Duke of Marlborough and the then Lord Macclesfield, adopted their politics (they were Whigs) and took an active part in the famous Oxfordshire election of Parker and Turner, who were Whigs, against Wenman and Dashwood, Tories. It is curious that my father wrote the electioneering verses and squibs for the Whigs at this election, and Sir W. Blackstone for the Tories. There are two copies of verses, each celebrating their rival colours, (blue and green). Blackstone's are by far the best, but my father's not amiss. All this must have made my father give up his clerical pursuits; and he must have published about this time one if not both of his political pamphlets viz : the one on a National Militia, and the other on Neutral Rights." My father has often told me that he was sent up to London by the then Duke of Marlborough and Lord Macclesfield with a strong recommendation to Lord Holdernese etc. He became confidential secretary to Lord Bute, and was highly esteemed and trusted by him as he afterwards was by Mr. Grenville, the Duke of Grafton, Lord North etc., but I do not believe nay I am certain that he did not carry on any correspondence between the King and Lord Bute for such never existed although on many critical occasions the King consulted him privately of which I have the proofs. He was also in the service, I think they called him Treasurer of the Princess Dowager of Wales until her death. He was very much in her confidence." Mr. Jenkinson, through the good services of the first Lord Harcourt, obtained an introduction at Court, as well as the favourable notice of the Earl of Bute, and during the next 40 years held many successive offices under various Ministries. He was M.P. for Cockermouth 1761 to Dec. 1766, and 1768, Appleby Jan. 1767-72, Harwich Aug. 1772-4, Hastings 1774-80, and Saltash 1780 until he was raised to the Peerage as Lord Hawkesbury 21 Aug. 1786. He was Under Secretary of State for the Northern Department March 1761-2, Private Secretary to Lord Bute, the Prime Minister, May 1762 to April 1763, Treasurer and Paymaster of the Ordnance June 1762-3, Joint Secretary to the Treasury April 1763 to July 1765, a Lord of the Admiralty Dec. 1766-7, a Lord of the Treasurg Dec. 1767 to Jan. 1773, Joint Vice Treasurer of Ireland Dec. 1772 to Oct. 1775, sworn a Privy Councillor in England 8 Feb. 1773, Writer of the Tallies and Counter Tallies and Clerk of the Pells in the Receipt of the Exchequer in Ireland 5 Aug. 1775-1801, and Secretary at War Dec. 1778 to March 1782, a Lord of Trade and Foreign Plantations 5 March 1784, Chancellor of the Duchy of Lancaster Aug. 1786 to Nov. 1803, and President of the Board of Trade 23 Aug. 1786 to June 1804. His Lordship was created Earl of Liverpool 1 June 1796, having previously succeeded his kinsman Sir Bankes Jenkinson as 7th Bart. 22 July 1790, and had an augmentation to his coat of arms of the arms of Liverpool 23 July 1796. He died at 26 Hertford St., Mayfair, 17 Dec. 1808, aged 81, having enjoyed the sinecure office of Collector of the

Customs, Inwards, in the Port of London, from 1789. Well known to possess the confidence of his Sovereign for many years, he was frequently described by political writers as the secret adviser of the King. On 18 Feb. 1761 he was granted permission to pass on horseback through the Horse Guards into and out of St. James's Park. (*Home Office Papers*).

His eldest son, the Hon. Robert Bankes Jenkinson, became even more distinguished in the political world than his father. Born 7 June 1770, he matric. Ch. Ch. Oxford 27 April 1787, was created M.A. 19 May 1790, and married (1) 25 March 1795 the Lady Louisa Theodosia Hervey (who d. 12 June 1821, buried at Hawkesbury) third dau. of Frederick Augustus 4th Earl of Bristol and Bishop of Derry, and (2) 24 Sept 1822 Mary 6th dau. of Charles Chester of Chicheley Hall, Bucks, (formerley Bagot), and niece of the first Lord Bagot, who survived him and dying s.p. 18 Oct. 1846 was buried at Kingston on Thames. Mr Jenkinson assumed the courtesy title of Honourable 21 Aug. 1786, and became Lord Hawkesbury on his father being made an Earl 1 June 1796. He was elected at the age of 20 both for Rye and Appleby in 1790, when he preferred to represent the former, for which he sat till he was called to the House of Lords in his father's Barony of Hawkesbury 15 Nov. 1803. His Lordship may be paid to have passed the whole of his life, after attaining his majority, in the service of his country. He was a Commissioner of the Board of Control for the Affairs of India June 1793-9, sworn a Privy Councillor 13 March 1799, and app. a Member of the Board of Trade the next day, Master of the Mint Feb. 1799 to April 1801, Secretary of State for Foreign Affairs Feb. 1801 to May 1804, for the Home Department May 1804 to Feb. 1806, and again March 1807 to Nov. 1809, and for War and the Colonies Oct. 1809 to June 1812, when he became First Lord of the Treasury and Prime Minister on the assassination of Mr Spencer Perceval, and held that coveted position until 30 April 1827, when failing health obliged him to retire into private life. This was the longest tenure of that office by any Prime Minister since the time of Lord Burleigh, with the exception of Mr. Pitt. Lord Liverpool was made Constable of Dover Castle and Warden Keeper and Admiral of the Cinque Ports 28 Jan. 1806, High Steward of Kingston upon Thames 1816, a Governor of the Charter House 15 Feb. 1805, an Official Trustee of the Britism Museum, a Fellow of the Royal Society 29 May 1794, a Knight of the Garter 9 June 1814, and held all these honours until his death. He received the rank of Colonel in the army 23 May 1794, so long as his regiment of Militia, the Cinque Ports Regiment of Fencible Cavalry was embodied for active service. He died s.p. at Fife House, Whitehall, on 4 Dec. 1828 aged 58, and was buried at Hawkesbury 18 Dec.

His Lordship's half-brother, the Hon. Charles Cecil Cope Jenkinson, succeeded him as third Earl of Liverpool 4 Dec. 1828. Born at 26 Hertford Street, Mayfair, on 29 May 1784, this Nobleman matric. Ch. Ch. Oxford 23 April 1801, and was created D.C.L. 15 June 1841. He was Page of Honour to George III. 1793-4, served as a Midshipman in the Royal Navy 1794-8, and fought in several naval actions, including the glorious 1 June 1784, was app. Cornet in the Surrey Yeomanry 20 Aug. 1803, afterwards entered the Diplomatic Service, and was app. Sec. of Legation at Vienna 13 July 1804, joined the Austrian Army as a Volunteer in 1805, and fought at Austerlitz 2 Dec. 1805. He was in charge of the Embassy at Vienna for a time during Sir A. Paget's illness in 1805-1806. He was adopted as his heir by his cousin the last Mr. Ottley of Pitchford, Salop, to whose estates in cos. Salop and Montgomery he succeeded on 16 Feb. 1807, when he took up his residence at Pitchford Hall, near Shrewsbury, and became D.L. Salop 8 Dec. 1807. He married at St. George's, Hanover Square, 19 July 1810 Julia Evelyn Medley, (who died at 10 (now 13) Portmann Square, London, 8 April 1814, aged 28, buried at Pitchford 24 April 1814,) only child of Sir George Shuckburgh-Evelyn Bart. by Julia Annabella dau. and heir of James Evelyn of Felbridge, Surrey, by Annabella dau. of Thomas and sister and in her issue sole heir of her brother George Medley of Buxted, Friston, and Coneyburrows all in co. Sussex, and had three daughters and co-heirs. He was M.P. for Sandwich 1807-12, Bridgnorth 1812-18, and East Grinstead 1818-28, and held office (under his brother) as Under Secretary of State for the Home Department Oct. 1807 to Feb. 1810, and for War and the Colonies Oct. 1809 to 1810. After the lapse of many years his Lordship again held office as Lord Steward of the Queen's Household Sept. 1841 to July 1846, and he was sworn a Privy Councillor 3 Sept. 1841, and made G.C.B. 11 Dec. 1845. He was Prothonotary of the County Palatine of Lancaster 1838-51, having been granted the reversion thereof previous to 1830, High Steward of Kingston on Thames from 1829, and a Governor of the Charterhouse 5 Feb. 1846. His Lordship, who was patron of two livings. died without male issue at Buxted 3 Oct. 1851, buried at Buxted 9 Oct., when the Earldom and Barony became extinct. The Baronetcy however devolved upon his cousin Sir Charles Jenkinson (M.P. Dover 1806-18), as 10th Bart., on whose death without male issue in 1855 it passed to his nephew Sir George Samuel Jenkinson, (M.P. North Wilts 1868-80, unsuccessful candidate for N. Wilts 1865, and for Nottingham in 1866,) the elder son of the Bishop of St. David's. His son Sir George Bankes Jenkinson the 12th and present Baronet succeeded his father in 1892.

Lady Selina Charlotte, the second daughter and co-heir, (the eldest to leave issue,) of the last Earl of Liverpool, married

.

(1) at St. George's, Hanover Square 15 August 1833 William Charles Viscount Milton, (son and heir of Charles Wm. 5th Earl Fitzwilliam K.G.,) who died v.p. and s.p.m. 8 Nov. 1835, and (2) at Wentworth in the private chapel 28 Aug. 1845 as second wife to George Savile Foljambe of Osberton Hall, Notts, and Aldwark, co. York, who died 18 Dec. 1869. The elder of their two sons, Cecil George Savile Foljambe of Kirkham Abbey, York, Haselbech Hall, Northampton and Ollerton, Notts, was born at Osberton 7 Nov. 1846, and was educated at Eton, entered the Royal Navy in 1860, served with the Naval Brigade in the New Zealand War of 1863-64, (medal, and mentioned in despatches), promoted to Lieut. 8 May 1867, and retired in 1870. He married (1) at St. James's, Piccadilly, 22 July 1869 Louisa Blanche (who d. at Compton Place, Sussex, 7 Oct. 1871, buried at Scopton, Notts, in the family vault,) eldest dau. of Frederick John Howard of Compton Place, Sussex, (grandson of the 5th Earl of Carlisle and Lady Fanny his wife only sister to the 7th Duke of Devonshire,) and (2) at the Chapel Royal, Whitehall, 21 July 1877 Susan Louisa eldest dau. of Col. William Henry Frederick Cavendish, cousin of the 7th Duke of Devonshire, by Lady Emily Augusta his wife dau. of John George 1st Earl of Durham, by Lady Louisa Elizabeth his wife, eldest dau. of Charles 2nd Earl Grey K.G., Prime Minister 1830-4. He was M.P. for North Notts 1880-5, and for the Mansfield Division 1885-92, a County Alderman Notts County Council 22 Oct. 1891-8, and was raised to the Peerage as Baron Hawkesbury of Haselbech, co. Northampton, and of Ollerton, Sherwood Forest, co. Nottingham, 24 June 1893, the former extinct Barony of his grandfather being revived in his person. His Lordship received an additional crest by Patent 10 Oct. 1893. He seconded the address in the House of Lords at the opening of the following session 12 March 1894, when Lord Rosebery became Prime Minister, and held office as a Lord in Waiting to the Queen from 30 April 1894 to 16 July 1895. He has issue by both marriages. His 2nd son, (the eldest by his 2nd wife,) was app. Second Lieut. 1st. Batt. Oxfordshire Light Infantry 15 February 1898.

1721. May 17. Henry Perrot of Northleigh, vice Herbert deceased. Only son of James Perrot, and nephew of Charles Perrot, (see Oxford University 1679,) he was born 1689, created D.C.L. Oxford 11 July 1733, m. Martha (who d. 11 Oct 1741) dau. of Brereton Bouchier of Barnsley, Cirencester. He voted against the employment of the Hessian Troops 1730, and the Excise Bill 1733, and sat for Oxon May 1721 until his death in Paris (?6) Jan. 1740. In 1740 he paid to Magdalen College a fine of £69 for certain tenements in All Saints, Oxford. He was churchwarden of Barnsley parish 1732, and patron and lord of that manor, and is supposed to have built the present mansion house in the park, the leaden pipes having his initials and the date 1721.

1722. April 2. Sir R. B. Jenkinson.
Henry Perrott.

1727. Aug. 30. Henry Perrot   T.
Sir W. Stapleton Bart. T.

Sir William Stapleton of Rotherfield Greys, matric. Ch.
Ch. Oxford 17 April 1714, aged 15, and succ. his father Sir
William S. of Nevis, as 4th Bart. He m. 28 April 1724 Catherine
dau. and heir of Wm. Paul of Braywick, Berks, voted against
Walpole on the matter of the Hessian Troops 1730, and the
Excise Bill 1733, and sat for Oxon 1727 till his death "at the
Bath " 13 Jan. 1740.

1734. May 1. The same.

1740. Jan 30. Sir James Dashwood Bart. of Kirtlington,
vice Stapleton deceased. Eldest surviving son of Robert Dashwood, he was born 1715, succ. his grandfather (see 1699) as 2nd
Bart. 14 July 1734, and m. 17 Feb. 1739 Elizabeth (who brought
him £70,000,) dau. and co-heir of Edward Spencer of Rendles-
ham, Suffolk, and sister to the Duchess of Hamilton. Sir James
was H.S. Oxon 1738, M.P. Jan. 1740 to April 1755, when unseated,
and 1761-8, and was a steward of the Anniversary Feast of the
Independent Electors of Westminster 1748. He succeeded to
the large jointure of his mother (Dorothea dau. and co-heir of
Sir James Read Bart. of Brocket Hall, Herts,) on her death 21
April 1753. He was created D.C.L. Oxford 25 Aug. 1743, and
was High Steward of the City of Oxford 1759 until his death 10
Nov. 1779.

1740. Feb. 27. George Henry Lee, Viscount Quarendon,
of Ditchley, vice Perrot deceased. This nobleman was born 21
May 1718, matric. St Johns Coll. Oxford 1 Jan. 1736, created
M.A. 14 Feb. 1737, Hon. D.C.L. 25 Aug, 1743, and D.C.L. by
diploma 27 Sept. 1762, and was M.P. for Oxon Feb. 1740 until he
succ. his father as 3rd Earl of Lichfield 15 Feb. 1743. He m. Diana
only dau. of Sir Thomas Frankland Bart. of Thirkelby, Yorks,
and was Custos Brevium in the Common Pleas, 1743-72, a Lord
of the Bedchamber to the King Dec. 1760-2, Captain of the Band
of Gentlemen Pensioners July 1762-72, sworn a Privy Councillor
14 July 1762, Deputy Ranger of Hampton Court Park July 1762-
72, was defeated by the Earl of Westmoreland for the office of
Chancellor of Oxford Univ. Jan. 1759, but was High Steward
thereof 19 Aug. 1760-2, and Chancellor of the Univ. 23 Sept.
1762-73 a Vice President of the Society of Arts, D.L. Oxon 17
Oct. 1763, and died 19 Sept. 1772. (M.I. Spelsbury). He founded
the Lichfield Clinical Professorship at Oxford by a bequest which
took effect in 1780.

1741. May 20. Viscount Quarendon T.
Sir James Dashwood T.

1743. March 23. Norris Bertie of Weston on the Green, *vice* Lord Quarendon called to the Upper House. Norreys Bertie was the son of James B. of Springfield, Essex, (who was the eldest son of Captain the Hon. Henry Bertie, see Oxford city 1685,) and was born 1718, matric. Magd. Coll. Oxford 5 Dec. 1734, aged 16, and was created M.A. *honoris causâ* 27 May 1738. He unsucc. cont. Westbury 1741 and 1747, but sat for Oxon March 1743-54, and died unmarried at Gwent 25 Oct. 1766, having spent several of the latter years of his life on the continent. " His estates of £2000 a year he has bequeathed to his brother Capt. Bertie," (*sic*, but should be great nephew or kinsman, son to the 3rd Earl of Abingdon).

1747. July 8. Sir James Dashwood T
          Norreys Bertie   T
1754. April 17. Lord Wenman   T 2033
          Sir J. Dashwood   T 2014
          Lord Parker   W 1919
          Sir E. Turner   W 1660

This was the great Oxfordshire contest, the poll being open 6 days, at the expense it is said of £40,000 each side. (See its "History" by *William Wing*.) Wenman and Dashwood fought for the Old Interest or Blues, receiving the support of the Duke of Marlborough, and the Earls of Guilford, Harcourt, and Macclesfield, while Parker and Turner were championed by the Earls of Abingdon and Lichfield,—the new Interest or Yellows. A great quantity of amusing literature was produced by both sides, and no expense was spared, but on petition Lord Parker and Sir E. Turner were declared duly elected by order of the House 23 April 1755.

Thomas Viscount Parker was born 12 Oct. 1723, the eldest son of George 2nd Earl of Macclesfield, whom he succ. in the title 17 March 1764, and matric. Hart Hall, Oxford, 10 May 1740, created Hon. M.A. 23 June 1743. and D.C.L. 7 July 1773, and m. 12 Dec. 1749 Mary dau. of Sir Wm. Heathcote Bart. He was M.P. Newcastle under Lyme 1747-54, Oxon 1754-61, and Rochester 1761-4, when he went to the Upper House, and became F.R.S. 19 Nov. 1747, a Governor and Guardian of the Foundling Hospital July 1752, D.L. Berks 22 Sept. 1758, and Oxon 15 Oct. 1763, and was High Steward of Henley 1764, until his death 9 Feb. 1795.

Sir Edward Turner of Ambroseden, was born 18 April 1719, matric. Ball. Coll. Oxford 7 Oct. 1735, aged 17, created M.A. 24 Oct. 1738, and D.C.L. 23 Aug. 1744, and ent. Lincolns Inn 2 July 1745. He m. April 1739 Cassandra eldest dau. of William, son of Theophilus Leigh of Addlestrop, co. Gloucester,

by Mary sister of the Duke of Chandos. He was M.P. Great
Bedwin 1741-7, Oxon 1754-61, and Penryn 1761 until his death at
Ambrosden 31 Oct. 1766, buried at Bicester. He was the only
surviving son of Sir Edward Turner, Chairman of the East India
Company, whom he succeeded as 2nd Bart. 19 June 1733. Two
of his daughters, Elizabeth and Cassandra, married Thomas
Lord Saye and Sele, and the 2nd Lord Hawke, respectively.
His son John assumed the surname and arms of Dryden 1791,
and was created a Baronet 1795, the two Baronetcies becoming
united in the person of his grandson in 1874.

Philip Viscount Wenman, elder son of Richard the 5th
Viscount, whom he succ. in the title 28 Nov. 1728, was born 23
Nov. 1719, matric. Oriel Coll. Oxford 9 June 1737, created D.C.L.
15 June 1741, and m. Sophia eldest dau. and co-heir of James
Herbert of Tythorpe, (see 1740.) He was M.P. Oxford city Nov.
1749-54, and Oxon 1754 until unseated April 1755, and died
at Thame Park 16 Aug. 1760, aged 41.

1761. April 8. Sir James Dashwood T
Lord Charles Spencer T

Lord Charles Spencer, of Wheatfield, was 2nd son of
Charles 3rd Duke of Marborough, and was born 31 March 1740,
matric. Ch. Ch. Oxford 28 April 1756, created M.A. 22 March
1759, and D.C.L. 7 July 1773. He was returned for Oxon at the
age of 21 in 1761, and sat till 1790, and again 1796 to 1801, and
seconded the Address in the House 25 Nov. 1762. He m. 2 Oct.
1762, Hon. Mary Beauclerk dau. of Vere 1st Lord Vere, third son
of the first Duke of St. Albans. Lord Charles was made Deputy
Ranger of Windsor Forest and Surveyor of Kensington Gardens
Dec. 1762, voted against Wilkes 1769, was made a Verdurer of
Whichwood Forest Sept. 1763, and was Col. of the Oxon Militia
28 May 1778 to 4 Oct. 1798, and received the rank of Col. in the
Army, 2 July 1778. He was sworn a Privy Councillor 20 April
1763, and was a member of various Ministries for many years,
being Surveyor of Gardens and Waters Jan. to April 1763,
Comptroller of the Household April 1763 to July 1765, a Lord of
the Admiralty March 1768 to July 1779, Treasurer of the
Chamber Sept. 1779, until the abolition of the office, June 1782,
a Vice Treasurer of Ireland Sept. 1782 to March 1784, Joint
Postmaster General Feb. 1801 to Feb. 1806, Master of the Mint
Feb. to Oct. 1806, and a Lord of the Bedchamber 1807 until his
death 16 June 1820.

1763. Jan. 12. Lord Charles Spencer, re-el. on being
Out Ranger of Windsor Forest, and surveyor of the King's
Gardens.

1763. April 4. Lord C. Spencer, re-el. on being app.
Comptroller of the Household.

1768. March 30. Lord Charles Spencer T
                  Viscount Wenman   W

Philip 7th Viscount Wenman, only surviving son of the
M.P. 1754, whom he succeeded 16 Aug. 1760, was born at Thame
Park, 1742, matric. Oriel. Coll. Oxford 1 Feb. 1760, aged 17,
created M.A. 29 Oct. 1762, D.C.L. 7 July 1773, and m. 7 July 1766
Lady Eleanor Bertie dau. of Willoughby 3rd Earl of Abingdon.
He voted for Wilkes 1769, sat for Oxon 1768-96, and died s.p.
26 March 1800, when the title became extinct.   He and his aunt
Mrs Herbert came into a jointure of £1000 a year on the death
on 36 May 1798 of Mrs Tate of Burleigh House, Loughborough,
co. Leicester, dau. of Mr. Butler, and relict (1) of Philip Herbert,
and (2) of —— Tate of Oxon.

1774. Oct. 19. The same.

1779. Dec. 22. Lord C. Spencer, re-el. after being made
Treasurer of the Chamber.

1780. Sept. 27. Rt. Hon. Lord C. Spencer T
                  Viscount Wenman   W

1782. Dec. 18. Lord C. Spencer, (as a Whig,) re-el. after
being app. a Vice Treasurer of Ireland.

1784. April 7. Rt. Hon. Lord C. Spencer W
                 Viscount Wenman   W

1790. June 24. Viscount Wenman   W
                 Marquis of Blandford T

George Spencer, Marquis of Blandford, of Blenheim
Palace, was the elder of the two sons of George 4th Duke of
Marlborough K.G., and was born 6 March 1766, educ. at Eton,
matric. Ch. Ch. Oxford 14 Jan. 1784, created M.A. 9 Dec. 1786,
and D.C.L. 20 June 1792.   He m. 17 Sept. 1791 Lady Susan
Stuart dau. of John 7th Earl of Galloway K.T.   Lord Blandford
was M.P. Oxon 1790-6, Tregony 1802-4, a Lord of the Treasury
Aug. 1804 to Feb. 1806, was called to the Upper House in his
father's lifetime as Baron Spencer of Wormleighton 12 March
1806, and took the additional name and arms of Churchill
by letters patent 26 May 1807.   He was made D.L. Berks 28 July
1798, Major 1st Reading Battalion of Volunteers 31 Dec. 1803
and 19 Nov. 1805, Lt. Col. Commandant 1st Reading Volunteers
1 Sept. 1808, and Lt. Col. Commanding 3rd Royal Berkshire
Militia 10 Sept. 1808.   His Lordship succeeded his father as 5th
Duke of Marlborough 30 Jan. 1817, and was elected F.S.A.,
High Steward of Oxford 1817, and also of Woodstock 1817, and
died 5 March 1840.

1796. June 3. Rt. Hon. Lord C. Spencer W
                John Fane.   T

John Fane of Wormsley, was the 2nd but eldest surviving son (by his third wife) of Henry Fane M.P., Clerk to the Privy Council, who was youngest brother to the 8th Earl of Westmoreland. He m. 16 Nov. 1773 Lady Elizabeth Parker eldest dau. of Thomas 3rd Earl of Macclesfield, (see 1754.) Mr Fane was created D.C.L. Oxford 28 June 1797, app. Major of the Oxfordshire Militia 4 June 1803, (not so in 1807,) Lt. Col. Commandt. 2nd Oxfordshire (Local) Militia 24 April 1809, and was M.P. for the County 1796 until his death in Westminster 8 Feb. 1824, being buried at Lewknor, Oxon. He was an eminent agriculturalist.

1801. March 6. Lord Francis Almaric Spencer, of Wychwood Park, *vice* his uncle Lord Charles Spencer app. Postmaster General. Lord Francis was the younger son of George 4th Duke of Marlborough, and brother to the M.P. 1790. Born 26 Dec. 1779, he matric. Ch. Ch. Oxford 20 Feb. 1797, was created D.C.L. 15 June 1803, and m. 25 Nov. 1800 Lady Frances FitzRoy dau. of Augustus 3rd Duke of Grafton K.G. who was Prime Minister 1766-70. Lord Francis became Captain in command of the Oxfordshire Cavalry Volunteers 13 July 1803, Captain in command of the Lewknor Hundred Vol. 3 Nov. 1803. Lt. Col. Cdt. 1st Oxfordshire Militia 14 April 1809, Lt. Col. Cdt. of the 1st or Queen's Own Oxfordshire Volunteer or Yeomanry Cavalry 12 Dec. 1818, and F.R.S. He was a Commr. of Control for the Affairs of India 13 Nov. 1809 to July 1810, sat for Oxon Feb. 1801 until created Baron Churchill 11 Aug. 1815, was Hereditary Ranger of Wychwood Forest, and died at Brighton 7 or 10 March 1845.

1802. July 14. Lord F. A. Spencer T.

John Fane T.

1806. Nov. 8. The same. Re-elected 12 May 1807, and 12 Oct. 1812.

1815. Oct. 12. William Henry Ashurst of Waterstock, *vice* Lord F. A. Spencer called to the House of Lords. Lord Sunderland, afterwards Duke of Marlborough (see Woodstock 1826,) was a candidate, but after a warm contest, retired without a poll. Mr Ashurst was born 19 Oct. 1778, and was the elder son of Sir Wm. Henry Ashurst Knt. a Justice of the King's Bench 1770-1800, and twice a Lord Commr. of the Great Seal, who died 1807. He matric. Worcester Coll. Oxford 26 Feb. 1796, B.A. 1798, created D.C.L. 6 July 1810, (then H.S of Oxon,) and m. (1) 10 Dec. 1806 Elizabeth eldest dau. of Oswald Mosley of Bolesworth Castle, Cheshire, and (2) 15 Aug. 1839 Selina widow of Sir Charles Mill Bart., and eldest dau. of Sir John Morshead Bart. Mr. Ashurst became Cornet of the Bullington, Dorchester, and Thame Cavalry Volunteers 1 Aug. 1798, and Lieut. thereof April 1806, was J.P. and D,L. Oxon, M.P. Oct. 1815-30, President of the Oxfordshire Agricultural Society 1837-46, a Trustee of

Dr. Radcliffe's Charity, and Chairman of the Oxon Quarter Sessions 1822 until his death at Waterstock 3 June 1846, aged 67.

  1818. June 24. John Fane.

               W. H. Ashurst.

  1820. March 13. The same.

  1824. March 8. John Fane of Wormsley, *vicc* his father deceased. Elder son of the M.P. 1796, he was born 9 July 1775, and m. 6 June 1801 Elizabeth dau. of Wm. Lowndes Stone of Brightwell Park, He was created D.C.L. Oxford 30 June 1824, was H.S. Oxon 1835, M.P. March 1824-31, and died 4 Oct. 1850, aged 75.

  1826. June 16. W. H. Ashurst   T   1329.

               John Fane   T   1268.

               G. F. Stratton   *W*   1058.

  The Poll lasted three days, and 2295 voted. The Plumpers given were for Ashurst 76, Fane 44, Stratton 815. The split votes were, Ashurst and Fane 1117, Ashurst and Stratton 136, Fane and Stratton 107. George Frederick Stratton of Great Tew, who was also defeated at Coventry March 1803, became Major Commandant Bloxham and Banbury Cavalry Volunteers 3 Sept. 1803 (so in 1825,) and died in greatly reduced circumstances in Long Island, North America. (*Wing's Annals of Steeple Barton.*)

  1830. Aug. 5. John Fane   T   1904.

               Lord Norreys   T   1618.

               Sir G. Dashwood *W* 1246.

  2762 voted at this election, the Plumpers being for Fane 94, Norreys 421, and Dashwood 241, while the Split Votes were Fane and Norreys 1001, Fane and Dashwood 809, Norreys and Dashwood 196. Sir George Dashwood 4th Bart., was the grandson of the M.P. 1699.

  Montague Bertie Lord Norreys, of Wytham Abbey, Berks, eldest son of Montague 5th Earl of Abingdon, was born 19 June 1798, educ. at Eton, M.A. Trin. Coll. Cambridge 1829, and m. 7 Jan. 1835 Elizabeth Lavinia only dau. of George Granville Harcourt, (see 1831.) Lord Norreys became Lieut. 1st Oxfordshire Yeomanry 9 July 1827, Captain 16 Dec. 1830, and was Mayor thereof 14 April 1847 to May 1855, D.L. Oxon, Hon. D.C.L. Oxford 11 June 1834, M.P. Oxon 1830-1, when defeated, and 1832-52, and Abingdon 1852 until he succeeded his father as 6th Earl of Abingdon 16 Oct. 1854. He was Lord Lieut. and Cus. Rot. of Berks 28 Feb. 1855 to 11 Aug. 1881, High Steward of Abingdon 1854-84, (both in succession to his father,) and High Steward of Oxford until his death in London 8 Feb. 1884, buried 13 Feb. at Wytham Abbey.

1831. May 9-12. G. G. V. Harcourt W 1782.
                  R. Weyland   W 1688.
                  Lord Norreys   *T* 1316.

This was the last election of an unreformed Parliament,
and 2934 voted, the Poll being kept open 3 days, and the enthusi-
asm of Reform won the two seats for the Whigs. 57 Plumpers
were given for Harcourt, 22 for Weyland, and 996 for Norreys,
while 1536 split their votes between Harcourt and Weyland, 189
between Harcourt and Norreys, and only 131 between Weyland
and Norreys.

George Granville Venables Vernon Harcourt of Nuneham
Park, eldest son of the Hon. and Most Rev. Edward Vernon
Harcourt, Archbishop of York 1807-47, (4th son of the 1st Lord
Vernon,) was born at Sudbury, co. Derby, 6 Aug. 1785, educ. at
Westminster, matric. Oriel Coll. Oxford 23 May 1803, student
1803-14, B.A. 1808, M.A. 1810. He m. (1) 27 March 1815 Lady
Elizabeth Bingham, (who died 9 Sept. 1838) eldest dau. of
Richard 2nd Earl of Lucan, and (2) 30 Sept. 1847 Frances Eliza-
beth Anne dau. of John Braham, and widow (1) of John James
Henry Waldegrave of Navestock, Essex, and (2) of George 7th
Earl of Waldegrave. (This lady re-m. fourthly in 1863 to Lord
Carlingford). On the death of the last Earl Harcourt he took the
name of Harcourt by Royal License 15 Jan. 1831, and became
tenant for life next to his father of the ancient Harcourt estates
at Newnham Courtney and Stanton Harcourt. He was M.P.
Lichfield 1806-30, and Oxon 1831-61, and died at Strawberry Hill,
Twickenham, 19 Dec. 1861, aged 76, buried 27 Dec. at Stanton
Harcourt.

Richard Weyland of Woodeaton, "a soldier of the finest
type," was the 2nd surviving son of John Weyland of Woodrising
Hall, Norfolk, (app. Major Oxon Militia 19 April 1779,) by
Elizabeth dau. and heiress of John Nourse of Woodeaton Hall.
Born 25 March 1780, he spent a short time at St. John's Coll. Cam.
bridge, and then entering the army, as Ensign 9th (East Norfolk)
Regiment 26 Dec. 1805, he became Lieut. therein 17 Dec. 1806, Lieut.
16th Light Dragoons 26 March 1807, Brevet Captain 18 July 1811,
Captain of a troop therein 5 Sept. 1811, and served with that
regiment throughout the Peninsular War, in Spain and Portugal,
(being A.D.C. to General Sir George Anson,) and at Waterloo,
for which he received the Waterloo Medal. He was made
Brevet Major 21 Jan. 1819, but retired from the army before 1822.
In 1825 he succeeded under the will of his maternal grandfather
to the Woodeaton estate, and in 1854 also succeeded his elder
brother in the Woodrising property. Major Weyland m. 12 Sept.
1820 Charlotte youngest dau. of Charles Gordon of Cluny, co.
Aberdeen, and widow of Sir John Lowther Johnstone 6th Bart.
M.P. of Westerhall, co. Dumfries. He was J.P. and D.L. Norfolk

and Oxon, H.S. Oxon 1830, M.P. 1831-7, and died 14 Oct. 1864, aged 84. His dau. Joanna m. in 1840 the 2nd Earl of Verulam. The Member must not be confused with another Richard Weyland, who became Ensign 53rd Foot 31 July 1806, and Lieut. 8th Foot 1 March 1809, (so in 1812).

    1832. Dec. 17. G. G. Harcourt W.

                Major R. Weyland W.

                Lord Norreys   T.

The celebrated Reform Act of 1832 gave a third Member to the County of Oxford.

    1835. Jan. 12. The same.

    1837. July 29. Lord Norreys   T 3002.

                G. G. Harcourt W 2835.

                T. A. W. Parker T 2767.

                Thomas Stonor *W* 1458.

This was the first instance in Oxfordshire of the county being divided into polling districts; 4125 voted out of 5253. Blue and White were the Colours of Lord Norreys, while Mr. Stonor's Colour was Yellow. Thomas Augustus Wolstenholme Parker of Sherborne Castle, only son of Hon. Thomas Parker, (who succ. his brother George, see Woodstock 1777, as 5th Earl of Macclesfield 20 March 1842,) was born 17 March 1811, educ. at Eton, and matric. Ch. Ch. Oxford 24 June 1829. He m. (1) 11 July 1839 Henrietta (who died 19 Nov. 1839) dau. of Edmund Turnor of Stoke Rochford, co. Lincoln, and (2) 25 Aug. 1842 Lady Mary Frances Grosvenor (Lady of the Bedchamber to the Princess of Wales,) dau. of Richard 2nd Marquis of Westminster K.G. He became Cornet 1st Oxfordshire Yeomanry 24 Jan. 1831, Captain 9 June 1837 to March 1850, D.L. Oxon 21 Aug. 1832, M.P. 1837-41, Viscount Parker by courtesy 20 March 1842, and succeeded his father as 6th Earl of Macclesfield 31 March 1850, and also as High Steward of Henley, which post he retained until his death 24 July 1896. He was patron of 6 livings.

    1841. July 5. Lord Norreys T.

              G. G. Harcourt W.

              J. W. Henley   T.

Joseph Warner Henley of Waterperry, only son of Joseph H. of London, merchant, was born at Putney 3 March 1793, educ. at Fulham, matric. Magd. Coll. Oxford 27 April 1812, B.A. 1815, M.A. 1834, created D.C.L. 28 June 1854, and m. 9 Dec. 1817 Georgiana 4th dau. of John Fane of Wormsley, (see 1824). He was in his father's office 1815-17, was for some years Vice-Chairman Oxon Quarter Sessions, then Chairman thereof 1846-63, and

M.P. Oxon 1841 until he accepted the Chiltern Hundreds Jan.
1878. Mr. Henley was sworn a Privy Councillor 27 Feb. 1852,
and held office as President of the Board of Trade Feb. to Dec.
1852, and Feb. 1858 to March 1859. He died at Waterperry 8
Dec. 1884, aged 91.

1847, Aug. 3. Lord Norreys   L.C.

G. G. Harcourt L.C.

J. W. Henley   C.

1852. March 10. Rt. Hon. J. W. Henley, re-el. on accepting office.

1852. July 12. Rt. Hon. J. W. Henley C.   2328.

Lt. Col. Sidney North   C.   2218.

G. G. Harcourt   L.C. 1313.

Lord Norreys   *L.C.* 681.

Lt. Col. Sidney North of Wroxton Abbey, was the 2nd son
of Lt. Gen. Sir Charles Wm. Doyle G.C.H., and was born at
Alnwick 28 May 1804, educ. at Sandhurst, became Ensigne 11th
Foot 1 Feb. 1821, Captain 87th Foot 22 Nov. 1827, went on half
pay 17 April 1835, and sold out of the Army 1837. He m. 18
Nov. 1835 Lady Susan North younger dau. of the 3rd Earl of
Guilford (see Banbury 1790,) in whose favour the abeyance of the
Barony of North was terminated 11 Sept. 1841. He assumed the
surname of North by Royal License 20 Aug. 1838, was created
D.C.L. Oxford 12 June 1839, became J.P. and D.L. Northants,
Middlesex, and Oxon, J.P. co. Warwick, D.L, co. Cambridge,
H.S. Oxon 1845, Lt. Col. 2nd Tower Hamlets Militia 1836, Lt.
Col. Oxfordshire Rifle Volunteers 1 May 1860-73, and Hon. Col.
thereaf 26 March 1873-94. He was sworn a Privy Conncillor 3
April 1886, sat for Oxon 1852-85, and died 11 Oct. 1894, aged
90.

1857. March 30. Rt. Hon. J. W. Henley C.

Lt. Col. Sidney North C.

G. G. Harcourt   L.

1859. March 6. Rt. Hon. J. W. Henley, re-el. after accepting office.

1859. May   2. Rt. Hon. J. W. Henley.

Lt. Col. Sidney North.

G. G. Harcourt.

1862. Feb.   3. Lt. Col. J. W. Fane C. 1909.

Sir H. Dashwood   L. 1722.

vice Harcourt deceased. Sir Henry Wm. Dashwood 5th Bart. was
the son of the defeated candidate 1830.

Lt. Col. John William Fane of Wormsley, eldest son of the M.P. 1824, was born 1 Sept. 1804, and married four times, (1) 30 Nov. 1826 Catherine (who d. 6 Nov. 1828) 12th dau. of Sir Benjamin Hobhouse 1st Bart. and sister to Lord Broughton (see *Williams' Gloucestershire Members,*) (2) 3 Nov. 1829 Lady Ellen Catherine Parker (who d. 23 Sept. 1844) 3rd dau. of Thomas 5th Earl of Macclesfield, and sister to the M.P. 1837 ; (3) 17 Nov. 1845 Charlotte (who d. 19 May 1855) youngest dau. of Theodore Henry Broadhead ; and (4) March 1856 Victoria youngest dau. of Wm. Temple. He was app. Major of the Oxfordshire Militia 2 May 1825, Lt. Col. 6 April 1847, Lt. Col. Commandant thereof 18 July 1862 to 22 May 1872, and during the Crimean War, he accompanied the service companies of the regiment to Corfu in 1855, and commanded them during their stay there. He was created D.C,L. Oxford 28 June 1854, J.P. and D.L. Oxon, H.S. 1854, M.P. Feb. 1862-8, ond died in London 19 Nov. 1875.

1865.	July 17.	Rt. Hon. J. W. Henley	C.
		Lt. Col. J, S. North	C.
		Lt. Col. J. W. Fane	C.
1868.	Nov. 18.	Rt. Hon. J. W. Henley	C.
		Lt. Col. J. S. North	C.
		W. C. Cartwright	L.

William Cornwallis Cartwright of Aynho, Northants, eldest son of Sir Thomas Cartwright G.C.H. many years Envoy to Sweden, who d. 1850, was born 24 Nov. 1825, and m. Fraulein Clementine Gaul. He became J.P. and D.L. Northants, H.S. 1890, sat for Oxon 1868-85, and is lord of the manors of Aynho, and Hinton in the Hedges.

1874.	Feb. 3.	The same.

1878. Feb. 5. Edward William Vernon Harcourt, of Nuneham Park, Berks, and Stanton Harcourt *vice* Henley, resigned. Elder son of Rev. Canon Wm. Vernon Harcourt of York, and nephew of the M.P. 1831, he was born 26 June 1825, matric. Ch. Ch. Oxford 19 Oct. 1843. student 1843-7, and m. 26 June 1849 Lady Susan Harriet Holroyd only dau. of George 2nd Earl of Sheffield. He was J.P. Berks, J.P. and D.L. Oxon, H.S. 1875, M.P. Oxon Feb. 1878-85, and South Oxon 1885-6, lord of the manors of Nuneham, Stanton Harcourt, Hinksey, Northmoor, Coggs, and Shifford, and Hon. Col. 1st Cinque Ports Artillery Volunteers 7 Aug. 1872 until his death 19 Dec. 1891.

1880.	April 1.	Lt. Col. J. S. North	C.
		W. C. Cartwright	L.
		Col. E. W. Harcourt	C.

Oxfordshire had 4721 registered electors in 1832, 7663 in 1868, and 6784 in 1884. At the Dissolution of Parliament 18 Nov. 1885, the provisions of the Redistribution of Seats Act 1885. came into operation, whereby Oxfordshire was divided into three Parliamentary Divisions, Mid. or Woodstock, North or Banbury, and South or Henley Divisions, each returning one Member. The High Sheriff of the County is the Returning Officer.

I. MID OXFORDSHIRE.

1885. Dec. 3. Francis W. Maclean L 4327.

   Viscount Valentia   C   4138.

Francis William Maclean, third son of Alexander Maclean of Barrow Hedges, Carshalton, Surrey, was born 13 Dec. 1844, educ. at Westminster, and graduated B.A. 1866, M.A. 1871, Trin. Coll. Camb. He entered the Inner Temple 1 Nov. 1864, where he was called to the bar 30 April 1868, and chosen a Bencher Nov. 1892, and became a Queen's Counsel May 1886. He m. 10 Aug. 1869 Mattie 2nd dau. of John Sowerby of Benwell Tower, Northumberland. Mr. Maclean was M.P. for Mid Oxon 1885 until he was made a Master in Lunacy April 1891, and from this office was promoted to be Chief Justice of the Supreme Court of Judicature of Bengal Oct. 1896, and received the honour of Knighthood 12 Oct. 1896. He was Chairman of the Central Committee at Calcutta for the relief of the sufferers from the famine in 1897-8, and made K.C.I.E. 11 Jan. 1898.

1886. July 6. Francis W. Maclean Q.C. L.U.

1891. April 21. G. H. Morrell C 4448.

   G. R. Benson   L   3768.

vice Maclean made a Master in Lunacy. George Herbert Morrell of Headington Hill Hall, eldest son of Rev. George Kidd Morrell D.C.L. of Adderbury, Oxon, vicar of Moulsford, Berks, was born 20 Feb. 1845, educ. at Rugby 1859-63, (winner of Challenge School Athletic Cup 1863,) and matric. Exeter Coll. Oxford 26 May 1863, B.A. 1867, B.C.L. and M.A. 1870, (winner of University Pair Oar Race 1866.) He entered the Inner Temple 29 April 1868, where he was called to the bar 26 Jan. 1871, and went the Oxford Circuit, and m. 4 Feb. 1874 Emily Alicia only child and heir of James Morrell of Headington Hill. He is author of the "Student's Manual of Comparative Anatomy, and Guide to Dissection." Col. Morrell has spent many years in the Volunteer Service, for he was a member of the Rugby School Cadet Corps 21 Feb. 1861 to 16 Oct. 1863, (Ensign 20 Feb. 1862, Lieut. 20 Aug. 1862, Captain 23 Oct. 1862 ;) of the Oxford Univ. Corps 17 Oct. 1863 to 11 Feb. 1869, (Ensign 6 July 1864, Lieut. 21 March 1865, Captain 7 Nov. 1665 to May 1868, Quarter Master Sergeant 9 May 1868 ;) and of the Inns of Court Volunteers 12 Feb. 1869 to

13 Nov. 1871. He was afterwards Lt. Col. Commandant of the Oxford Univ. Corps 22 Jan. 1879 to 1 Nov. 1897, receiving the rank of Hon. Col. 1895, and was presented the Volunteer Decoration by H.R.H. the Duke of Cambridge in 1894, (First List). He formed one of the Rugby team which won the Ashburton Shield 1861, and of the Oxford Univ. team which won the Chancellor's Plate, against Camb. Univ. in 1866. Col. Morrell was a member of the Oxford Local Board 1871-83, and of the Oxford School Board 1873-7, was President of the Oxford School of Science and Art 1884-91, made J.P. Berks 1876, J.P. Oxon 1877, Dep. Lieut. Oxon Jan. 1885, High Sheriff of Oxon 1885, and has been an Alderman of the County Council since 1889. He was elected for Mid Oxon April 1891, but lost his seat the following year, but has again represented the Division since 1895.

1892. July. G. R. Benson G.L. 4278.

G. H. Morrell   C   4167.

Godfrey Rathbone Benson, 4th son of William B. of Alresford, Hants, was born in 1864, and matric. Ball. Coll. Oxford 16 Oct. 1883, aged 18. He sat for Mid Oxon 1892-5, but was defeated April 1891, and 1895.

1895. July 19. G. H. Morrell C 4669.

G. R. Benson   L   3740.

Mid Oxon had 9767 electors in 1895.

II. NORTH OXFORDSHIRE.

1885. Dec. 4. Sir Bernhard Samuelson L 4436.

Llewelyn Malcolm Wynne C 2944.

Sir Bernhard Samuelson of Bodicote Grange. Banbury, son of Samuel Henry S. of Liverpool, merchant, was born 22 Nov. 1820, educ. at Skirlaugh, Yorkshire, and m. (1) 20 July 1841 Caroline (who d. 16 April 1886,) dau. of Henry Blundell of Hull, and (2) 6 April 1889 Lelia Mathilda dau. of the Chevalier Leon Serena, and widow of Wm. Denny of Dumbarton. He was an extensive ironmaster at Middlesborough, and agricultural implement manufacturer at Banbury, a member of the Institution of Civil Engineers, of the Institute of Mechanical Engineers, Past President of the Iron and Steel Institute, and became a Knight of the Legion of Honour 1878. He was M.P. Banbury Feb. to April 1859, when defeated, and 1865-85, and for North Oxon 1885-95, and was created a Baronet in 1884, and sworn a Privy Councillor in 1895. Sir Bernhard is a County Alderman of Oxon, and F.R.S.

1886.	July 13.	Sir B. Samuelson	G.L.	3677.
		L. M. Wynne	*C.*	3184.
1892.	July	Sir B. Samuelson	G.L.	3640.
		L. M. Wynne	*C.*	3453.
1895.	July 22.	Albert Brassey	C.	4057.
		C. Thornton	*L.*	3047.

Albert Brassey of Heythrop Park, Chipping Norton, son of Thomas Brassey an eminent railway contractor, and brother to Thomas Lord Brassey, Governor of New South Wales, was born 22 Feb. 1844, and matric. Univ. Coll. Oxford 18 Oct. 1862, B.A. 1867. He m. 13 Jan. 1871 the Hon. Matilda Maria Helena Bingham eldest dau. of John 4th Lord Clanmorris. Mr Brassey entered the Army as Cornet 14th Hussars 21 Aug. 1867, and was Lieut. thereof 3 April 1869-71. He became Captain Oxfordshire Yeomany 6 April 1872, (Hon. Major in 1889,) and was Lt. Col. thereof 21 April 1892-4, (rank of Hon. Col. 1893.) He is a J.P. for Oxon, was High Sheriff 1878, Mayor of Chipping Norton 9 Nov. 1898, and has been M.P. for North Oxon since 1895.

North Oxon had 8145 electors in 1895.

III. SOUTH OXFORDSHIRE.

1885.	Dec. 2.	Col. E. W. Harcourt	C.	3778.
		Fred. Wm. Maude	*L.*	3258.
1886.	July 15.	Hon. Francis Parker	C.	3674.
		Sir W. Phillimore	*G.L.*	2600.

Hon. Francis Parker was born 15 Aug. 1851, the 4th son of Thomas 6th Earl of Macclesfield (see 1837,) and was educ. at Eton, matric. Ch. Ch. Oxford 13 Oct. 1869, S.C.L. and B.A. 1873, M.A. 1879, entered the Middle Temple 3 Aug. 1871, went to the Inner Temple 6 Nov. 1871, and was called to the bar at the Inner Temple 26 Jan. 1875, and went the Oxford circuit. He m. 16 Feb. 1882 Henrietta 3rd dau. of Henry Lomax Gaskell of Kiddington Hall, Woodstock, and was M.P. for South Oxon 1886-95.

1892.	July.	Hon. F. Parker	C	3688
		Sir W. Phillimore	*G L*	3269
1895.	July 24.	R. T. Hermon-Hodge	C	3831
		H. Samuel	*L*	3470

Robert Trotter Hermon-Hodge of Wyfold Court, Reading, eldest son of George Wm. Hodge of Newcastle on Tyne, was born in 1851, educ. at Clifton College, matric. Worcester Coll.

Oxford 17 Oct. 1870, S.C.L. and B.A. 1873, M.A. 1881. He m. in 1877 Francis Caroline only daughter of Edward Hermon M.P. of Wyfold Court, and assumed the prefix surname of Hermon in 1885. He is J.P. for Berks and Oxon, was a County Alderman of Oxon 1889-95, became Second Lieut. Oxfordshire Yeomry 9 Nov. 1878, Lieut. 1 July 1881, Captain 5 May 1892, (rank of Hon. Major 1894), and was M.P. Accrington Division of North East Lancashire 1886-92, but was defeated there 1885, 1892, and Dec. 1893. Since 1895 he has sat for South Oxon. He moved the Address at the opening of the Session in 1891.

South Oxon had 8932 registered electors in 1895.

THE CITY OF OXFORD.

The first Parliament of England was summoned by King John to meet at *Oxford* on 15 Nov. 1213, and since that remote period other Parliaments were ordered to meet in the Loyal City in 1439, and April 1554, (when however the place of meeting was afterwards altered in each instance to Westminster.) Furthermore the Royalist Members of the famous Long Parliament held their assembly, called the Junta, at Oxford in 1643-4, and " in consequence of the Great Plague raging in London, the Parliament met in the great Hall of Christ Church in Oxford on 9 Oct. 1665, and a gay Court surrounded the King there." And a little later on " a new Parliament met at Oxford 21 March 1681, because the University was devoted to the Crown." For the first three or four centuries most of the City Members appear to have been selected from the ranks of the leading merchants and principal men of Oxford, and included many Mayors, while several of the Recorders were also returned. Since that period however the City went further afield for its Representatives, inasmuch as it commenced to elect scions of the County Families of Oxfordshire, and during the last century a still greater change is witnessed by the election of distinguished strangers.

The many disputes between Town and University are instanced in the references to John de Bereford (1344,) and Thomas Wentworth (1604.) The proverbial loyalty of Oxford was never more exhibited than during the Cival War, when its Members Whistler and Smith were disabled to sit ; but, on the other hand Col. Cooper and Ald. Nixon were staunch Roundheads, and the famous lawyer Bulstrode Whitlocke, and Unton and Richard Croke were also firm supporters of Parliament. In later times among its distinguished Members have been Sir George Nares, Justice of the Common Pleas, Field Marshal Earl Harcourt, General St. John, Sir Charles Wetherell, Solicitor General, Sir William Erle, Chief Justice of the Common Pleas, Lord Hatherley, Lord Chancellor, Viscount Cardwell, Secretary for War, and Lord Justice Chitty. Oxford in fact has shewn a decided preference for electing distinguished lawyers, which is still further demonstrated by the mention of George Caulfield, Matthew Skinner and Francis Burton, who were Welsh Judges. Sir William Harcourt has been Chancellor of the Exchequer and Leader of the House, and the present Member, Viscount Valentia, is Comptroller of Her Majesty's Household. Mr. Thackeray was the best known of the rejected Candidates.

1295. Thomas de Sowy.
Andrew de Pyrie.

These are the earliest known Citizens for Oxford, although the City was in all probability previously represented in the Parliaments of 1265, and Jan. and Sept. 1283. Even after this date instances have occurred as in 1297, May 1300 and 1316, when no Members were summoned for cities and boroughs. In 1285 Thomas de Sowy, clerk, held as tenant for the King. (*Oxford City Documents, edited by J. E. Thorold Rogers.*) He was Mayor of Oxford 1294, 1301, 1302, 1303, and was app. with three others and divers merchants with the Sheriff of Oxford to purchase specified quantities of wool, 30 July 1297. (*Patent Rolls*). His colleague was Mayor of Oxford 1297, M.P. 1295, 1300, 1301, 1302, 1305, 1306, 1309, 1311, 1313, and one of the City Constables in 1305. There are references to four members of the Pyrie family in the *Patent Rolls* 1307-13.

1298. Christopher de Oxon.
John de Weston.

In the *Patent Rolls* 1281-1292 there are references to Henry, John, Mosseus, and James de Oxon or Oxonia, Christopher was one of the two Bailiffs of Oxford on 25 December 1298. It is doubtful if his colleague was the same person as the following:—2 Jan. 1282, Licence at the instance of John de Weston, for Felicia, late the wife of William de Cheney, tenant in chief, to marry whomsoever she will of the King's allegiance. 26 April 1286, Protection with clause *volumus* until All Saints, for John de Weston going beyond seas with the King. 8 Jan. 1291, Grant to J. de W. of the marriage of William son and heir of Bartholomew de Brienzun, tenant in chief. 16 Aug. 1297, Protection with clause *volumus* for one year for John de Weston going beyond seas with Elizabeth Countess of Holland. 2 Nov. 1309, Exemption for life for J. de W. of Lybre from being put on assizes juries or recognizances against his will. Master John de Weston was app. Chamberlain and Receiver of Scotland 14 March 1309, was Steward of the Household of the King's brothers the next year, and Constable of the Tower of London 1323-6.

1300. March. Andrew Pirie.
John le Orfevre.
1301. Andrew de Pirie.
John Aurifaber.

The latter was given as Lorfevre in the Enrolment of the
Writ *de Expensis*, and was the same as the M.P. 1300, 1302, 1309,
1313, 1314, and 1321. He was also M.P. for Newbury 1302. *Wood*
gives him as John Goldsmith. 20 Oct. 1289, Writ *de intendendo*
directed to the bailiffs burgesses and good men of Oxford for
Nicholas le Orfevre, elected Mayor, whose fealty the King has
taken. Ten of this name are referred to in the *Patent Rolls*
1281-92. 5 Dec. 1285, Commission of oyer etc. on complaint by
the Prior of Merton that Amicia de Ewell, having been taken
with stolen goods at Molesey within the liberty wherein he has
pleas of theft, by Thomas le Sergaunt of Molesey and Wm. le
Messier, his servants, and imprisoned, the said prison was broken
and the said Amicia taken away by Edw. Lovekin, John le
Orfevre, and several others. 6 April 1327 Order to the Mayor
and Bailiffs of Oxford to deliver to John, Bishop of Ely, or to his
attorney, the £65 1 0 found upon John le Orfevre of Oxford and
William le Taillour of Oxford, who with others lately robbed the
Bishop of certain sums of money, the said John and William
having been taken and imprisoned at Oxford at the suit of
Walter atte Hull, the Bishop's servant, and they have confessed
certain felonies, as the King has given the above sum to the
Bishop. *(Patent Rolls.)*

1302.	Andrew de Pyrie.
	John le Orfevere.
1305.	Andrew de Pirye.
	Christopher son of Simon.
1306.	Andrew de Purye.
	Christopher son of Simon.
1307. Jan.	Andrew de Pyrye.
	Christopher son of Simon.
1307. Oct.	Andrew de Pirie.
	William Deveneys.

Appointment 5 April 1308 of William Deveneys to be
Chief Justice of the Bench, Dublin, having the same place on the
Bench as he had hitherto held. *(Patent Rolls)*.

1309.	Andrew de Purie.
	John le Orfevre.
1311. Aug.	Andrew de Pyrie.
	John de Fallele.
1311. Nov.	The same.

Wood gives Thomas Farthing and William de Carswell as
the Members 5 Edw. II., J. Culvere and J. Minekan 6 Edw. II., but
if correct, the summonses to Parliament Feb. 1312, were revoked

before the Return, and the *Official Returns* mention no Member for Oxford in the next Parliament, Aug. 1312·

1313. March. Andrew de Pyrie.

John le Orfevre.

1313. Sept. Andrew de Purie.

John Aurifaber.

1314. Sept. John Aurifaber.

John de Fallele.

1315. John son of William le Spicer.

John de Falele.

William le Espicer was Mayor of Oxford 1285. *Wood* calls the Member J. Fitz William. Fallele was Member 1311, 1314, 1315, 1320, 1321, 1322, 1324, and Bailiff 1329.

1318. John Mymecan.

John de Cudelynton.

On 10 June 1312 Alan son of Wm. Fitz Warin going to Ireland had letters nominating Peter Fitz Warin and John Mymekan his attorneys for one year. Mymecan was again Member 1328, 1332, 1334, 1336, 1338.

1319. John son of William Bost.

William de Spaldyng.

The former again sat 1322, 1324, 1325, 1327, 1328, 1336, 1337, 1340, 1341. John son of John Bost is mentioned in the *Patent Rolls* 28 Aug. 1336. On 9 Aug. 1327, Commission to Wm. de Burncestr, John de Oxon and two others to enquire by juries of counties Oxford and Berks touching kidels in the Thames, and cause them to be removed, and the nets and engines to be burned, and to fine and punish offenders therein. On 25 June 1309 complaint by Thomas, Abbot of Brunne, (Bourne,) and William de Spaldyng, canon of that house, that certain persons assaulted the said W. de S. at Brunne, co. Lincoln, threw him into a pit full of water, and tore his habit. 26 Jan. 1335, Appointment of Wm. de Spaldyng and three others in Holand, co. Lincoln, to see that the men of that county are duly furnished with arms according to their estate, pursuant to the King's late proclamation and the statute of Winchester ; and to array them for the defence of the realm. W. de S. and two others were app. to keep the King's peace there 26 July 1325. William son of Richard de Spaldyng was returned for Spalding Borough as one of the most discreet wool merchants "to attend the King at York for counsel and advice" 20 Jan. 1328. W. de S. was granted exemption for life from being put on assizes juries or recognisances and from appointment as mayor sheriff escheator coroner or other bailiff or minister of the King against his will, and on 8 June 1336 was granted exemption from Knighthood for two years, and was pardoned 8 July 1336 for not having taken the Order of Knighthood within the times specified in the King's two proclamations, and of any issues forfeited by him on account of the default.

1320. Richard Cary.
John de Fallele.

Cary was Mayor of Oxford 1328, 1335, 1340, 1341, 1343, 1345, and on 18 May 1329 he (as Mayor) and Fallele (as one of the Bailiffs) witnessed the Enrolment of an Indenture of a grant to St. Mary's House, Oxford. He was again Member 1335, 1339. 6 Jan. 1327, Commission of Oyer to John de Stonore and others, on complaint by the abbot of Abyndon that Thos. de Legh 'tounclerc,' Rd. Cary, Thos. de Leghe of Oxford, 'bakere," And. le Wormenhale (1325,) Thos. de Denton of Abyndon, Wm. de. Pirie, Simon de Gloucestr and others, with a multitude of other persons, in warlike manner besieged the abbey, burned the gates, and entering the abbey carried away books chalices vestments church ornaments and other goods and divers charters writings obligatory agreements and other muniments. They took Rt. de Halton the prior then sick within the abbey, and carried him to Baggeleye Wood, in Radeleye, and there threatened him with the loss of his head unless he would do their will, afterwards they carried him back to the abbey, broke a certain coffer in which was the common seal, and under fear of death made him seal three writings obligatory—by one of which the abbot and convent became bound to them in £1000—and also other writings of release and quit-claim of all trespasses from the beginning of the world till the date of sealing.

1321. John Aurifaber.
John de Falele.

1322. May. John de Falele.
John son of William Bost.

1322. Nov. John Aurifaber.
John Fallele.

1324. Jan. John de Fallee.
John son of William Bost.

1325. Andrew de Wormenhale.
John son of William Bost.

The former was Mayor of Oxford as Knt. 1327, and again Member 1331, 1332, 1336, 1337, 1339, and was of the same family as Andrew de W. who was Mayor 1279, Robert de W. the Mayor 1298, and Philip de W. who was Bailiff on 25 Dec. 1298, and Mayor 1310. Writ *de intendendo* for Andrew de W., elected

Mayor of Oxford, on his having taken the oath in the Chancery, 30 Sept. 1327. Master John de O. parson of the Church of Walpol, going beyond the seas on the King's service has letters nominating A. de Wormenhale and Henry de Todenham his attorneys in England until Easter, 6 Oct. 1337.

1327.   The same.

1318. Feb. Andrew de Wyrcestre.

John son of William de Oxon.

1328. April. John Culverd.

John son of William Bost.

Culverd was a wine seller and coroner of Oxford in 1285, Mayor 1285, 1292, (and as Culvert) 1293, M.P. 1328, 1330, 1331, 1332, founded a chantry in All Saints, and died about 1334. His wife was named Christina. 6 Oct, 1337, Pardon to the Carmelite Friars of Oxford for acquiring in mortmain from John de Croxford (see County 1312,) John Culvered and three others, for the enlargement of their dwelling place, divers plots in Oxford containing one acre of land, held in chief, and entering therein without the licence of Edw. II. (*Patent Rolls*).

1328. July. John Mymkan.

John son of William Bost.

Writ to the Bailiffs of Oxford for payment to John Mynikan and John son of William Bost, burgesses of that city, of their expenses in coming to the treaty at York on Sunday after St. James last, to wit 18 days, 6 Aug. 1328. (*Close Rolls*).

1330. March. John Culverd.

Stephen de Adynton.

The latter was again M.P. 1337, and Mayor 1338..

1330. Nov. Andrew de Wormenhale.

Henry de Stodlegh.

The latter was M.P. for Oxford 1330, 1332, 1336, 1339, and Mayor 1337, 1344. Writ *do intendendo* in favour of H. de Stodelegh, mayor elect, who has taken the oath of office before the King at Westminster, 1 Oct. 1337.

1331. Sept. Andrew de Wormenhale.

John Culverd.

1332. March. Andrew de Wormenhale.

Henry de Stodler.

1332. Sept. John Culverd.

John Mynekan.

1332.. Dec, The same.

1334. Feb. John Mymcan.

John de Falle.

The latter was apparently not the same as the M.P. 1311, but was Member 1334, 1346, 1448, 1351.

1335. Richard Cary.

John de Persshore.

The latter again sat 1338. On 2 March 1328 a commission issued to try John de Pershore for the assault upon Abingdon Abbey, (see under Rd. Cary 1320).

1336. March. Henry de Stodeleye.

John Mymkan.

1336. Sept. Andrew de Wormenhale.

John son of William Bost.

1337. Jan. Andrew de Wormenhale.

John Bost.

It is curious that Oxford was not one of the 17 Towns directed to send Members to the preceding Parliament summoned to meet at London 3 Jan. 1337.

1337. Sept. Stephen de Adynton.

Andrew de Wormenhale.

By Writs dated at Westminster 18 August, the Mayor and Bailiffs of Oxford, (among other towns,) were directed to send three or four persons to attend this Parliament, and Stephen de Adynton, Andrew de Warmenhale, and John Mimmecan were accordingly elected. They were however merely summoned to advise with the King upon some special matter, and were not regular Members of Parliament.

1338. Feb. John de Pershore.

John Mymekan.

1338. July. John Mymmekan.

Nicholas de Publesbury.

Nicholas again sat 1341, 1344.

1339. Jan. Richard Cary.

Andrew de Wormenhale.

1339. Oct. Henry de Stodlee.

John son of William Bost de Oxon.

1340. Jan. Simon de Gloucestr.

John son of William Bost.

Writ *de intendendo* 23 Sept. 1336 in favour of Simon de Gloucestr elected Mayor of Oxford who has taken his oath of office before the King at Nottingham. (*Patent Rolls*).

1340.   March.   John son of William Bost.
        John de Bybury.

John de Bibury is mentioned in the *Patent Rolls* 8 March
1337. He was again Member 1346, 1348. John Bybury and
Alice his wife paid ijs as Poll Tax in 1380.

1341.   John son of William de Oxon.
                Nicholas de Peblesbury.

1344.   John de Bereford.
                Nicholas de Peplesbury.

Commission of Sewers 28 Feb. 1328 to John de Bereford
and four others for the water of Wythum and the dykes and
places by which water, in the parts of Morland, in the Wapentake
of Lovedon, co. Lincoln, flows from Claypol to the city of Lincoln, and thence into the river. (*Patent Rolls*). Probably
however he was not the Member for Oxford, who, according to
the *Oxford City Documents*, kept a tavern where commenced the
famous fray on St. Scholastica's Day 10 Feb. 1354. He it was
who organised the attack on the scholars, some of whom were
murdered by the mob, the affray lasting for three or four days,
and for which Bereford was excommunicated. He however was
afterwards elected Mayor the same year, having previously
served that office 1348, 1349, 1350, 1351. (*Wood's Ancient and
Present State*). He was M.P. 1344, 1346, 1348, 1451, and (as
Wereford) 1353.

1346.   John de Bybury.
                John de Falle.

1348.   Jan.   John de Falle.
                John de Aleston.

1348.   March. John de Bereford.
                John de Bybury.

1351.   John de Bereford.
                John de Falle.

1353.   John de Wereford.
                John de Stodle.

John de Stodle was seemingly son of the M.P. 1330. He
was again M.P. 1358, 1361, 1371, and was Mayor 1353, 1357, 1358,
1359, 1360, 1361, 1365, 1368. His colleague was evidently
John de Bereford the former Member.

1355.   John de Seynte Fredeswyth.
                Henry de Malmesbury.

Wood gives John de Fridiswida as Mayor of Oxford 1352,
1355, 1356, and there is a reference to him in the *Oxford City
Documents* as Mayor on 17 July 1355 as John de St. Frideswyde.

1358. John de Stodle.

John de Sancta Frideswida.

1360. Peter le Paynter.

John de Wyndesore.

The latter was a collector (with John Gibbes, and Wm. Codeshale, see 1369,) of a lay subsidy in Oxford temp. Edw. 3, and Rich. 2. He again sat for the city 1362, 1363, 1372, and may have been a kinsman of John de Wyndesore, King's clerk, who was Keeper of the King's Exchanges (or Mint) at Canterbury and London in 1335.

1361. John de Stodle.

John de Bereford.

1362. John de Wyndesore.

Galfridus de Brehull.

Geoffrey Brehull, cordwainer, and Margaret his wife, with their three servants John, John, and Alice, paid the Poll Tax in 1380. Perhaps of kin to Henry de Brehull who was ordered to be arrested as a suspected person and imprisoned in Warwick goal 8 Aug. 1336.

1363. Richard Wydehay.

John Wyndesore.

Richard de Wodehay was Mayor of Oxford 1362, 1363, 1364, 1366, and again Member 1365.

1365. Richard Wodehay.

John Hertewelle.

The name of John de Hertwell appears as Mayor 1367, 1372.

1366. John de ———

William Northern.

William Northern was a great benefactor to the city, of which he was Member 1366, 1372, 1382, 1383, and Mayor 1369, and 1376, being Knighted at the Coronation of Richard II, which occurred during his Mayoralty in 1377. Alderman W. le Northern and Margaret his wife, and his servants Peter, John, John, John, John, Richard, William, Alice, Alice, and Alice, were assessed to the Poll Tax in 1380, the sum of xijd. being paid for each man, and iiijd. for each maid-servant. He must therefore have been a person of great wealth and influence at Oxford. He died in 1383, (M.I. St. Peter's le Bayley Church,) being buried with his wife under the same marble.

1368. John Dadynton.

John de Benham.

John Dadyntone, cutler, and Joan his wife, paid a Poll Tax

of xijs in 1380, and his apprentice Richard Haclitt iiijd., and his servants John and Roesia iiijd.

1369. William de Codesale.

John Gibbes.

The former was a brewer at Oxford, and employed two carters, a brewer, and a maltman. He was again M.P. 1371, 1373, 1376, 1377, Mayor 1370, 1371, 1373, 1374, 1375, 1379, and was an Alderman in 1380, when he paid Poll Tax for himself, his wife Alice, seven men-servants, and one maid-servant.

John Gibbes was one of the most prominent citizens of Oxford of his day. He was member 1369, 1376, 1377, and Mayor 1377, 1378, 1383, 1384, (and as Sir 5, Gybbes Knt.) 1413, 1414, 1415, (unless the three latter dates referred to his son.) A Commission issued to John Gibbes, as Mayor, John Shawe (1388) and Thomos Somerset (1379), as Bailiffs, and others, 15 July 1378, on the information of John de Dodeford, prior to St. Frideswide's, Oxford, that four fellow canons of his seized and put in chains his steward deputed in his absence, and carried away his goods, to arrest and deliver them to the said prior to be chastised according to the rule of their order. (*Patent Rolls.*) Alderman John Gibbes, vintner, and Joan his wife were assessed for the Poll Tax in 1380 at xiijs. iiijd, while xijd. and iiijd. were paid for their servants Robert and Matilda. *(Oxford City Documents.)* On 8 March 1382 John Gibbes, Wm. Dagvyle (see 1373,) Wm. Godesale, (1369) and Richard Mercer (1380,) were made Commissioness of the Peace for Oxfordshire. 30 June 1380, Writ of aid for John Gibbes, John Hereford, serjeant at arms. and three others, appointed to arrest and deliver to their prior John Ryal, Richard de Brakley, and John Kent, apostate canons of St. Frideswide's, Oxford. 8 July 1382, Commission of the Peace and of Oyer and terminer in co. Oxford to John Gibbes, Wm. Godeshale, and Rd. Mercer, and again 21 Dec. 1382. Appointment 3 July 1383 of Rd. Forster, J. Gibbes, and others to take stonemasons carpenters and other workmen for the repair of the King's two mills before the castle of Oxford. (*Patent Rolls.*)

1371. Feb. William Coteshale.

John de Stodle.

1371. June. William Coteshale.

(One Member only.) The Sheriff was directed to send certain specified Knights, Citizens, and Burgesses, who were at the last Parliament.

1372.   William Northern.

John de Wyndesore.

1373.   William de Codeshale.

William Dagevyll.

William Dagvile was Mayor 1380, 1381, 1385, 1394, and Member 1373, 1377, 1383, J.P. for the city and county, and when Mayor 1380 was assessed for the Poll Tax with Juliana his wife at xiij.s. iiijd., and his servants John and Robert at iiijd. each. He died "6 Juyn ——," (M.I. All Saints,) and is said to have been eight (?) times Mayor. About his time the Oxford Members appear to have been joined in the Commission of the Peace for the county, for Dagvyle was so named 8 March and 21 Dec. 1382, with other of his colleagues.

1376.		William de Codeshale.
		' John Gibbes.
1377.	Jan.	Richard de Garston.
		William Dagevyll.

R. Gerston's name is given by *Wood* as Mayor 1386, 1395, 1396, and as Sir R. Gerston Knt. 1399, 1411. He was again Member 1390, 1393.

1377.	Oct.	William de Codeshale.
		John Gibbes.
1378.		William Dagevill.
		Alan le Spicer.
1379.		Thomas Somerset.
		Edmund Kenyan.

Thomas Somerset, draper, and Ellen his wife paid a Poll Tax of xiijs. iiijd. in 1380, and iiijd. each for his apprentice Philip, and his servant Elizabeth. He was one of the two Bailiffs of Oxford on 15 July 1378, as previously mentioned, and Mayor 1392. Edmund Kenyan, hosteller, was Mayor (as E. de Renyan) 1401, 1404, 1412. He and his wife Elizabeth paid a Poll Tax of iijs. iiijd. in 1380, besides iiijd. each for his servants Joan and Christina. He was again Member 1380, 1381, 1385, 1386, 1390, 1391, 1394.

| 1380. | Jan. | Richard Mercer. |
| | | John Hikkes. |

Alderman Richard le Mercer and his wife Juliana paid a Poll-Tax of xiijs. iiijd. in 1380, and xijd. for his servant Geoffrey and Sarah his wife, besides xiijd. and iiijd. for his other servants Walter and Thomas. He was Mayor 1382, 1387, 1388, 1390, 1391, 1393, and made a Commr. of the Peace for the county 8 March, 8 July, and 21 Dec. 1382. John Hickes, spicer, and Alice his wife paid a Poll Tax of 14s. 4d. in 1380 besides 12d. for his apprentice John Dobbe, 12d. each for his four men-servants, (one a maltman,) and 4d each for his two maid-servants. He sat for Oxford again in 1383, 1384, 1388.

1380. Nov. Richard de Adyngton.

Edmund Kenyan.

The former was assessed with his wife Margaret at vjs. viijd. for the Poll Tax in 1380, and his servants William, Agnes, and Haubere at 8d. each.

1381.   Edmund Kenyan.

Walter Bon.

Walter Bone, draper, and Agnes his wife paid a Poll Tax of vs. in 1380, and vjd. for his servant Alice.   He was Mayor (as W. Bowne) 1397, 1398,

1382. May. The same.

1382. Oct. Walter Dagevill.

William Northerne.

Walter was probably an error for William Dagevill.

1383. Feb. William Northern.

William Dagevill.

1383. Oct. William Dagvill.

John Hickes.

1384. April. } The same.
1384. Nov. }

1385.   ·   Peter Welynton.

Edmund Kenyan.

Peter Welynton, mercer, and Maud his wife were assessed at xijd. in the Poll Tax of 1380, and his servants John and Robert at iiijd. each.

1386.   Edmund Kenyan.

Thomas Houkyn.

1388. Feb. John Hickes.

Thomas Somersete.

1388. Sept. John Shawe.

Thomas Baret.

John Shawe, fishmonger, and Maud his wife paid a Poll Tax of 6s. 8d. in 1380, and 4d. each for his servants William, Henry, and Maud. He was one of the two Bailiffs of Oxford on 13 July 1378, M.P. 1388, 1414, and Alderman in 1428. On 20 April 1385 licence was granted for the alienation in mortmain by Nicholas Spicer and John Shawe both of Oxford of a messuage in Oxford, to the abbot and convent of Oseneye. (*Patent Rolls.*) Thomas Baret, spicer, and Margery his wife paid a Poll Tax of iijs. in 1380, and 4d. each for his servants John and Robert.

1390. Jan. Richard Garston.

Alan Lekenesfeld.

The latter was a mercer, who with his wife Katherine was rated at vs. for the Poll Tax in 1380, besides 4d. each for his apprentices Thomas and Henry, and his servants Maud and Agnes.

1390. Nov. Edmund Kenyan.

Adam de la River.

The latter with his wife and his servants Robert and Alice were assessed for a lay subsidy in the 14th century. He was again M.P. 1395, 1397, 1401.

1391. Edmund Kenyan.

John Utteworth.

The latter is written Vyteworth in the Enrolment of the Writ de Expensis. As John Otteworth he was a collector in 1409 of one entire tenth and the moiety of a tenth, granted 11 Hen. 4 within the town and suburbs of Oxford. He was again M.P. 1397, 1406.

1393. Richard Garston.

John Merston.

John Garston apppears in the Enrolment of the Writ de Expensis, but this was probably a clerical error. John Merstone, chandler, paid xijd. to the Poll Tax of 1380. and was Mayor 1400, 1403, and M.P. 1393, 1401, 1404, 1414. Perhaps father of the John Merston who was assessed as " servant " to W. Codeshale (see 1369) in the Poll Tax of 1380.

1394. Edmund Kenyan.

John Forster.

John Forster, shoe-maker, paid xijd. to the Poll Tax in 1380.

1395. John Lodelowe.

Adam de la Ryver.

John Lodelowe's name appears in the list of those subject to the Poll Tax in 1380, when he was assessed at iiijd. as apprentice to Richard Chichestre, apothecary, Oxford.

1397. Jan. Adam de la Ryver.

Walter Benham.

Walter Benham, fishmonger, and Emma his wife paid a Poll Tax of 12d. in 1380, and 4d. each for their servants Elizabeth and Ellen. He paid ijs. rent for a house. He was again M.P. 1402, and was seemingly son of the Member in 1368.

1397.   Sept.   Adam de la Ryver.
                   John Otteworth.
1399.   John Spicer.
                   John Burbrigge.

John Spicer, tailor, and Alice his wife paid a Poll Tax of
3s. in 1380, and 4d. for his servant Joan.   He again sat for
Oxford 1402, 1403.

1400.   Thomas Forsthull.
                   Adam Ryver.

The former was perhaps brother to Philip Forsthull, a
juror in 1402.

1402.   Sept.   John Spicer.
                   Walter Benham.
1403.   John Spycer.
                   Thomas Coventre.

The latter was a hosier in 1380, when with his wife Joan
and Juliana her mother, he was assessed to the Poll Tax at xijd.,
and his servant Isabel at iiijd.   He was Mayor of Oxford 1419,
1427, 1427, 1428, 1429, and an Inquisition was made before him
as such on 27 April 1428.   He again sat for the city 1407, 1410,
1413, 1414, 1417, 1419, 1420, 1421, 1422, 1423, 1427, 1429, 1431.

1404.   Oct. 1.   John Merston.
                   Michael Salesbury.
1406.   Thomas Couele.
                   John Otteworth.

Thomas Couele, hostiler, and Agnes his wife paid a Poll
Tax of 5s. in 1380, and 4d. for his servant Agnes.   It is very
doubtful whether he was the same as Thomas Couele, who was
Escheator of Beds and Bucks in 1383 and 1385, and was made a
Commr. of the Peace for Bucks 14 Dec. 1381, and 9 March and 21
Dec. 1382.

1407.   Oct.   Thomas Coventre.
                   Hugo Benet.

Hugh Benet was a juror at an Inquisition in 1402, and
again M.P. 1410. 1413. 1417.

1410.   Jan. 12. ⎫
1413.   April.   ⎬ The same.
                 ⎭
1414.   April 24. John Shawe.
                   Walter Colet.
1414.   Oct. 15.   John Merston.
                   Thomas Coventre.

1416. Feb. William Brampton.

The Return is torn, and the name of the other Member unknown. Brampton was in 1401 a collector of a tenth granted 2 Hen. 4, within the town of Oxford and its suburbs. As Sir W. Brampton Knt. he was Mayor 1420, 1421, 1422, 1425, 1430, 1431, 1436, 1439, and again sat for the city 1419, 1421. 1425.

1417. Nov. Thomas Covyntre.
Hugo Benet.

1419. Oct. Thomas Coventre.
William Brompton.

1420. Nov. 20. Thomas Coventre.
William Offord.

Offord was again M.P. 1421, 1422, 1426, Mayor 1424, 1426, Alderman in 1428, and died 1432, leaving a charity of 6s. 4d. to the city and revenues for the chaplains of St. Peter's in the Baily to celebrate for him and his three wives Alice, Elizabeth, and Margery, all buried with him at St. Peter's.

1421. April 20. William Brampton.
Thomas Coventre.

1421. Nov. 20. William Offord.
John Quarame.

1422. Oct, 20. Thomas Coventre.
William Offord, or Ufforde.

1423. Oct. 1. Thomas Coventre.
Thomas Wilde.

Wilde was again Memberr 1425, 1432.

1425. April 12. William Brampton.
Thomas Wilde.

1426. Feb. 4. William Offord.
Thomas Goldesmyth.

On 28 June 1381 a Commission issued to the Sheriff of Berks and others to arrest and imprison Thomas Goldsmyth of Abyndon and others, insurgents against the King, seize their goods and certify the same in Chancery, (*Patent Rolls*,) but it is very doubtful if he was related to the Member.

1427. Sept. 12. Thomas Coventre.
Thomas Swanne.

1429. Sept. 12. Thomas Coventre.
Richard Wythigg.

Swanne and Wythigg were the two Bailiffs of Oxford on 14.Feb. 1423.

1431. Jan. 8.   Thomas Coventre.

                  Richard Wythigge.

1432. May 5.   William Herberfeld.

                  Thomas Wylde.

Herberfield was Mayor 1432, 1433.

1433. June 20.   Thomas Daggevyle.

                  John Estbury.

The former was presumably the son of the M.P. 1373. He was one of the two Bailiffs of Oxford on 27 April 1428, when there was an Inquisition concerning a robbery, and was Mayor 1434, 1435.

1435. Sept. 24.   Thomas Daggevile.

                  Thomas Coventre.

1436. Dec. 25.   John Buntyng.

                  Thomas Bailly.

Thomas Bayley was Mayor 1440, 1441, 1442, 1443, and perhaps son of the John Bailly mentioned as a brewer in the Poll Tax of 1380.

1442. Jan. 12.   Thomas Bailly.

                  John Michell.

Michell was one of the two Bailiffs on 27 April 1428.

1477. Jan. 26.   Thomas Dagfeld.

                  Robert Walford.

The former was apparently the same as the M.P. 1433. Walford was a juror in 1428, and Mayor 1444, 1445.

1449. Jan. 29.   Alderman Thomas Wythyg.

                  William Dagvile.

The former was presumably son or brother of the M.P. 1429, while the latter bore the same relation to the M.P. 1433, and was seemingly the same as Wm. Dagvile who was a collector in 1488 of the second fifteenth and tenth subsidy granted 3 Hen. 7. If he was the same as the M.P. 1467, then he was Mayor of Oxford 1465, 1466, 1467, 1470, 1472, 1474, and made a Commissioner of the Peace for the town 20 July 1461.

1449. Oct. 8.   William Newman.

                  Oliver Urry.

Newman again sat for Oxford 1450, 1453. Pardon of outlawry dated Westminster 16 Oct. 1461, to Oliver Skynner of Oxford, 'husbondman,' *alias* Oliver Urry of Oxford, skinner, for not appearing to answer Andrew Jamys and Thomas Beleter, citizen and mercer of London, touching debts of 100s. and £12 15s. 4d. respectively. Pardon of outlawry 3 May 1463 to Oliver Urry of the town of Oxford, skynner, for not appearing before John Prysot and his fellows, justices of the Bench of the late King to answer John Warendorp, merchant, of Almain, touching a debt of £13 10s. (*Patent Rolls.*)

1450.	Oct.	William Newman.
		John Fitzaleyn.

The latter was Mayor 1449, 1450.

1453.	Feb. 22.	Robert atte Wood.
		Willlam Newman.

Robert Attwode *alias á* Wode, was Mayor 1454, 1455, 1456, 1457, 1458, and M.P. 1453, 1460.

1455.	June.	Return lost.
1459.	Nov. 12.	John Kenyngton.
		Reginald Skyres.
1460.	Sept. 28.	Richard Spragat.
		Robert atte Wode.

John Spraget who was Mayor of Oxford 1447, 1448, was probably the father or elder brother of the Member, Richard Spragat, who was Mayor 1451, 1452, 1453, (and as Sir R. Spraget Knt.) 1461, 1462, 1464, 1471, (and if the same, as R. Spraget 1473.) He was made a Commissioner of the Peace for the city of Oxford 20 July 1461. (*Patent Rolls.*)

1451.	June	No Returns found.
1463.	Jan.	
1467.	May 26.	William Bedston.
		William Dagvile,

Commission dated at Westminster 29 May 1461, to Thomas Sakevyle and William Bedston esquires to arrest John Suthwyk esq. and bring him before the King in Council. (*Patent Rolls.*)

1470.	Nov.	Return lost.
1472.	Sept. 25.	John Goylyn.
		Stephen Havell.
1478.	Jan. 9.	John Seman.
		Henry Gay.

Seman was Mayor 1476, 1477, 1482, 1486, and was assessed in All Saints parish at £4 10 0, and his 8 men servants at 12d. or 4d. each. Pardon of outlawry 13 Nov. 1465 to Robert Curson of London, 'gentilman,' mainpernor of Wm. Fraunceys late of Kymburley, Norfolk, ' husbondman,' of his outlawry in Middlesex for not appearing before John Prysot and his fellows, justices of the Bench of the late King, to answer for his ransom for not holding the said William before the said Justices one month after Easter 30 Hen. 6, to answer Henry Gay esq. on a plea of debt, provided that he satisfy the King of his ransom, he having surrendered to the Flete prison, as Robert Danby, Chief Justice of the Bench, has certified. (*Patent Rolls.*)

    1483, 1484, 1485, 1487. Returns lost.
    1491. Oct.   Edward Woodward.
                  Robert Caxton.

Woodward was Mayor 1480, 1481, 1483, 1487, 1494, and died 20 Oct. 1496, (M.I. St. Martin's Church, Oxford.) "He was the owner of the Inn called the King's Head in this parish, and had several sons and daughters. The youngest dau. Margaret married Wm. Cogan, (son of Wm. Cogan, Mayor of Bristol,) which William and Margaret succeeding Woodward in the said Inn, kept it to the time of their death."   Their dau. Agnes married Ald. Raffe Flaxney. Woodward's relict Maude re-m. to Wm. Balcombe, Mayor of Oxford 1503, 1507, 1509, who died 4 Oct.—Robert Caxton was perhaps father of Thomas mentioned by Turner as follows, "1523. It', payd to Thomes Caxton for hys Coot xxd.—It', Rec' of hym a byll and a sword."

    1495, 1497, 1510, 1512, 1515, 1523. Returns lost.

An ordinance passed requiring persons to have a residence of three years within the boundaries before they could be elected Members for the city. (*Turner's Records of Oxford.*)

    1529. Oct.   John Latton.   ·
                  Ald. William Flemyng.

Fleming was an Oxford " Grosser," (grocer,) and his wife was named Joan. He compounded for the offices of Chamberlain and Bailiff 6 Oct. 1522, was an Alderman in 1524 and 1540, Mayor 1525, 1526, 29 Sept. 1527, and 1528, one of the two Coroners 29 Sept. 1528, an Member 1529 to April 1536. On 6 April 1537 the city refused to pay his costs and expenses as a Member, on the ground that at his election in 1529 he had promised, as others did, to pay his expenses himself. He was made a Commr. to collect the Subsidy in Oxford town 1 Aug. 1524, and was assessed to such, as an Alderman, in St. Martin's parish, at £3, and on 26 April 1515 was fined 3s. 4d. on presentation by the Jury—" Item, that he usith contynually unlawfull mesures, that is to say, an unlawful yerde, in the great diseyte of the king's liege people." (*Turner.*). He made his will 28 April, and it was inrolled 7 May 1540.

John Latton of Kingston Bagpuze, Berks, which he purchased 1542, son and heir of Wm. L. of Chilton, was made a

Commr. to collect the Subsidy in Berks 1 Aug. 1524, a Commr. of the Peace for Berks 18 Feb. 1525, 6 Feb. 1526, and 24 Nov. 1530, and a Commr. of Gaol Delivery for Oxon and Berks 20 June 1530. He was adm. to the Inner Temple without dispensation 20 Feb. 1510, called to the bar in due course, and was a Bencher thereof in 1529, Autumn Reader 1524-5, Lent Reader 1535, and Treasurer 1534.

| 1536. May | } No Returns found. |
| 1539. April | |

1541. Dec. 26. William Lenthall.

The name of his colleague is unknown. William Lenthall of Lachford and Great Haseley, son and heir of Thomas L., m. Katherine dau. of John Badly, and sat for Oxford 1541-4. He is styled *armiger* in the Return. and was " of a reverent age in 1584."

1545 Jan. Return lost.

1547. Sept. 15. Ald. Ralph Flaxney.

Edward Freurs.

The former was the son of Ald. Richard Flaxney, and m. Agnes dau. of Wm. Cogan. He became one of the Common Council of Oxford 29 Sept. 1531, Chamberlain 29 Sept. 1538, Bailiff 29 Sept. 1542, Alderman 19 May 1549, Member 1547-52, Mayor 29 Sept. 1551, 1552, 1562, and 1577. " He gave a scarlett cloak unto this citie."

Edward Freurs was the second son and heir of Wm. F. (Mayor of Oxford 1530, 1531, 1535, 1536, 1541,) and m. Anne dau· of John Bustard of Adderbury. He was elected one of the eight Assistants to the Mayor 18 Sept. 1554, but was dismissed from the Council 19 June 1562, and d. 13 Jan. 1665.

1553. Feb. 22. Christopher Edmonds.

Edward Glynton.

The former is styled *armiger* in the Return, and was perhaps the father of Sir Christopher Edmonds of Leuknor, who was Knighted 1592, M.P. Wallingford 1584-5, and Buckingham 1586-7, m. Dorothy dau. of Christopher Lidcott of Rushcombe, Berks, and left a sister and co-heir Francisca a Maid of Honour to Q. Elizabeth, who m. John Doyley of Chiselhampton. Glynton or Glymton was admitted to the Freedom of the city 1530, elected a Common Councillor 29 Sept. 1533, compounded for Chamberlain 7 Oct. 1535, Bailiff 1539, M.P. 22 Feb. to 31 March 1553, and March to May 1554, Alderman 26 Sept. 1553, and was a Coroner in 1556.

1553. Aug. 15. John Wayte.

Ald. Thomas Wylliams.

John Wayte, 'Paynter,' (? son of Thomas Wayte, wax-chandler,) was adm. to the Freedom of the city in 1538, Bailiff 29 Sept. 1552, Assistant 9 Sept. 1554, 4 Sept. 1561, and 16 Sept. 1562, Mayor 1555, 1561, disfranchised 31 July 1578, was a haberdasher in 1569, M.P. 15 Aug. to 5 Dec. 1553, Oct. 1554 to Jan. 1555, and Sept. to Dec. 1555, and J.P. for Oxford in 1574.

His colleague was the son of Alexander Williams, and m. Mary dau. of Henry Doyley of Wallingford Castle, ' councellor at Lawe.' He and Thomas Mallyson (see 1554) and two others were app. to have the custody of the armour in Oxford 26 April 1548. He became one of the two Bailiffs 29 Sept. 1546, an Assistant 9 Sept. 1554, Alderman 27 April 1557, Mayor 29 Sept. 1557, 1565, 1576, M.P. Aug. to Dec. 1553, and app. a Vintner 15 Sept. 1558. On 27 Sept. 1558 "Thomas Willyams, Mayre, dyd tender one peny gylted according to the old custome, for the wch he shall make one of his children ffre when he comethe to full age, takyng his othe to this Towne." (*Turner.*) When Mayor he received the Queen at Oxford 31 Aug. 1566. He was accused in 1576 by Ald. Noble (see 1584) of not doing his duty to the 'Queen and Comon welth,' and appeared before the Privy Council touching the matter on 26 May 1577. He was J.P. for Oxford in 1579, and "gave to the City a paule or burying clothe of velvytt."

1554. March 27.   Ald. Thomas Mallynson.

Ald. Edward Glynton.

Ald. Mallynson was adm. to the Freedom of the city in 1535, became a Common Councillor 29 Sept. 1541, compounded for Chamberlain 10 Nov. 1542, became Bailiff 1545, 1548, M.P. March to May 1554, and Alderman 19 May 1549 to 27 April 1557, when he seems to have been dlscharged from office, and on 27 May 1557 he was fined 3s. 4d. " for opprobrious words spoken against Mr Mayer at thys day yn the Councell howse." He is said to have given £200 to the city.

1554. Oct. 23.   John Wayte.

William Tylcock.

Tylcock was a baker, and was adm. to the Freedom of the city in 1537, became Chamberlain 29 Sept. 1542, Collector 1546, Bailiff 1545, 1548, M.P. Oct. 1554 to Jan. 1555, an Assistant to the Mayor 9 Sept. 1554, one of the two Coroners 29 Sept. 1556, Alderman 3 Oct. 1557, and Mayor 1556, 1560, 1568, 1575, was dismissed from the Council (with Freurs and Pantre) 19 June 1562, but appears to have remained Alderman, as he is given that rank in his appointment with others to survey the banks about the South Bridge 17 June 1575. He d. 22 June 1578, aged 74. (M. I. St. Thomas's Church.)

1555. Sept. 14.   John Wayte.
William Pantre.

Thomas Pantre who was bedel 1524, may have been father of this William Pantre, who was adm. to the Freedom of the city, as gentleman, 1544, Chamberlain 1545, Bailiff 1554, Member Sept. to Dec. 1555, but was "dismissed from the Council House and ordered to behave himself honestly amongst his neighbours" 19 June 1562.

1558. Jan. 7.   John Barton.
Richard Williams.

Both styled *generosns* in the Return.   Barton was adm. to the Freedom of the city as a 'Bochar,' (butcher,) in 1537, Chamberlain 1541, Bailiff and Collector 1546, one of the eight Assistants to the Mayor 8 July 1556, and M.P. 1556.

Richard Williams was admitted to the Freedom of the city, in 1536 or 1537. Chamberlain 1547, Bailiff 1550, an Assistant 28 May 1554, and 28 May 1557, Mayor March and 29 Sept. 1571, and 1578, Alderman 31 July 1577, and died just before his last Mayoralty finished, on 19 Sept. 1579, buried in St. Tole's Church. His wife was named Johan or Joan.

1559. Jan. 7.   Thomes Wood.
Roger Tayller.

This Parliament was dissolved 6 May 1559.   "Yt ys agreyd at a Cowncell holden the 27 of January, yt Mr Mayre (John Wayte) and Mr. Wood shall goo unto London a bowt the suete of Saynct Mary Colledg." (*Council Minute* 27 Jan. 1562.) "Yt ys further agreed at thys Counsell that Mr. Wood shall be rewarded for hys fryndshipp shewed to thys Cytie in the Commyssyon of Sewers, as by Mr. Mayor the Aldermen and Assocyatts shalbe thoughte good." (*Idem* 19 Oct. 1576.)   Wood was M.P. Jan. to May 1559. and Dec. 1562 to Jan. 1567.

Roger Tayller, gentleman, became Chamberlain 1552, Bailiff 29 Sept. 1554, an Assistant 20 Aug. 1560, and 16 Sept. 1562, Mayor 1563, 1569, 1574, and Alderman 31 July 1577.   In 1575 Ald. Noble charged with not doing his duty.

1562. Dec. 6.   William Page.
Thomas Wood.

The Council Minutes for 7 Dec. 1562 contain the following interesting entry:—" Item. William Page, gent. admitted into the liberties of the City etc. at the request of the Lord the Earl of Bedford, and the same day was elected one of the Burgesses of Parliament.'

1571. April 2.   Edward Knollys
William Frier.

Edward Knollys was the third son of Sir Francis K. (see County 1662,) and was probably a commoner of Magdalen College, Oxford, in and before 1564. He entered the Middle Temple 1565, and was M.P. for Oxford 1571 and 1572 until his death in Ireland in 1575. In order to qualify him for representing Oxford, he was specially admitted to its Freedom, as appears by the following *Minute,*—" 12 March. 1571. And yt ys also agreed at this said Counsell that Mr. Edward Knoles, Esquire, shall be recorded as free w^{th}in this Cyttie, who hath taken his oth and was admytted to be inrowled." The ordinance requiring three years reeidence had prebably become obsolete by this period.

William Frere or Fryer of Watereaton, (? son of the M.P. 1547,) was H.S. Oxon 1597, and had a son Edward who was made a Baronet 1620.

1572.   April 14.   Edward Knolles.

William Owen.

Both styled esquire in the Return. William Owen, 'carier,' second son of George Owen (? the M.P. for the County 1558,) was adm. Hanester in 1566 or 1567, and m. Anne dau. of John Rawley of Billesby, Northants. He sat for Oxford 1572-83.

1575.   Dec.   Francis Knolles, *vice* his brother Edward deceased. The new Writ was dated 24 Dec., and on 29 Dec. it was " agreed at the Council that he shalbe chosen so soone as he shall have taken hys othe to the lyberties of thys Cytie." Francis Knollys was the sixth son of Sir Francis K. (see County 1562,) and was probably a commoner of Magdalen College, Oxford, in and before 1564. He was created M.A. 10 July 1598, entered Grays Inn 1565, was Knighted 1587, and was well known at Court as " young Sir Francis." He married (by license dated 21 Dec. 1588) Lettice dau. of John Barrett of Hanham, co. Gloucester, and leased from the Crown the manor of Battel near Reading. He was M.P. for Oxford Dec. 1575-83, 1584-5, 1586-7, 1588-9, Berks 1597-8, 1604-11, 1625, and Reading March to May 1640, and Oct. 1640 until his death, his will being proved 5 May 1648.

1584.   Oct. 23.   Francis Knollys.

Ald William Noble.

Ald. Noble was a well-known citizen of Oxford, where he lived in the house known as ' Le Swynstock ' in St. Martin's parish. He was admitted Hanester in the first year of Queen Mary's reign, (as late apprentice of Robert Cogeyn, mercer,) and became a Common Councillor 29 Sept. 1559, but was dismissed the Council House 19 June 1562, on which date, "It was agreed by the hole Counsaill that William Noble shall go to warde uppon a slaunder agaynst the Mayre, Aldermen, and ten of Assistaunce." (*Council Minute*). Notwithstanding this he was elected Chamberlain 1571, and Bailiff 1573, and when holding the latter office he led the opposition for the City against the University, and was imprisoned for twelve days by the Vice Chancellor of the University, (for shutting the Guildhall door against him and others when they came to keep a Court Leet there,) until Sir Francis Knollys (see County 1562,) gave his word for his appearance before them. This made him very popular in the city, and on 19 Oct. 1574 he was app. to go to London with the Mayor etc. on City business before the Privy Council. Smarting however under the sting of a false imprisonment Noble commenced suits in the Star Chamber against the University, and presented petitions both against that body and the Mayor and citizens. In April 1575, he exhibited Articles to the Privy Council against the University, and against the Town, but on 18 Sept. 1583, "he, the Mayor, and Mr Frere made up their quarrels." Noble was one of the three persons licensed by the city of Oxford to sell wines there 13 Dec. 1575, and this monopoly was further increased by a renewal of the license on 11 Nov. 1578 to him and one other person only. He was elected Alderman 5 Nov. 1579, Coroner the next day, Mayor 1581, M.P. 1584-5, and was buried in St. Martin's Church 1593.

1586. Sept. 22. Francis Knollys.

George Calfielde.

George Caulfeild, Calfhill, or Callfilde, as his name was variously spelt, was the son of Alexander C. of Great Milton, Oxon, and was of Ch. Ch. Oxford 1561, student 1564, B.A, 25 June 1566, ent. Grays Inn 1568, called to the bar 9 Feb. 1581, Ancient 26 May 1584, Pensioner 22 April 1594, Autumn Reader 6 May 1597, Bencher 15 Nov. 1597, and m. Martha second dau. of Richard Taverner of Woodeaton, (and quære aunt of the M.P. for Woodstock 1626). Caulfield was a Justice of the Great Sessions for the counties of Brecknock, Glamorgan, and Radnor (fee £50 a year,) July 1600-8, Recorder of Oxford, M.P. Wycombe 1584-5, and Oxford 1586-7, 1588-9, 1593, 1597-8, and Sept. to Dec. 1601. His dau. Dorothy m. 30 Oct. 1606 R. Coventrie of Cassington, Oxon, at which date Caulfield was still Recorder. His brother Toby was created Lord Charlemont of Ireland 1620.

1588. Oct. 10. Sir Francis Knollis jun. Knt.

George Cawfeild.

1593. Jan. Hon Sir Edmund Carye Knt.

George Calfeilde.

Sir Edmund Carey was the 7th son of Henry 1st Lord Hunsdon K.G., who was first cousin to Queen Elizabeth, and Lord Chamberlain of her Household, and brother to the wife of Sir Francis Knollys, (see County 1562.) He was adm. an Hanaster of Oxford 1573, adm. (? specially) to Grays Inn 1580, Knighted by the Earl of Leicester when serving as a soldier in the Low Countries 1587, M.P. for Newport, (Isle of Wight) 1588-9, Oxford Jan. to April 1593, Wilts Sept. to Dec. 1601, Calne Jan. 1606-11, and d. 12 Sept. 1637, aged 80, having m. (1) Mary dau. of Christopher Cooker of Croft, Lincolnshire, (2) Elizabeth dau. and co-heir of John Lord Latimer, and relict of Sir John Danvers, and (3) Judith dau. of Laurence Humphrey D.D. Dean of Winchester, and President of Magdalen College, and widow of Sir George Rivers of Chafford, Kent. His brother Robert was created Earl of Monmouth. His grandfather William Carey's elder brother Sir John was grandfather of the first Viscount Falkland. The *Cal. State Papers* for July 1588, the year of the Armada, contains a reference to " The number or men appointed to be drawn together out of various shires for an army for defence of Her Majesty's person, with the names of the Colonels appointed to lead them, Sir William Knolles, Sir Francis Knollys, Sir Edmund Carey, and six others."

1597. Aug. 29. Anthony Bacon.

George Callfeild.

Anthony Bacon was the fourth son of Sir Nicholas Bacon, Lord Keeper of the Great Seal 1558-79, (being his elder son by his second wife,) and elder brother to the still more celebrated lawyer, Sir Francis Bacon, Lord Chancellor 1618-21, who was created Lord Verulam, and Viscount St. Albans. He was adm. to Grays Inn (" de societate magistrorum " 27 June) 1576, M.P. Wallingford Jan. to April 1593, Oxford Aug. 1597 to Feb. 1598, Ambassador to Venice, and d. unm. May 1601. Bacon was evidently employed abroad in the service of Government for several years, as is gathered from the following letters in *Cal. State Papers*:—" 15 Jan. 1581. Bourges. Anthony Bacon to Lord Burghley. All the letters he has received from England, mention the honourable and fatherly dealing of Burghley towards him, for which he offers his devoted service. Is grateful for his assistance in prosecuting his right to Pinner Park." There was another letter dated 13 Feb. 1581, and on 24 March 1588 Bacon wrote from Montaubon to Secretary Walsingham :— " Now that I am convalescent I hope soon to be with you." " 6 April 1589, Examination of Richard Gest of Chester. Details his services under several masters. Was with Mr. Anthony Bacon two years, under whom he wrote a great volume of matters of importance." On 28 June 1599 John Chamberlain wrote to Dudley Carleton :—" The Queen hears that the Earl of Essex has given Essex House to Anthony Bacon, which displeases her ; I believe it is but instead of £2000 he meant to give him, with a clause of redemption for the same." " Examination of Henry Cuffe 2 March 1601.—Often heard that Anthony Bacon was an agent between the Earl of Essex and the King of Scots."

Finally on 27 May 1601 Chamberlain wrote to Carleton at the Hague :—Ant. Bacon has died so deep in debt that his brother (Fras. Bacon) is little the better by him. •

1601. Sept. 20. Francis Leighe.

George Calfyld.

Francis Leigh of Newnham Regis, co. Warwick, was the son of Sir William Leigh of Stoneleigh, co. Warwick, and m. Mary dau. of Thomas Egerton, Viscount Brackley, Lord Chancellor 1603-17. He was made K.B. at the Coronation of James I. on 25 July 1603, M.P. Oxford Sept. to Dec. 1601, and 1604-11, and Warwickshire Nov. 1621 to Feb. 1622, and was a member of the Derby House Society of Antiquaries, together with Sir Henry Spelman, Sir Robert Cotton and Camden. He was an intimate friend of the latter, who left him by will £4 for a memorial ring. Grant 12 Feb. 1608 to Sir Francis Leigh and his heirs to keep a weekly market and two yearly fairs at Dunchurch, co. Warwick. He was living 1625. His son Francis was created Earl of Chichester in 1644.

1604. March 1. Sir Francis Leigh Knt.

Thomas Wentworth.

Son of Peter Wentworth of Lillingston Lovell, Oxon, he matric. Univ. Coll. Oxford 30 Oct. 1584, aged 16, ent. Lincolns Inn 23 Oct. 1585, was called to the bar 9 June 1594, "to be published next moote in this term," called to the Bench of that Society 8 June 1609, " to be published next moote," sat as such 17 Oct. 1609, and was Lent Reader 1612, and Treasurer of Lincoln's Inn 1621. Wentworth was app. Recorder of Oxford Sept. 1607, (until his death,) and as such took a very active part— " behaved himself so turbulently "—in the numerous disputes of the City and the University for which he was discommoned by the University in 1611, but was restored after two years. He was M.P. for Oxford 1604-11, March to June 1614, 1620-2, 1624-5, April to Aug. 1625, Jan. to June 1626, and 3 March 1628 until his death in or about that year. He was, (said *Wood*) " a troublesome and factious person, who was more than once imprisoned in Parliament." *Wood* says he died in Sept. 1627, an error perhaps for Sept. 1628. He m. Dorothy dau. of Thomas Keble of Newbottle, Northants.

1614. March. Sir John Ashley Knt.

Thomas Wentworth.

Sir John Ashley of Kent, son of John Ashley, Master of the Jewel House, was Knighted at the Charterhouse 11 May 1603. He m. Katherine dau. of Anthony Bridges, and as Deputy Master of the Revels was commissioned 6 May 1622 to take up for the King's service embroiderers tailors and other artificers.

Demise 10 Jan. 1608 to Thomas Elliot for the use of Sir John Ashley of the King's two parts of the manors of Broadway and Whaddon, and other lands in Notts and Dorset forfeit by the recusancy of Mary Gerard, widow. Ashley was granted the reversion of the Mastership of the Revels 1612, and succeeded Sir George Buck (who had gone mad) in that office 22 May 1622, but appears to have sold his interest therein to Henry Herbert by Aug. 1623. He died 13 Jan, 1641.

<blockquote>
1621.   Feb. 15.   Sir John Brooke Knt.   ———

Thomas Wentworth.   ———

Sir Francis Blundell.   ·———
</blockquote>

The "Official Returns" state that the name of Sir Francis Blundell Knt. is given on the back of the Writ instead of that of Wentworth.   Sir F. Blundell petitioned against Wentworth 8 Feb. 1621, but the next day the House resolved "that Wentworth is duly elected, and that the Mayor be sent for to answer for his misdemeanour." Sir F. Blundell was dead before 20 Sept. 1625, when Sir Francis Annesley undertook to pay £500 to his widow and executrix.

Sir John Brook, of Hekington, son of Hon. Henry B. (who was 5th son of George 4th Lord Cobham,) was Knighted Jan. 1612, was the senior Teller of the Exchequer in May 1626, M.P. Gatton 1614, Oxford 1621-2, Bedwin 1625, and Appleby Oct. 1640-3, when disabled to sit as a royalist, and m. (1) Anne ——— (who d. Feb. 1625,) and (2) Frances dau. of Sir Wm. Bamfield. He was created Lord Cobham 3 Jan. 1645, and was buried at Wakerley, Northants, 20 May 1660.   Dudley Carleton wrote from Paris to John Chamberlain 24 Oct. 1601—"Sir John Brooke, with Coppinger, a Kentish gentleman, lately came to learn the language, and are the logs in our French school." Grant 16 June 1607 to Sir John Brook of a pension of £100 per annum for life.   On 31 March 1610 he wrote from Carmina to Lord Salisbury,—"Could not bear the seas, and not being allowed to land in Spain for fear of the plague, they put in at a small town in Portugal." On 7 April 1611 Sir Thomas Lake, Secretary of State, informed Lord Salisbury, that "the Lord Chancellor of Scotland has permission to pass over his pension to Sir John Brook and Sir John Burlacy who have bought it," and accordingly they had a grant of £200 a year each on 21 May 1611.

<blockquote>
1624.   Jan. 19.   Thomas Wentworth.

John Whistler.
</blockquote>

Son and heir of Hugh Whistler of Milton Parva, Oxon, he matric. Trin. Coll. Oxford 14 Oct. 1597, aged 17, B.A. 17 Feb. 1601, ent. Grays Inn 4 May 1601, was called to the bar 1611, and chosen Treasurer thereof 1640.   Whistler in 1622 was made Deputy Recorder of Oxford to Wentworth, whom he succeeded as

Recorder on his death on Monday before the Feast of St. Matthew, 3 Car. I. He was M.P. Oxford 1624-5, 1625, 1626, 1628-9, and Oct. 1640, until he was disabled to sit for his loyalty (probably in Jan.) 1644, and died 1646. On 1 Nov. 1645 he " Petitions as sometimes an unworthy member of the Commons Ho. of Parl. His delinquency was in being present at the meeting of some members of Oxford, whither he had gone on the commission for regulating of forests, being a member thereof shortly after the battle of Edgehill, was taken prisoner to Oxford and after he had given bail for £2000, was again imprisoned 7 weeks, during which time his house was taken from him. Was released on new bail for £2000 to appear at the Assizes, but the day before he was again imprisoned and taken to Hungerford, on purpose to cause him to forfeit his bail. Got out of Oxford 1 June 1644, was examined by Sir Wm. Waller courteously treated and dismis ed. Went to Combe, co. Hants, and lived with his brother who had served at Edgehill on the Parliament's side, until he was carried prisoner to Whitchurch near Reading, and thence to London to Mr Speaker, from whom he stands referred to the Committee at Goldsmith's Hall.—No reference."

1625. April. The same, re-elected 23 Jan. 1626, and 3 March 1628.

1640. March 3. Charles Lord Howard.

Ald. Thomas Cooper

Charles Howard, Viscount Andover, eldest son of Thomas 1st Earl of Berkshire K.G., was created K.B. 1 Feb. 1625, and m. Dorothy 2nd dau. of Thomas Viscount Savage. 9 Nov. 1633, Warrant to allow Charles Lord Howard, and Thomas Howard, sons of the Earl of Berkshire, about to travel for three years, to embark with them one horse and two geldings,—With note that they were embarked in the " Mayflower " of Dover on above date. (*Cal. State Papers.*) He was M.P. Oxford March to May 1640, and Oct. to Nov. 1640, when he was summoned to the House of Lords as Baron Howard of Charlton, and introduced as such Nov. 20. He signed the Loyal Declaration at York 15 June 1642, was impeached by Denzill Hollis the next day, and was a Lord of the Bedchamber to Prince Charles in 1648. On 27 Jan. 1644 he and John Whistler signed at Oxford the Loyal Letter to the Earl of Essex. On 1 May 1649 he " begs to be joined in his father's composition. Left the King's party 4 years since, and went beyond seas, where he still remains. 19 July, Begs to compound for himself on Exeter Articles, his estate being but £250 a year for life. Sept. 25, Fine £375. 4 June 1650, Fine increased to £625, at one-sixth. 26 July, Fine allowed to stand on Exeter Articles at £500, on certificate of Lord Fairfax." He succ. his father as 2nd Earl of Berkshire 16 July 1669, and died and was buried in Paris April 1679. " When does Lord Andover go

Ambassador to the Emperor?" (Francis Crane to Robert
Francis, 14 Feb. 1669.) 9 June 1669, Warrant to the Treasury
Commrs. to pay £500 to Charles, Lord Andover, out of the
Privy Seal Dormant of 2 Oct. 1668, as the King's free gift.

Ald. T. Cooper was of an ancient and respectable family,
which had held the manor of South Weston, Oxon, for several
centuries, and was Mayor of Oxfor 1630, and M.P. March to May
1640. He was one of the seven Assistants or Common Coun-
cilmen at the Visitation 12 Aug. 1634, (as Thomas Cowper.) He
was an active soldier during the Civil War, and the *Cal. State
Papers* contains many references to him as follows :—25 Sept.
1645, Order made at the Committee of the House of Commons for
the reduced officers, (under the order of the House of 8th inst.
for £400 to be disposed of for arrears to the Reformadoes who
were with the Lord General Essex in Cornwall,) to pay to Lieut.
Thomas Cooper £8 10s. od. His receipt for the same was dated
29 Sept. On 9 July 1648 the Committee of both Houses at Derby
House ordered that an order be given to Major Cooper to muster
the horse under Col. Butler that are app. for the guard of the
Parliament from day to day and return the musters to this Committee, for which service he shall be allowed 5s. per diem. The
Council of State ordered 27 Jan. 1651, that—Denis Gauden having
contracted to furnish bread for 20,000 men, being 4800 cwt. of
biscuit every month, until the end of July next, for the army in
Scotland,—license be given to Thomas Palmer, Henry Wright,
and Thomas Cooper, who are employed for that purpose, to buy
the corn necessary without molestation. The Council wrote on
13 Sept. 1651 to Col. Cooper at Worcester,—" Lord Mordington,
now prisoner at Manchester, writes the Lord General that he !eft
a bag with 115 old double pieces in the house of Thomas
Demetrius at Worcester. Make diligent search for it, and
examine Demetrius about it, and if you can discover it seize and
sent it up to the Council."—The money was found. He went
with Cromwell's Army to Scotland as Col. of Foot and on 4 Nov.
1651 the letter of Col. Cooper from Hull, with the bill of exchange
for transporting his regiment to Scotland, was referred to the
Scotch Committee to take order for payment. He was Governor
of the Orkney Islands in Dec. 1652 and June 1653. On 29 April
1653 the Council ordered T.C. and four others to examine the
state of the prison of the Upper Bench and to propound regula-
tions for its management, and on 5 May following Colonels
Cooper and Pride, Mr. Hyland and Major Allen were ordered to
suppress bear baiting, bull baiting, and playing for prizes by
fencers in Southwark and other places as great evils and abomina-
tions. He was Col of a regiment at Ayr in Feb. 1654, when some
curious correspondence took place about the cheese supplied his
soldiers. Thomas Cooper app. one of His Hi4hness's Council in
Scotland for the government of that nation was given his

instructions as such 30 March 1655. He was Governor of Ayr on 12 March and 7 Aug. 1655, and on 21 Dec. following the Council advised a warrant for £200 to Col. Cooper for his journey to Ireland on the State's service, which Cromwell approved. He was afterwards sent to Ireland, and was M.P. for cos. Down, Antrim, and Armagh 1656, until he was made one of Cromwell's House of Lords as Lord Cooper 10 Dec. 1657. His name afterwards appears under the order for proclaiming Richard Cromwell as Protector 1658, and he petitioned the Protector for his regiment 16 Nov. 1658. The Committee for Safety and for the nomination of Officers resolved that T.C. should have a Foot Regiment 16 June 1659, and four days later nominated him to be a Corporal of the Guard for Parliament, and on 30 June 1659 added Col. Cooper to the Committee of Officers to whom Petitions were referred to consider who were deserving men and fit for employment in the Army. He was ordered to be made Col. of a Horse regt. (late Lord Fleetwood's) 8 July 1659 and afterwards served in Ireland, as on 14 Sept. following he wrote from Dublin to Col. Clarke. He survived the Restoration.

1640. Oct. 12. Charles Lord Howard.

John Whistler, Recorder.

1640. Nov. 30. John Smith of Oxford, *vice* Lord Howard called to the Upper House. This Member was third son of Ald. Oliver Smith, Mayor of Oxford 1619, 1624, who d. 13 April 1637, and grandson of Ald. Thomas Smith, Mayor 1585, 1590, 1595, 1600, who d. July 1601, (4th son of Robert S. of Cuerdley, Lancashire, son and heir of Robert S. of that place, eldest son of Robert S. of Polehouse, who was eldest son to William Smith, Bishop of Lincoln 1495-1513, the Founder of Brasenose College and President of Wales. His eldest brother Ald. Thomas Smyth was Mayor of Oxford 1631, 1643, and d. 20 April 1646. John Smith ent. Grays Inn 16 March 1641, and was Mayor of Oxford 1639, and Member Nov. 1640 until disabled to sit as a Royalist (probably in Jan.) 1644. On 12 Nov. 1646 he "begs to compound on Oxford Articles for delinquency. Sat in the Assembly there. Dec. 3, Fine at one-tenth £220." On 26 Sept. 1646 the House of Commons resolved "that this House doth accept of the sum of £220 for a Fine for the delinquency of John Smith of the City of Oxford, Gent. His offence, that being a Member of the House of Commons he deserted the Parliament. He rendered upon the Articles of Oxford. His estate in fee per annum, in possession £107 6 8; in reversion per annum £3 ; in goods and debts £150; and he owes £600. His fine at a tenth is ——. An Ordinance for granting a pardon unto John Smyth of the City of Oxford, Gent., for his delinquency, and for taking off the sequestration of his estate was this day read, and upon the question, passed, and ordered to be sent to the Lords for their concurrence." (*Journals*). On 27 Jan. 1651 he was also assessed at £100 by the

Committee of Advance of Money, but no further proceedings were taken in the matter. He died 4 Nov. 1657. (M.I. St. Tole's Church, Oxford). His dau. Alice m. R. Holloway of that parish, counsellour at law, who d. 7 Sept. 1672.

1646.   Dec. 14.   Ald John Nixon.

John Doyley.

vice Whistler and Smith disabled to sit. The former was the son of John Nixon of Blechington, husbandman, and acquired a considerable fortune by much industry. He settled as a mercer at Oxford, where he was adm. a Freeman 3 Feb. 1625, entered the City Council 1627, and of which he was Mayor 1636, 1646, and 1654, and M.P. Dec. 1646-53. He was an Alderman in 1657 when John Corbet was sworn Register of Oddington before him as a J.P. at Oxford. He m. Joane Simpson or Stevenson. Nixon was zealously devoted to the Puritans, and was a witness against Archbishop Laud on his trial. He founded the Free School in the Guildhall Yard 1658, and died 14 April 1662, being buried in St. Mary's Church. The House of Commons " continued him " as Mayor of Oxford 29 Sept. 1647, " till the House take further order," added him to the Commrs. of Assessment for the City 24 July 1649, and app. him, Richard Croke, (see 1654,) and Ald. Wm. Wright (see 1679,) Assessment Commrs. for the City 16 Feb. 1660. The House having ordered " that Mr. Nixon now Mayor of Oxford, have leave to go down to Oxfordshire ; and that the thanks of this House be given to the said Mr. N. for his good service, and good affections testified thereby to the Parl. Mr. Speaker gave the thanks of this House to the said Mr. N. accordingly." (*Commrs. Journal.*)

John Doyley of Chislehampton, eldest son of Sir Cope Doyley Knt. of that place, was born 1602, matric. Wad. Coll. Oxford 27 Nov. 1618, aged 16, and m. Mary dau. and co-heir of Sir John Shirley Knt. of Isfield, Sussex. He was H.S. Oxon 1638, M.P. Oxford Dec. 1646 until secluded Dec. 1648, a Parliamentary Commr. for the visition of the University, and died about 1660.

1653.   June.   No Members nominated for Oxford.

1654.   July.   Bulstrode Whitelocke.

One Member only was returned by the Loyal City in 1654, and 1656. The celebrated Bulstrode Whitlocke of Phillis Court, Henley, was the only son and heir of Sir James Whitlock (see Woodstock 1609,) and was born in Fleet Street 6 Aug. 1605, adm. to Merchant Taylors' School 1615, matric. St. John's Coll. Oxford 8 Dec. 1620, ent. the Middle Temple 9 Aug. 1619, called to the bar 24 Nov. 1626, elected an Associate to the Bench 21 April 1648, and a Bencher of that Society 27 Oct. 1648. He was M.P. Stafford 1626, Great Marlow Nov. 1640-53, Oxford, Bedford, and

Bucks 1654, but preferred to represent Bucks till Jan. 1655, and again 1656 until made one of Cromwell's House of Lords as "Lord Whitlock " 10 Dec. 1657.   On the outbreak of the Civil War he became Captain of a Troop of Horse for the Parliament, and was Governor of the garrison of his own residence at Phillis Court, which he held against the King's party.   Whitlock was held in the greatest esteem and respect as a lawyer by the Parliament, who made him a Dep. Lieut. of Bucks 1642, Attorney of the Duchy of Lancaster 1644, a member of the Assembly of Divines, one of the Committee of the Admiralty 15-28 April 1645, a Serjeant at law in Oct. 1648, (but which appointment was declared illegal 1660,) Lieut. to the Earl of Pembroke as Constable of Windsor Castle, and Forest 1648, Keeper of the King's medals and library July 1649, and a member of the first five Councils of State 14 Feb. 1649 to 15 Feb. 1650, 16 Feb. 1650, to 15 Feb. 1651, 17 Feb. to 24 Nov. 1651, 25 Nov. 1651 to 24 Nov. 1652, and 1 Dec. 1652, to 19 April 1653.   Whitlock was a Commr. of the Great Seal 12 April 1648 to 8 Feb. 1649, First Commr. thereof from then to 30 May 1654, and 14 July 1654 to 15 Jan. 1656, a Commr. thereof 22 Jan. to 14 May 1659, and Lord Keeper thereof 1 Nov. 1659 to 13 Jan. 1660.   He was also Ambassador to Sweden (£1000 a year) Nov. 1653 to July 1654, President of the Council of State Aug. 1659, Col. of the Berks Militia 1 Sept. 1659, one of the Committee of Safety Oct. 1659, Speaker of the House of Commons *pro tem.* 1656, High Steward of Oxford June 1649-60, Recorder of Oxford until 1653, Chairman of the Oxfordshire Quarter Sessions, 1653, and High Steward of Reading 1654-60.   Forseeing the speedy downfall of the Commonwealth Whitlock retired to the country 30 Jan. 1660, where he lived a quiet life, until his death at Chilton Park, Wilts, 28 Jan 1676.   He was buried at Fawley, Bucks.   Owing to his moderation, several Members spoke in his favour at the Restoration, and he was allowed the benefit of the Act of General Pardon in June 1660.

1654.   Nov. 16.   Richard Croke of Marston, *vice* Lord Commr. Whitlock who made his election to represent Bucks. This Member was the 2nd but eldest surviving son of Serjeant Unton Croke (see 1659,) was born about 1623, aged "abont 11 " in 1634, and m. Elizabeth dau. of Martin Wright, Alderman and Goldsmith of Oxford.   He was adm. to the Inner Temple 24 Jan. 1635, where he was called to the bar 5 Nov. 1646, Autumn Reader 1670, Bencher 23 Nov. 1662, was M.P. Oxford Nov. 1654 to Jan. 1655, 1656 to Jan. 1658, Jan. to April 1659, and 1661-79, made a Serjeant at law 21 April 1675, Knighted at Oxford 16 March 1681, and was a Commr. to survey and sell the King's manors and lands at Woodstock 1649, Dep. Steward of that manor Oct. 1649, a Commr. tor settling the Militia for Oxfordshire 1659, for the Assessment of Oxford City 16 Feb. 1660, and Recorder of Oxford 1653 until his death 14 or 15 Sept. 1683, aged 59 or 60.

" He alwaies ran with the times and his religion was as venal as his tongue. He was hated by many for his smooth, false, and flattering tongue." (*Wood*). Richard and his brother Unton Croke were among the Parl. Commrs. who were driven from Woodstock in Oct. 1649 by the strange noises and wonderful achievements of some royalist wags.

1656. Aug.   Richard Croke.

1659. Jan. 13.   Unton Croke.

Richard Croke.

Father and son. Unton Croke of Marston, near Oxford, was the fourth son of Sir John Croke of Chilton, Bucks, a distinguished Judge of the King's Bench 1607, (see *Williams' Welsh Judges*,) and was born 1594, matric. Ch. Ch. Oxford 2 March 1610, aged 15, (subscribed as Umpton Croke). He was adm. to the Inner Temple 16 Nov. 1609, where he was called to the bar 26 Jan. 1617, Bencher 14 June 1635, Lent Reader 1639, and m. 8 Nov. 1617 Anne dau. and heir of Richard Hore of Marston. He was M.P. Wallingford 1626, and March to May 1640, and Oxford Jan. to April 1659, and rendered great service to the Parliamentary cause. He was made a Sergeant at law 21 June 1655, Deputy Steward of Oxford University, (under Lord Pembroke,) a Commr. for security of the Protector 1656, and for the trial of persons charged with treason without a jury 1656, and J.P. for Oxfordshire. On 2 Oct. 1655 a letter was written to the Protector by Dr. John Owen (see Oxford Univ. 1653) recommending Croke for a Judgeship 1655, but he was never raised to the Bench. He died at Marston 28 Jan. 1671, aged 77, and was buried there. (M.I.) " Bond 29 Dec. 1660 of Unton Croke of Marston and Unton Croke of Oxford in £4000 for the peaceable demeanour of the latter." (*Cal. State Papers*). " On 3 July 1654 Edward Lyde, *als* Joyner, of Horspath parish, and Dorothy, one of the daughters of John Robinson of Whately, yeoman, were married by and with the consent of the said John Robinson in this parish before Unton Croke, Justice of the Peace, according to the Statute. (Signed) Unton Croke." (*Marston Parish Register*.) The Serjeant at law must not be confused with his second son Major Unton Croke, for whose peaceable behaviour such large bail was given, and who was a very active soldier under the Commonwealth. It is somewhat doubtful in fact whether it was the father or the son who was the Unton Croke elected for Oxford in 1659, but although the author of the *History of the Croke Family* states it was Major Unton Croke the son, yet it appears on the whole more probable that the Member was Serjeant Unton Croke, the father, as otherwise the son would have been distinguished as 'junior.' The latter was made Captain of a Troop of Horse in the early part of the Civil War (or about 1648,) created B.C.L. Oxford 5 June 1649, and for his great zeal in suppressing John Penruddock's rising at Salisbury in March 1655 he was made Major and given £200 a year. As Unton Croke jun. he was app. Captain of the Foot Militia in Oxfordshire 2 April 1650, accompanied his kinsman Bulstrode Whitelocke (see 1654) in his Embassy to Sweden 1653, made a Commr. of Woodstock manor Oct. 1655, and High Sheriff of Oxon 1658. Major Croke proclaimed Richard Cromwell as Protector at Oxford 1658, and was app. by Parl. Colonel of Berry's Regiment 11 Jan. 1660, but with his regiment declared in favour of General Monk, in London 29 Feb. following. He m. (1) the dau. of Sir Charles Wise, and (2) the dau. of——— Mallet of Exeter, merchant, and was living in or near London in a gouty condition in 1690.

1660.   April   5.   Viscount Falkland.

James Haxley.

As to Lord Falkland see the County 1659.   James Huxley was M.P. Oxford April to Dec. 1660. "Mr. Huxley, a presbyterian chiefman, lived in the fair stone house behind Pembroke College on the south side" (Wood.) On 30 May 1660, Request by Col. Alexander Popham and James Huxley to Lord Chancellor Hyde in behalf of Wm. Clewer, that he would present to the King, Clewer's petition for presentation to the rectory of Green's Norton, Northants, who had lost his grant of Blisworth by refusing to keep the thanksgiving day for the victory of Worcester, and praying for His Majesty after it had been forbidden. The Member was apparently not of kin to Sir John Huxley H.S. Beds 1666, J.P. Middlesex, who was Knighted at Whitehall 16 March 1662, and was the elder son of John Huxley of Eaton Bray, Beds., whose other son was named Thomas.

1661.   April 16.   Richard Croke, Recorder.

Brome Whorwood.

Viscount Falkland and James Huxley also stood   Brome Whorwood was the eldest son of Sir Thomas Whorwood Knt. of Heddington, Oxon, and Sandwell Hall, co. Stafford, by Ursula Sde dau. and heiress of George Brome of Halton, and was student and fellow commoner of Trin. Coll. Oxford in 1634, and created D.C.L. 1 (or 2) Nov. 1642. He was licensed at the age of 19 on 22 Sept. 1634 to marry Jane Rider dau.-in-law of the Right Worshipful James Maxwell, (one of the esquires of H.M.'s bedchamber.) He was seated at Holton, Oxon, and had also an estate at Sandwall, co. Stafford, for which on 28 Nov. 1645 he was assessed by the Committee for Advance of Money at £2000. "Nov. 28, Order that he be brought up in custody to pay his assessment. Had lands in counties Worcester and Stafford. Nov. 1645, He petitions that though not conscious of delinquency he has been sequestered during his absence in France, yet wishing to take the opportunity of the favour of Parliament, he came in with the Speaker's pass." Information was laid against him 21 Sept. 1646, "That having many arms in his house he refused to part with them for Parliament, said he would keep them for the King and send them to Warwick. When the Earl of Northampton beseiged the Castle,— some of his neighbours threatened to stop them, and he said, "Let them do so if they durst." He said that he and others had £500 each in their hands and would spend it all for the King, and when that was gone he would find as much more, for the King was in the right way, and Parliament's courses were destructive, and he would spend his blood before the King should be beaten. He cursed the adherents of Parliament and swore he would lose his whole estate rather than they should prevail." Later on, on 14 Feb. 1648, Being adjudged a a delinquent by the Committee for Sequestrations he begs to compound. Has taken the National Covenant and Negative Oath. Feb. 28, Fine at one-tenth, £872." On 16 Dec. 1659 appears the following sharp letter from Humphrey Robinson to Williamson,—" Mr. Whorwood owes me money, can none of the college persuade him to be honest." He was M.P. for Oxford in four Parliaments 1661-81, was removed from the Commission of the Peace for Oxfordshire 13 Jan. 1680, and died in the Old Palace Yard at Westminster 12 April, and was buried at Holton 24 April 1684, aged 69. In 1656 Williamson, (afterwards Sir Joseph, and Sec. of State 1674-9,) was travelling tutor to the sons of Brome Whorwood and Sir Edward Norris. Having separated from his wife, she obtained a decree in Chancery for alimony against him, and there are several references in the *Cal. State Papers* to the matter, which the King himself endeavoured to settle:—"23 June 1669. Whitehall, Petition of Broome Whorwood to the King, showing that in June 1659 he was ordered by a decree in Chancery to pay his wife £300 a year, from Feb. 1657, during their separation; that although he filed a bill of error, he was served with process to execute the said decree, when on his petition His Majesty, on 18 Feb. 1664, ordered him to settle £300 a year on his wife, and pay £1000 for all arrears; that having done this he was again prosecuted for expenses on his wife's petition, and a decree given 12 June 1667 that he should pay all that is still unpaid, on which his opponents advance their bills. Requests a reference and re-hearing of his case that he may not be further molested." (Lord Arlington called him "my old friend" on 7 June 1669.) June 30. Reference to the Lord Keeper of the petition of Brome Whorwood, that a stop may be put to all proceeding in the affair between him and his wife till the Judges report. Whorwood wished the King to personally settle the matter, but his wife would not agree to this.

1679.   Feb. 12.   William Wright.

Broome Whorwood.

"Georg Pudsey of Ellsfeild, then stood and received the canvass, which cost him they say about £300." (*Wood's Life and Times.*)

Aldermam William Wright was perhaps brother to Martin Wright, Mayor of Oxford 1635, 1655, and m. Mary widow of Edward Dewe (of the Bampton family,) and dau. of John Banks of Abingdon, (by Mary 2nd dau. of Robert Perrot of Northleigh, organist and bailiff of Magdalen College,) or m. (1) Christian dau. of John Smith M.P. (see 1640.) He was a leading man at Oxford, of which he was an Alderman at the Visitation of 1634, Mayor 1656 and 1667, app. an Assessment Commr. 16 Feb. 1660, M.P. in three Parliaments 1679-81, re-app. an Alderman by the new Charter Sept. 1668, and died 26 or 30 Oct. 1693, aged 98. He was H.S. Oxon 1674, and J.P. until left out of the commission 14 June 1685. This William Wright was 'a great-cocker,' i.e. patron of cockfighting. On 25 June 1683 "Lord Norreys and — Pudsey of Elsfeild with constables searched Ald. W. Wright's house, and King the glover's, for armes." On 17 July the Alderman's house was again searched, an "armour cap a pee for one man" being found there, and he was released on bail 30 Nov. Wright appeared in the Court of King's Bench before Lord Chief Justice Jeffreys 16 April 1684, for publishing scandalous libels "that the King and Duke are brothers in iniquity," and though he pleaded not guilty, he was found guilty and committed to custody.

1679. Aug. 25. William Wright. —— ——
Brome Whorwood. ——
George Pudsey. —— ——

"George Pudsey lost it by 20 votes." (*Wood.*)

1681. Feb. 7. William Wright. —— ——
Brome Whorwood. ——
George Pudsey. —— ——

"Pudsey lost it by nearly an 100 votes," the Duke of Buckingham (who slept at Wright's house,) and Lord Lovelace actively assisting his opponents.

1685. March 9. Hon. Henrie Berty.
Sir George Pudsey Knt.

Captain the Hon. Henry Bertie of Chesterton, third son (by his 2nd wife) of Montagu 2nd Earl of Lindsey, was M.P. Westbury Feb. 1678 to Jan. 1679, Nov. 1701 to July 1702, when defeated, but was seated on petition Nov. 1702 and sat till 1715. He also sat for New Woodstock Feb. to March 1681, and for Oxford 1685-7, and 1689-95. He became Capt. of a company in Lord Gerard's regt. of horse 15 Feb. 1678, which was disbanded in Jan. and March 1679, and was Captain of the Horse Troop of

Militia of Oxon in March 1681 and 1685. He was app. Captain of an Independent Troop of Horse 18 June 1685, but it was disbanded after the battle of Sedgemoor in that year. He and his half brother Richard (see Woodstock 1685,) had their commission taken from them in Nov. 1685, "because not forward in the parliament to vote up the popish officers." *(Wood)*. He m. (1) Philadelphia eldest surviving dau. of Sir Edward Norreys of Weston on the Green, (see the County 1675,) and so acquired that estate and (2) Catherine sister of Sir Henry Fetherstone Bart. He was made Dep. Lieut. Oxon 30 May 1689, and died at a very advanced age at Chesterton 5 Dec. 1734. His grandson was M.P. for the County 1742.

"The loyall and generous" Sir George Pudsey of Elsfield, who was Knighted by the King at Oxford on 15 March 1681, being then D.L. for Oxon, and "one of the Captaines of the Militia company," *(Wood)* was the son of George P. of Langley, co. Warwick, and kinsman to William Pudsey who succeeded Bulstrode Whitlock as Chairman of the Oxon Quarter Sessions. He "never togated in any University," *(Wood)* but ent. the Middle Temple 18 Nov. 1663, bar. at law 25 May 1666, Serjeant at law 23 Jan. 1683, and, having twice unsucc. cont. Oxford, represented it 1685-7, and was its Recorder 17 Sept. 1683 to Sept. 1688. He was app. a Commr. for the regulation of the city of Oxford 1688, and died about 1691 in the Fleet. He m. the dau. of Sir Thomas Coghill Knt. of Blechingdon, and she d. 12 Feb. 1689. He was the last of the family to reside at Ellesfield, which manor and estate, of about £1200 a year, he sold to Lord North for £25000. The lordship of Ellesfield came to the Pudseys about the beginning of the reign of Hen. 7, for Edith (aged 40 in 7 Hen. 8,) niece and heir to the last Gilbert Hore, and dau. of John Hore, m. (1) Thomas Fulthorpe of Bernard's Castle, and (2) Rowland a younger son of Henry Pudsey of Barfold, and Bolton, Yorkshire. Hugh de Pute, or Pudsey, Bishop of Durham 1153, was of the same family. Gilbert de Ellesfield (see the County 1295,) was lord of the manor temp. Edw. I, and his descendant and heir Johanna married John Hore, de Childerley, 8 Hen. 4.

      1689. Jan. 11.   Hon. Henry Bertie   T.
                Sir Edward Norreys Knt.   T.

    As to Sir E. Norreys, see the County 1675. William Wright and Thomas Horde were candidates but apparently did not take a poll.

      1690. Feb. 19.   The same.
      1695. Oct. 24.   Sir E. Norreys   T.   ———
                Thomas Rowney   T.   ———
                William Wright   W.   ———
                Ald. Henry White.   W.   ———

Ald. Henry White, 2nd son of Sir Sampson Wright, was called "Squire White" to distinguish him from his father. He was a draper at Oxford, Mayor 1691-2, and m. Katherine dau. of Ald. Wm. Wright, (see 1679). The other defeated candidate was his brother-in-law, the Recorder of Oxford 1688-1721, (as to whom see *Williams' Welsh Judges*).

Thomas Rowney of Oxford, was the son of Thomas R. an Attorney of Oxford, who was on intimate terms of friendship with Anthony Wood. He matric. St. John's Coll. Oxford 15 May 1684, aged 16, was H.S. Oxon (as T. R. jun.) 1691, and called to the bar at the Inner Temple 20 May 1694. He was licensed by the Vicar General 27 May 1691 to marry Elizabeth dau of Edward Noel of St. Clement Danes, Middlesex. He sat for Oxford 1695-1722, and died 26 Aug. 1727.

1698. July 23. The same.

1701. Jan. 6. Thomas Rowney   T.

              Francis Norreys   T.

The latter was the younger son of Sir Edward Norreys, (see the County 1675,) matric. Queen's Coll. Oxford 31 March 1683, aged 17, and entered Lincolns Inn 1684. He was app. Ensign of Capt. Richard Bertie's Independent Troop of Horse 18 June 1685, which, after Sedgemoor, was incorporated into the Earl of Peterborough's regt. of horse. He was seated at North Weston, and sat for Oxford 1701 until his death 6 June 1706.

1701. Nov. 25. The same, re-elected 17 July 1702, and 8 May 1705.

1706. Dec. 11. Sir John Walter Bart. of Sarsden, *vice* Norreys deceased. This Member was 2nd but eldest surviving son of Sir William W. whom he succ. as 3rd Bart. 5 March 1693, and grandson of Sir Wm. Walter, (see the County 1663). He matric. Queen's Coll. Oxford 21 Aug. 1691, created D.C.L. 27 Aug. 1702, was a Clerk Comptroller of the Board of Green Cloth Feb. 1711 to Feb. 1716, and m. Elizabeth dau. of Sir Thomas Vernon Knt. He sat for Appleby Dec. 1694-5, and Dec. 1697 to Dec. 1700, and for Oxford Dec. 1706 nntil his death s.p. 11 June 1722. His widow re-m. to Viscount Harcourt, the Lord Chancellor, (see *Williams' Parl. Hist. of Wales*). The title expired with his brother Sir Robert 20 Nov. 1731.

1708. May 3. Thomas Rowney   T.

              Sir John Walter   T.

1710. Oct. 4. The same.

1711. Feb. 26. Sir John Walter, re-el. after accepting an office of profit under the Crown.

1713. Aug. 22. Thomas Rowney.

              Sir John Walter.

1715. Jan. 24. The same.

1722. March 22. Sir John Walter   T.

Thomas Rowney   T.

This Thomas Rowney of Dean Farm was the son of the M.P. 1695, and matric. St. John's Coll. Oxford 5 July 1709, aged 16, and entered the Inner Temple 1709. He was High Steward of Oxford City July 1743-59, and the Town Hall was built in 1751 nearly at his own expense. He m. 10 March 1756 Miss Trollope, voted against the employment of the Hessian Troops 1730, and the Excise Bill 1733, and sat for Oxford 1722 until his death 27 Oct. 1759, buried in St. Giles' Church, Oxford, 4 Nov. He and his father held one of the seats for Oxford for a period of 64 years without interruption.

1722. Oct. 24. Francis Knollys of Thame, *vice* Walter deceased. This Member was the son of Francis Knollys M.P. for Reading, who died of the small pox 1701, by Elizabeth youngest dau. and co-heir of John Stribblehill of Thame. He sat for Oxford Oct. 1722-34, and died unmarried 24 June 1754. He voted against the Excise Bill 1733, under the following circumstances,—"On the Call of the House his excuse was not allow'd, and he was order'd to be taken into Custody of the Serjeant at Arms; but being discharged appeared on the Report, and voted against the Bill."

1727. Aug. 16. Thomas Rowney   T

Francis Knollys   T

1734. April 23. Thomas Rowney   T

Matthew Skinner   W

Serjeant Skinner was the third and youngest son of Robert S. of Welton, Northants, bar. at law, and law reporter, and was born 22 Oct. 1689, educ. at Westminster, matric. Ch. Ch. Oxford 18 June 1709, aged 19, and having entered Lincolns Inn 20 June 1709, was called to the bar 21 April 1716. He was one of the four Common Pleaders of the City of London 1719-22, Recorder of Oxford 30 May 1721-49, made a Serjeant at law 1 Feb. 1724, one of the King's Serjeants 11 June 1728, and His Majesty's Prime (or First) Serjeant 12 May 1734, being Treasurer of Serjeants Inn 1728. He m. 1719 Elizabeth dau. of Thomas Whitfield of Watford Place, Herts. He unsucc. cont. Andover 1727, but was M.P. for Oxford 1734 till made Chief Justice of Chester 26 Nov. 1738, and held that judicial post until his death at Oxford 21 Oct. 1749, aged 60 years all but a day. He resided at Oxford 1722-39.

1739. Feb. 8. James Herbert of Kingsey, Bucks, (Tory,) *vice* Skinner made C. J. of Chester. Elder son of James Herbert of Tythorpe and Kingsey, who was drowned 1721, (see the

County 1715,) he merely sat for Oxford Feb. 1739 until his death unmarried 21 Nov. 1740, at an early age.

1740.   Dec. 3.   Philip Herbert of Kingsey, *vice* his elder brother James deceased.   Third son of James H. of Tythorpe (see the county 1715,) he was adm. to Lincolns Inn 25 Jan. 1735, called to the bar 20 June 1740, m. Mary dau. and heir of Edward Butler (see Oxford University 1737,) and sat for Oxford Dec. 1740 until his death s.p. at Kingsey 21 July 1749, aged 32.   He left two sisters and co-heirs, Sophia who married the 6th Viscount Wenman, (see the County 1768,) and died a widow 20 July 1787, aged 70, and Agnes who died unmarried in 1810, aged 91.

1741.   May 4.   Thomas Rowney   T

Philip Herbert   T

1747.   June 26.   The same.

1749.   Nov. 21.   Viscount Wenman (see the County 1754) *vice* Herbert deceased.

1754.   April 15.   Thomas Rowney   T

Hon. Robert Lee.   T

Hon. Robert Lee of Charlbury, 13th and youngest son of Edward 1st Earl of Lichfield, was born 3 July 1706, and m. 21 Jan. 1748 Catherine daughter of Sir John Stonehouse Bart. of Radley, Berks.   He was nominated D L. Oxon 9 June 1762, was M.P. Oxford 1754-68, and succ. his nephew George (see the County 1740) as 4th and last Earl of Lichfield 19 Sept. 1772.   He was Hereditary Custos Brevium in the Common Pleas 1772 until his death s.p. 3 Nov. 1776, when the title became extinct.

1759.   Nov. 19.   Sir Thomas Stapleton of Bray, Berks, and Rotherfield Greys, *vice* Rowney deceased.   Eldest son of Sir Wm. S. of Grays, (see the County 1727,) whom he succ. as 5th Bart. 13 Jan. 1740, he was born 24 Feb. 1727, matric. St. Mary Hall, Oxford 27 Feb. 1744, created D.C.L. 3 July 1754, and m. 27 Nov. 1765 Mary 2nd dau. of Henry Fane M.P. of Wormsley, (see the County 1796.)   He sat for Oxford Nov. 1759-68, and died 1 Jan. 1781.   The Barony of Le Despencer was terminated in favour of his eldest son Thomas in 1788.

1761.   March 25.   Hon. Robert Lee   T

Sir T. Stapleton   T

In 1768 the Mayor and Aldermen of Oxford offered to re-elect them, provided they advanced £7500 to discharge a debt upon the city.   The two Members, however, on 26 Jan. 1768, laid the latter before the House of Commons, who sent ten of the offending persons to Newgate for five days, and only discharged them after a very severe reprimand, upon their knees, from the Speaker.   During their brief imprisonment, it is said, however, that the guilty parties completed another bargain for the City with the Duke of Marlborough and Lord Abingdon, whose nominees were returned.

1768. March 17.	George Nares	T	592
	Hon. W. Harcourt	T	562
	William Craven	W	332
	Sir J. Cotter	W	80

Mr. Craven became 6th Earl Craven March 1769, and died 1791. Sir James Cotter 1st Bart. of Rockforest, co. Cork, died 1770.

George Nares was the younger son of George Nares of Albury, Oxon, who was Steward to the 2nd. and 3rd. Earls of Abingdon, and was born at Hanwell, Middlesex, in 1716, educ. at Magdalen College School, adm. to New Coll. Oxford, created D.C.L. 7 July 1773, adm. to the Inner Temple 19 Oct. 1738, where he was called to the bar 12 June 1741. He m. 23 Sept. 1751 Mary dau. of Sir John Strange, Master of the Rolls 1750-4. He was Town Clerk of Oxford 8 Sept. 1746 to 5 July 1756, made a Serjeant at law 6 Feb. 1759, and a King's Serjeant 1759, Recorder of Oxford 1766-71, voted against Wilkes 1769, M.P. Oxford 1768 until sworn in a Justice of the Common Pleas 26 Jan. 1771, and was Knighted the next day. Mr. Justice Nares sat on the Bench until his death at Ramsgate 20 Jul/ 1786. He was buried at Eversley, Hants. His son Rev. Edward Nares D.D., m. 1797 Lady Charlotte Spencer 3rd dau. of the 3rd Duke of Marlborough K.G.

Hon. William Harcourt, 2nd son of Simon 1st Earl Harcourt, (great grandson of the M.P. for the County 1679,) was born 20 March 1743, and m. 3 Sept. 1778 Mary widow of Thomas Lockhart of Craig House, Scotland, and dau. of Rev. W. Danby D.D. of Farnley, Yorkshire. One of the few military men who sat for Oxford, he entered the army at the age of 16 as Ensign 1st Foot Guards Aug. 1759, became Captain 16th Light Dragoons 27 Oct. 1759, (raised at his father's expense,) and backed by great family interest, saw rap'd promotion, becoming Captain 3rd King's Own Dragoons 30 June 1760, Lt.-Col. 31st Foot (from half-pay) 28 Nov. 1764, Lt.-Col. 4th Light Dragoons 19 April 1765, Lt.-Col. 16th Light Dragoons 24 June 1768, A.D.C. to the King with the rank of Colonel 29 Aug. 1777, Col. of the 16th Light Dragoons 20 Oct. 1779, Major Gen. 12 Nov. 1782, Lt.-Gen. 12 Oct. 1793, Gen. 1 Jan. 1798, and Field Marshal 19 July 1821. He was M.P. for Oxford 1768-74, an Equerry to the Queen Consort 5 Sept. 1761-6, Extra Groom of the Bedchamber to the King 29 Nov. 1766 to 1808, Governor of Fort William 29 March 1794, Commander of the British Cavalry in the war in Flanders and Holland 1793-4, and of the army there 1794-5.

Governor of Hull 15 July 1795-1801, Gov. of the Royal Military College at High Wycombe and Great Marlow 23 June 1801-10, Dep. Lieut. Berks 22 Nov. 1801, and Gentleman and Master of the Robes to the King 26 Nov. 1808 to 5 June 1809. General Harcourt succeeded his brother George as 3rd Earl Harcourt 20 April 1809, and was Master of the House to the Queen April 1809 till Her Majesty's death in 1818, Gov. of Portsmouth 30 July 1811-30, Keeper of Windsor Great Park 11 Nov. 1815, G.C.B. 20 May 1820, Gov. of Plymouth 1 Jan. 1827, Dep. Lieut. of Windsor Forest, Dep. Ranger of Windsor Great Park, and Lieut. of Windsor Forest 1782, and a Commr. of the R. Mil. Coll. Sandhurst. His Lordship died 17 June 1830, at his seat St. Leonard's Hall, Berks, aged 87, when the title became extinct. He was A.D.C. to Lord Albemarle at the capture of Havannah 1762, took his regiment to America, and in 1776 took prisoner the American General, Charles Lee.

1771. Jan. 31. Lord Robert Spencer, *vice* Nares made a Judge. Third son of Charles, 2nd Duke of Marlborough, he was born 3 May 1747, matric. Ch. Ch. Oxford 10 April 1762, created M.A. 6 May 1765, and D.C.L. 7 July 1773. He had an extensive Parliamentary career, being M.P. for Woodstock 1768-71, when he resigned his seat to stand for Oxford, which he rep. till 1790, and was also M.P. Wareham 1790 till he resigned Feb. 1799, for Tavistock March 1802-7, and March 1817-18, and again for Woodstock 1818-20. Lord Robert held office as a Lord of Trade Aug. 1772 to Dec. 1781, Joint Vice Treasurer of Ireland May 1782 to April 1783, and Surveyor General of Woods and Forests Feb. 1806 to Dec. 1807. He m. 2 Oct. 1811 Henrietta only dau. of Sir Everard Fawkener K.B., and relict of Hon. Edward Bouverie, and died s.p. 23 June 1831, aged 84.

1774. Oct. 5.   Lord R. Spencer   T
            Hon. Peregriue Bertie   W

Captain the Hon. Peregrine Bertie of Yattenden, Berks, and Weston on the Green, was the third son of Willoughby 3rd Earl of Abingdon, and was born 13 March 1741. He entered the Royal Navy, and, according to the custom of that day, he attained (through family influence) the rank of Captain 6 Nov. 1762, and was appointed to the " Shannon." He m. 7 May 1790 Miss Hutchins of Yattenden, and sat for Oxford 1774 until his death at his seat at Frilsham, Berks, 20 Aug. 1790.

1780. Sept. 8. The same.

1782. June 3. Lord R. Spencer, re-el. on being made Vice Treasurer of Ireland. He was now a Whig.

1784. March 30. Lord R. Spencer   W
            Hon. P. Bertie   W

1790. June 16. Hon. P. Bertie   W

Francis Burton   T

Francis Burton of Edworth, Beds, was the son of Col.
Francis Burton, of St. George's, Westminster and was born 1744,
and matric. Ch Ch. Oxford 9 Dec. 1760, aged 16, B.A. 1764, M.A.
30 April 1767. He was adm. to Lincolns Inn 4 May 1761, called
to the bar there and gave the usual bond 10 Feb. 1768, called to
the Bench of that Society 12 Feb. and sat as such 6 May 1778,
Treasurer 1792, and was made a King's Counsel in Trinity term
1792. He was M.P. Heytesbury Dec. 1780-4, Woodstock 1784-90,
and Oxford 1790-1812, Chairman of the Oxfordshire Quarter
Sessions 1771-7, Recorder of Woodstock 1780-1802, and of Oxford
1797 until July 1801, when he resigned on account of loss of
sight. Mr. Burton was Puisne Justice of Chester July 1788 to
1817, when he resigned. He m. Jan. 1778 the eldest dau. of
Nlcholas Halhead of Woodstock, and died in London 28 Nov.
1832, aged 88, being then the senior King's Counsel, and having
been blind for many years. (See *Williams' Welsh Judges.*)

1790. Dec. 21. Arthur Annesley 613

———— *Ogilvie* 103

vice Captain Bertie who died before the meeting of Parliament.
Arthur Annesley of Bletchingdon, was the only son of Arthur
Annesley (H.S. 1765,) and matric Ch. Ch. Oxford 27 May 1779,
aged 18, was H.S. Oxon 1784, M.P. Oxford Dec. 1790-6, when
defeated, and unsucc. cont. Woodstock 1806. He m. 1785
Catharine dau. of Admiral Sir Charles Hardy Knt., and died 20
Jan. 1841, aged 80. His son Arthur became 10th or 11th
Viscount Valentia in 1844.

1796. May 27. Henry Peters   T   658

Francis Burton   T   504

Arthur Annesley T 461

This poll lasted 3 days, when 890 voted. The Plumpers
given were for Peters 91, Burton 56, Annesley 10. After this
date nearly every election was vigorously contested at Oxford.

Henry Peters of Betchworth Castle, Surrey, was a London
merchant, and a partner in Masterman & Co., bankers. He sat
for Oxford 1796-1802, and died in London 21 Dec. 1827. His
eldest son Henry m. 25 Jan. 1814 Caroline Mary Susannah eldest
dau. of John Campbell, Master in Chancery.

1802. July 9. J. A. Wright   T   836

F. Burton   T   812

J. I. Lockhart   T   454

The poll lasted four days, and 1186 voted. The Plumpers
were, for Wright 56, Burton 85, Lockhart 126.

John Atkyns Wright of Crowsley Park, son of — Atkyns, of Ketteringham, Norfolk, was created D.C.L. Exeter College, Oxford, 18 June 1801, having assumed the name of Wright. He was M.P. Oxford 1802-7, and 1812-20, H.S. Oxon Feb. 1798, Major Commandant Henley and Binfield Volunteers 16 Sept. 1803 to April 1806, Recorder of Henley on Thames, and Chairman of the Oxfordshire Quarter Sessions Jan. 1819 until his death at Crowsley Park 5 March 1822.

1806.	Dec. 9.	F. Burton	T	836.
		J. A. Wright	T	760.
		J. I. Lockhart	*T*	715.

1353 electors voted, the poll being kept open 6 days. The Plumpers were, for Burton 54, Wright 45, Lockhart 221.

| 1807. | May 4. | Francis Burton. |
| | | J. I. Lockhart. |

John Ingram Lockhart of Sherfield House, Hants, and Great Haseley House, Oxon, youngest son of James Lockhart of Melchett Park Wilts, and London, (a partner in Lockhart, Wallace, and Co., bankers, Pall Mall,) matric. Univ. Coll. Oxford 5 May 1783, aged 17, created D.C.L. 14 June 1820, ent. Lincolns Inn 7 May 1783, bar. at law 14 June 1790, and went the Oxford circuit, of which he became a distinguished member. Mr. Lockhart possessed great retentiveness of memory. He m. 14 Jan. 1804 Mary only child and heir of Francis Wastie of Cowley, and Haseley House, and took the name of Wastie in lieu of Ingram-Lockhart by Act of Parliament 12 Oct. 1831. He unsucc. cont. Oxford 1802, 1806, 1818, and 1830, but rep. it 1807-18, and 1820-30. He was Recorder of Romsey till Oct. 1834, app. Deputy Recorder of Oxford to Sir Wm. Elias Taunton in 1830, and succeeded that distinguished Judge as Recorder of Oxford March 1835, but died at Great Haseley 13 Aug. following, aged 70.

1812.	Oct. 17.	J. A. Wright	T	863.
		J. I. Lockhart	T	828.
		Hon. George Eden	*W*	794.
		H. R. Curzon		104.

1538 voted, the poll being prolonged for 9 days. Mr. Curzon resigned at the close of the second day's poll. 79 Plumpers were given to Wright, 142 to Lockhart, and 241 to Eden, while the Split Votes were, between Wright and Lockhart 435, Wright and Eden 308, Lockhart and Eden 229.

1818.	June 22.	J. A. Wright	850
		Gen. F. St. John	675
		J. I. Lockhart	448

The Poll lasted 4 days, and 1143 voted. The Split Votes
were, between Wright and St. John 414, Wright and Lockhart
374, St. John and Lockhart 42, while Wright received 62
Plumpers, St. John 219, and Lockhart 32.

General the Hon. Frederick St. John was the 2nd surviving
son of Frederick 2nd Viscount Bolingbroke, by Lady Diana
Spencer eldest dau. of Charles 2nd Duke of Marlborough. Born
20 Dec. 1765, he entered the army as Ensign 31 Aug. 1779, and
became Lieut. 85th Regt. 7 Feb. 1780, Capt.-Lieut. and Captain
88th Regt. 12 Dec. 1780, Capt. 95th Foot 22 Aug. 1781, Major 8
April 1783, (then 104th Regt.), on half-pay in 1786, Major 45th
Foot 13 June 1789, Lt. Col. of the 2nd. Foot 23 Feb. 1791, Col. 21
Aug. 1795, Major Gen. 18 June 1798, (" on full pay of late 117th
Foot,") was on half-pay in 1804, Lt. Gen. 30 Oct. 1805, and
General 4 June 1814. He served in the West Indies until 1781,
in Jersey and Guernsey until 1783, at Gibralter, throughout (as
Brigadier and Major Gen.,) the Rebellion in Ireland in 1798, and
afterwards in India under Lord Lake with much distinction,
taking part in the two campaigns against the Mahrattas, where
he was second in command, being engaged in seven sieges and
two general actions, for which he received the thanks of
both Houses of Parliament. He m. (1) 8 Dec. 1788 Lady Mary
Ker (who d. 6 Feb. 1791) 3rd dau. of Wm. 5th Marquis Lothian ;
(2) 6 April 1793 Hon. Arabella Craven (who d. 8 June 1819,) 4th
dau. of Wm. 6th Lord Craven, (see 1768 ;) and (3) 14 Nov. 1821
Caroline Elizabeth youngest dau. of J. Parsons. General St.
John was M.P. Oxford 1818-20, when defeated, and died at
Chailey, Sussex, after a few hours' illness 19 Nov. 1845, aged 79,
being then the senior General, with the exception of Sir George
Nugent Bart.

1820. March 10.	C. Wetherell	T	907
	J. I. Lockhart	T	737
	General F. St. John		623

1267 voted at this election, the Poll being open 3 days. 14
Plumpers were given to Wetherell, 71 to Lockhart, and 182 to
St. John. The Split Votes were as follows, Wetherell and
Lockhart 559, Wetherell and St. John 334, Lockhart and St.
John 107.

The distinguished lawyer, Charles Wetherell, was the 3rd
son of the Very Rev. Nathan Wetherell, Master of University
College, and Dean of Oxford, and was baptised at Oxford 6
March 1770, educ. at St. Paul's School, matric. Univ. Coll.
Oxford 14 Jan. 1786, aged 15, demy Magd. Coll. 1788-91, B.A. 2.
June 1790, M.A. 9 July 1793, created D.C.L. 13 June 1834.
Entering the Inner Temple 1790, he was called to the bar 4 July
1794, became K.C. 23 March 1816, a Bencher 21 June 1816,
Reader 1824, and Treasurer of his Inn 1825. He m. (1) 28 Dec.

1826 his cousin Jane Sarah Elizabeth (who died 21 April 1831,)
2nd dau. of Sir Alexander Croke Knt. of Studley Priory, Judge
of the Vice Admiralty Court in North America, and (2) 27 Nov.
1838 Harriet Elizabeth 2nd dau. of Col. Francis Warneford of
Warneford Place, Wilts. Wetherell was defeated at Shaftesbury
Oct. 1812 but seated on petition Feb. 1813-18, and sat for Oxford
1820-6, (where defeated 1832,) Hastings June to Sept. 1826,
Plympton Dec. 1826-30, and Boroughbridge 1830-2, and unsucc.
cont. Birmingham Jan 1840. He defended Watson for the Spa
Field riots 1817, was Knighted 10 March 1824, Solicitor General
Jan. 1824-6, and Attorney General Sept. 1826 to April 1827 and
Feb. 1828 to June 1829, when he resigned owing to his opposition
to Catholic Emancipation. He was Recorder of Bristol from
before 1830 to 1846, Temporal Chancellor of the County Palatine
of Durham from March 1835 to 1846, Counsel to Magd. Coll.
Oxford 1804-46, Counsel to Oxford Univ. 1830-46, and Deputy
High Steward of Oxford from May 1846 until his death (from a
fall from his carriage ten days before) at Preston Hall, Kent, 17
Aug. following, aged 76, buried in the Temple Church 25 Aug.
He was said to be worth over £200000, and to have left no will.
During the Reform excitement, Wetherell, although advised not
to do so, persisted in attending as Recorder of Bristol to open
the Quarter Sessions as usual in Oct. 1831, and being well-known
for his opposition to the burning question of the day, his
presence gave such offence to the mob, that they broke out into
the most serious rioting, which was only quelled, after enormous
damage had been done, by the severest exertions.

1824. Feb. 29. Charles Wetherell, re-el. on being made
Solicitor General.

1826. June 16. J. H. Langston W 1054

J. I. Lockhart W 760

W. H. Hughes W 729

The Poll was kept open for 4 days when 1575 voted.

James Haughton Langston, son of John L. of Sarsden
House, (H.S. 1804, who purchased the Sarsden and Churchill
estates from Sir Wm. Walter Bart. and d. 1812.) was born 1797,
educ. at Eton, matric. Ch. Ch. Oxford 23 May 1814, aged 17,
created D.C.L. 23 June 1819, and m. 6 July 1824 the Lady Julia
Moreton 2nd dau. of Thomas 2nd Earl Ducie, (see *Williams'
Gloucestershire Members*.) Upon attaining his majority he
re-built Churchill Parish Church in 1819. He was H.S. Oxon
Oxon 1819, M.P. Woodstock 1829-26, and Oxford 1826-34, and
1841-63, Verdurer of Wychwood Forest in 1830, and died at
Sarsden House, Chipping Norton, 19 Oct. 1863, aged 66.

1830. Aug. 4. J. H. Langston   W   1108
                W. H. Hughes   W   1054
                J. I. Lockhart   T   750

Poll prolonged to 5 days, during which 1779 voted. Langston had 85 Plumpers, Hughes 424, Lockhart 137, while the Split Votes were, for Langston and Hughes 520, Langston and Lockhart 503, Hughes and Lockhart 110.

William Hughes Hughes, eldest son of John Hewitt, of Clapham Common, Surrey, was born 1792, assumed the name of Hughes 25 May 1825, ent. Lincolns Inn as W. Hughes-Hewitt (aged 29) on 5 June 1822, and was called to the bar 26 June 1827. He was H.S. Hants, and an Alderman of the City of London for Portsoken Ward March 1832 till discharged upon a writ of *quo warranto* the same year, and again for Bread Street Ward 18 Oct. 1843 till he resigned his gown A..ril 1848. He sat for Oxford 1830-2, and March 1833-7, being defeated 1832 and 1837, was a director of the London and Greenwich Railway in 1846, and died at Ilkley Wells House, Yorkshire, 10 Oct. 1874.

1831. May 2.   J. H. Langston.
                W. H. Hughes.

1832. Dec. 13. J. H. Langston   W   1260.
                 Thomas Stonor   W   953.
                 W. H. Hughes   W   919.
                 Sir C. Wetherell   T   523.

Sir C. Wetherell resigned on the first day. 2139 voted out of 2312 on the register. The Plumpers given were, for Langston 104, Stonor 109, Hughes 184, and Wetherell 146. The Split Votes were, Langston and Stonor 476, Langston and Hughes 456, Langston and Wetherell 224, Stonor and Hughes 207, Stonor and Wetherell 81, Hughes and Wetherell 72. On petition Mr. Stonor was unseated March 1833.

Thomas Stonor of Stonor Park, eldest son of Thomas Stonor of that place, was born in London 22 Oct. 1797, and m. 25 July 1821 Frances dau of Peregrine Edward Towneley of Towneley Hall, Lancashire. He was J.P. and D.L. Oxon, H. S. 1836, M.P. Oxford 1832 till unseated March 1833, unsucc. cont. the City 1835, and the County 1837, and was summoned to Parliament by writ dated 14 Sept. 1839 as senior co-heir to the Barony of Camoys, dormant since 1426. His Lordship held office as a Lord in Waiting to the Queen July 1846 to Feb. 1852, Jan. 1853 to Feb. 1858, June 1859 to July 1866, and Dec. 1868 to Feb. 1874, and died at Stonor 18 Jan. 1881.

1833. March 18. W. Hughes Hughes   W   803
                  Charles Townley   W   702
                  Donald Maclean   T   462

vice Stonor, whose election was declared void. 1966 voted out of 2312.

1835.	Jan. 10.	W. H. Hughes	T	1394.
		Donald Maclean	T	1217.
		Thomas Stonor	*W*	1022.

2200 voted out of 2424. Hughes had 166 Plumpers, Maclean 320, and Stonor 281, while the Split Votes were, Hughes and Maclean 672, Hughes and Stonor 536, Maclean and Stonor 205.

Donald Maclean was the youngest son of General Sir Fitzroy Maclean 8th Bart. of Morvaren Argyllshire, and was born in 1800, educ. at Eton, and matric. Ball. Coll. Oxford 6 April 1818, aged 18, Snell Exhibitioner 1822, B.A. 1823, M.A. 1827, created D.C.L. 20 June 1844. He took a leading part in the formation of the Union Society, ent. Lincolns Inn 12 July 1820, aged 20, bar at law 9 Feb. 1827, sat for Oxford 1835-47, having failed March 1833, m. 8 Sept. 1827 Harriet younger dau. of General Frederick Maitland, (grandson of the 6th Earl of Lauderdale), and died at Rome 21 March 1874. ✦

1837.	July 26.	Donald Maclean	T	1348.
		William Erle	W	1217.
		W. Hughes Hughes	*T*	897.

2115 voted out of 2773. The Split Votes were, for Maclean and Erle 492, Maclean and Hughes 672, Erle and Hughes 135. The Plumpers given were 184 to Maclean, 572 to Erle, and 90 to Hughes.

William Erle was another of the many lawyers returned for Oxford. Born at Fifehead Magdalene, Dorset, 1 Oct. 1793, the son of Rev. Christopher Erle of Gillingham, Dorset, he was educ. at Winchester, matric. New Coll. Oxford 15 Nov. 1811, B.C.L. 1818, D.C.L. by decree of Convocation 18 June 1857, Fellow 1811-35, and Hon. Fellow 1870-80. He was called to the bar at the Middle Temple 26 Nov. 1819, adm. *ad eundem* to the Inner Temple 11 June 1822, and elected a Bencher thereof 18 Nov. 1834, Reader 1843, and Treasurer 1844, and m. 30 Sept. 1834 Amelia eldest dau. of Rev. David Williams D.C.L. Warden of New Coll. Oxford, and Prebendary of Winchester. He became a K.C. 7 July 1834, Counsel for the Bank of England 1844, M.P. Oxford 1837-41, a Serjeant at law 7 Nov. 1844, Knighted 23 April 1845, a Justice of the Common Pleas 6 Nov. 1844-6, a Justice of the Queen's Bench Oct. 1846-59, and Lord Chief Justice of the Common Pleas 24 June 1859 to 26 Nov. 1866, when he retired from the Bench. Chief Justice Erle became a Privy Councillor 6 July 1859, F.R.S. 22 Nov. 1860, was a member of the Trades Union Commission 1867-8, and author of the " Law relating to

Trades Union," 1869. He died at Bramshott Grange, Liphook, Hants, 28 Jan. 1880, aged 86.

1841. June 30.   J. H. Langston   W. 1349.
                Donald Maclean   T. 1238.
                Neil Malcolm   *T.* 1041.

2374 voted out of 2787. Langston had 1087 Plumpers, Maclean 30, and Malcolm only 7, while the Split Votes were, for Langston and Maclean 219, Langston and Malcolm 44, Maclean and Malcolm 984. Langston's Colour was Purple, Hughes' Red and Blue, and Maclean and Malcolm's Colours were Blue and White.

1847. July 29.   J. H. Langston   L
                W. Page Wood   L

William Page Wood was the 2nd son of Sir Matthew Wood 1st Bart. M.P. Lord Mayor of London 1815-17, and was born in London 29 Nov. 1801, educ. at Winchester 1812-18, went to Trin. Coll. Camb. 1820, scholar 1822-5, B.A. 24th Wrangler 1824, fellow 1824-30 M.A. 1827, created L.L.D 1864, ent. Lincolns Inn 1 March 1824, bar. at law 27 Nov. 1827, elected a Bencher 15 April 1845, and Treasurer 1867. He m. 5 Jan. 1830 Charlotte only dau. of Major Edward Moore of Great Barlings, Suffolk. Page Wood became Q.C. Feb. 1845, a Bencher of his Inn 15 April 1845, Vice Chancellor of the County Palatine of Lancaster 7 May 1849-51, Knighted 14 April 1851, M.P. Oxford 1847-42, created D.C.L. Oxford 3 July 1851, Hon. Student of Ch. Ch. 1867-81, Solicitor General March 1851 to Feb. 1852, and 28 Dec. 1852 to 10 Jan. 1853, a Vice Chancellor Jan. 1853-68, and a Lord Justice of Appeal in Chancery March to Dec. 1868. He was sworn a Privy Councillor 28 March 1868, created Lord Hatherley 9 Dec. 1868, and was Lord High Chancellor of England Dec. 1868 to Oct. 1872. His Lordship was elected F.R.S. 22 Dec. 1834, and became a member of the Council and a Vice President thereof, and died 10 July 1881.

1851. April 3.   W. Page Wood re-el., after taking office.
1852. July 6.   J. H. Langston.
               Sir W. Page Wood.
1853. Jan. 4.   Rt. Hon. Edward Cardwell,

vice Sir W. Page Wood raised to the Bench. This distinguished statesman was born 24 July 1813, the elder son of John Cardwell of Liverpool, merchant, and was educ. at Winchester, matric. Ball. Coll. Oxford 25 March 1831, scholar 1832, B.A. (double first class) 1835, M.A. 1838, fellow 1835, created D.C.L. 17 June 1863. He entered the Inner Temple 19 Nov. 1833, was called to the bar 16 Nov. 1838, and chosen a Bencher 28 April 1868, and m. 14

Aug. 1838 Anne dau. of Charles Stuart Parker of Fairlie, Ayr-shire. Cardwell unsucc. cont. Clithero 1841, but was seated on petition 21 March 1842, and sat till 1847, was defeated at Liverpool 8 July and for Ayrshire 22 July 1852 but sat for Liverpool 1847-52, and for Oxford Jan. 1853-7, when defeated, and July 1857 until created Viscount Cardwell 6 March 1874. He was Financial Secretar/ to the Treasury Feb. 1845 to July 1846, President of the Board of Trade (as a Peelite) Dec. 1852 to Feb. 1855, a Privy Councillor for England 28 Dec. 1852, and for Ireland 5 July 1859, attained a seat in the Cabinet 1859, and was Chief Secretary for Ireland June 1859-61, Chancellor of the Exchequer of the Duchy of Lancaster July 1861-4, Secretary of State for the Colonies April 1864 to June 1866, and for War Dec. 1868 to Feb. 1874. As such he re-organised the army by abolishing the purchase system 20 July 1871, and introducing the short service system. Lord Cardwell was a member of the Senate of London University, an Ecclesiastical Commr. until Nov. 1882, President of the Commission on Vivisection 23 June 1875 to March 1876, and died at Torquay 15 Feb. 1886.

1857.	March 31.	J. H. Langston	L	1671
		Charles Neate	L	1057
		Rt. Hon. E. Cardwell	*L.C.*	1016
		Serjeant Gaselee	*L*	245

Serjeant Stephen Gaselee (1807-73), whose father was a Justice of the Common Pleas, also unsucc. cont. Bridgwater 1847, and Portsmouth March 1855 and 1868, but sat for the latter 1865-8.

Charles Neate was the second son of the Rev. Thomas Neate, rector of Alvescot, Oxon, and was born at Adstock, Bucks, 13 June 1806, educ. at the College Bourbon, Paris, matric. Lincoln Coll. Oxford 2 June 1824, scholar 1826-8, B.A. 1828, M.A. 1830, fellow of Oriol Coll. 1828-79, lecturer on law and history 1856, senior treasurer 1845, ent. Lincolns Inn 30 June 1827, bar. at law 27 Jan. 1832. When engaged in a case as junior to Sir Richard Bethell, (afterwards Lord Chancellor, as Lord West-briry,) Neate took the opportunity of offering frequent suggestions to his learned leader, which so annoyed Bethell, that he said loudly, " Hold your tongue." On the rising of the Court Neate assaulted Bethell, and so ruined his own chance at the bar. He was Secretary to Sir Francis Baring when Chancellor of the Exchequer 1839-41, M.P. Oxford March to June 1857, when unseated for bribery, and again Nov. 1663-8, Drummond Pro-fessor of Political Economy at Oxford 1857-62, and Clerk of the Market until his death at Norham Manor, Northumberland, 7 Feb. 1879, buried at Alvescot 13 Feb. Professor Neate was the author of several lectures and pamphlets, and resided at Oxford 1868-79, being the senior Fellow at his death.

138   MEMBERS FOR OXFORD.

1857. July 21. Rt. Hon. E. Cardwell L.C. 1085.
               W. M. Thackeray   L.   1018.
vice J. H. Langston whose election was declared void. William
Makepeace Thackeray was the celebrated novelist.

1859. April 29. J. H. Langston   L.
               Rt. Hon. E. Cardwell L.

1859. June 27. Rt. Hon. E. Cardwell, re-el. after being
made Irish Secretary.

1861. July 30. The same, re-el. after being app. Chancellor of the Duchy.

1863· Nov. 7. Charles Neate, *vice* Langston deceased.

1864. April 9. Rt. Hon. E. Cardwell, re-el. after being
made Colonial Secretary.

1865. July 11. Rt. Hon. E. Cardwell L
               Charles Neate   L

1868. Nov. 8. Rt. Hon. E. Cardwell L 2765
               W. V. Harcourt Q.C.   L 2636
               J. P. Deane Q.C.   C 1125

The Rt. Hon. Sir James Parker Deane Knt. Q.C. was born
1812, and is Vicar General of the Archbishop of Canterbury.

William George Granville Venables Vernon Harcourt of
Malwood, New Forest, Hants, was born 14 Oct. 1827, and is the
younger of the two son of the Rev. Canon William Vernon
Harcourt of Nuneham Park, and brother to Col. E. W. Harcourt,
(see the County 1878.) He graduated B.A. 1st clrss classics and
Senior Optime 1851, M.A. 1869, Trin. Coll. Camb., ent. the Inner
Temple 2 May 1851, was called to the bar 1 May 1854, and made
a Queen's Counsel 10 Jan. 1866. He m. (1) 5 Nov. 1859 Maria
Thérése (who d. 31 Jan. 1863) dau. of Thomas Henry Lister of
Armitage Park, co. Stafford, the first Registrar General 1837-42,
and (2) 2 Dec. 1876 Elizabeth dau. of J. Lothrop Motley American
Minister at St James', and widow of T. P. Ives. He was made
Counsel to the Treasury 1864, Professor of International Law at
Camb. Univ 1869-87, a member of numerous Royal Commissions,
author of " Letters of ' Historicus ' on International Law,"
unsucc. cont. Kircaldy Burghs 1859, sat for Oxford 1868 to May
1880, when he was defeated after taking office, for Derby May
1880-95, when he lost his seat, and has represented West Monmouthshire from 1895. Sir William Harcourt was Knighted 12
Dec. 1873, sworn a Privy Councillor 28 April 1880, and held office
as Solicitor General Nov. 1873 to Feb. 1874, Secretary of State
for the Home Department April 1880 to June 1885, and Chancellor of the Exchequer Feb. to July 1886, and Aug. 1892 to June
1895. He became a member of the Council of Education for

Scotland 1881, and succeeded Mr. Gladstone as Leader of the Liberal Party in the House of Commons March 1894, but retired from that position 8 Dec. 1898.

1868. Dec. 22. Rt. Hon. E. Cardwell, re-el. after being made Secretary of War.

1873. Dec. 6. W. V. Harcourt, Q.C., re-el. after being made Solicitor General.

1874. Feb. 3.	Sir W. Harcourt	L	2332
	Rt. Hon. E. Cardwell	L	2281
	A. W. Hall	C	2198
1874. March 16.	A. W. Hall	C	2554
	J. D. Lewis	L	2092

vice Cardwell called to the Upper House. John Delaware Lewis sat for Devonport 1868-74, when defeated.

Alexander William Hall of Barton Abbey, eldest son of Henry Hall of that place, by the Hon. Catherine Louisa Hood 4th dau. of Alexander 1st Viscount Bridport, was born in London 25 June 1838, matric. Exeter Coll. Oxford 15 Oct. 1858, aged 20, from Eton, and m. 27 Aug. 1863 Emma Gertrude 2nd dau. of Edward Jowett of Eltofts, Yorkshire. Mr Hall unsucc. cont. Oxford Feb. 1874 and April 1880, but represented it March 1874-80, May to July 1880 when unseated on petition, and again 1885-92. He became J.P. Oxon 1865, Dep.-Lieut. 1867, High Sheriff 1867, and has been County Councillor for the Barton Division since 1889.

1880. April 3.	Sir W. Harcourt	L	2701
	J. W. Chitty Q.C.	L	2669
	A. W. Hall	C	2659

Joseph William Chitty was the 2nd and only surviving son of Thomas Chitty, of London, an eminent special pleader, and was born 27 May 1829, educ. at Eton, matric. Balliol Coll. Oxford 23 March 1847, B.A. 1851, Vinerian scholar, fellow of Exeter Coll. 1852-8, M.A. 1855, and three times stroked the Oxford Eight in the inter-University Boatrace, and afterwards acted as Umpire for some years. Mr Chitty entered Lincoln's Inn 15 Nov. 1851, where he was called to the bar 30 April 1856, made a Queen's Counsel 5 Feb. 1874, and elected a Bencher of his Inn 2 Nov. 1875. He m. 7 Sept. 1858 Clara Jessie 6th dau. of Rt. Hon. Sir Frederick Pollock 1st Bart. Lord Chief Baron of the Exchequer 1844-66. He was Major of the Inns of Court (14th Middlesex) Rifle Volunteers 5 Nov. 1869 to Dec. 1876, and M.P. for Oxford from 1880 till he was raised to the Bench as a Justice of the Chancery Division of the High Court of Justice 6 Sept. 1881, receiving the honour of Knighthood 7 Dec. 1881. He was elevated to the position of Lord Justice of Appeal and was sworn a member of the Privy Council 15 Jan. 1897, and died in London 15 Feb. 1899, leaving behind him the highest reputation as a most excellent Judge.

    1880. May 10. A. W. Hall   C 2730

                      Sir W. Harcourt L 2681

vice Sir W. Harcourt appointed Home Secretary. On petition this election was declared void July following, and in consequence of the report of the Royal Commissioners appointed to inquire into the matter, no further writ was issued for Oxford during the duration of this Parliament.

    1881. Sept. Mr. Chitty was made a Justice of the High Court at this date, but no writ issued to fill the vacancy, the City remaining without a Member till the Dissolution 18 Nov. 1885, when, by the provisions of the Redistribution of Seats Act of that year. Oxford was only allowed one Member.

    1885. Nov. 26. A. W. Hall   C 3312

                      Chas. Alan Fyffe L 2894

    :, 1886. July 1   A. W. Hall

    1892. July   Sir G. T. Chesney C 3278

                      Robinson Souttar L 3156

Robinson Souttar was elected for Dumfriesshire 1895.

Sir George Tomkyns Chesney, son of Captain Charles Cornwallis Chesney, Bengal Artillery, was born in 1830, and m. in 1855 Annie L. dau. of George Palmer of Purneah, Bengal. Entering the Bengal Engineers as Second Lieut. 8 Dec. 1848, he became First Lieut. 1 Aug. 1854, Capt. 27 Aug. 1858, Brevet Major next day, Brevet Lt. Col. R. E. 14 June 1869, Col. 1 Oct. 1867, Major Gen. in 1886, and Lt. Gen. 10 March 1887, and fought in the Indian Mutiny 1857-9, present at the battle of Budleekesari, served as Brigade Major of Engineers throughout the siege of Delhi, and was twice severely wounded at the assault (mentioned in despatches, medal with clasp, and Brevet of Major.) He was President of the Indian Civil Engineering College at Cooper's Hill 1870-80, Secretary to the Government of India in the Military Department 1880-6, made C.S.I. 1883, C.I.E. 1886, C.B. 1887, and K.C.B. 1890. Sir George served in the Burmese War 1886, (medal and clasp,) and was a Member of the Governor General of India's Council 1886-61, and M.P. for Oxford 1892 until his death, suddenly, of heart disease, 31 March 1895, having been made Colonel Commandant Royal Engineers 28 March 1890.

    1892. April 20. Viscount Valentia C 3745

                  J. F. Little   L 3143

Arthur (Annesley,) Viscount Valentia, of Bletchington

Park, only son of Hon. Arthur Annesley who died s.p. 27 Oct. 1844, was born 23 Aug. 1843, and succeeded his grandfather as 11th Viscount Valentia in the Peerage of Ireland 30 Dec. 1863. His Lordship became Cornet 10th Hussars 10 May 1864, and Lieut. 2 May 1868, but retired 1872, and was made Captain of the Queen's Own Oxfordshire Hussars (Yeomanry) 26 March 1873, (Hon. Major 1887,) Major in 1891, and Lt. Col. thereof 19 Dec. 1894, (Hon. Col.) He m. 30 Jan. 1878 Laura Sarah youngest dau. of Daniel Hale Webb of Wykeham Park, Banbury, and widow of Sir Algernon William Peyton 4th Bart. of Swift's House, Bicester. Lord Valentia is patron of one living, J.P. Oxon, High Sheriff 1874, Vice Chairman of the County Council from 1889, and has represented the City of Oxford since April 1892. He accepted office as Comptroller of Her Majesty's Household Oct. 1898, when he was sworn of the Privy Council.

  1895. July 17. Viscount Valentia C 3623

       T. H. Kingerlee L 2975

  1898. Nov. 4. Viscount Valentia, re-elected after accepting office.

  There were 2312 registered electors for Oxford in 1832, 5000 in 1868, 6495 in 1884, and 7637 in 1895. The Mayor is the Returning Officer.

THE UNIVERSITY OF OXFORD.

Although the University was summoned to return Members to the Parliament of 1301, unfortunately the Return is hopelessly lost, and the names of its earliest Members are therefore unknown. After a lapse however of three centuries the right of representation was again restored in the first Parliament of James I, by diploma dated 12 March 1604, the right of election being granted to "the Doctors and actual Masters of Arts." The voting still remains unaffected by the provisions of the Ballot Act 1872, and may be either by word or mouth, or by proxy, but though it has been said that "the Candidates are put to no expense," this rule only applies to uncontested returns, for where there is a contest the Candidates pay their own expenses as in other constituencies. The poll may be kept open for 5 days. The University has returned very many eminent Members, and especially at the first it made an especial point of being represented by Civilians, including such men as Crompton, Marten, Jenkins and Scott, Judges of the Admiralty. Then again Dun, Bennett, Edmondes, Wake, Roe, and Trumball, were Envoys to Foreign Courts, Calvert and Windebank were Secretaries of State, and Stuart was Vice Admiral. Curiously enough though the University was always so eminent for its loyalty, yet one of its Members, the ungrateful Danvers, was a notorious Regicide, and John Selden the lawyer, and Dr. Owen, the Vice Chancellor were strong supporters of Parliament. Other eminent Members were Sir Matthew Hale, Lord Chief Justice of England, the Earl of Rochester, Lord High Treasurer, the Earl of Nottingham, Lord Chancellor, William Bromley and Lord Colchester who were Speakers of the House of Commons, and Sir Robert Peel and Mr Gladstone the Prime Ministers. The Earl of Cranbrook has been Secretary of State, and Sir John Mowbray was the "Father of the House." Sir Christopher Wren, the first Earl of Liverpool, Sir George Hay and Sir John Nicholl, were among the defeated candidates.

MEMBERS FOR OXFORD UNIVERSITY.

1301. Return lost.

.   .   .   .   .

1604. March 16. Sir Daniel Dunne.
Sir Thomas Compton.

Sir Daniel Dun was the son of Robert Dun, descended from a Radnorshire family, and became Fellow of All Souls Coll. Oxford, 1567, B.C.L. 14 July 1572, D.C.L. 20 July 1580, and Principal

MEMBERS FOR OXFORD UNIVERSITY.

of New Inn Hall 1580. He was admitted an Advocate of the
College of Doctors of Laws 22 Jan. 1582, and became an eminent
Civilian, entered Grays Inn 9 Aug. 1599, and was a Commr. for
the Danish treaty 1602-3, a Master of the Court of Requests 1598,
Judge of the Prerogative Court of Canterbury in 1605, (but not in
1611,) and Dean of the Arches 1598—1617. On 2 Oct. 1602 John
Chamberlain wrote to Dudley Carleton in Paris, stating that
" Lord Eure, Sir John Herbert, Dr. Dunn, (made Master of
Requests for this voyage,) and Le Sieur, are gone to treat with
the King of Denmark and the Hanse Towns at Bremen, where
they are safe lodged till spring or longer." He was re-incor-
porated at Camb. Univ. 1603, Knighted 23 July 1603, Joint
Commr. of the High Court of Admiralty 7 Feb. 1609-17, a Commr.
named by James I for adjusting an Union with Scotland, M.P.
Taunton 1601, and Oxford Univ. 1604-11, and March to June
1614, and died 15 Sept. 1617. He married Joan third dau. of
Wm. Aubrey LL.D. (see *Williams' Parl. Hist. of Wales.*)
Nath. Brent to Carleton 11 Oct. 1617,—"The Spanish Ambassador
angry that Sir Hen. Marten succeeds Sir Dan Dun as Judge of the
Admiralty, Marten having ever been against him." Commission
3 Jan. 1599 to Dr. Dan Dunn, Judge of the Audience Court of
Canterbury, and others, to decide without appeal all disputes
between the English and the subjects of the French King in
reference to piracies and depredations committed at sea. Commission 31 July 1599 to him and others to enquire for and punish
all offenders in aiding and receiving pirates. Grant 6 Sept. 1604
to Sir Dan. Dunn, Master of Requests, of a pension of £100 per
annum for life.

Sir Thomas Crompton of London, son of Sir Thomas
Crompton Knt., was born 1558, matric. St. Alban Hall, Oxford,
(entry under date 20 Dec. 1577,) aged 19, B.A. from Merton Coll.
28 Jan. 1579, M.A. 1 Dec. 1581, B.C.L. and D.C.L. 11 July 1589.
He was adm. an advocate of the Doctor's Commons 25 April
1605, " but must have previously acted in our Courts as he was
Advocate General to Queen Elizabeth," (*Coote's Civilians,*) and
was Judge of the High Court of Admiralty 1589-1608, Judge of
the Consistory Court and Chancellor of the diocese of London
1607-8, a Master in Chancery 2 June 1608-8, and Vicar General
to the Archbishop of Canterbury. He was Knighted 23 July
1603, M.P. Boroughbridge 1597-8, Whitchurch 1601, and Oxford
Univ. 1604 until his death at the latter end of 1608, being buried
in St. Gregory's Church, by St. Paul's. *Wood* insinuates that
he was concerned in the schemes of the Earl of Essex, but
adduces no proof of his guilt, and in fact as there were two or
three Sir Thomas Cromptons at this period, it is very possible
that they may have been confused together. (See *Williams'
Parl. Hist. of Wales.*) It is doubtful if Crompton was married.
Grant 31 May 1603 to Dr. Thomas Crompton of the office of

King's Advocate General in Ecclesiastical Causes, which he held until his death. He must not be confused with Thomas Crompton of the Middle Temple, Protbonotary of the Common Pleas, whose will was dated 12 Nov. 1612, with a codicil 15 May 1614.

1609. Oct. 21 William Bird, *vice* Crompton deceased. Son of William Byrd of Walden, Essex, he was born 1561, matric. All Souls Coll. Oxford 28 Nov. 1581, aged 20, fellow 1578 to 22 June 1604, B.C.L. 4 July 1583, and D.C.L. 13 Feb. 1588, and was adm. a member of the College of Advocates 9 Oct. 1590. He was Official Principal and Dean of the Arches Oct. 1618-24, M.P. Oxford Univ. Oct. 1609-11, Knighted at Bedford 22 March 1617, a Master in Chancery 1621-4, and Judge of the Prerogative Court of Canterbury 29 June 1622 until his death s.p. 28 Aug. 1624, being buried in Christ Church, Newgate, 5 Sept.

1614. March. Sir Daniel Dun.

Sir John Bennett.

Second son of Richard Bennett of Clapcot, Berks, he became a student of Ch. Ch. Oxford 1573, B.A. 11 June 1577, M.A. 15 June 1580, proctor 1585, B.C.L. and D.C.L. 6 July 1589, entered Grays Inn 2 Feb. 1599, and was adm. an Advocate 21 Jan. 1604. He was a Commr. to repress heresy in the latter part of Queen Elizabeth's reign, was Knighted at Whitehall 23 July 1603, Vicar General and Chancellor to the Archbishop of York, a Judge of the Prerogative Court of Canterbury (in 1611), until June 1622, Chancellor to Anne of Denmark Queen to James I, a Master in Chancery 18 March 1608 to July 1621, one of the Councel of the North, Prebendary of Langtoft in the Church of York, and Ambassador to Brussels March 1617. Sir John m. Ann dau. of Christopher Weekes of Salisbury, and (2) Leonora ——— who survived him and died 30 Sept. 1638, (M.I. Uxbridge). He was a distinguished speaker in the House, and sat for Ripon 1597-8, and 1604-11, York 1601, and Oxford Uni. March to June 1614, and 1620 until he was expelled the House 24 April 1621 for receiving bribes and committing various acts of rapacity, ("for divers exorbitant oppressions and bribery.") "Sir John Bennett is convicted of corruption, but he is sick, and his sentence awaits his appearance to answer for himself." (Sir Dudley Diggs to Carleton, 18 April 1621. *Cal. State Papers.)* *Camden* says he was fined £20000 in 1622, but this is doubtful, as the *Parl. Hist. of England* states that he was merely required to find security in that amount for his appearance to answer the charges against him. Bennett however was pardoned by the indulgent King. He resided at Dawley, Middlesex, and died 15 Feb. 1627. His grandson was the celebrated Earl of Arlington, and the Earl of Tankerville now represents the family. On 20 March 1617 Geo. Gerrard wrote to Carleton,———"His Majesty then gave the Great Seal to Sir Fras. Bacon, who got it cheaply,

Sir John Bennet having offered £30000 for it"; and on 20 Nov. 1617 Sir Horace Vere informed Carleton that Sir Thos. Edmonds, Sir John Bennet, Sir Hum-May etc. were aspirants to the Secretary's place.

1620. Dec. 20.   Sir John Bennett.

Sir Clement Edmondes.

Sir Clemont Edmonds of Salop, the son of a yeoman, matric. All Saints Coll. Oxford 8 July 1586, aged 19, B.A. 5 Nov. 1589, fellow 1590, M.A. 10 July 1593, and m. by license dated 15 Feb. 1598, Mary (an attendant upon the Lady Stafford at Court) dau. of Robert Clerk of Grafton, Northants. He was app. Assistant Remembrancer of the City of London 5 May 1601, succ. Dr. Giles Fletcher as Remembrancer 2 July 1605-9, and was a Master of Requests, Knighted 29 Sept. 1617, and app. Clerk of the Privy Council for life 13 Aug. 1609. "Sir Clement Edmondes not sworn Secretary (of State) as expected." (Locke to Carleton, 31 Aug. 1622.) He was promoted to be Sec. of State, but he prevented from entering upon its duties by his death. He sat for Carnarvon Nov. 1609-11, and Oxford Univ. 1620-2, and died of an apoplexy etc. in St. Martin's in the Field 12 Oct. 1622, aged 58, buried at Preston, Northants. He was "a learned person, was generally skilled in all arts and sciences, and famous as well for military as for politic affairs, and therefore esteemed by all an ornament to his degree and profession," (*Wood.*) 9 Oct. 1604, Warrant to pay to Clemt. Edmondes, solicitor for the city of London, £20, for relieving and conveying out of the realm certain strangers, long detained as captives, and freed at the late recovery of Sluys, in Flanders. On 30 March 1608 he was styled Secretary of the City of London. On 25 Sept. 1610 he was granted the benefit of the recusancy of Sir Edw. Mansfield of Bucks, Augustine Belson of Oxon, and Charles Townley and Dorothy Brookesby of Lincolnshire; and on 4 Oct. the office of Muster Master General for life. He was sent to treat with the States of Holland about the East India trade and Greenland Fishery in Dec. 1614, and in Aug. 1618 was sent down by the Council to survey the drains and outfalls of the Fens. Sir Clement Edmondes and Lord Brooke were Secretaries to the "last Lord Commissioners of the Treasury" before 1618.

1621. May 29.   Sir John Danvers Knight, of Chelsea ("the Regicide,") *vice* Bennett expelled the House. Third and youngest son of Sir John Danvers Knt. of Dauntsey, Wilts, and Danby Castle, Yorks, he was born 1585, matric. from Bras. Coll. Oxford, 10 Jnly 1601, aged 16, and was of Lincoln's Inn 1612. He m. (1) Magdalen youngest dau. of Sir Richard Newport Knt. of High Ercall, Salop, and relict of Richard Herbert M.P. of Montgomery Castle, (see *Williams' Parl. Hist. of Wales,*) (2)

Elizabeth Dauntsey, and (3) Grace Hawes. He was Knighted at
Royston 3 March 1609, M.P. Arundel May 1610 to Feb. 1611,
Montgomery March to June 1614, Oxford Univ 1620-22, April to
August 1625, Jan. to June 1626, 1628-9, March to May 1640,
Newport (Isle of Wight) 1624-5, and Malmesbury Oct. 1640 to
April 1653. Danvers was for some years a Gentleman of the
King's Privy Chamber, but became a Col. in the Parliamentary
Army 1642, was one of the Committee of both Houses at Derby
House in June 1648, and not only sat as a member of the
infamous High Court of Justice which tried and condemned
King Charles I. to death. but was one of those who actually
signed the death warrant in Jan. 1649. He was one of the first
Council of State 14 Feb. 1649 to Feb. 1650, and died at Chelsea 16
April 1659, aged 74. Lord Clarendon called him " a proud
formal, weak man." His disloyal conduct so offended his
brother Henry, Earl of Danby, a most gallant soldier, that at his
death in 1644, he left all his estates to his sister Elizabeth
ancestress of the Dukes of Leeds. He was attainted at the
Restoration.

> 1624.   Jan. 8.   Sir George Calverte.
>
> Sir Isaac Wake.

The former was the son of Leonard Calvert, and was born
at Kipling, Yorks, about 1579, and matric. Trin. Coll. Oxford 28
June 1594, aged 14, B.A. 23 Feb. 1597, a student in municipal
law, created M.A. 30 Aug. 1605. and entered Lincolns Inn 16
Aug. 1598. After leaving Oxford he travelled for a time, and on
his return became Secretary to Sir Robert Cecil when Secretary
of State, and was one of his (Lord Salisbury's) executors June
1612. He was made Clerk of the Crown in the province of Con-
naught and County Clare 10 July 1610, a Clerk of the Council
Jan. 1608, Knighted at Hampton Court 29 Sept. 1617,
and Secretary of State 15 Feb 1619 to April 1625, when he
resigned on becoming a Roman Catholic, but was allowed to sell
his office to Sir Albert Morton for £6000. He was M.P. Bossiney
Oct. 1609-11, Yorkshire 1620-2, and Oxford Univ. 1624-5, granted
a pension of £1000 a year on the Customs 2 May 1620, and was
created Lord Baltimore 16 Feb. 1625. He m. Anne dau. of
George Mynne of Hertingfordbury, Herts, and she died just before
10 Aug. 1622, when Locke informed his friend Carleton of her
death. He received a grant on 3 May 1620 of the increased custom
on silk for 21 years, and on 30 March 1623 " re-grant to Sec. Calvert
of a territory in Northumberland, with alteration and addition of
some particular points, for better encouraging that plantation."
(Cal. State Papers.) His Lordship obtained while Sec. of State
a grant of the province of Avalon in Northumberland with the
most extersive privileges, and expended £25000 in settling it.
Owing to the encroachments of the French he was obliged to

abandon it, whereupon he obtained in 1632 a similar grant of
the province of Maryland in America from Charles I, He died
15 April 1632, and was buried in St. Dunstan in the West. " Sir
Geo. Carew answers the French letters, Levinus Munch those of
the Low Countries, Mr Calvert the Spanish and Italian, and Sir
Thos. Lake the home letters." (Chamberlain to Carleton, 17
June 1612.) On 3 Feb. 1614 Chamberlain informed Carleton that
he " finds no truth that he (Carleton) is to be recalled (from
Paris,) and Calvert to succeed him. Sir Thos. Edmondes has
returned without leave, hoping for provotion in the coming
appointments," and on 12 May that " Calvert is spoken of for
Holland."

Sir Isaac Wake of Hants, 2nd son of Rev. Canon Arthur
Wake of Oxford, rector of Billyng, Northants, matric. Ch. Ch.
Oxford, 25 May 1593, aged 12, B.A. 23 July 1597, fellow of Merton
Coll. 1598, M.A. 22 Feb. 1603, public orator 1604-21, and entered
the Middle Temple 1604. He travelled abroad until 1609, then
was Secretary to Sir Dudley Carleton, (Secretary of State,) being
so in 1613, and was Knighted 9 April 1619, and M.P. Oxford
Univ. 1624-5. He was granted the reversion of the Keepership
of the Hospital of Ewelme, for life 3 July 1607. " Isaac Wake
is to reside at Turin in the place of Albert Morton." (John
Chamberlain to Alice Carleton, 6 April 1615.) He was Agent in
Savoy in Feb. 1618, and went Ambassador to Venice, Savoy etc.
April 1619, and was still there in April 1629, and died in Paris in
the King's service July 1632.

1625.   April 16.   Sir Thomas Edmundes.

Sir John Danvers.

Sir Thomas Edmondes, 5th son of Thomas E. of Fowey,
Cornwall, was born at Plymouth about 1563, his father being
Mayor there 1582.   He enjoyed the patronage of Sir Francis
Walsingham, (see Banbury 1558,) and was English Agent to
Henry 4 at Paris 1592-96, in Oct. 1597, and July 1598 to June
1599. He was then made Sec. to the Queen for the French
tongue 17 May 1596, a Clerk of the Privy Council 1598, M.P.
Liskeard Sept. to Dec. 1601, Wilton 1604-11, Oxford Univ.
1625, and Jan. to March 1626, when voided, Knighted 20 May
1603, Ambassador at Brussels April 1605-9, and at Paris May
1610-16, April 1617, and June to Sept. 1629. 3 May 1604, Grant to
Sir T. E. in reversion after Sir Geo. Coppin, of the office of
Clerk of the Crown in Chancery, (of which office he entered
into possession in 1620.)   He was French Secretary in 1603. "Sir
T. E. thought of as Secretary," (Chamberlain to Carleton 22 Oct.
1612 ;) " likely to be Secretary," (ditto 27 Oct. 1613 ;) " it is
thought he will have the place of Chancellor of the Duchy of
Lancaster," (31 May 1616.)   He m. (1) May 1601 Magdalen who
died at Paris 31 Dec. 1614, dau. and co-heir of Sir John Wood,

Clerk of the Signet, and (2) by license dated 11 Sept. 1626 Sara dau. of Sir James Harrington of Exton, Rutland, and widow of Francis Lord Hastings, and of Edward 11th Lord Zouche. He died 20 Sept. 1639, aged about 76.

1626. Jan. 17. The same.

1626. March 23. Hon. Sir Francis Stuart K.B. *vice* Edmondes, whose election was declared void 17 March 1626. On 19 April 1626 it was ordered that the right of election for the University be referred to the Committee of Privileges. Third son of James 2nd Earl of Moray, he matric. Ch. Ch. Oxford 15 May 1604, aged 15, B.A. 26 Feb. 1606, and was created M.A. 8 July 1616. He was granted a pension of £400 a year 7 March 1617, was Vice Admiral to the Earl of Oxford in Feb. 1622, and on 15 April 1623 was made Admiral (on board the St. George, at 20s. a day,) of the two ships sent to Spain. Grant to Sir F. Stewart of the office of keeping the walks in Cranbourne Chace, etc. Berkshire, for life, 17 Sept. 1616. "Sir Hen. Rich and Sir F. Steward have gone over to Calais to fight a duel, but a messenger is despatched by Council to arrest them. (Edw. Sherburn to Carleton, 26 Oct. 1616.) He was made K.B. 2 June 1610, M.P. Liskeard 1626, and 1628-9, and Oxford Univ. March to June 1626. On 30 May 1625 Sir John Hippisley informed Sec. Conway that "Sir Francis Stuart has made stay of a ship of Dunkirk in the Downs, laden with corn and bullion," and there are several references to this matter in the *Calendar of State Papers* for that year. He seemed to be in command of the English ships in the Straits of Dover and the Channel, and to have been an active seaman. On 14 Aug. 1625 he wrote to Buckingham replying to the complaints of the Western gentlemen of his negligence in searching the coast which had been molested by Turkish pirates from Sallee. "The Earl of Warwick, with Sir Francis Stewart his Vice Admiral arrived on the 19th April 1627 at Plymouth," (Sir James Bagg to Buckingham.) "The Earl of Warwick sailed from that port on 9 May with 5 ships, Sir F. Steward being his Vice Admiral in the "Hector," against the Spaniards." "He was a learned gentleman, was one of Sir Walter Raleigh's club at the Mermaid tavern in Friday street in London, and much venerated by Ben Johnson, who dedicated to him his comedy of 'The Silent Woman.' He was a person also well seen in marine affairs, was a captain of a ship, and, as I have been informed by those who remember him, did bear the office for sometime of a vice, or rear, admiral." *(Wood's Fasti).*

1628. Feb. 20. Sir Henry Marten.

Sir John Danvers.

Sir Henry Marten Knt. of London, the son of Anthony Marten of London, a member of a Berkshire family, was born in

London 1563, educ. at Winchester School, matric. New Coll. Oxford 24 Nov. 1581, aged 19, scholar 1580, fellow 1582, B.C.L. 15 June 1587, and D.C.L. 5 June 1592. He entered Grays Inn 9 Feb. 1581, was adm. an advocate of the College of Doctors of Laws 16 Oct. 1596, and became King's Advocate General 3 March 1609. Official to the Archdeacon of Berks, Chancellor of the diocese of London 1616-27, Judge of the High Court of Admiralty Oct. 1617-41, Dean of the Arches Sept. 1624-34, and Judge of the Prerogative Court of Canterbury Sept. 1624 until his death. Marten was an able speaker in Parliament, and sat for Wilton 1586-7, Wootton Bassett 1604-11, St. Germans 1625, Oxford Univ. 1628 to March 1629, and St. Ives March to May 1640. He was Knighted 21 Dec. 1616, or 16 Jan. 1617, (*D.N.B.*) was of Lincolns Inn 1623, appointed a Commr. for the repair of St. Paul's 10 April 1631, and died "very aged and wealthy" 26 Sept. 1641, aged 81, and was buried at Longworth, Berks. He m (1) Elizabeth (who died 19 June 1618,) dau. of ———, and (2) a second wife who died 1677, and his elder son Henry Marten the Regicide was a leading Member of the Long Parliament.

1640. March 7. Sir Francis Windebanke.

Sir John Danvers.

Sir Francis Windebank Knt. of London, and Hurst, Wilts, son and heir of Sir Thomas W. of St. Martin's in the Fields, matric. St. John's Coll. Oxford (entry dated) 18 May 1599, aged 13, B.A. 26 Jan. 1602, and entered the Middle Temple 1602. He was travelling in France and Germany 1606, was in Paris in Feb. 1606, and in Italy 1607, and returned home Feb. 1608. The *Cal. State Papers* contain many letters referring to him in 1606. "Grant to Francis Windebank 21 Feb. 1605 in reversion, after Levinus Munck and Francis Gale who are also in reversion, of a Clerkship of the Signet." He had entered into possession of this office before Dec. 1624, and as such was made a Commr. with Sir Robert Pye (see Woodstock 1640,) Sir Henry Marten (see 1628,) and many others for the repair of St. Paul's, London, 10 April 1631. He was Knighted 18 June 1632, (his fees to H.M.'s servants amounting to £56 18 8 by account dated 17 June,) sworn one of the two principal Secretaries of State 15 June 1632, and held this important office till 1641, and was also a Lord of the Treasury 1635-6, and a Lord of the Admiralty 20 Nov. 1632, and 16 to 23 March 1636. He was J.P. Wilts, M.P. St. Germans 1625, Oxford Univ. March to May 1640, and Corfe Castle Nov. 1640 till he fled the Kingdom the following month, and died in Paris 1 or 11 Sept. 1646. He was brother in law to Robert Reade of Linkenholt, Hants. His eldest son was made a Baronet in 1645.

1640. Oct. 17. Sir Thomas Roe.

John Selden.

Sir Thomas Roe of Cranford, Middlesex, and co. Gloucester, son and heir of Robert Roe of London, (by Elinor who d.
1629, having re-m. to Richard Berkeley of Stoke and Rendcombe,
(see *Williams' Gloucestershire Members*,) matric. Magd. Coll.
Oxford 6 July 1593, aged 12, (then of Bulwick, Northants,) ent.
the Middle Temple 1597, and m. Eleanor dau. of Sir Thomas
Cave of Stanford, Northants. Roe was Knighted 23 July 1604,
Ambassador to the Great Mogul Nov. 1614-17, (being sent at the
East India Company's expense, as Chamberlain wrote to Carleton
24 Nov. 1614,) and at Constantinople 1621, a Privy Councillor,
M.P. Tamworth March to June 1614, Cirencester 1620-2, Oxford
Univ. Oct. 1640-4, and Chancellor of the Order of the Garter 5
Dec. 1636 until his death 6 Nov. 1644, aged 64. In 1637 he gave
a rent-charge of £25 a year to Cirencester out of lands at Mous-
well, 40s. for a sermon or prayers on the 13th Sept. in every year
for ever, and the rest to apprentice poor children.

The learned lawyer and antiquary John Selden was the
eldest son of John Selden a common fiddler of Salvinton, West
Tarring, Sussex, and was born 16 Dec. 1584, bred at Chichester,
matric. Hart Hall, Oxford 24 Oct. 1600, entered at Clifford Inn
1602, adm. to the Inner Temple May 1604, where he was called
to the bar 14 June 1612, fined for refusing to be Reader 1624, and
chosen a Bencher 3 Nov. 1633. He was M.P. Lancaster
March 1624-5, Ilchester and Great Bedwin Jan. 1626, when
he preferred the latter, till June 1626, Ludgershall 1628-9,
and Oxford Univ. Oct. 1640-53, and was imprisoned by the
King for some months in 1628, and was also on 4 March
1629 (with eight other Members) sent to the Tower, and
he remained a prisoner till May 1631. He was a lay member
of the Assembly of Divines 1643, Master of Trinity Hall Aug.
1645, Keeper of the Rolls and Records in the Tower, 27 Oct.
1643-54, a Commr. of the Admiralty 15 to 28 April 1645, a
member of the Committee appointed by both Houses, a Commr.
of the Admiralty April 1645, and had £5000 voted him for his
" sufferings " Jan. 1646, but being then very wealthy, he refused
to accept, and " kept his conscience." Selden died unmarried 30
Nov. 1654, and was buried 14 Dec. in the Temple Church. He
was long Steward to Henry Grey 9th Earl of Kent, and after the
Earl's death, to the Countess till her death in 1651, and was
author of ' Titles of Honour,' 1614, and the ' History of Tythes,'
1617, and many other learned works. His ' Table Talk,' com-
posed by his Secretary Robert Milward, appeared in 1689.

1653. June. No member was appointed to represent the
University in Barebones' Parliament, and only one Member was
returned 1654, and 1656.

1654. June 27. John Owen D.D. ·

This reverend gentleman was the only clergyman that

ever represented an Oxfordshire constituency. Born 1615, the
son of Rev. Henry Owen of Stradham, Oxon, he was educ. at
Westminster, matric. Queen's College, Oxford 4 Nov. 1631, aged
16, B.A. 11 June 1632, M.A. 27 June 1635, ordained soon after 1635,
Dean of Ch. Ch. Oxford, 18 March 1651 until deprived 15 March
1660, Vice Chancellor of the Univ. 9 Sept. 1652 to Oct. 1658, First
Commr. to execute the office of Chancellor of the Univ. 16 Oct.
1652, M.P. 1654, but was unseated on account of his orders, (his
renunciation of which was invalid,) created D.D. by diploma 23
Dec. 1653. He was sometime rector of Fordham, Essex, and m.
(1) at Fordham, —— (who d. 1676,) and (2) was licensed as a
widower 21 June 1677 (then of St. Andrew Undershaft, London,
to marry Dorothy Doyley of Stepney, widow, of Thomas Doyley
of Chislehampton. He was minister of the Congregational
Chapel in Leadenhall Street, and dying at Ealing 24 Aug. 1683,
aged 67, was buried in Bunhill Fields among the Dissenters.
Dr. Owen was app. preacher to the Council of State 8 March
1650, and preached Henry Ireton's funeral sermon in Westminster Abbey 6 Feb. 1652. The Council of State on 15 Aug.
1659 ordered him to raise a troop of well-affected volunteer horse
for defence of Oxford Univ. and parts adjacent. On 16 April
1672 Robert Harbin, clerk of the Leathersellers' Company,
certified that the freedom of their hall was granted to Dr. Owen
and Mr. John Loder to preach there, if they obtained the King's
license, which was granted; and on 28 March Dr. Owen (who
was one of the leaders of the Nonconformists,) was one of
the Ministers who thanked the King for the Declaration of
Indulgence, as to which he is said to have been consulted the
year before.

1656.   Aug. 22.   Rt. Hon. Nathaniel Fiennes.

As to this Member, see the County 1654.

1659.   Jan.   4.   Matthew Hale.

John Mills.

That most pious upright and learned Judge, Sir Matthew
Hale, was the only son of Robert Hale of Alderley, co.
Gloucester, where he was born 1 Nov. 1609. He matric. Magd.
Hall, Oxford, 20 Oct. 1626, ent. Lincolns Inn 8 Sept. 1628, bar at
law 17 May 1636, invited to the Bench 6 Feb. 1649, " to be called
next Moate," and took his seat two days later. Hale was made
Serjeant at law 23 Jan. 1654, M.P. for Gloucestershire 1654-5, and
April to Nov. 1660, and Oxford Univ. Jan. to April 1659, and was
made a Justice of the Common Bench 25 Jan. 1654, but threw up
his post about Sept. 1658. He took an active part in the
Restoration, and was made Serjeant at law 22 June 1660, a
Commr. to try the Regicides 7 Nov. 1660, Knighted 30 Jan.
1661, and was Lord Chief Baron of the Exchequer 7 Nov. 1660-71,
and Lord Chief Justice of England 18 May 1671 until he

resigned Feb. 1676. Sir Matthew distinguished himself as one of the Counsel for Archbishop Laud Nov. 1643, was placed on the Committee of Law reform 20 Jan. 1652, and on the Committee for Trade 1 Nov. 1655. He m. (1) Anne dau. of Sir Henry Moore 1st Bart. of Fawley, Berks, and (2) after 1664 Anne dau. of Joseph Bishop of Fawley, presented to Alderley 1665, was a great benefactor to Gloucester Abbey Library, and dying 25 Dec. 1676, was buried at Alderley churchyard. (M. I.)

John Mills of Southants, matric. Ch. Ch. Oxford 12 Oct. 1621, aged 17, student from Westminster School, B.A. 6 Feb. 1623, M.A. 13 June 1626, B.C.L. 23 July 1631, created D.C.L. 5 Jan. 1649, a Canon of Ch. Ch. Oxford 1648-51, when deprived, restored 1659-60, when ejected by Charles II, but was Chancellor of Norwich 1661-73. He was adm. an Advocate of Doctor's Commons (as Mylles) 3 July 1650, and was a Parliamentary Commr. to receive the surrender of Oxford 1646, a Parl. Visitor of the Univ. 1647, Judge Advocate of the Parl. Army 1644-51 and 1659-60, and M.P. Oxford Univ. Jan. to April 1659, and April to Dec. 1660. He died in London in or about 1676.

> 1660. April   Thomas Clayton
> John Mills

Thomas Clayton of La Vache, Bucks, was the son of Thomas Clayton M.D. of Oxford, (Master of Pembroke Coll. 1624-47,) and matric. at that College 25 May 1627, aged 15, B.A. 22 Jan. 1629, M.A. 17 Oct. 1631, B. Med. 18 July 1635, and D. Med. 19 June 1639. He was of Grays Inn 1633, Regius Professor of Medicine at Oxford Univ. (fee £40 a year) 1647-65, M.P. April to Dec. 1660, Warden of Merton College 1661-93, and was Knighted 27 March 1661. He m. Bridget dau. of Sir Clement Cotterell Knt. and died 4 Oct. 1693. On 6 May 1658, the Council of State ordered "The Trustees for the Maintenance of Ministers to settle an Augmentation of £80 a year on Dr. Clayton, Professor of Physic at Oxford University," which was approved 3 June 1658. He petitioned the King 9 Sept. 1660, having "hazarded his life and spent much money for the Restoration," for a letter to the Sub-Warden and Fellows of Merton College in favour of his election to the Wardenship, and the King in Feb. 1661 asked the Archbishop of Canterbury to elect him. He was however refused admission to the College, the doors being bolted against him 2 April 1661, and the violent opposition offered by all of the Fellows to Clayton's admission as Warden, gave rise to memorable scenes, and continual disputes afterwards took place between him and them concerning his administration of the College.

> 1661. April 1.   Hon. Lawrence Hyde
> Sir Heneage Finch Knt. and Bart.

The former was the second son of Edward 1st Earl of
Clarendon, the celebrated Lord Chancellor aud historian, and
was born in March 1641, M.A. Oxford by diploma 4 Feb. 1661,
created D.C.L. 7 Oct. 1700, and m. 1665 Lady Harrietta Boyle 5th
dau. of Richard 1st Earl of Burlington.   He became " Honourable " 3 Nov. 1660, entered the Middle Temple 1660, was M.P.
Newport (Cornwall,) at the age of 19, from Aug. to Dec. 1660,
Oxford Univ. 1661-79, Wootton Bassett Feb. 1679 to Jan. 1681, and
was created Viscount Hyde 23 April 1681, and Earl of Rochester
29 Nov. 1682.   He was Master of the Robes to the King 21 May
1662 to July 1675, and "has had in Boons £20000," (*Seasonable
Argument* etc. 1677,) was Extra Gentleman of the Bedchamber to
the King (in 1682 and) till 1685, Ranger to Richmond Park 10
Oct. 1683, a Governor of the Charterhouse 24 June 1685, K.G.
29 June 1685, Dep. Speaker of the House of Lords 4 Aug. 1685,
Postmaster General 13 Aug. 1685-7, Chancellor and Lord Keeper of
the Great Seal to the Queen in 1686, a Commr. for Ecclesiastical
Causes in England and Wales 22 Nov. 1686 to 12 Jan. 1687, a
Commr. of Greenwich Hospital 20 Feb. 1695, a Privy Councillor
19 Nov. 1679 to Dec. 1688, and again 1 March 1692, Ambassador
Extraordinary to John III of Poland 11 June to Oct. 1676, Joint
Ambassador to the Congress of Nimeguen Jan. 1677 to 22 Sept.
1678, Secret Envoy to the Prince of Orange Sept. 1677, Envoy
Extraordinary to the Hague 12 Aug. 1678, Chancellor of the
Exchequer and a Lord of the Treasury 26 March to 21 Nov. 1679,
First Lord of the Treasury 21 Nov. 1679 to 9 Sept. 1684, and Lord
High Treasurer of England 16 Feb. 1685 to 4 Jan. 1687. Lord
Rochester was made K.G. 29 June 1685, Recorder of Salisbury
27 Feb. 1685, Lord President of the Conncil Aug. 1684 to Feb.
1685, and again Sept. 1710 to May 1711, app. Lord Lieut.
of Ireland Oct. 1684, (but did not proceed there then,) and
Dec. 1700 to Feb. 1703, Lord Lieut. of Herts 1686-9, and
of Cornwall 15 Sept. 1710-11, and High Steward of Oxford
Univ. 20 Nov. 1709, until his death 2 May 1711, aged 69.   In Jan.
1687 he was granted a pension of £4000 a year for two lives, and
of forfeited Irish lauds valued at about £2000 a year in addition.
On 30 Oct. 1661, " Pass for Lord Crofts and Lawrence Hyde to go
to France on the King's service."   " He is of a middle stature,
well-shaped, of a brown complexion," (*J. Macky*, 1704.)   " He
was thought the smoothest man in the Court, and speaks not
ungracefully," (*Burnet*,) but " had an assuming manner."

His equally celebrated colleague, Sir Heneage Finch, was
born in Kent 23 Dec. 1621, the eldest son of Sir Heneage Finch
Knt. of Kensington, and was educ. at Westminster, matric. Ch. Ch.
Oxford 18 Feb. 1636, created D.C.L. 7 Nov. 1665, and m. 30 July
1646 Elizabeth eldest dau. of Daniel Harvey M.P. of Folkestone,
a Turkey merchant of London.   He was Assessed by the Committee for Advance of Money at £150 on 10 March 1645, but on

18 April was respited "till his estate comes to him, or till further
order, not having £100, on affadavit." He was called to the bar
at the Inner Temple 30 Jan. 1646, Bencher 29 June 1660,
Treasurer 1661-72, and was Knighted and made a Baronet 7 June
1660, Solicitor General 6 June 1660-70, Attorney General 10 May
1670-4, Councillor to the Queen Consort 1670, M.P. Canterbury
and St. Michaels April 1660, when he preferred the latter till Dec.
1660, Beaumaris and Oxford Univ. 1661 when he preferred to sit
for the latter until created Baron Finch of Daventry 10 Jan. 1674.
He was Keeper of the Great Seal 9 Nov. 1673-5, and Lord
High Chancellor 19 Dec. 1675 till his death. His Lordship
was furthermore created Earl of Nottingham 12 May 1681,
and was Chamberlain of Chester 1673-6, sworn a Privy Councillor of England 9 Nov. 1673, and again 21 April 1679, when
the Council was freshly constituted, a Privy Councillor of
Scotland 18 May 1674, made a Governor of the Charterhouse 17
July 1674, a Lord Commr. of the Admiralty 14 Sept. 1677 to 14
May 1679, and was specially app. Lord High Steward of England
for the trials of Charles Lord Cornwallis 30 June 1676, Philip
Earl of Pembroke 18 March to 4 April 1678, and Wm. Viscount
Stafford 30 Nov. to 7 Dec. 1680. Lord Nottingham died 18 Dec.
1682, aged 61. He was a man well versed in the laws, and an
official of the greatest probity and discretion, besides being a
great orator.

1674. Jan 16.   Thomas Thynne   203
                Sir Christopher Wren   125
                Sir George Croke " very few "
                Thomas Bourchier   20

vice Sir H. Finch made Lord Keeper and a Peer. Of the defeated
Candidates, Sir Christopher Wren Knt. P.R.S., the eminent
architect who rebuilt St. Paul's, was M.P. Plympton 1685-7,
Windsor 1689 and 1690 but unseated each time, Weymouth 1701-2,
Surveyor General of the King's Works 1669-1719, and d. 25 Feb.
1723, aged 91. Sir George Croke Knt. of Waterstock, H.S. 1664,
(whose candidature was hardly known,) d. 1880. Thomas
Bouchier D.C.L. was Regius Professor of Civil Law 1672-1712,
and Principal of St. Alban Hall 1679 till his death at his ancient
seat at Hanborow May 1723, aged 89. John Edisbury also stood
in 1674, "but being soundly jeered and laughed at for an
impudent fellow, desisted." (*Wood.*)

Thomas Thynne of Kemesford in Agro, co. Gloucester,
was the eldest son of Sir Henry Fred Thynne 1st Bart. of Kemps-
ford, co. Gloucester, whom he succ. in the title 6 March 1670,
and matric. Ch. Ch. Oxford 21 April 1657. He m. Lady Frances
Finch dau. of Heneage 2nd Earl of Winchilsea, and was approved
by the King as Dep. Lieut. of Wilts 12 May 1672, sat for Oxford
Univ. Jan. 1674 to Jan. 1679, and for Tamworth in three

Parliaments Feb. 1679 to March 1681, and was created Viscount
Weymouth 11 Dec. 1682. He was sworn a Privy Councillor 18
June 1702, was a Lord of the Board of Trade 1705-6, and died 28
July 1714, aged 74. *Wood* in his *Life and Times* styled him,—" a
gentleman of the Bedchamber to the Duke of York, turned from
his service for baseness and ingratitude—a person now much
against the King's interest in Parliament—a hot head."

1679. Feb. 27. John Edisbury   245
              Hon. Heneage Finch   243
              Dr. John Lamphire   209
              Dr. Thomas Boucher   7

Mr. Finch was the 2nd son of the 1st Earl of Nottingham,
(see 1661,) and was born 1649, educ. at Westminster School,
matric. Ch. Ch. Oxford 18 Nov. 1664, aged 15, created D.C.L. 22
May 1683, and m. Elizabeth dau. and heir of Sir John Bankes of
Aylesford. He was called to the bar at the Inner Temple 23
Nov. 1673, Bencher 28 Oct. 1677, King's Counsel 10 July 1677,
Solicitor General to the Duke of York, Solicitor General to the
King 13 Jan. 1679 to April 1686, leading Counsel for the seven
Bishops 1686, Guildford 1685-7, Oxford Univ. Feb. to July 1679,
1689-98, and Jan. 1701 till created Lord Guernsey 15 March 1703.
His Lordship was sworn a Privy Councillor 20 May 1703, but his
name was erased from the Council 20 May 1706. He was how-
ever re-sworn a P.C. 14 Oct. 1714, and held office as Master of the
Jewel Office 1711-14, and Chancellor of the Duchy of Lancaster
14 Oct. 1714 to 29 Feb. 1716. He was created Earl of Aylesford
26 Oct. 1714, and died 22 July 1719. In appearance he was, " a
tall thin black man." *(J. Macky's Characters)*.

John Edisbury was the son and heir of John E of Pentre-
clawdd, Denbighshire, and was born 1646, matric. Bras. Coll. Oxford 9 Nov. 1661, aged 15, B.A. 1665, M.A. 1668, B.C.L. and D.C.L.
1672, and entered Grays Inn 22 Dec. 1654. He was admitted an
Advocate of the College of Doctors of Laws 5 Nov. 1672, and was
M.P. Oxford Univ. Feb. to July 1679, Chancellor to the Bishop
of Exeter 1692, and a Master in Chancery 15 May 1684 till he
resigned July 1708. " Dr. Edisbury the civilian 'tis said is to goe
Ambassador to Spain and not the Lord Lexington," wrote
Luttrell in his *Diary* 31 Dec. 1691.

1679. Aug. 19. Charles Perrott   224
              Sir Leoline Jenkins Knt. 204
              Dr. William Oldys   104
              Hon. James Lane   45

"The black potman carried it for Perrott,—a thorough
paced soaker." *(Wood.)* Oldys was Admiralty Advocate 17
July 1668 to 17 Sept. 1693 and Lane was the Earl of Lanes-
borough's son.

Sir Leoline Jenkins was the son of Leoline Jenkins of Llanblethian, Glamorgan, and was educ. at Cowbridge School, and matric Jes. Coll. Oxford, 4 June 1641, aged 16, fellow 1660, D.C.L. 12 Feb. 1661, and was Deputy Professor of Civil Law 1662, Assessor to the Chancellor's Court, and Principal of Jes. Coll. 1 March 1661 to April 1673. In 1661 he became Commissary of the Deanery of the peculiar of Bridgnorth, Salop, and Registrar of the Consistory Court of Westminster Abbey, and was made by Archbishop Sheldon his Commissary and Official (and probably his Vicar General) for the diocese of Canterbury. During the Civil War he "bore arms among the academic youth," in the royalist army in Wales. He retired in June 1653 to the continent where he spent three years in travel, in France, Holland, and Germany. He was adm. an Advocate of Doctors Commons 11 Nov. 1664, entered Grays Inn 10 Aug. 1667, became Deputy to Dr. George Sweit in the Court of Arches 1664, and was Knighted 7 Jan. 1670, sworn a P.C. 11 Feb. 1680, Assistant Judge of the High Court of Admiralty 21 March 1665-8, and Judge thereof 1668-73, and Keeper or Master of the Prerogative Court of Canterbury Jan. 1669-85. Sir Leoline who was one of the most capable statesman of the day, was sent upon various diplomatic missions, being a Plenipotentiary to the Congress at Cologne 5 May 1673 to May 1674, and at Nimeguen 20 Dec. 1675 to Feb. 1679, Resident Ambassador to the States General 14 Feb. 1679, sole representative at Nimeguen 20 Feb. to 11 July 1679, Secretary of State 26 April 1680 to 14 April 1684, P.C. 11 Feb. 1680, M.P. Hythe Feb. 1673 to Jan. 1679, and Oxford Univ. Aug. 1679-81, and March 1685 until his death unmarried at Hammersmith 1 Sept. following, aged 62. He became a manager of the Univ. Press 1672, and was a Commr. for the suggested Union with Scotland 1678. He received a bounty of £5000 on quitting office in 1684. He was a munificent benefactor to Jes. Coll. Oxford, in whose chapel he was buried, bequeathing to it the bulk of his property.

His colleague was the third son of James Perrott of Northleigh, Oxon, and was born 1639, subscribed St. John's Coll. Oxford 29 Oct. 1657, B.A. 1661, fellow (till his death,) B.C.L. 10 March 1664, and D.C.L. 23 June 1669. He was adm. an Advocate of Doctors Commons 26 May 1671, and was Clerk to Secretary Williamson in 1670 and Jan. 1672. He sat for Oxford Univ. Aug. 1679-81, and 1685 until his death unmarried in his College at Oxford 10 June 1686, aged 47. (M.I. Fifield). His Will was proved at Oxford 14 July.

1681. Feb. 3. The same, re-el. 17 March 1685.

1685. Nov. 23. George Clarke. — ——

Dr. William Oldish. ———

vice Jenkins deceased. Clarke had a majority of about 80 votes.

(*Wood*). Born in 1660, the only son of Sir Wm. Clarke, of London, (who was Secretary at War during the Commonwealth, and to Charles II, till he died of his wounds received in the sea fight off Harwich 4 June 1666,) he matric. Bras. Coll. Oxford 15 Dec. 1675, aged 15, B.A. 27 June 1679, fellow of All Souls Coll. Nov. 1680 till his death, M.A. 18 April 1683, B.C.L. 28 April 1686, D.C.L. 12 July 1708. Clarke was Judge Advocate General 1684-1705, was app. Sec. of War in Ireland 27 May 1690, and acted as Sec. to General de Ginckel during the Irish campaign. He was app. "Secretary at War to all the Forces both Horse and Foot, during the King's absence from England" 3 March 1692, and discharged the duties of that post for Mr. Blathwayte during the latter's absence abroad with the King until Sept. 1695, and was afterwards Acting Secretary at War until April 1704. He was also Secretary to Prince George of Denmark May 1702 to Oct. 1705, Assistant or Joint Secretary to the Admiralty May 1702 to Oct. 1705, and a Lord of the Admiralty Dec. 1710 to Oct. 1714, and must therefore have been a most industrious official. He was elected M.P. for Oxford Univ. Nov. 1685, but never sat in that Parliament as the House was prorogued until it was dissolved in 1687. Clarke was afterwards M.P. Winchilsea 1702-5, East Looe 1705-8, Launceston 1710-13, and Oxford Univ. Dec. 1717 until his death 22 Oct. 1736, aged 75. He was a virtuoso and a man of taste.

1689. Jan. 7. Hon. Heneage Finch   T
             Sir Thomas Clarges Knt.   T

The latter was of Flemish extraction, and the son of John de Glargés or Clarges of Hainult. *Hearne* says he was an apothecary. In 1654 his sister Anne married General George Monk, afterwards Duke of Albemarle, and in 1658 Richard Cromwell employed Clarges to carry despatches to Monk in Scotland, and the General then gradually communicated to him his intention of restoring the monarchy. Clarges then acted as Monk's correspondent in London, and in Feb. 1660 was made Commissary General of the Musters, and also Clerk of the Hanaper about the same time. On 2 May 1660 he was commissioned by Parliament to carry the message inviting Charles II to return home and ascend the throne, and leaving England three days later, he reached Breda on 8 May, where the King at once Knighted him. He was sworn a member of the Irish Privy Council 1660, and was re-app. to his office of Muster Master General after the Restoration in Dec. 1660, with a fee of 10s. a day and 2s. 6d. for a Clerk, and still held that post in 1667, but not in Jan. 1670. He m. Mary 3rd dau. of George Proctor and sister and co-heir of Edward P. of Nowell Woodhouse, Notts, Clarges was a frequent speaker in the house, and sat for Ross, Sutherland, and Cromarty 1656-8, Banff, Cullen, etc. and Peebles, Selkirk, etc. Jan. to April 1659, Tregony April 1660 till void, Westminster

April to Dec. 1660, Southwark March, 1666-79 Christchurch Feb.
1679-81, and 1685-7, and Oxford Univ. 1689 until his death 4 Oct.
1695. He was adm. to Grays Inn 7 Aug. 1662, and was of Wad.
Coll. Oxford 4 Jan. 1689, D. Med. His son was made a Baronet
1674, but the title expired with the 4th Bart. 1734.

 1690. Feb. 19. The same.

 1695. Oct. 21. Hon. Heneage Finch.   T
       Sir William Trumball Knt. W

 Trumball was "the eminentest of all our civilians, and
was by much the best pleader in those Courts, and was a learned,
a diligent, and a virtuous man." *(Bishop Burnet)*. The son and
heir of William Trumball M.P. of East Hamstead, Berks, he was
born 1638. matric. St. John's Coll. Oxford, 5 April 1655, fellow of
All Souls 1657, B.C.L. 1659, D.C.L. 1667, and entered the Middle
Temple 1657. He m. (1) Katherine dau. of Sir Charles Cotterell,
and (2) Judith dau. of Henry 4th Earl of Stirling. Trumball was
adm. an Advocate of Doctors Commons 28 April 1668, and was
Chancellor of the Diocese of Rochester, Judge Advocate of the
Fleet 1683-4, a Clerk of the Signet Jan. 1683 to Jan. 1716, Clerk
of the Deliveries of the Ordnance Feb. 1684 to May 1685, Knighted
at Whitehall 21 Nov. 1684, Envoy Extraordinary to France May
1685 to Sept. 1686, and Ambassador to the Ottoman Porte 1687 to
April 1690. He was sworn a P.C. 5 May 1695, M.P. East Looe
1685-7, and Oxford Univ. 1695-8, a Lord of the Treasury May
1694 to Nov. 1695, Secretary to the Lords Justices May to Oct.
1695, and Northern Secretary of State May 1695 to Dec. 1697.
He died 14 Dec. 1716, aged 78. In Aug. 1660 he petitioned
Charles II to render effectual a grant made to him by the late
King of the fourth reversion of a Clerkship of the Signet, which
by death of diver clerks he is made capable to enjoy.

 1698. July 23. Sir Christopher Musgrave Bart. T.

       Sir William Glynn Bart.   T.

 Sir Christopher Musgrave of Hartley, Westmoreland, 3rd
son of Sir Philip Musgrave 2nd Bart. of Edenhall, in that county,
was born in 1631 or 1632, matric. Queen's Coll. Oxford 10 July
1651, B.A. same date, and entered Grays Inn 18 Oct. 1654. He
was Captain of the Guards, Knighted in 1671, Mayor of
Carlisle 1672, Gov. of Carlisle *vice* his father, deceased, 1677. He
suffered imprisonment in the Tower and other places for his
loyalty, and was concerned in the rising of 1655, and in Sir
George Booth's rising in 1659. His father was Governor of Carlisle, and Christopher was Lieut. of the garrison in 1661, and on
25 Jan. 1662 a commission was given to Simon Musgrave to be
Lieut. in the Governor's company at Carlisle in the room of
Christopher Musgrave made Captain of a company. His company
was however disbanded Sept. 1667, and on the 19th of that month

he writes from Carlisle to Williamson, "trusting that when an employment offers he will intercede with His Majesty for him, a poor younger brother." As Clerk of the Robes to the Queen (app. 1663) he was on 13 April 1664 " to be allowed immediate livery and £40, and so each year." He had a grant of the office of Searcher at Berwick in June 1668, and received a commission as Captain in the 1st Foot Guards 5 Nov. 1669. On the 1 April 1672 he wrote from Carlisle to Williamson—"Some of our Northern Members, I hear, are Commrs. for Prizes in the North. If I could be crowded in I would act so that the meeting of the Parliament should not frighten me." He was Master of the Robes to the Queen Dowager (Henrietta Maria), and succeeded his brother Richard as 4th Bart. in 1687. He was Governor of Carlisle in 1685, and Captain of an Independent Company forming its garrison till 17 Feb. 1685, when he became Captain of an Independent Company in 'Our Tower of London,' a Commr. to execute the office of Master of the Horse 1679 to July 1681, Lieut. General of the Ordnance July 1681 to July 1687, a Teller of the Exchequer June 1702 to July 1704, and a Commr-for the Union with Scotland Oct. 1702-4. He was M.P. Carlisle 1661-81, 1685-7, and 1689-90, Westmoreland 1690-5, Appleby 1695-8, Oxford Univ. 1698 to Dec. 1700, Oxford Univ. and Westmoreland Jan. 1701, and preferred the latter till Nov. 1701, Totness Dec. 1701-2, and Westmoreland again 1702 until his death of apoplexy in London 29 July 1704. He m. (1) 31 May 1660 Mary (who d. at Carlisle Castle 11 July 1664) dau. and co-heir of Sir Andrew Cogan Bart. of Greenwich, and (2) 1671 Elizabeth dau. of Sir John Franklin of Willesden, Middlesex.

Sir William Glynn of Ambrosden, third but eldest surviving son, succeeded his father Sir William as 2nd Bart. He was born 1663, matric. St. Edmund Hall Oxford 5 Dec. 1679, aged 16, created D.C.L. 26 April 1703, was appointed Dep. Lieut. Oxon 30 May 1689, H.S. 1706, and sat for Oxford Univ. 1698 to Dec. 1700. He m. Mary 2nd dau. and co-heir of Sir Edward Evelyn Bart. of Long Ditton, Surrey, presented to Ambrosden 26 July 1682, 19 June 1685, and Sept. 1721, and to Bicester 1 Aug. 1691, and died 3 Sept. 1721. *Kennett,* whose patron he was, gives him an excellent character. The title expired in 1874 on the death of Sir Stephen 9th Bart, brother-in-law to Mr Gladstone, (see 1847).

1701. Jan 3. Hon. Heneage Finch.   T
        Sir C. Musgrave   T

1701. March 21. William Bromley of Bagington, co.Warwick, *vice* Musgrave who elected to serve for Westmoreland. Eldest son of Sir Wm. Bromley K.B. of Baginton, he was born there 1663, matric. Ch. Ch. Oxford 12 April 1679, aged 15, B.A. 5 July 1681, created D.C.L. 27 Aug. 1702, and entered the Middle Temple 1683. He m. Hon. Elizabeth Stawell, 2nd dau. of Ralph 1st

Lord Stawell.   Bromley was a Commr. of Public Accounts
Feb. 1696 (probably till April 1705), Chairman of the Committee
of Privileges and Elections Oct. 1702 to April 1705, Speaker of
the House of Commons 25 Nov. 1710 to July 1713, (for which he
had been defeated by John Smith by 43 majority in 1705,) and
Northern Secretary of State July 1713 to Sept. 1714.   He
presented to Baginton 27 Sept. 1699, was M.P. Warwickshire
1690-8, and Oxford Univ. March 1701 until his death 13 Feb.
1732, aged 68.

    1701.   Nov. 25.   Hon. Heneage Finch   T

                      William Bromley   T

    1702.   July   17.   The same.

    1703.   Nov. 22.   Sir William Whitelock Knt. of Phillys
Court, Henley, *vice* Finch made a Peer.   This Member was the
2nd son of the celebrated Bulstrode Whitlock, (see Oxford 1654,)
being his eldest son by his 2nd wife, and therefore half-brother
to Sir James Whitlock, (see the County 1654.)   He was born
1636, adm. to the Middle Temple 4 June 1647, called to the bar 6
6 Feb. 1654, (when under age,) Bencher 11 Nov. 1671, Lent Reader
1676, and Treasurer of his Inn 29 Oct. 1680.   He had Phillis Court
from his father, and m. 1671 Mary dau. of Sir Thomas Overbury.
He was Knighted 10 April 1689, made K.C. to William III 1689,
but " turned out" Hilary term 1696, K.C. by Queen Anne 24
June 1702, and George I in 1714, D.L. Oxon by warrant 30 May
1689, M.P. West Looe Jan. to April 1659, and Oxford Univ. 1703,
until his death, being buried at Fawley Nov. 1717, aged 81.
Whitelock was a violent Tory, and greatly attached to old
fashions, even to his shoe-strings.   Speaking on some question
in Parliament, he used the words—" as black as——," " As your
shoe-strings," interrupted a member on the other side.   " Sir,
I remember when there were more shoe-strings and fewer cox-
combs in this assembly," was Whitelock's reply.   His 3rd but
eldest surving son William m. 11 March 1696 Ann dau. and
co-heir of Edward Noel of the Inner Temple, (Sir William
having settled upon his son the manor of Remenham by deed
the day before,) but d. v. p. and was buried at Fawley 27
July 1709.

    1705.   May   9.   Sir W. Whitlock   T

                 W. Bromley.   T

    1708.   May   3.   The same, re-elected 4 Oct. 1710, 25 Aug.
1713, and 24 Jan. 1715.

    1715.   Dec. 4.   George Clarke (see 1685,) *vice* Whitelocke
deceased.

1722. March 22.	W. Bromley	T	337
	George Clarke	T	278
	William King	T	159

Smith's Parliaments gives the poll as, Bromley 278, Clarke 213, and King 142, and says that King had 75 Plumpers, and the others one each 455 voted. Dr King who was Principal of St. Mary Hall 1717-63, and was a staunch Jacobite, petitioned 25 Oct. 1722.

1727. Aug. 18. W. Bromley.

George Clarke.

1732. Feb. 26. Henry Hyde, Viscount Cornbury, *vice* Bromley deceased. Third but eldest surviving son of Henry 5th Earl of Clarendon and Rochester, and grandson of the M.P. 1661, he was born at the Cockpit, Whitehall, 28 Nov. 1710, matric. Ch. Ch. Oxford 21 May 1725, and was created D.C.L. 6 Dec. 1728. He m. Nov. 1737 Frances dau. of George 2nd Earl of Lichfield, was made a Gentleman of the Bedchamber to the Prince of Wales 1738, and sat for Oxford Univ. Feb. 1732 until summoned to the House of Lords as Baron Hyde of Hindon by writ 22 Jan. 1750, and died s.p. at Paris 26 April 1753, being killed by a fall from his horse. He was buried at Westminster Abbey 12 June. He was a great Jacobite, and entertained the Young Pretender.

| 1734. April 26. | George Clarke. | T |
| | Viscount Cornbury. | T |

1737. Feb. 9. William Bromley of Bagginton, (Tory) *vice* Clarke deceased. Born 1701, 2nd but eldest surviving son of the M.P. 1701, he went to Westminster School 1714 matric. Ch. Ch. Oxford 27 Feb. 1717, aged 15, went to Oriel College, and was created D.C.L. 19 May 1732. He m. the dau. of —— Frogmerton. He sat for Warwich 1737-34, when defeated, and Oxford Univ. 9 Feb. 1737 until his death s.p. 12 March following, aged 35. On 13 March 1734 he proposed the famous motion to repeat the Septennial Act.

1737. March 31. Edward Butler, *vice* Bromley deceased. Born 1686, son of Robert Butler of London, he (? entered the Middle Temple 1697,) matric. Magd. Coll. Oxford 13 Oct, 1702, aged 16, demy 1702-10, B.A. 27 May 1706, M.A. 13 May 1709, fellow 1710-22, Bursar 1720, a student of medicine 1722, and D.C.L. 22 June 1722. He m. 9 July 1723 " Mrs. Mary Tate (third dau. of Anthony Tate of Burleigh Park, co. Leicester and sister-in-law to the famous Dr. Sacheverell), a lady of about £500 per annum fortune," who brought him Burleigh Park. Butler was President of Magd. Coll. 29 July 1722-45, Vice Chancellor of Oxford Univ. 4 Oct. 1728 to 6 Oct. 1732, and M.P. March 1737 till his death 29 Oct. 1745.

1741.   May 4.   Viscount Cornbury   T

Edward Butler   T

1745.   Nov. 12.   Peregrine Palmer, *vice* Butler deceased Second son of Nathaniel Palmer, M.P. of Fairfield, Stoke Courcy, Somerset, who d. 1717, by Frances dau. of Sir Wm. Wyndham Bart. M.P. of Orchard Wyndham, Somerset, he succ. his brother Thomas in the estates early in life, and matric. Ball. Coll. Oxford 3 July 1719, aged 16, B.A. 1723, M.A. from All Souls Coll. 1727, and was created D.C.L. 12 April 1749, then of Fairfield, Somerset. He m. the heiress of ·—— Longman, and sat for Oxford Univ. Nov. 1745 until his death 30 Nov. 1762. Being the last survivor of his name and family, he left his estates to his next of kin, Arthur Acland, 2nd son of Sir Hugh Acland Bart. of Columb John, Devon.

1747.   June 27.   Viscount Cornbury

Peregrine Palmer

1750.   Jan. 31.   Sir Roger Newdigate   T   184

——— *Harley*   126

Sir Edward Turner   67

vice Lord Cornbury called to the Upper House. As to Sir E. Turner, see the County 1754. *Smith* gives his poll as 47. Hon. Robert Harley M.A., 2nd son of the 3rd Earl of Oxford, became a bar. at law Lincoln's Inn 21 Nov. 1751, and was Recorder of Tewkesbury 1756 until his death unm. at Bath 5 Jan. 1760, aged 32.

That fine old English gentleman and antiquary Sir Roger Newdigate of Arbury co. Warwick, was the 7th and youngest son of Sir Richard N. 3rd Bart. of Arbury, and was born 30 May 1719 adm. to Westminster School 1732, and while there succ. his brother Sir Edward as 5th Bart. 14 April 1734. He matric. Univ. Coll. Oxford 9 April 1736, created M.A 16 May 1738, and D.C.L. 13 April 1749, and was M.P. Middlesex 1741-7, and Oxford Univ. Jan. 1750-80. He m. (1) 1743 Sophia dau. of Edward Conyers of Copped Hall, Essex, and (2) 1776 Hester dau. of Edward Mundy of Shipley, Derbyshire. Sir Roger was a Steward of the Anniversary meeting of the Independent Electors of Westminster 1746, and became Major of the Warwickshire Militia on its being embodied, July 1759, (and was so in 1769.) He died s.p. 23 Nov. 1806, aged 86, when the title became extinct.

1754.   April 15.   Peregrine Palmer   T

Sir R. Newdigate   T

1761.   March 27.   The same

1762.   Dec. 16.   Sir Walter Wagstaffe Bagot Bart. of Blythfield, co. Stafford, (Tory) *vice* Palmer deceased.   He was born 23 Aug. 1702, (? 1704,) matric. Magd. Coll. Oxford 27 April 1720, "aged 15," and was created D.C.L. by diploma 17 May 1737. He was the only surviving son of Sir Edward Bagot M.P. whom he succ. as 5th Bart. 1712, m. 1724 Lady Barbara Legge eldest dau. of Wm. 1st Earl of Dartmouth, and was M.P. Newcastle under Lyme Nov. 1724-7, Staffordshire 1727-54, and Oxford Univ. Dec. 1762 until his death 20 Jan. 1768. He voted against Walpole, and was made a Trustee of Dr. Radcliffe's library at. Oxford March 1737, and a Governor of the Foundling Hospital Dec. 1739.

1768. Feb. 3. Sir William Dolben Bart. of Finedon, Northants, *vice* Bagot deceased. Only son of Rev. Sir John Dolben, Prebendary of Durham, whom he succ. as 3rd Bart. 20 Nov. 1756, he was educ. at Westminster, matric. Ch. Ch. Oxford 28 May 1744, aged 17, gained a studentship, and was created D.C.L. 7 July 1763. He m. (1) 17 May 1748 Judith dau. and sole heiress of Somerset English, and (2) 14 Oct. 1799 Charlotte dau. of Gilbert Affleck of Dalham Hall, Suffolk, and widow of John Scotchmer. He sat for Oxford Univ. 3 Feb. to 11 March 1768, and again 1780-1806, and for co. Northampton 1768-74. He voted against Wilkes 1769, ("has a son in the army,") was made a Verderer of Rockingham Forest July 1765, and died 20 March 1814, aged 88. The title expired with his only son in 1837.

1768. March 23.   Sir R. Newdigate   T   352
                  Francis Page   T   296
                  Charles Jenkinson   198
                  George Hay   62

Charles Jenkinson became the first Earl of Liverpool, (see the County 1717.) Dr. George Hay who was Dean of the Arches 1768-78, and Knighted 11 Nov. 1773, sat in Parliament for various places 1754 until his death 6 Nov. 1778, and was a well-known politician.

Francis Page of Middle Aston, was the son of Richard Bourne of Ombersley, co. Worcester, by Isabella only niece and heir of Judge Page, and matric. New Coll. Oxford 29 April 1743, aged 16, created M.A. 1 Aug. 1747, and D.C.L. 14 April 1749. He was H.S. Oxon 1752, M.P. Oxford Univ. 1768 until he resigned in 1801, and died unmarried at Middle Aston 24 Nov. 1803. On 1 and 2 Aug. 1740 the estate at Barton of Sir Francis Page Knt. a well-known Judge, was conveyed in trust for Francis Bourne, son of his niece Isabella, on condition of his changing his name to Page. In 1803 the property passed to Francis Page's brother Richard Bourne of Elmsley Castle, co. Worcester, who had previously assumed the name of Charlett.

1774.   Oct. 14   Sir R. Newdigate.
                  Francis Page.

1780. Sept. 11. Francis Page   T
                  Sir W. Dolben   T
   1784. April 1. The same, re-el. 21 June 1790, and re-el.
28 May 1796.

   1801 March 23. Sir William Scott Knt. of Univ. Coll.
Oxford, *vice* Page who accepted the Stewardship of the Chiltern
Hundreds. Born 17 Oct. 1745, the elder son of William Scott of
Heworth, co. Durham, and brother to John 1st Earl of Eldon,
Lord High Chancellor 1807-27, (see *Williams' Herefordshire
Members,*) he matric. Corpus Christi Coll. Oxford 3 March 1761,
aged 15, scholar 1761, B.A. 20 Nov. 1764, fellow of Univ. College,
M.A. 17 June 1767, B.C.L. 30 May 1772, D.C.L. 23 June 1779, and
was Camden Professor of Ancient History 1773-85. He was adm.
an Advocate of Doctors Commons 3 Nov. 1779, adm. to the
Middle Temple 24 June 1762, where he was called to the bar
11 Feb. 1780, Bencher 5 July 1794, Treasurer 1807, and was
Knighted 24 Sept. 1788, Admiralty Advocate 21 May 1782 to May
1788, Judge of the Consistory Court 30 Aug. 1788 to 14 Aug. 1820,
and Vicar General of the Province of Canterbury 24 Sept. 1788—
1821, and Judge of the High Court of Admiralty Oct. 1798 to
Feb. 1828. He m. (1) 7 April 1781 Anna Maria (who d. 4 Sept.
1809) eldest dau. and co-heir of John Bagnall of Earley Court,
Berks, and (2) 10 April 1813 Louisa Catherine, Dowager Marchion-
ess of Sligo, and dau. of Admiral Earl Howe. Sir William was
sworn a P.C and app. a member of the Board of Trade 31 Oct.
1798, elected F.R.S. and F.S.A., Registrar of the Court of
Faculties 1783, Master of the Faculties 3 April 1790, Chancellor
of London, Official Commissary of the cities and dioceses of
Canterbury and London, a Trustee of the British Museum, M.P.
Downton April to July 1784 when unseated, and 1790—1801,
when he resigned his seat in order to stand for Oxford Univ.
which he rep. until he was created Lord Stowell 17 July 1821,
(being returned for the University and Downton 1818, when
he preferred the former.) His Lordship who was seated at
Earlycourt, Berks, died 28 Jan. 1836, aged 90. He held the
highest rank as a civilian, and Admiralty Judge, and left
personalty sworn under £200000, and landed property bringing
in £12000 a year.

   1802. July 5. Sir W. Dolben   T
                   Sir W. Scott   T
   1806. Nov. 6. Sir W. Scott   T   651
                   Charles Abbot   T   404
                   Richard Heber   *T*   275
   Charles Abbot sat for Oxford Univ. 1806 to 3 June 1817,
when he was created Lord Colchester. Born at Abingdon 14
Oct. 1757, the son of Rev. John Abbot D.D. rector of all Saints,

Colchester, he was sent to Westminster School March 1763,
matric. Ch. Ch. Oxford 14 June 1775, aged 17, Vinerian scholar
1781, and fellow 1786-92, B.C.L. 1783, D.C.L. 1793, and was called
to the bar at the Middle Temple 9 May 1783, and joined the
Oxford circuit. He m. Dec. 1796 Elizabeth eldest dau. of Sir
Philip Gibbes. He was Clerk of the Rules in the King's Bench
(£2700 a year) 1794 to May 1801, Deputy Recorder of Oxford
till 1801, Recorder July 1801 till he resigned in Nov. 1806,
M.P. Helston in a Double Return 21 June to 23 Dec. 1790,
when unseated, and again June 1795-1802, and Woodstock 1802-6,
Chief Secretary for Ireland May 1801 to Feb. 1802, Keeper of the
Signet or Privy Seal in Ireland May 1801 to May 1829, P.C. in
Ireland May 1801, and in England 21 May 1801. He was
Speaker in the House of Commons 11 Feb. 1802 till he resigned
in June 1817, (on a pension of £4000 a year for himself, and
£3000 for his immediate successor,) and was then raised to the
Peerage. Lord Colchester was F.R.S. and F.S.A., an Official
Trustee of the British Museum, an extra Trustee 1817, and a
Trustee of the Hunterian Museum, and was seated at Kidbrook,
Sussex. He died 7 May 1829, aged 71. As Speaker in 1805 he
gave the casting vote in favour of Mr. Whitbread's motion
impugning the conduct of Lord Melville as Treasurer of the
Navy. He must not be confused with Charles Abbott, created
Lord Tenterden 1827, who was Recorder of Reading 1812-16,
and Lord Chief Justice of the King's Bench 1818-32.

1807. May 8. Sir W. Scott.
　　　　　　Charles Abbot.
1812. Oct. 7. The same.

1817. June 10. Robert Peel of Drayton Park, co.
Stafford, *vice* Abbot called to the Upper House. This distinguished statesman was the eldest son of Sir Robert Peel 1st
Bart. M.P. of Bury, Lancashire, an eminent cotton-spinner, and
was born 5 Feb. 1788, was at Harrow Jan. 1801 to Dec. 1804,
matric. Ch. Ch. Oxford 21 Oct. 1805, B.A. 1808, M.A. 1814, and
created D.C.L. 18 June 1817. He seconded the Address in the
House 23 Jan. 1810, and was M.P. Cashel April 1809-12, Chippenham 1812-17, when he resigned to stand for Oxford Univ. which
he rep. till Feb. 1829, when he resigned his seat in consequence
of being converted to the principle of Catholic Emancipation.
He succ. his father as 2nd Bart. 3 May 1830, and m. 8 June 1820
Julia youngest dau. of General Sir John Floyd Bart. Peel was
M.P Westbury March 1829-30, and Tamworth 1830 until his death
in 1850, was sworn a P.C. for England and Ireland 13 Aug. 1812,
and held office as Under Sec. of State for War and the Colonies
June 1810-12, Chief Secretary for Ireland Aug. 1812 to Aug. 1818,
Secretary of State for the Home Department Jan. 1822 to April
1827, and Jan. 1828 to Nov. 1830, First Lord of the Treasury and

Chancellor of the Exchequer Dec. 1834 to April 1835, and First Lord of the Treasury Sept. 1841 to July 1846. His action in repealing the Corn Laws led to the breaking up of the Tory Party into the ' Peelites,' and ' Protectionists' or Conservatives. Sir Robert was made an Ecclesiastical Commr. Feb. 1835, an Elder Brother of the Trinity House 1835, and elected Lord Rector of Glasgow Univ. Nov. 1836. He died on 2 July 1850, aged 62, from the effects of being thrown from his horse when riding down Constitution Hill. Owing to the Metropolitan Police Force being established in 1829, when Peel was Home Secretary, the members of the Force have since been familiarly known as ' Bobbies ' or ' Peelers.' Sir Robert Peel was regarded as a most moderate and conscientious statesman, who during many years upheld the highest traditions of his position.

1818.	June 18.	Sir W. Scott	T	
		Robert Peel	T	
1820.	March 8.	The same.		
1821.	Aug. 24.	Richard Heber	T	612
		Sir John Nicholl	*T*	519

The Poll lasted 3 days. The defeated candidate Sir John Nicholl of Merthyr Mawr, Glamorganshire, 2nd son of John Nicholl of Llanmaes, was born 16 March 1759, educ. at Cowbridge School, and Bristol, matric. St. John's Coll. Oxford 27 June 1775, elected to a founder's kin fellowship, B.C.L. 15 June 1780, D.C.L. 6 April 1785, and became a bar. at law of the Middle Temple 3 May 1793. He was adm. an Advocate 3 Nov. 1785, app. a Commr. to inquire into the state of the law of Jersey 1791, was Knighted 31 Oct. 1798, and succ. Sir William Scott (see 1801) as King's Advocate 6 Nov. 1798 to Jan. 1809. Sir John was M.P. Penryn 1802-6, Hastings 1806-7, Great Bedwin and Rye 1807 but preferred the former, for which he sat in 7 Parliaments 1807-32. In Aug. 1821 he vacated his seat for Great Bedwin in order to stand for Oxford Univ., where he was defeated, but was re-elected without opposition for Great Bedwin Feb. 1822, the seat having been kept vacant for him. He was Dean of the Arches and Judge of the Prerogative Court of Canterbury Jan. 1809-34, sworn a Privy Councillor and app. a member of the Board of Trade 6 Feb. 1809, and was Judge of the High Court of Admiralty May 1833-8 and Vicar General to the Archbishop of Canterbury 1834 until his death at Merthyr Mawr 26 Aug. 1838 aged 79. Nicholl m. 8 Sept. 1787 Judy youngest dau. of Peter Birt of Wenvoe Castle, Glamorgan. He was F.R.S. and F.S.A., app. Lt.-Col. Commandant of the St. George's, Bloomsbury Volunteers 3 Aug. 1803, and was made a member of the Judicial Committee of the Privy Council 14 Aug. 1833.

Richard Heber was born 5 Jan. 1773, and was the eldest son of Rev. Reginald Heber, rector of Chelsea, and then of Malpas,

Cheshire, and Hodnet, Salop, and half-brother of Reginald **Heber**
the pious Bishop of Calcutta 1823-6. He matric. Bras. Coll.
Oxford 14 Dec. 1790, aged 16, B.A. 1796, M.A. 1797, created
D.C.L. 19 June 1826, unsucc. cont. Oxford Univ. 1806, but rep. it
Aug. 1821 until he resigned his seat Feb. 1826. He succ. his
father in 1804 as lord of the manors of Wicklewood Ampnors,
Norfolk, of Hodnet and others in Salop, and of West and East
Marton, Stainton, Hartlington, and Buckden in Craven, Yorkshire, and was Lt.-Col. of a regiment of Yeomanry raised in
Craven in 1801, and app. Ensign Salop Volunteers 10 March
1804, Capt. 9 July 1803. He was seated at Marton, and Hodnet,
H.S. Salop 1821, and dying unmarried 4 Oct. 1833, aged 59, was
buried at Hodnet. Heber acquired the reputation of an accomplished scholar in the literary world, and his library consisting of
above 200000 vols. was one of the most extensive and rare
collections in Europe.

1822. Feb. 12. Rt. Hon. R. **Peel**, re-el. after being made
Home Secretary.

1826. Feb. 22. Thomas Grimston Bucknall **Estcourt** of
Estcourt, co. Gloucester, *vice* Heber who accepted the Stewardship of the Chiltern Hundreds. Eldest son of Thomas Estcourt
of Estcourt, he was born 3 Aug. 1775, matric. Corpus Christi
Coll. Oxford 11 April 1793, created M.A. 15 June 1796, and D.C.L.
27 June 1827, ent. Lincolns Inn 9 March 1795, and was called to
the bar 20 June 1820. He was M.P. Devizes Jan. 1805 to Feb.
1826, when he resigned his seat and was elected for Oxford Univ.
which he rep. till 1847, being thus a member of the House for 42
years. He m. 12 May 1800 Eleanor 2nd dau. of James Sutton of
New Park, Wilts. Mr Estcourt was J.P. and D.L. cos. Gloucester
and Wilts, Chairman of the Wilts Quarter Sessions till 1837,
Recorder of Devizes in 1837, and F.S.A. He died at Estcourt 26
July 1853, aged 77.

1826. June 14. Rt. Hon. R. Peel   T

                T. G. Bucknall Estcourt   T

1828. Feb. 4. Rt. Hon. R. Peel, re-el. on being made
Home Secretary.

1829. Feb. 28. Sir R. H. Inglis   T 755
                Rt. Hon. R. Peel   *T* 609

vice Peel who had accepted the Chiltern Hundreds on account of
his adopting Catholic Emancipation. On seeking re-election he
was defeated, but a seat was immediately found for him at
Westbury. The Poll was kept open on this occasion for 3 days.

Sir Robert Harry **Inglis** of Milton Bryant, Beds, only son
of Sir Hugh, whom he succ. as 2nd Bart. 21 Aug. 1820, was born
in London 12 Jan. 1786, educ. at Winchester, matric. Ch. Ch.
Oxford 21 Oct. 1803, aged 17, B.A. 1806, M.A. 1809, created

D.C.L. 7 June 1826, and was called to the bar at Lincolns Inn 8 June 1818. He was Private Secretary to Lord Sidmouth in early life, a Commr. for settling the affairs of the Carnatic 1814-30, Recorder of Devizes, Chairman Beds Quarter Sessions, M.P. Dundalk May 1824-6, Ripon Feb. 1828 to Feb. 1829, when he vacated his seat and ousted Mr Peel from Oxford Univ., which he rep. till Jan. 1854, when he retired from Parliament. Sir Robert Inglis who was called 'the Champion of the Protestant Church,' and was an elegant scholar, was elected F.R.S. 4 March 1813, and F.S.A. 22 Feb. 1816, (Vice Pres. 1846-54,) was app. a Commr. of the Public Records 12 March 1831, a Royal Commr. to build Churches, a Life Governor of King's College, London, Professor of Antiquity in the Royal Academy 1850-5, sworn a Privy Councillor 11 Aug. 1854, and was a Trustee of the British Museum 1834 until his death in London 5 May 1855.

 1830. July 30. T. G. Bucknall Estcourt T
        Sir R. H. Inglis   T

 Both these Members were re-elected without opposition 2 May 1831, 12 Dec. 1832, 8 Jan. 1835, 25 July 1837, and 29 June 1841.

 1847. Aug. 3. Sir R. H. Inglis   P. 1700.
       Rt. Hon. W. E. Gladstone L.C. 997
       Charles Gray Round C. 824

 The Poll was kept open 5 days, when 1851 voted. The Split Votes were, between Inglis and Gladstone 870, Inglis and Round 798, Gladstone and Round 2, while 32 Plumpers were given to Inglis, 125 to Gladstone, and 24 to Round. Mr Round was of Birch Hall, Essex, bar. at law Lincoln's Inn 24 June 1822, Recorder of Colchester, M.P. North Essex 1837-47, and d. 1 Dec. 1867.

 William Eward Gladstone of Hawarden Castle, Flintshire, —the leading man of the age—was born 29 Dec. 1809, the fourth son of Sir John Gladstone 1st Bart., an eminent Liverpool merchant, educ. at Eton, matric. Ch. Ch. Oxford 23 Jan. 1828, student 1829-39, B.A. double first class 1832, M.A. 1834, Hon. Student 1867-98, created D.C.L. 5 July 1848, Hon. fellow All Souls 1858, and became a student of Lincolns Inn 25 Jan. 1833, but did not proceed to the bar. He m. 25 July 1839 Catherine eldest dau. of Sir Stephen Richard Glynne 8th Bart. M.P. of Hawarden Castle, and heir of her brother Sir Stephen the last Bart. Mr. Gladstone was M.P. for Newark (as a Tory) 1832 to Dec. 1845, when he became converted to Free Trade, and vacated his seat, and sat for Oxford Univ. 1847-65, when he was defeated. He also unsucc. cont. Manchester 1837, and South West Lancashire 1868, but was M.P. for South Lancashire 1865-8, Greenwich 1868-80, Leeds and Midlothian 1880, when he made his election to represent the latter, for which he sat until 1895, when he quitted Parliamentary life, owing to failing eye sight. He was sworn a Privy Councillor 3 Sept. 1841, and held in succession the offices of a Lord of the Treasury Dec. 1834 to March 1835, Under Sec. of State for War and the Colonies March to April 1835, Master of the Mint Sept. 1841 to Feb. 1845, Vice Pres. of the Board of Trade Sept. 1841-3, President of that Board May 1843 to Feb. 1845, Secretary of State for War and the Colonies Dec. 1845 to July 1846, Chancellor and Under Treasurer of the Exchequer and a Lord of the Treasury Dec. 1852 to Feb. 1855, June 1859 to June 1866, Aug. 1873 to Feb. 1874, and April 1880 to Dec. 1882, Special Lord High Commissioner to the Ionian Islands Nov. 1858 to Feb. 1859, First Lord of the Treasury and Prime Minister Dec. 1868 to Feb. 1874, April 1880 to June 1885, Feb. to July 1886, and for the fourth time Aug. 1892 to March 1894, being also Lord Privy Seal Feb. to July 1886, and Aug. 1892 to March 1894. Mr. Gladstone was Lord Rector of Edinburgh Univ. 1859-65, and of Glasgow Univ. 1877-80, elected an Elder Brother of the Trinity House 1861, Professor of ancient history at the Royal Academy March 1876, presented with the freedom of the City of Dublin 1877, of Aberdeen 1871, and of the Turners' Company of London 1876, D.L. Flintshire, a member of the Institute of France 1865, a Governor of the Charterhouse, and a Life Governor of King's College, London. Mr. Gladstone, who declined an Earldom in June 1885, died 19 May 1898, and was accorded a state funeral in Westminster Abbey 30 May. For a great number of years he held an unique position among the politicians of this country, and while his wonderful genius, his stores of learning, and his brilliant oratory attracted the attention of the world, the unequalled power which he possessed in a surprising degree of winning the hearts of the humblest of his followers, made the name of ' Gladstone ' a household word in the land.

1852.   July 15.   Sir R. H. Inglis   C   1369

                Rt. Hon. W. E. Gladstone   L.C.   1108

                R. Bullock Marsham   C   758.

Robert Bullock Marsham D.C.L. bar. at law Lincolns Inn 1813, was Warden of Merton College 1826 until his death 27 Dec. 1880, aged 94.

1853.   Jan. 20,   Rt. Hon. W. E. Gladstone   L.C.   1034

                Dudley Perceval   C   885

Dudley Montagu Perceval, 4th son of Spencer Perceval the Prime Minister who was shot 1812, was Deputy Teller of the Exchequer 1828-34, and died 2 Sept. 1856.

1854.   Feb. 7.   Sir William Heathcote Bast. of Hursley Park, Winchester, *vice* Inglis who accepted the Stewardship of the Manor of Northstead. Born at Worting, Hants, 17 May 1801, the only son of Rev. Prebendary William Heathcote of that place, he was educ. at Winchester, matric Oriel Coll. Oxford 30 Oct. 1817, (where John Keble was his tutor), B.A. 1821, fellow of All Souls 1822-5, B.C.L. 1824, created D.C.L. 28 May 1830, Hon. Fellow 1858, and became a student of the Inner Temple 1822. He succ. his uncle Sir Thomas as 5th Bart. 22 Feb. 1822, and m. (1) 8 Nov. 1825 Hon. Caroline Frances Perceval (who d. 3 March 1835) youngest dau. of Charles 1st Lord Arden, and (2) 18 May 1841 Selina dau. of Evelyn John Shirley of Ettington Park, co. Warwick. He was M.P. for Hants 1826-31, North Hants 1837 to March 1849 when he accepted the Chiltern Hundreds, and Oxford Univ. Feb. 1854-68. He was for many years Chairman of the Hants Quarter Sessions, was sworn a Privy Councillor 9 Aug. 1870, and died at Hursley Park 17 Aug. 1871, aged 80. "A fine old English Gentleman of the best and worthiest type."

1857. March 27. Rt. Hon. W. E. Gladstone   L C
                  Sir W. Heathcote   C

1859. Feb. 12. Rt. Hon. W. E. Gladstone, re-el. after being made Special Lord High Commissioner to the Ionian Islands.

1859. April 29. Rt. Hon. W. E. Gladstone   L
                  Sir W. Heathcope   C

1859. July 1. Rt. Hon. W. E. Gladstone   L   1050
                Marquis of Chandos   C   859

vice Gladstone, made Chancellor of the Exchequer. Lord Chandos succ. his father as 3rd and last Duke of Buckingham and Chandos 1861, and was Lord President of the Council 1866-7, Secretary for the Colonies 1867-8, Governor of Madras 1875-80, and Chairman of Committees in the House of Lords 1886 until his death 1889, when the Dukedom became extinct.

1865. July 18. Sir W. Heathcote   C   3236
                 Gathorne Hardy   C   1904
                 Rt. Hon. W. E. Gladstone L   1724

Gathorne Hardy of Hemsted Park, Staplehurst, Kent, third and youngest son of John Hardy of Dunstall Hall, Staffordshire, Recorder of Leeds, and a Bencher of the Inner Temple, who was one of the first members for Bradford 1832-7, and 1841-7, by Isabel dau. of Richard Gathorne of Kirkby Lonsdale, Westmoreland, was born at Bradford 1 Oct. 1814, educ. at Shrewsbury School, and matric. Oriel College, Oxford, 22 Nov. 1832, B.A. Nov. 1836, M.A. 1861, and was created D.C.L. 13 June 1861. Having entered the Inner Temple 16 Nov. 1831, he was called to the bar 1 May 1840, and elected a Bencher of his Inn 28 April 1868. On 29 March 1838 he married Jane (C. I.) dau. of

James Orr of Hollywood House, county Down. Having unsuccessfully contested Bradford, 1847, Mr. Gathorne Hardy sat for Leominster Feb. 1856-65, and his return for Oxford University in that year, when he ousted Mr. Gladstone from his seat, was one of the sensational events of that general election. Accepting office under Lord Derby he was Under Secretary for the Home Department March 1858 to June 1859, sworn a Privy Councillor 6 July 1866, and was President of the Poor Law Board July 1866-7, Home Secretary May 1867 to Dec. 1868, Secretary of State for War Feb. 1874-8, and for India April 1878 to April 1880. He quitted his seat for the University on being raised to the House of Lords as Viscount Cranbrook 4 May 1878, and was furthermore created Earl of Cranbrook in August 1892. His Lordship again held office as Lord President of the Council June 1885 to Feb. 1886, and July 1886 to July 1892, being also Chancellor of the Duchy of Lancaster 3 to 16 Aug. 1886. Lord Cranbrook, who assumed the prefix surname and arms of Gathorne by Royal License 11 May 1878, is a J.P. and D.L. for Kent and the West Riding of Yorkshire, and patron of two livings. He was Chairman of the West Kent Quarter Sessions till he resigned Oct. 1867, and was created G. C. S. I. 20 April 1880, and Hon. L.L.D. of Cambridge University. His eldest brother, Sir John Hardy M.P. was created Baronet in 1876.

1866. July 12. Rt. Hon. Gathorne Hardy, re-elected on appointment as President of the Poor Law Board.

1867. May 20. The same, re-elected after being made Home Secretary.

1868. Nov. 18. Rt. Hon. Gathorne Hardy   C

Rt. Hon. J. R. Mowbray   C

John Robert Mowbray of Warenne's Wood, Mortimer, Reading, only son of Robert Stribling Cornish of Exeter, architect, was born at Exeter 3 June 1815, educ. at Westminster, matric. Ch. Ch. Oxford 23 May 1833, student 1834-47, B.A. 1837, M.A. 1839, created D.C.L. 30 Nov. 1869, Hon. student 1876, and Hon. Fellow of Hertford College 1875. He was admitted to the Inner Temple 25 Oct. 1834, called to the bar 19 Nov. 1841, and joined the Western circuit, He assumed the name of Mowbray in lieu of Cornish by Royal License 26 July 1847, and m. 19 Aug. following Elizabeth Gray only child of George Isaac Mowbray of Bishopwearmouth, Durham, and Mortimer, Berks. Entering Parliament for Durham in June 1853, Mr. Mowbray sat for that City until 1868, when he was returned for Oxford University, and represented that constituency until his death. He was sworn a Member of the Privy Council 6 April 1858, and held office as Judge Advocate General March 1858 to June 1859, and again July 1866 to Dec. 1868, and was Second Church Estates Commissioner Aug. 1866 to Feb. 1869, and Third Church Estates

Commissioner April 1871 to Nov. 1892. He was created a Baronet 3 May 1880, elected a member of the Council of King's College, London, 1877, a County Councillor for Berks 1889, and app. a D.L. for Devon. Sir John Mowbray was the " Father of the House of Commons " from 16 Jan. 1898 until his death on 22 April 1899, aged 83.

     1874. Jan. 31. The same.

     1874. March 14. Rt. Hon. Gathorne Hardy, re-elected on being app. Secretary of State for War.

     1878. May   17.   John Gilbert Talbot   C   2687

                 Professor H. J. S. Smith   L   989

vice Rt. Hon. Gathorne Hardy, called to the Upper House.

     John Gilbert Talbot of Falconhurst, Kent, elder son of Hon. John Chetwynd Talbot Q.C., M.P., Attorney General to the Prince of Wales, was born 24 Feb. 1835, educ. at the Charter-house. matric. Ch. Ch. Oxford 18 May 1853, B.A. 1858, M.A. 1860, and was created D.C.L. 26 June 1878. He m. 19 July 1860 Hon. Meriel Sarah Lyttleton eldest dau. of George 4th Lord Lyttleton. Mr. Talbot is J.P. for Kent, Sussex, Middlesex, and London, D.L. Kent, Chairman of the West Kent Quarter Sessions from 1867, and County Councillor for the Sevenoaks Division since 1889. He unsuccessfully contested Kidderminster May 1862, and Malmesbury 1865, but was M.P. for West Kent 1868 to May 1878, when he vacated his seat in order to stand for Oxford University, which he has since represented. He held office as Secretary to the Board of Trade April 1878 to April 1880, was appointed an Eccleslastical Commissioner, and was sworn a Privy Councillor 7 July 1897.

     1880. April   1.   Rt. Hon. J. R. Mowbray   C

                 J. G. Talbot   C

     1885. Nov. 24.   Rt. Hon. Sir J. R. Mowbray Bart.

                 John Gilbert Talbot.

     1886. July   2.   The same, re-elected July 1892, and 13 July 1895.

     1899. May 11. Sir W. R. Anson Bart.   L.U.

vice Mowbray deceased. Sir William Reynell Anson of All Souls' College, Oxford, is the eldest son of Sir John William Hamilton Anson 2nd Bart. of Birch Hall, Lancashire, and Warbleton, Sussex, whom he succeeded in the title 2 Aug. 1873. Born 14 Nov. 1843, he matric. from Balliol College, Oxford, 5 May 1862, B.A. 1866, Fellow of All Souls' College 1867, M.A. 1869, Moderator 1870, Vinerian Law Reader 1874-81, Public Examiner in Jurisprudence 1876-8 and 1882, B.C.L. by degree 3 June 1875, D.C.L. 1881, and has been Warden of All Souls' since 1881. Sir William entered the Inner Temple 2 Nov. 1866,

MEMBERS FOR OXFORD UNIVERSITY. 173

was called to the bar 17 Nov. 1869, and is author of *Principles of the Law of Contract*, and *Law and Custom of the Constitution*. He is J.P. for Oxon, Chairman of the Quarter Sessions from 1894, unsuccessfully contested West Staffordshire 1880, and was Vice Chancellor of Oxford University from 1898 until he resigned in order to enter Parliament for the University in May 1899.

The University of Oxford had 2522 electors on its register in 1832, 4214 in 1868, 5382 in 1884, and 6154 in 1895. The Vice Chancellor is the Returning Officer.

BURFORD.

1306. Thomas de Lincoln.

Commission of oyer and terminer issued to Justices 5 April 1284, on complaint by Humphrey de Bohun, Earl of Hereford and Essex, that, while he was under the King's protection and in his service in Wales, his men were assaulted and imprisoned at Norwich, and his goods carried away by Thomas de Linc' and others.

This is the only instance recorded of a member being returned for the Borough of Burford, and it is presumed, that like other small Boroughs, the privilege was afterwards withheld from it in compliance with the expressed wishes of its principal inhabitants, who in those days considered the wages of two shillings a day paid to their representatives in Parliament as a great burden. For similar reasons the other Oxfordshire Boroughs of Chipping Norton, Dadington, Witney, and Woodstock, were also disfranchised, and only in the case of Woodstock was the privilege ever afterwards renewed.

CHIPPING NORTON.

1300. March. John Mayheu.
Robert le Hurre.

Browne Willis gives these names, which do not appear in the *Official Returns* at this date.

1302. John Maheu.
Robert de la Hurne.

The *Patent Rolls* contain references to John and William de la Hirne in 1298, and to Robert Maheu "sometime King's approver at Warrewyk" on 16 Oct. 1301. On 26 April 1285 Gilbert de Bohun staying in England had letters nominating John Mahun and Nicholas de Tykehull his attorneys in Ireland for one year.

    1305. Richard Aleyn.

          William Aleyn.

DADINGTON.

    1302. Robert de Elseffeld.

          Henry Durnal.

The former was of kin to the Member for the County 1295.

    1305. John Tankrevy.

          William Gyllot.

There are two references to John Giliot or Gylot of Yorkshire in the *Patent Rolls* 1283 and 1285. William Gillot of Rothewell was one of the merchants appointed 30 July 1297 to purchase specified quantities of wool in Northants and Rutland. License 28 July 1312 for the alienation in mortmain to the Abbot and Convent of St. Albans by William Gilot and Cicely his wife of two messuages and 1½ acre of land in the town of St. Albans.

WITNEY.

    1305. John de Hustone.

          Walter Raulyn.

    1306. Walter Raulyn.

    1311. No Return made.

    1314. Walter de Foresta.

          Henry le Plower.

    1315. John de Stanlake.

          John Savage.

William and Thomas de Stanlake were bakers in Oxford on 2 March 1328, when the *Patent Rolls* mentions them in a riot in Abingdon Abbey.

    1330. Thomas de Munstre.

          John de Welewe.

THE BOROUGH OF BANBURY.

Previous to the year 1832 the Boroughs of Banbury, Abingdon, Bewdley, Higham Ferrers, and Monmouth, were the only English Boroughs that returned but one Member each. " By the labor and dilygent sewte " of Thomas Denton, and others, Banbury was granted the privilege of returning a Burgess to Westminster, by Queen Mary's Charter to the town dated 26 Jan. 1554, and Mr Denton was in gratitude chosen its first representative. Several of its Members, of the families of Cope and Fiennes also sat for the County. The Norths afterwards supplied seven Members, including Lord North the Prime Minister, and his two sons. Sir Francis Walsingham, Secretary of State to Queen Elizabeth, was one of the earliest Members for Banbury, and among the Defeated Candidates, the most famous were Sir John Hawles, Solicitor General, and Edward Miall the advocate of Disestablishment.

MEMBERS FOR BANBURY.

1554. March. Thomas Denton.

The first Member for Banbury also sat for the County 1558.

1554. Oct. ———— Denton.

1555. Sept. Return lost.

Although the Returns for the two last Parliaments have been lost, yet *Beesley's History of Banbury* gives Thomas Denton as the Member in the second and third Parliaments called by Mary, and therefore it seems probable that Thomas Denton also sat for Banbury Oct. 1554 to Jan. 1555, and Sept. to Dec. 1555.

1558. Jan. John Denton.

John Denton of Appleton Berks, and Ambroseden, Oxon, was the only brother of the first Member, and the younger son of Thomas Denton of Sunderfield, Bucks. On 25 Oct. 1542 the patronage of the Church of Ambrosden and the manors of Ambrosden and Blackthorn were granted by the King to John

Denton then resident at Blackthorn, who presented to Ambrosden 20 July 1547. He was High Sheriff of Oxon and Berks 1557, and m. (1) Margaret dau. of Sir John Brome of Halton, Oxon, and (2) Theodora 2nd dau. of John Blundel of London, mercer. After Denton's death, she re-m. 17 Eliz. (or before) to Justiman Champney.

1559. Jan.   Francis Walsingham.

The name is supplied by *Browne Willis*, and *Beesley* also give Francis Walsingham as the Member at this date, stating he was then aged 22.

1562. Dec. 26. Francis Walsingham, one of the most trustworthy and useful of Queen Elizabeth's Statesmen, was the third and younger son of William Walsingham of Scadbury, Chislehurst, Kent, where he was born in 1536. Having been educated at King's College, Cambridge, he spent some time in travelling abroad, where he acquired various languages, which proved of great service to him in his future career. He then became Agent to William Cecil, Lord Burleigh, then Secretary of State and afterwards Lord Treasurer, who discovered his abilities and sent him as Ambassador to France. Walsingham again proceeded to France in Aug. 1570 as Ambassador to treat of a marriage between Queen Elizabeth and the Duke of Alencon, and although this was not brought about, he remained there dealing with other matters until April 1573. After his return home he was made a Privy Councillor, and appointed Secretary of State 1574, which office he discharged with the greatest diligence until 1586. He was also Chancellor of the Order of the Garter 22 April 1578 till he resigned in or before April 1588, one of the three keepers of the Great Seal 15 to 29 April 1587, and Chancellor of the Duchy of Lancaster 15 June 1577 until his death. He was Ambassador to the Netherlands in 1578, and again to France July to Dec. 1581, was sent on an Embassy to King James of Scotland in 1583, and was a Commissioner to Mary Queen of Scots Oct. 1586. Walsingham had the honour of entertaining Queen Elizabeth at his house at Barn Elms. He was Recorder of Colchester, Knighted at Windsor Nov. 1577, M.P. Banbury 1559, Banbury and Lyme Regis 1562, but preferred the latter till 1567, Surrey (about) 1573-83, 1584-5, 1586-7, and 1588-9. "17 August 1585, an abstract of the articles passed from the Queen's Majesty to Sir F Walsyngham for the farming of all the Customs subsidy and other duties for all manner of goods within the ports of Plymouth, Exeter, Poole, Bristol, Bridgewater, Gloucester, and other places." Walsingham married Anne elder dau. of Sir George Barne, Lord Mayor of London 1552, and widow of Alexander Carlyell. On 1 July 1580 Sir Francis Knollys (see the County 1562,) wrote to Walsingham, to condole with him on the death of his daughter. He died in Seething Lane, London, 6 April 1590, and, so far from having amassed a fortune, he spent his patrimony in the service of his country, and was buried at night at the expense of his friends, who feared that his body might be arrested for debt. "He was buried the next day in St. Paul's Church, near the body of Philip Sidney his son in law. He died greatly in debt." *(Cal. State Papers.)* The statement in the *Dictionary of National Biography* that he was Knight of the Garter, is incorrect. His only surviving daughter married three husbands, the celebrated Sir Philip Sidney, the Earl of Essex, and the Earl of Clanricarde, in succession.

1563. (about Feb.) Owen Brereton, *vice* Walsingham, who made his election to sit for Lyme. Owen Brereton was adm. to Grays Inn 1523. (Quaere son of John B. of Burras, Salop, by Anne sister of Sir Jevan Lloyd of Yale.)

1571. April. Anthony Cope.

As to this Member, see the County 1614.

1572. April 14. The same.

1584. Nov. 29. Richard Fenys.

As to Mr. Fiennes, see the County 1586.

1586. Oct. 18. Anthony Cope.

He was re-elected 4 Oct. 1588, and as Sir A. Cope Knt., Jan. 1593, 16 Sept. 1597, and 3 Oct. 1601.

1604. March 1. Sir William Cope Knt.

He also will be found as Member for the County 1624. He was re-el. for Banbury March 1614, and as Sir W. Cope Knt. and Bart. 22 Dec. 1620.

1624. Jan. 24. Sir Erasmus Driedon Bart.

Seated at Canons Ashby, Northants, this Member was the second son of John Dryden, by Elizabeth dau. of Sir John Cope Knt. of Canons Ashby. He matriculated from Magdalen Coll. Oxford, (entry under date) 1571, aged 18, demy 1571-5, fellow 1575-80, B.A. 11 June 1577, of the Middle Temple 1577, and m. Frances 2nd dau. and co-heir of William Wilkes of Hodnel, co. Warwick. He was H.S. Northants 1599 and 1618, created a Baronet 16 Nov. 1619, M.P. for Banbury 1624-5, and died 22 May 1632. In Feb. 1605 he prays the King to be released from prison, as the Northamptonshire petition was only a testimonial of the godliness of the preachers in the county. In Feb. 1627 Sir Erasmus Dryden, Sir Edmond Hampden, Sir Wm. Wilmer, Sir John Pickering, and John Hampden, prisoners in the Gatehouse in Westminster for 17 days, "being much afflicted with the sense of His Majesty's heavy displeasure, and much prejudiced both in their health and estates by this restraint," petitioned the Council to mediate with the King "to vouchsafe them his wonted favour, and to free them from their imprisonment."

1625. April 30. Sir W. Cope Knt. and Bart.

On petition this election was declared void.

1625. July 19. Hon. James Fenys, *vice* Cope unseated.
Mr. Fiennes will be found under the County 1626.

1626. Jan.   Calcott Chambre.

This Member was seated at Williamscott, Oxon, and was
the son of George C. of Petton, Salop, by Judith dau. and heir of
Walter Caldecott or Calcot of Williamscott.   Born in 1581, he
matric. Bras. Coll. Oxford 13 Nov. 1590, aged 19, and sat for
Banbury Jan. to June 1626.   By the Charter granted to Banbury
28 June 1608, he was appointed an " Assistant " of the Corporation for life.   He was also of Denbigh and Carnowe, Wicklow,
and died 29 Oct. 1635, and was buried at Carnowe.   His younger
dau. Mary m. 1632 Edward 2nd Earl of Meath, who was drowned
in the passage to England 1675.   His son Calcot Chambre may
have been the personage referred to in the following curious
proceedings :—" Calcott Chambers, New Soaphouse, Foxhall,
Surrey, 9 Oct. 1648. Depositions to the effect that there was
treasure hid in his house, for which he had been offered £25000;
that it had been a coining place, where money had been coined
for the King, and that the Queen had come to mass there
weekly, and taken the accounts of the coiners, but that those
who had been employed therein, or were likely to discover the
treasure, being 12 persons, had been poisoned.   Oct. 17, Chambers
petitions the Committee for Advance of Money. Overtures were
made me by Thomas Wells to discover treasure hidden in my
house 14 years ago, and I was at first over-credulous, but finding
their vanity and falsehood, I refused to neglect my employment
and follow his fancies.   Thereupon he and others framed accusa-
tions against me and my wife, pretending out of zeal to the
State, to discover treasure belonging to Papists hid in my house,
whereas he had long sought, by advice oft astrologers and
magicians, to find the fancied treasure, and thereupon he
accused me and my wife before Speaker Lenthall.   We attended
Lenthall on summons, and the falseness of the accusation was so
apparent that we were released and also Mrs Sherwin, committed
on the same matter.   But though, by the Speaker's order, a
thorough search was made in and about the house for days
together, and nothing found, yet a fresh order had been procured
(dated 6 Oct.) to dig in my house, which interferes in my
employment of soap-boiling, and I and my family are disquieted
and plundered It is most improbable that money should be hid
in my house 14 years ago, before any rumour of war, therefore I
beg to know-- 1st.   Who is to repair my house after the digging ?
2nd.   What is to be the limit of the time allowed for digging in
my house, that I may not always be subject to be insulted over

by malicious people? 20 Oct. 1648, The officers to proceed no further, and the informers to make good all damage done in the search."

1628. March 10. John Crew.

John Crew of Steane, Northants, son and heir of Sir Thomas Crew, Serjeant at Law, and Speaker of the House of Commons, was born in 1598, matric. Magd. Coll. Oxford 26 April 1616, aged 18, B.A. 18 Jan. 1617, ent. Grays Inn 30 Jan. 1615, and was called to the bar 1624. He was app. a Commr. to levy the first two subsidies in Cheshire 1 Feb. 1640. He m. about 1623 Jemima dau. and co-heir of Edward Waldegrave of Lawford, Essex. He was Recorder of Banbury in 1634, sat for Agmondesham 1624-5, and 1625, Banbury 1628 to March 1629, Brackley Jan. to June 1626, and Oct. 1640 till secluded Dec. 1648, and Northants March to May 1640, 1654-5, and April to Dec. 1660. Although made Chairman of the Committee of Religion by Parliament in 1640, a member of the Derby House Committee of both Houses 3 Jan. 1648, and one of "Cromwell's House of Lords" as Lord Crewe 10 Dec. 1657, he was Knighted by Charles II in 1660, and created Baron Crewe 20 April 1661. His Lordship died 12 Dec. 1679, aged 81. He was imprisoned by Cromwell 6 to 29 Dec.1648 for opposing the trial of the King, and was a member of the Council of State 23 Feb. to May 1660.

1640. March 9. Hon. Nathaniel Feines.

1640. Oct. 21. Hon. Nathaniel Fiennes.

As to Mr Fiennes, see the County 1654. It is a matter of note that so many of the Members should also represent the County.

1653. June ⎫
1654. Aug. ⎬ No Members summoned from Banbury.
1656. Aug. ⎭

1659. Jan. 3. Hon. Nathaniel Fiennes.

1660. April. Sir Anthony Cope Bart.

See the County 1661.

1661. April 1. John Holman.

This Member, who was described as of Banbury, and Weston Flavell, was the 2nd son of Philip Holman who had been a scrivener in London, but in 1629 bought the estates of the Chetwodes at Warkworth and Grimsbury. He sat for Banbury in the four Parliaments 1661 to 1681, was made a Baronet 1 June, 1663, and m. Jane dau. of Samuel Forbes of Kew, but died s.p.m. in 1704, when the title became extinct. His dau. and heiress Mary became the third wife of Sir William Portman, 3rd Bart, K.B.

1679. Feb. 17. ⎫ Sir John Holman Bart.
1679. Aug. 19. ⎭

1681. Feb. 5.   Sir John Holman.   ———

Thomas Wise.   ———

Mr. Wise petitioned 25 March 1681, but the Parliament was dissolved three days afterwards.

1685. March 9. Hon. Sir Dudley North Knt.   T.

Sir Dudley, who was seated at Glenham Parva, Suffolk, was the third son of Dudley 4th Lord North, and was born in London 16 May 1641. When a child he was stolen by a beggar in London, but was after some time recovered, and restored to his parents. He was bound as an apprentice to a Turkey merchant, and was afterwards removed to Constantinople, where he became entrusted with the chief management of the English Factory there, as Treasurer to the Levant Company, and made a large fortune. On his return home he became well-known as one of the leading London merchants, and in Parliament he became manager of all the affairs of Government which related to the Revenue. He was Sheriff of London June 1682, Alderman of Farringdon Without Ward 14 Dec. 1682 till he res. Sept. 1689, and unsuccessfully contested that city 1681, Knighted 11 Feb. 1683, was a Commissioner of the Treasury 26 July 1684 to 16 Feb. 1685, and of the Customs (£1200 a year) 7 March to 1 August, 1684, and again 2 April 1685 to 20 April 1689. Sir Dudley m. Anne eldest dau. of Sir Robert Cann Bart. of Bristol (see *Williams'* *Gloucestershire Members*) and widow of Sir Robert Gunning. He was the author of "Discourses upon Trade," and died 21 Dec. 1691. His eldest son Dudley North married Catherine eldest dau. of Elihu Yale, Governor of Fort St. George, and was M.P. for Orford 1722 until his death 4 Feb. 1729. His only surviving son, another Dudley North, was born 1706, and m. 3 Oct. 1730 Lady Barbara Herbert only dau. of Thomas 8th Earl of Pembroke. He died 6 June 1764, and his 2nd daughter and co-heir Mary m. Charles Long, father of the M.P. 1796.

1689. Jan. 14. Sir Robert Dashwood Knt. and Bart.

See the County 1699.

1690. Feb. 24. Sir R. Dashwood.   10.

John Hawles.   140.

Sir John Hawles K.C., was Solicitor General June 1695 to June 1702. On 31 March 1690 Nathaniel Wheatley and others petitioned in his favour, on the ground that he had been denied a poll, but Dashwood was declared duly elected 29 Dec. 1691.

1695. Oct. 22. Sir R. Dashwood.

1698. July 23. James Isaacson.   W.

This member, who is believed to have been a London
stockbroker, sat for Banbury 1698 until he was expelled the
House on 10 Feb. 1699, as appears from the following entry in the
Commons Journals of that date :—" Ordered that Mr Isaackson, a
Member of this House, do attend this House, in his place, immediately. · And he, being come into the House, was heard in his
place, and then withdrew into the Speaker's Chamber. Ordered
that James Isaackson, esquire, having since his being elected to
serve in this Parliament been concerned and acted as a Commissioner in managing the duties upon Vellom, Paper and Parchment contrary to the Act made in the 5th and 6th years of His
Majesty's reign for granting several duties upon Salt, Beer, Ale,
and other liquors, be expelled this House," and a new writ was
ordered the same day. A few days afterwards four other Members
were similarly expelled, being adjudged incapable of sitting in
the House, on account of being concerned in the management of
the public revenues, but of course this did not affect their personal
character, and did not bear the construction applied in the present
day to the term ' expulsion from the House.' *Luttrell's Diary*
has several references to the subject, but his mention of the
rumour that Isaacson intended to surrender his Commissionership
in order to stand again for Banbury in Feb. 1699 was not carried
into effect. It was James Isaacson who drew up the proposals for
managing the duty on parchment, paper, etc., which were laid
before Parliament, *(Treasury Papers*, 1693,) and on the passing of
the Act, he was placed in the first Commission for the Board of
Stamps 21 May 1694, and retained the position until removed, on
the King's death, 6 June 1702. He was also 'the King's Warehouse
Keeper of the Customes in the Port of London ' in Feb. 1697 and
1699. On 11 Jan. 1700 *Luttrell* relates that " Sir John Conway, Sir Richard Middleton, and other M.P.'s have entered a
caveat at the privy seal to stop a grant passing of all the marshes
and wasts by the sea side in Flint and Denbighshire to Mr
Isaacson," (probably as trustee for the Earl of Portland, the King's
Favourite). He was afterwards a Commissioner of Customs
for Scotland (£400 a year) 5 June 1707 till he resigned in July
1710. Perhaps son of Anthony Isaacson, who was Navy Agent
and Correspondent at Newcastle to Secretary Williamson in
1672, and Collector of the Port of Newcastle in 1690, and kinsman
to Sir Charles Isaacson, Clerk of the Green Cloth till April 1702.

1699.   Feb. 23.   Sir John Cope Bart.

Again see under the County 1679.

1701.   Jan.   6. { John Dormer   W
                  { Hon. Charles North   T

This was a Double Return by two contending Mayors of
Banbury, but on petition the Return in favour of Mr. Dormer
was taken off the file by order of the House 13 March 1701.

Hon. Charles North was the younger of the two sons of Francis 1st Lord Guilford, Lord Keeper of the Great Seal, and was therefore nephew to the M.P. 1685. He was Member for Banbury in 6 Parliaments 1701-13, and died unm. 10 Dec. 1714, aged 37.

John Dormer, second son of William D. of Ascot, (H. S. 1666, who died 1683, by the sister of Sir Charles Cotterell Knt. of Wylsford, co. Lincoln, Master of the Ceremonies,) matric. Ch. Ch. Oxford 15 March 1678, aged 16. and m. Catherine youngest and 4th surviving dau. and co-heir of Sir Thomas Spencer 3rd Bart. of Yarnton, (see County 1661.) 29 April 1689, Warrant for the appointment of John Dormer as Assistant Master of the Ceremonies. (*Calendar of State Papers.*) He had previously been app. to the post in Dec. 1686, and occupied it until May 1715. Mr. Dormer died 5 March 1728, and his widow re-m. to Lieut. Gen. the Hon. Henry Mordaunt, brother to Charles 3rd Earl of Peterborough, (see 1722.) "Sir Rd. Kennedy was some days since killed by one Mr. Dormer in a quarrel at Woodstock." (*Luttrell*). Another John Dormer, Lieut.-Col. in the Army, born 1669, eldest son of Robert D. of Rousham, by Anne eldest dau. of Sir Charles Cotterell, M.C., was made a Groom of the Bedchamber to the King May 1699, and was killed at Almanza in Spain 14 April 1707, unmarried.

| 1701. | Nov. | 27. | Hon. Charles North. |
| 1702. | July | 20. | |

| 1705. | May | 8. | Hon. Charles North | ——— |
| | | | *Toby Chauncy* | ——— |

| 1708. | May | 4. | Hon. Charles North. |
| 1710. | Oct. | 6. | |

1713. Aug. 25. Jonathan Cope   W.

Jonathan Cope of Brewerne Abbey, Hanwell, and Ranton, co. Stafford, was the eldest son of Jonathan Cope M.P. of Ranton Abbey, who died 1694, and matric. Ch. Ch. Oxford 18 Feb. 1708, aged 16. He was created a Baronet at the age of 21, on 1 March 1714, and sat for Banbury 1713-22. He m. Mary youngest dau. of Sir Robert Jenkinson 2nd Bart. of Walcot, (see County 1689). He inherited the Hanwell estate in 1721, and died at Orton Longville, Hunts, on 28 March 1765, aged 75, and was buried at Hanwell.

1715. Jan 26. Sir Jonathan Cope Bart.

| 1722. | March 24. | Monoux Cope | ——— |
| | | *Sir W. Codrington* | ——— |

Sir William Codrington presented a petition 25 Oct. 1722, but did not proceed with it. Sir John Cope M.P. charged Sir Francis Page, the Judge, with attempting to bribe the electors of

Banbury in order to secure Sir W. Codrington's return, and the matter being brought before the House, the Judge only escaped censure by 128 votes to 124.

Monoux Cope of Hanwell, Hants, kinsman of the last Member, was the elder son of Sir John Cope 6th Bart. M.P., by Alice dau. of Sir Humphrey Monnoux Bart. of Wotton, Beds. He was M.P. for Banbury 1722-7, and for Newport, Isle of Wignt, 1741-7, and succeeded his father in the title 8 Dec. 1749. Sir Monoux m. Penelope dau. of Lieut. Gen. the Hon. Harry Mordaunt, (see 1713,) and died 29 June 1763, aged 77.

1727. Aug. 19.   Hon. Francis North   T.

Born 13 April 1704, the eldest son of Francis 2nd Lord Guilford, this Member matric. Trin. Coll. Oxford 25 March 1721, and sat for Banbury 1727 till he succeeded his father as 3rd Lord Guilford 17 Oct. 1729. He married three times, (1) 26 June 1728 Lady Lucy Montagu (who died 7 May 1734) only dau. of George 2nd Earl of Halifax, (2) 17 Jan. 1736 Elizabeth (who d. 21 April 1745) relict of George Viscount Lewisham, and dau. of Sir Arthur Kaye Bart., and (3) 13 June 1751 Lady Mary Finch dau. of Daniel Earl of Winchelsea and Nottingham, and widow of Thomas 1st Marquis of Rockingham, (and mother of the Prime Minister 1765-6.) Lord Guilford also succeeded his cousin William as 7th Lord North 31 Oct. 1734, and was styled under the senior title as Lord North until he was created Earl of Guilford 8 April 1752. His Lordship was a Lord of the Bedchamber to Frederick Prince of Wales Oct. 1730 until the Prince's death 20 March 1751, and is said by the *Gentleman's Magazine* to have been made a Lord of the Bedchamber to the King the following month. If so, he resigned the office previous to 1757. He was also Governor and Tutor to Prince George of Wales (afterwards George III.,) 30 Sept. 1750 to April 1751, and Treasurer and Receiver General to the Queen 29 Dec. 1773-90. He became a Dep. Lieut. for Oxon 17 Oct. 1763, was elected a Vice President of St. George's Hospital, and was High Steward of Banbury 1766 until his death 4 Aug. 1790.

1730. Jan. 21.   Toby Chauncy.

Tobias Chauncy of Edgcote, Northants, was the son of Toby C. of that place, and was born 2 Feb. 1674, and matric. Corpus Christi Coll. Oxford 6 Nov. 1690. Having been called to the bar at the Inner Temple 28 June 1699, he was made Recorder of Banbury and Daventry, and m. 1725 Anne 4th and youngest dau. of William Holbech of Farnborough, co. Warwick, and Radston, Northants. Her nephew was elected for Banbury in 1794 Mr. Chauncy (or his father) was the defeated candidate and petitioner at Banbury 1705, but represented it Jan. 1730 until his death 27 March 1733.

1733. April 9. William Viscount Wallingford, *vice* Chauncy deceased. William Knollis, commonly called Viscount Wallingford, elder son of Charles 4th Earl of Banbury, was First Major of the 1st Troop of Life Guards July 1737-40, voted for the Convention 1739, being then styled a Major in the Horse Guards, (£500 a year,) m. Mary Catherine dau. of John Law the Financier, and sat for Banbury April 1733 until his death v.p. in France 6 June 1740. His father Charles Knollys, 4th Earl of Banbury, was the son of Nicholas 3rd Earl of Banbury, (see the County 1584,) and was baptized at Boughton 3 June 1662, and married (1) Elizabeth dau. of Edward Lister of Barwell, co. Leicester, and (2) Mary dau. of Thomas Woods of St. Andrew's, Holborn. On no less than four occasions, on 10 June 1685, Jan. 1698, 19 May 1712, and 1727, did he unsuccessfully petition the House of Lords for a writ of summons as 4th Earl of Banbury. He killed his brother-in-law Capt. Philip Lawson in a duel in 1692, and being indicted for murder 7 Dec. 1692 as 'Charles Knollys, Esquire' he petitioned the House of Lords' that as Earl of Banbury he was entitled to a trial by his Peers. After considerable argument, in Trinity term 1694 Lord Chief Justice Holt and the three other Judges of the Court of King's Bench unanimously quashed the indictment and set the defendant free on the ground that he was the Earl of Banbury, and that his name was wrongly entered.

1734. April 26. Viscount Wallingford T.

1740. Nov. 25. William Moore of Pollesden, Surrey, *vice* Viscount Wallingford deceased. This Member sat for Banbury Nov. 1740 until his death 22 Oct. 1746.

1741. May 6. William Moore T.

1746. Nov. 26. John Willes, *vice* Moore deceased. Eldest son of Sir John Willes Knt. of Astrop, Northants, Lord Chief Justice of the Common Pleas 1737-61, (see *Williams' Welsh Judges*,) he matric. Worcester Coll. Oxford 3 March 1738, aged 16, and was created M.A. 4 July 1741, and D.C.L. 12 April 1749. Mr. Willes sat for Banbury Nov. 1746-7, and for Aylesbury 1754-61, and having been appointed by his father in Dec. 1752 Filazer to the Court of Common Pleas for London and Middlesex, held the office until his death at his seat at Astrop 24 Oct. 1784.

1747. June 29. John Willes W.

1754. April 15. Frederick Lord North T.

Frederick North, commonly called by courtesy Lord North, of Wroxton Abbey, was the son of the M.P. 1727, and was born 13 April 1732, educ. at Eton, matric. Trin. Coll. Oxford 12 Oct. 1749, and was created M.A. 21 March 1750. He m. 20 May 1756 Anne dau. and heir of George Speke of White Lackington, Somerset, who brought him a fortune of £4000 a year, and was made a Dep. Lieut. of Northants 15 March 1755, of Kent 7 Sept. 1757, Somerset 5 June 1758, and of Oxon 9 June 1762. He was created L.L.D. Camb. Univ. 3 July 1769, and held office as a Lord of the Treasury June 1759 to July 1765, Joint Paymaster of the Forces Aug. 1766-7, and Chancellor and Uader Treasurer of the Exchequer and a Lord of the Treasury Oct. 1767-70. Lord North was sworn a Privy Councillor 10 Dec. 1766, and was First Lord of the Treasury and Prime Minister for over 12 years from Jan. 1770 to March 1782. It was during his government that the unhappy War of Independence broke out in the American Colonies in 1775. Although a Tory, Lord North was afterwards Home Secretary in the Duke of Portland's Coalition Ministry April to Dec. 1783. He was M.P. for Banbury 1754 until he succeeded his father as 2nd Earl of Guilford 2 Aug. 1790. As became a Prime Minister his Lordship was the recipient of numerous honours and offices, for he was chosen Recorder of Gloucester 1770, made a Governor of the Charterhouse 4 Feb. 1771, Ranger and Warden of Bushey Park 14 June 1771, an Elder Brother of the Trinity House 1771, K.G. 18 June 1772, Chancellor of Oxford Univ. 3 Oct. 1772, created D.C.L. by diploma 10 Oct. 1772, appointed Lord Lieutenant and Custos Rotulorum of Somerset 15 March 1774, Recorder of Saltash 1774, and of Taunton 26 Nov. 1774, and Constable of Dover Castle and Lord Warden and Admiral of the Cinque Ports 16 June 1778, all of which he held until his death. He was also President of the Foundling Hospital from 1771, Governor of the Turkey Company from 1777, President of the Asylum from 177—, and a Vice President of St. George's Hospital. His Lordship died 5 Aug. 1792. He had seats at Bushy Park, Middlesex, Dollington, Somerset, and Waldershare, near Dover.

1759. June 4. The same, re-elected after being made a Lord of the Treasury.

1761. March 27. The same. He was re-elected 17 Nov. 1766 on being made Paymaster General of the Land Forces, and 30 Nov. 1767 after accepting office as Chancellor of the Exchequer.

1768. March 18. The same.

1774. Oct. 7. The same. He was re-elected 9 June 1778 on being made Warden of the Cinque Ports.

1780. Sept. 8. The same. On 9 April 1783 he was re-elected after being appointed one of the Principal Secretaries of State.

1784. April 3. } The same.
1790. June 18. }

1790. Dec. 21. George Augustus Lord North W. *vice* his father become Earl of Guilford. Eldest son of the last

Member, he was born 11 Sept. 1757, matric. Trin. Coll. Oxford
1 Nov. 1774, created Hon. M.A. 4 June 1777, and m. (1) 30 Sept.
1785 Lady Maria Anne Hobart (who died 23 April 1794) 4th dau.
of George 3rd Earl of Buckinghamshire, and (2) 28 Feb. 1796
Susan eldest dau. of Thomas Coutts the banker.   His Lordship
was M.P. for Harwich April 1778-84, and for Wootton Bassett
1784-90, and was returned for Petersfield as the Hon. G. A.
North June 1790, but accepted the Chiltern Hundreds in order to
stand for Banbury, which he represented from Dec. 1790 until he
succeeded his father as 3rd Earl of Guilford 5 Aug. 1792.   He
became Lieut.-Col. Commandant of the Cinque Ports Militia 23
July 1779, F.R.S. 17 Jan. 1782, was Secretary and Comptroller of
the Queen's Household Jan. 1781-3, Under Secretary of State for
the Home Department (to his father) April to Dec. 1783, and was
made a Manager for the House of Commons to impeach Warren
Hastings 3 April 1787.   His Lordship was Colonel of the Cinque
Ports Volunteers in 1793, Captain of Deal Castle 1795-9, became
a Dep. Lieut. for Kent 11 Aug. 1797, and was High Steward of
Banbury (in succession to his father,) Dec. 1794 until his death
at Mr. Coutt's, in Stretton Street, Piccadilly, on 29 April 1802.
The long and painful ill state of his Lordship's health arose from
a fall from his horse, a few years before, at Cheltenham, owing to
the animal taking fright as his Lordship was presenting a basket
of fruit to Miss Coutts, afterwards Countess of Guildford.   By
this accident, it is supposed the spine of his back was affected,
which occasioned the bodily sufferings under which he lan-
guished during the remainder of his life.   He left estates to the
amount of £18000 per annum, which devolved upon his brother
and successor Francis.

1792.   Sept. 21.   Hon. Frederick North, (W) *vice* his
brother Lord North called to the Upper House. He was the
third son of the 2nd Earl of Guilford (see 1754,) and was born 7
Feb. 1766, matric. Ch. Ch. Oxford 18 Oct. 1782, was created Hon.
D.C.L. 5 July 1793, and D.C.L. by diploma 30 Oct. 1819.   He was
M.P. for Banbury Sept. 1792 till he was made Comptroller of the
Customs in the Port of London Feb. 1794, F.R.S. 6 Feb. 1794,
and one of the two Chamberlains of the Exchequer 13 Dec. 1779
until he surrendered the patent 10 Oct. 1826, when the office was
abolished.   He was also Secretary of State in Corsica 9 Jan. 1795
until that island was restored to France in 1797, Governor of
Ceylon 26 March 1798 to Jan. 1805, and Vice Admiral of Ceylon
1799-1805.   He succeeded his brother Francis as 5th Earl of
Guilford 11 Jan. 1817, and as High Steward of Banbury, was
made Chancellor of the Univ. of Corfu in the Ionian Islands
1819, G.C.M.G. 26 Oct. 1819, L.L.D. Camb. 1821, and died
unmarried 14 Oct. 1827.   Lord Colchester in his *Diaries*,
described him as, " A pleasant but very singular man."

1794.   March 5.   William Holbech of Farnborough, co.

Warwick, *vice* Hon. F. North who accepted an office in the Customs. Son of Hugh Holbech of Mollington, who died 1765, he was born 1748, matric Trinity Coll. Oxford 27 Nov. 1766, aged 18, created M.A. 30 June 1770, and m. 1772 Anne dau. of William Woodhouse M.D. of Lichfield. Mr. Holbech's aunt was the wife of Toby Chauncy (see 1727.) He succeeded his uncle William Holbech in his estates of Farnborough, co. Warwick, and Radston, Northants, in 1771, sat for Banbury March 1794-6, as *locus tenens* for the Norths, and died 6 July 1812. His grandson Hugh was defeated at Banbury 1841.

 1796. May 30. Dudley North.

 Dudley North of Glemham Hall, Ipswich, was M.P. for Great Grimsby 1790-6, and for Banbury 1796-1806. He was defeated at Banbury in 1806, but was elected in a Double Return 1807, and a fresh election being ordered, he was once more returned Feb. 1808, and sat till 1812. He had however been also chosen for Newtown, Isle of Wight, on 7 May 1807, but accepted the Chiltern Hundreds and vacated that seat in order to stand for Banbury in Feb. 1808. He was M.P. for Richmond, (Yorkshire,) 1812-18, and again for Newtown 1820 until he once more accepted the Chiltern Hundreds in Feb. 1821. Mr. North was the second son of Charles Long of Saxmundham, Suffolk, (see 1685,) and cousin to Lord Farnborough. He was baptized 14 March 1748, educ. at Bury St. Edmunds, and graduated B.A. 1771, M.A. 1774, Emmanuel Coll. Camb. Under the will of his aunt who died in 1789, he took the name of North, in lieu of his patronymic, and m. 5 Nov. 1802 Hon. Sophia Anderson-Pelham eldest dau. of Charles 1st Lord Yarborough. On the death however in 1812 of his elder brother Charles Long of Hurts Hall, he took the name and arms of Long in addition to those of North. He was a friend of Dr. Samuel Johnson, and died s.p. at Brompton 21 Feb. 1829, aged 80.

 1802. July 7. The same.

 1806. Nov 1. William Pread   W   10
       Dudley North   W   6

 This is the only instance (save 1831) in which a North was unsuccessful at Banbury. William Praed of Tyringham, Bucks, and Trevethoe, Cornwall, was the son of Humphrey Mackworth Praed M.P. of Broughton, co. Stafford, and grandson of William Mackworth (who took the name of) Praed M.P., third son of Sir Humphrey Mackworth of Gnoll, Glamorgan, (see *Williams' Parl. Hist. of Wales.*) He was born 24 June 1749, matric. Magd. Coll. Oxford 2 March 1767, aged 17, and m. 19 June 1778 Elizabeth Tyringham, dau. of Barnaby Backwell of Tyringham, Bucks, and St. Clement Danes, banker. He was senior partner in the London banking house of Hallidays, Duntze, Praeds and Co., and also in the Truro and Falmouth banks, and was Recorder of St. Ives in 1792 and 1807, M.P. St. Ives 1774 until void 1775, and 1780-1806, and Banbury 1806 until void 1808 when he was defeated. He died 9 Oct. 1833, aged 84. His grandson Wm. Backwell Tyringham M P. Bucks 1835-7, took the name of Tyringham 1859. The Member must not be confused with his kinsman William Mackworth Praed, Serjeant at law, Chairman of the Board of Audit, who was father of the poet.

1807.   May   5. { Dudley North.   9
                  { William Praed.   9

There was a Double Return of both candidates, but on petition the election was declared void, and a new writ issued, which resulted

1808.   Feb. 16.   Dudley North   5
        William Praed   3
1812.   Oct. 5.   Hon. F. S. N. Douglas   T.

Hon. Frederick Sylvester North Douglas, of the Pheasantry, Middlesex, was born 8 Feb. 1791, and was the only son of Sylvester Lord Glenbervie, (Recorder of Banbury,) by Lady Catharine Ann North eldest dau. of the 2nd Earl of Guilford, the Prime Minister, (see 1754.)   He matric. Ch. Ch. Oxford, 24 Oct. 1806, aged 15, student 1806-18, B.A. and M.A. July 1813, and was of Lincolns Inn 1807.   He m. 19 July 1819 Harriet eldest dau. of William Wrighton of Cusworth, Yorkshire, and was Captain in Major Stratton's squadron of Yeomanry Cavalry.   This young and talented Member was the means of establishing the Banbury National School Society, of which he became President 1817. He represented Banbury 1812 until his death in London 21 Oct. 1819, aged 28.

1818.   June 19.   The same.

1819.   Nov. 22.   Hon. Heneage Legge, *vice* Douglas deceased.   Second son of George 3rd Earl of Dartmouth, K.G., by Lady Francis Finch dau. of Heneage 3rd Earl of Aylesford, he was born 29 Feb. 1788, educ. at Eton, matric. Ch. Ch. Oxford 24 Oct. 1805, fellow of All Souls Coll. 1812-18, B.C L. 1812, D.C.L. 1818, and was called to the bar at Lincolns Inn 1815.   Mr. Legge m. 19 July 1821 Mary dau. of Major Johnstone, and sat for Banbury Nov. 1819 until made a Commissioner of the Customs Feb. 1826.   He held this office until his death 12 Dec. 1844.

1820.   March 10.   Hon. Heneage Legge   T

At this date a riot occurred at the hustings, and the Corporation were unable for some time to leave the Town Hall.

1826.   Feb. 10.   Hon. Arthur Charles Legge, (T.) *vice* his brother Heneage made a Commissioner of the Customs.   Born on 25 June 1800, the third son of the third Earl of Dartmouth, he

entered the army as Ensign 28th Foot 23 May 1816, became Ensign
and Lieut. Coldstream Guards 27 Feb. 1817, when on half-pay 25
Dec. 1818, Lieut 1st Life Guards 31 July 1820, Captain thereof 17
Jan. 1822 until placed on half-pay 23 June 1837, received the rank
of Major 10 Jan. 1837, Lt. Col. 11 Nov. 1851, Col. 28 Nov. 1854,
Major Gen. 28 Aug. 1865, Lt. Gen. 26 Jan. 1874, and General 1
Oct. 1877, being still on half pay as Captain in 1872.   He m. (1)
14 June 1827 Lady Anne Frederica Catherine Holroyd (who died
31 Aug. 1829) third dau. of John 1st Earl of Sheffield, and grand
dau. of the 2nd Earl of Guilford, (see 1754,) and (2) 29 Aug. 1837
Caroline 4th dau. of James Charles Philip Bouwens.   General
Legge became D.L. Kent 1852, Lt. Col. 3rd Battalion Staffordshire
Rifle Volunteers 1860, and was Col. 1st Staffordshire R. Volunteers
8 May 1868 until his death at Caynton, Shifnal, 18 May 1890.

1826.   June 10.   The same.

1830.   July 30.   Henry Villiers Stuart   T.

Henry Villiers-Stuart of Dromana, co. Waterford, was born
in London 8 June 1803, and was the eldest son of Lord Henry
Stuart the 2nd son of John 1st Marquis of Bute.   He enjoyed the
North influence at Banbury through his uncle the 2nd Marquis
of Bute who married the eldest dau. of the third Earl of Guilford,
(see 1790,) and was chosen High Steward of Banbury 1827.
Having been educated at Eton, Mr. Stuart matric. Ch. Ch. Oxford
15 Dec. 1820, and took the additional surname of Villiers by sign
manual 17 Nov. 1822.   He was M.P. for co. Waterford 1826 to
Feb. 1830 when he vacated his seat, and for Banbury 1830-1, and
was sworn a Privy Councillor in Ireland 1836, and created Lord
Stuart de Decies 10 May 1839.   His Lordship married Madame
de Ott.   He became Col. of the Waterford Art. Militia 30 Dec.
1839, and was Lord Lieut. of co. Waterford 1831 until his death
23 Jan. 1874, when the title became extinct.

1831.   May 2.   John Easthope   W   6

         Hon. H. Hutchinson   T   2

The number of electors at Banbury at this date was 18.
Smith says the poll only lasted one day, and that 6 voted for
Easthope, and 3 for Hutchinson.

Lt.-Col. the Hon. Henry Hely Hutchinson of Weston
Wedon, Northants, brother of the third Earl of Donoughmore,
was born 26 March 1790, married 26 April 1825 the widow of the
Hon. F. S. N. Douglas, (see 1812,) and died 2 July 1874.   He
fought at Waterloo.

John Easthope was the 2nd surviving son of Thomas E. of
Tewkesbury, where he was born 29 Oct. 1784.   He became a
London stockbroker in 1818, and made £150000 in a few years.
(*Boase's Modern Biography*).   He purchased the *Morning Chronicle*
for £16500 in 1834 which he owned till 1847, and was made a

Baronet 24 Aug. 1841. He unsuccessfully contested St. Albans Jan. 1821, Southampton 1835, Lewes 1837, and Bridgnorth 1847, but was MP. for St. Albans 1826-30, Banbury 1831-2, and Leicester 1837-47. Sir John m. (1) 1807 Anne dau. of Jacob Stokes of Leopard House, near Worcester, and (2) 19 Sept. 1843 Elizabeth eldest dau. of Col. Skyring R.A., and widow of Major John Longley R.A. He was a director of the London and South Western Railway in 1846, and died at Fir Grove, Weybridge, Surrey, 11 Dec. 1865, aged 81, when the title became extinct, his son having pre-deceased him. (See *Williams' Gloucestershire Members*).

1832. Dec. 11. Henry William Tancred   W

This Member was the 2nd son of Sir Thomas Tancred 5th Bart. of Boroughbridge, Yorks, and was born 1780, B.A. Jes. Coll. Camb. 1804, M.A. 1807, ent. Lincolns Inn 4 May 1799, bar. at law 11 May 1804, invited to the Bench of that Society 14 Nov. 1831, and sat as such 11 Jan. 1833, and became a Queen's Counsel in Trinity Vacation 1831. He was made a Commissioner to inquire into the state of registers of births marriages and deaths, not being parochial registers, 13 Sept. 1836, sat for Banbury 1832 till he accepted the Chiltern Hundreds Jan. 1859, and died at Margate 20 Aug. 1860. Mr. Tancred was one of those who rallied around Lord Brougham in his efforts to found the Society for the Diffusion of Useful Knowledge. He was a zealous, upright, and inflexible Whig, a staunch member of Brook's Club, and one of the first to join the Reform Club on its being founded. He was author of several political works.

| 1835. Jan. 5. | H. W. Tancred | W | 203 |
| | *E. L. Williams* | *T* | 43 |

Edward Lloyd Williams was a barrister of the Midland circuit. *Smith's Parliaments of England* gives the poll as Tancred 205, Williams 45, and styles the latter a Radical.

| 1837. July 25. | H. W. Tancred | W | 181 |
| | *Henry Tawney* | *T* | 75 |

Mr. Tawney was a banker at Banbury.

1841. June 30.	H. W. Tancred	W	124
	Hugh Holbech	*T*	100
	Henry Vincent	*Ch.*	51

Henry Vincent the Chartist, was a printer at Bath. He was also defeated at Ipswich Aug. 1842, and 1847, Tavistock March 1843, Kilmarnock May 1843, Plymouth July 1846, and York May 1848, and 1852.

| 1847. July 31. | H. W. Tancred | L | 226 |
| | *James Macgregor* | *C* | 164 |

James Macgregor was born at Liverpool 1808, was M.P. Sandwich 1852-7, when defeated, and was Chairman of the South Eastern Railway 1848 until his death in London 5 Sept. 1858.

1852. July 9. H. W. Tancred.

1857.	March 28.	H. W. Tancred	L	216
		Edward Yates	C	58
1859.	Feb. 9.	Bernhard Samuelson	L	177
		John Hardy	C	176
		Edward Miall	L	118

vice Tancred resigned. John Hardy of Dunstan Hall, Staffordshire, unsuccessfully contested Plymouth 1857, and East Staffordshire 1880, but sat for Midhurst 3 March to 23 April 1859, when Parliament was dissolved, was the last Member for Dartmouth Nov. 1860-8, and sat for South Warwickshire 1868-74. He was brother to the Earl of Cranbrook, (see Oxford Univ. 1865,) and was born 23 Feb. 1809, m. 13 Aug. 1846 Laura 3rd dau. of William Holbech of Farnborough, (see 1794,) and was made a Baronet 23 Feb. 1876. He died in 1888.

Edward Miall also failed for Southwark Sept. 1845, Halifax 1847, and Tavistock Sept. 1857, but sat for Rochdale 1852-7, when he was defeated, and for Bradford March 1869-74, having been defeated there Oct. 1867 and 1868. He was born 8 May 1809, was the well-known advocate of Disestablishment, and died 29 April 1881.

Sir Bernhard Samuelson will be found under North Oxfordshire 1885.

1859.	April 30.	Sir C. E. Douglas	L	235
		B. Samuelson	L	199

Sir Charles Eurwicke Douglas Knt. was the son of Rt. Hon. Charles Philip Yorke M.P., and was born 12 May 1806, educ. at Harrow, and graduated B.A. 1828, M.A. 1831, St. John's Coll. Camb. He m. 1832 Jane Mary Anne eldest dau. of Sir Charles Des Voeux 2nd Bart., and was Private Secretary to Viscount Goderich, Colonial Secretary Nov. 1830 to March 1833, King at Arms of the Order of St. Michael and St. George 1832-59, and a Commissioner of Greenwich Hospital 8 Aug. 1845 to July 1846. He was Knighted 12 Oct. 1832, made C.M.G. 1832, K.C.M.G. 1859, M.P. for Warwick 1837-52, unsuccessfully fought Durham June 1853, and sat for Banbury 1859-65, when he lost his seat. He died in London 21 Feb. 1887.

1865.	July 12.	B. Samuelson	L	206
		Charles Bell	C	165
		Sir C. E. Douglas	L	160

Charles Bell was elected M.P. for the City of London in Nov. 1868, but died the following February.

1868.	Nov. 17.	B. Samuelson	L	772
		J. Stratton	C	397
1874.	Feb. 3.	B. Samuelson	L	760
		Lt.-Col. J. J. Wilkinson	C	676

Col. Josiah Wilkinson was also defeated at Norwich March 1875.

1880.	April 1.	B. Samuelson	L	1018
		T. Gibson Bowles	C	583

Thomas Gibson Bowles also unsuccessfully contested Darlington 1874, and South Salford 1885, but has sat for King's Lynn since 1892.

At the Dissolution in Nov. 1885 the Borough of Banbury ceased to return a Member of Parliament, but was merged in the Northern or Banbury Division of the County. It had 329 electors in 1832, 1529 in 1868, 1952 in 1874, and 1881 in 1884.

THE BOROUGH OF WOODSTOCK.

The most eminent of the Members for the Royal Borough of Woodstock were William Cooke, Judge of the Admiralty, Sir James Whitlock, Judge of the King's Bench, Sir Robert Pye, Auditor of the Exchequer, Sir Edward Atkyns and Sir John Skynner who were both Lord Chief Barons, Sir Thomas Littleton, Speaker of the House, the famous soldier Earl Cadogan, Viscount Bateman, and the Earl of Macclesfield who were Courtiers, Lord Auckland the statesman and diplomatist, and his son the Earl who was Viceroy of India, Lord Henry Spencer, the Envoy to Prussia, Lord Lavington, Governor of the Leeward Islands, the philanthropic Earl of Shaftesbury, Lord Chelmsford the Lord Chancellor, the Duke of Marlborough, Viceroy of Ireland, and his son Lord Randolph Churchill, Chancellor of the Exchequer and Leader of the House. As might be expected, some of the earlier Members, such as George Whitton and the Fleetwoods, were officials of the Royal Park at Woodstock. Col. Packer and Sir Jerome Sankey were noted soldiers of the Commonwealth.

MEMBERS FOR WOODSTOCK.

1302. Edmund de Parco

John Beneit

The former Member was probably of kin to Sir Thomas de Parco, (see the County 1298.) It is doubtful whether the following paragraph in the *Patent Rolls* refers to the Member for Woodstock :—20 Oct. 1290, Pardon to John Beneit of Wodenese, detained in the prison of Oxford, for the death of Alice de Wodenose, his wife, and Mariota and Alice his daughters, as it appears by the record of Henry de Rale and his fellows, justices appointed to deliver the said gaol, that he killed them in a fit of madness, while labouring under acute disease.

1305. John de Wappenham

Reginald Bene

194   MEMBERS FOR WOODSTOCK.

The former may have been a native or resident of
Wappenham in Northamptonshire, as his name implies that he
or his family were connected with the place.

.   .   .   .

After this date Woodstock was relieved of the burden of
returning and paying two Burgesses, for two centuries and a half.
Henry 6 by his Charter dated 24 May 1453, declared "that the
same Mayor and commonalty of the Borough of New Woodstock
and their successors shall not be compelled to choose any burgesses for the Borough aforesaid to come to any Parliament of us
or our heirs hereafter to be held, but shall be exempted for ever."
Just a century afterwards, however, when the right of representation was becoming regarded as a privilege instead of a burden,
the Borough was again enfranchised in the first year of Queen
Mary, to return two Members.

1553. Sept. 6. William Cooke
        Sir John Chamberleyn

William Cooke was one of the many eminent Civilians
returned by Oxfordshire constituencies. A member of New
College and All Souls College, Oxford, he graduated B.C.L. 18
July 1530, and D.C.L. 11 Oct. 1536, and was admitted a member
of the College of Advocates 15 Oct. 1537. (Quaere if he was the
William Cooke admitted to Grays Inn in 1528.) He was Rector
or Warden of Elmeley, Kent, Principal or chief moderator of the
Civil Law School in St. Edward's parish 1537, Dean of the
Arches 1545-9, Judge of the Prerogative Court of Canterbury
1548, Judge of the Admiralty 1554-8, and Custos of Ilford
Hospital, Essex, 1551. Cooke was M.P. for Woodstock Sept. to
Dec. 1553, and was perhaps the William Cooke who was M.P.
for Portsmouth April to May 1554. He was buried 23 Aug.
1558, and probaby died unmarried.

Sir John Chamberlayne was the third son of Richard C.
and brother to Sir Edward C. of Shirburn Castle (who died 1543,)
and uncle to Sir Leonard, (see the County 1554.) He was
Knighted before 1553, M.P. Woodstock, Sept. to Dec. 1553, and
had two sons George and Edmund.

1534. March. Sir Ralph Chamberleyn.
        William Johnsun.

Sir Ralph was the third son of Sir Edward C. of Sher-
borne, nephew to Sir John the last member, and brother to Sir
Leonard, (see County 1554.) He m. Elizabeth dau. of Sir Robert
Fiennes, was Knighted 1553, and died after 1575. On 15 July
1558 the Queen gave directions to Sir Clement Higham and Sir
John Sulyarde to take inventories &c. of the goods &c. of Sir
Ralph Chamberlayne and others, and to make account of their
revenues since the loss of Calais. (*Calendar of State Papers.*)

It is doubtful whether his colleague was the William Johnson of Leighton Buzzard who in 1574 married Mary dau. and co-heir of Edmond Harmon of Taynton, Oxford.

1554. Oct. 24. Anthony Restwold.

George Chamberleyne.

The former was M.P. Woodstock Oct. to Dec. 1554, and Aylesbury Oct. to Dec. 1555. He was a son of Edward Restwold of the Vache in Chalfont St. Giles, Bucks, by Augusta or Agnes 2nd dau. of John Cheyney of Drayton, and died s.p. and v.p.

George Chamberlayne of Bodington, Northants, elder son of Sir John C. (see 1553,) m. Dorothea dau. of John Butler of Aston in yᵉ Wall, Northants. Oct. 1560, Answers by George C. of Wickham, to interrogatories touching his intercourse with Papists beyond the sea. Letters received by him from Lady Dormer, the Countess Feria, &c. (*Cal. State Papers.*) Another George C. was 2nd son of Sir Leonard (see County 1554.) Quaere died 10 Feb. 1565, Inq. p. m. 25 Oct. 1565.

.   .   .   .

No returns have been found for the Parliaments elected in Sept. 1555, Jan. 1558, Jan. 1559, and Dec. 1562, and *Browne Willis* expressed his belief that no Members were returned by Woodstock to those Parliaments. As there is distinct evidence, from a discussion in the House, (see *Commons Journals*,) that Woodstock did *not* make a Return to the Parliament of 1562, it is probable that *Willis* was correct, and the Borough returned no Member after 1554, until the privilege was again revived in 1571.

1571. April. Thomas Penniston.

Martin Johnson.

Thomas Peniston of Beaconsfield, Bucks, M.P. Woodstock 1571, m. Elizabeth dau. of Humphrey Ashfield of Heathcop. His grandson was made a Baronet in 1612. On 28 Aug. 1571 the Constables of the Hundred of Wootton certified to T. P. that they had caused privy watch and search to be made throughout the said Hundred, and specified the vagrants apprehended and punished. On 20 April 1592, Exemplification, at the request of Marten Colpeper, widow, upon a bill and answer, in a cause between her and Thomas Penyston, defendant. *(Cal. State Papers.)*

Martin Johnson was M.P. Woodstock 1571, and (as Johnsleyne) 1572-83. He was probably son or brother of the M.P. 1554, and father of William J. of Oxford city, whose son Martin Johnson matric. Ball. Coll. 17 July 1640, aged 16.

1572. April 15. George Whytton.

Martin Johnsleyne.

George Whitton was for many years Surveyor of the Royal
Manor of Woodstock, and as such was engaged in several disputes with his neighbours. Although at first sight it appears as
if he was of a tyrannical and cantankerous disposition, yet from
the fact that his son or grandson John Whitton was app. Comptroller and Surveyor of Woodstock 8 May 1607, and held the
same office in 1642, it may not unreasonably be inferred that
Whitton was a good and faithful servant, and caused offence
chiefly by fearlessly discharging his duty. Many references are
made to him in the *Calendar of State Papers*, as follows :—1579,
Petition of John Osbaston and John Preedy to the Council.
Complain of the extreme dealings of George Whitton of Woodstock, in taking unfair advantage of their bonds for money bor-
rowed of him. Articles of their suit against Mr Whitton.—
Dec. 1580, Complaint by George Whitton, Comptroller and
Surveyor of the manor and park of Woodstock against Sir
Hen. Lee. Being angry with me for accusing him of
deer-stealing 10 years ago, when Fras. Chamberlain was
Lieutenant of Woodstock, and later for reproving him for
leaving workmen unpaid &c., he declared he would make me
weary of my office ; Sir Henry has defrauded me of 20 marks a
year, granted by Her Majesty's warrant, and for 6 or 7 years has
retained from me the woodwardship of the manor of Spillsberry,
given in recompense of service by Edward 6, and worth 20 marks
yearly, besides the fees appertaining to my office of comptroller
of Her Majesty's manor and park of Woodstock aforesaid.—Dec.
1580, Answer of Sir Henry Lee to certain allegations of George
Whitton relative to a transaction about some venison and deer
stealing 16 years since. Prays to be protected from Whitton's
slanderous clamours, and to be released from imprisonment.—
1583, The answer of William Skelton, Mayor of New Woodstock,
to the complaint of Geo. Whitton touching the election of Mayor
and the corrupt dealing of W.S. in that behalf, &c. On 18 May
1604 Pardon was granted to Mr Bolton "for killing George
Whitton," who may have been this Member. Geo. Whitton of
Woodstock Park was the fourth son of William W. of Nethercote,
and m. Dorothy, younger dau. of Thomas Peniston, (see 1571).
He was M.P. Woodstock 1572-84, and Brackley 1584-5 and 1586-7.

1584. Oct. 26. Lawrence Tannefeld.

Henry Umpton.

As to Sergt. Tanfield, see the County 1604. Henry Unton
or Umpton was the second son of Sir Edward Unton M.P. of
Wadley and Farringdon, Berks, by Anne daughter to Edward
Seymour, Duke of Somerset, and Protector of England. He m.
Dorothy dau. of Sir Thomas Wroughton of Brodhinton, Wilts.,
was Knighted 29 Sept. 1586, M.P. Woodstock 1584-5 and Berks
1593, gained distinction at the siege of Zutphen 1586, and went
as Ambassador to France 1591 and 1595, dying there s.p. 23 **May**

1596, whenthe male branch of his family became extinct. He challenged the Duke of Guise for making slighting remarks concerning Queen Elizabeth. He was buried at Farringdon 8 July 1596. Oct. 1582, Considerations to move Her Majesty to grant Mr Henry Unton's suit for the custody of his mother, Anne Countess of Warwick, wife of the late Sir Edward Unton, the said relict having the same month been declared of unsound mind. 15 Jan. 1583, Report of Henry Unton and other, arbitrators app. by the Council to settle the controversies between Sir John Conway and Anthony Bowrne. Willingness of both parties to come to agreement. Intermarriage of their children.

> 1586. Oct. 11. Lawrence Tanfeild.
>
> Francis Stoner.

Francis Stonor of Stonor Park, High Sheriff of Oxfordshire 1592 and 1621, was the son and heir of Sir Francis Stonor by Cecily dau. of Sir Leonard Chamberlain, (see County 1554.) He was Knighted Sept. 1601, sat for Woodstock 1586-7, and built and endowed an alms house at Upper Assendon, near Stonor Park, for 10 poor persons, and endowed it wiih a rent charge of £61 a year. He and his family were consistent Roman Catholics. Sir Francis was born in 1553, and married Martha dau. of John Southcote, Judge of the Queen's Bench. He wrote to Lord Salisbury on 22 Feb. 1606, recommending a general survey of the King's woods and offering to rent them at £10000 a year above the present revenue; and on 18 May 1610 begging that his lease of Watlington Park may be granted according to promise, relying on which he had purchased the land in the park which would be of little value to him without the woods.

> 1588. Nov. 4. Lawrence Tanfeilde.
>
> John Lee.

Quære if this John Lee was the 4th and youngest son of Richard Lee of Quarendon, and ancestor of the Lees of Binfield, Berks, or 2nd son of Thomas Lee M.A. and Bachelor of physick, fellow of Magd. Coll. Oxford. A John Lee was adm. to Grays Inn 25 Nov. 1581.

> 1593. Jan.
> 1597. Oct. 17 } The same.
>
> 1601. Oct. 5. Lawrence Tanfeild.
>
> William Scott.

Scott was styled ' gentleman ' in the Return.

> 1604. March 1. Sir Richard Lee.
>
> Thomas Spenser.

Sir Richard was the son of Sir Antony Lee, and younger brother of Sir Henry Lee K.G. of Ditchley, Master of the

Ordnance. He m. (1) the widow of Sir ———— Hall, Knt. and (2)
Lady Croker of Hook Norton, and sat for Woodstock 1604 till
his death 22 Dec. 1608. On 25 July 1588, Lord Henry Seymour
wrote from 'The Revenge,' in Dover Road, to Secretary Walsyngham, (see Banbury 1558,) as follows:—Is happy to hear of the
beginning of victory, but grieved that he cannot be an actor in
it. If Parma intends anything he will now shew his courage.
Many gentlemen have come to venture their lives in the Queen's
service.   Their names are Richard Lee, and three others.
On 2 Oct. 1602 John Chamberlain wrote to Dudley Carleton in
Paris,—The commencement at Oxford was very famous . . .
specially for the confluence of cut purses, whereof ensued many
losses, Mr. Bodley lost his cloak, Sir Rich. Lea two jewels of 200
marks, which he and Sir Harry Lea meant to bestow on the
bride, Mr. Tanfield's daughter.

Thomas Spencer of Yarnton, a branch issuing from the
stock of the noble houses of Marlborough and Spencer, was the
elder son of Sir William Spencer Knt. who died 18 Dec. 1609. In
Dec. 1604 Thomas Spencer and Sir Rich. Spencer were Keeper of
the Writs and Rolls, in the Common Pleas. Thomas Spencer
petitioned Lord Salisbury 29 Dec. 1610 for an order to the Woodward of Whittlewood Forest, Northants, to allow his right of 40
loads of wood yearly, as his " estovers " as lord of the manor.
He married Margaret dau. of Richard Brainthwait, Serjeant at
law, and was made a Baronet 29 June 1611, and afterwards
Knighted at Whitehall 24 May 1612. He was famous for his
great hospitality, and rebuilt the tower at the west end of
Yarnton Church, as also a noble mansion house near the old one.
He died 16 or 17 Aug. 1622, and was buried the next day in a
chapel he had erected on the south side of the chancel of
Yarnton Church.

1609.   Dec. 6. James Whitelock

vice Sir R. Lee deceased. This distinguished Judge was the
youngest son of Richard W. a London merchant, and was born
23 or 28 Nov. 1570, educ. at Merchant Taylors School, became a
scholar of St. John's Coll. Camb. 1588, B.C.L. 1594, and was a
Fellow till June 1598.   Having been admitted to the Middle
Temple 2 March 1593, he was called to the bar 24 Oct. 1600, and
served as Autumn Reader 1619. He was Recorder of Bishop's
Castle (fee 40s. a year) in 1609, of Ludlow 1621-4, and of Bewdley
1621-4, made Steward of the lands of St. John's Coll. Camb.,
Recorder of Woodstock 1606, Steward and Counsel of Eton
College 1609, and also of Westminster School 1610, and was M.P.
Woodstock Dec. 1609-11, Woodstock and Corfe Castle March
1614, but probably preferred to sit for the former till June 1614,
and again 1620-2.   On 18 May 1613 Whitelock was summoned
before the Council and sent to the Fleet, where he remained a
prisoner till 13 June. This however did not bar his promotion to

the Bench, for he was made a Serjeant at law 18 June 1620, Knighted 29 Oct. 1620, and the same day app. Chief Justice of Chester and of the counties of Denbigh, Flint, and Montgomery. On 9 Nov. 1620 Chamberlain wrote to his friend Carleton, stating that "Sir James Whitelock has brought the Receivership of the Wards." He was an active member of the Council of the Marches of Wales till 18 Oct. 1624, when he became a Justice of the King's Bench, and this judicial post he filled until his death at his mansion at Fawley Court 21 June 1632. He married 9 Sept. 1602 Elizabeth dau. of Edward Bulstrode of Bulstrode. (See *Williams' Welsh Judges*).

1614. March. James Whitelock, Recorder.

Sir Philip Carye Knt.

Sir Philip Cary of Caddington, Beds, and Hunslet, Yorks, 3rd son of Edward C. of Berkhamstead, Herts, matric. Queen's Coll. Oxford 22 Feb. 1594 aged 14, and ent. Grays Inn 9 Aug. 1590. He was Knighted 23 May 1605, sat for Woodstock March to June 1614, 1620-2, 1624-5, April to Aug. 1625, and was buried at Aldenham 13 June 1631. Grant to Sir Phil. Carey, Wm. Pitt, and John Williams, in fee simple of the manor and lordship of Minster, Kent, 26 Nov. 1611. Grant to Sir Philip Carey of the office of keeping Marybone Park, Middlesex, for life, 27 Feb. 1615.

1620. Dec. 7. Sir James Whitlock Knt., Recorder.

Sir Philip Carye Knt.

1624. Jan. 14. Sir Philip Cayre.

William Lenthall, Recorder.

As to William Lenthall, the Recorder of Woodstock at this date, see the County 1654.

1625. April 20. Sir Philip Carye Knt.

Sir Jerrard Fleetwood Knt.

Sir Jerrard Fleetwood of Crawley, Hants, was the son of Thomas F., and brother to Sir William F. of Missendon, Bucks, M.P. Bucks and Middlesex, Receiver of the Court of Wards. He was therefore uncle to the M.P.'s 1628 and 1640. He was Knighted July 1603 and M.P. for Woodstock April to Aug. 1625, and Jan. to June 1626, and Ranger of Woodstock Park 1611. On 22 Feb. 1646, he " Begs a moderate composition. Resides in co. Hants which was long under the King's forces, and was obliged to be a Commissioner of Array, and sometimes to go to Winchester, but disliked the business, and was never in arms. His lands formerly worth £250 a year, have been sequestered three years, and lie waste and in the King's power, so that he has no maintenance, yet is willing to submit to a fine. 7 April, Fine £500. In addition to this, he was assessed by the Committee of

Advance of Money at £400 on 29 Jan. 1647, but as it appeared on
16 Nov. 1648 that his debts amounted to £4476, his assessment
was taken off on 24 November " as his debts are much more than
the whole value of his estate." 30 Aug. 1625, Warrant to pay to
Sir Gerard Fleetwood 12d. a day for looking to the game within
the manor of Woodstock and within 10 miles about the same.
He was living in 1651.

> 1626.   Jan. 14.   Sir Gerard Fleetwood.
>
> Edmund Taverner.

Richard Taverner of Wood Eaton was High Sheriff of Oxon
1568, while John Taverner of Soundess, (Nettlebed,) was Sheriff
1662, and died 1674, aged 85. Edmund Taverner who sat for
Woodstock Jan. to June 1626 and 1628-9, was doubtless of the
same family, and was perhaps the son of John Taverner,
Surveyor of the King's Woods in 1605. There are many references to him in the *Calendar of State Papers*. 2 Nov. 1626, Warrant to pay to Edmund Taverner £200 for a diamond sold to His
Majesty and given to Mons. Frogan. 24 Nov. 1626, Warrant to
pay to E.T. £400 for provision for the Queen's Masque shortly to
be performed. 11 Feb. 1628, Warrant to pay to E.T. £600 towards
the expenses of a Masque to be presented shortly before the King
at Whitehall. There are several letters to and from him during
1628-31. He was Secretary to the Lord Chamberlain, Philip Earl
of Pembroke and Montgomery, in Dec. 1630, and still so in 1637.
Sir James Perrott wrote from Haroldston to Secretary Nicholas
23 June 1631, in reference to his Vice Admiralty accounts—" Mr
Taverner is so just a man that he will not deny what the writer
paid. Taverner dealt then in those businesses as Mr Oldisworth
does now." He was cousin to Wm. Strode the merchant, of
Barrington, Somerset.

> 1628.   March.   Sir Miles Fleetwood Knt.
>
> Edmund Taverner.

Sir Miles Fleetwood of Ardwinkle, Northants, and Cranford,
Middlesex, was the eldest of the three sons of Sir William F. of
Cranford, Receiver of the Court of Wards, and brother to Sir
Wiliam (see 1640,) and to Sir George who was a famous General in
Sweden. He was adm. to Grays Inn 9 Jan. 1588, was Knighted
at Dublin 29 April 1602, and m. Anne dau. of Nicholas Luke of
Woodend, Beds. He sat for Westbury 1621-2, Bletchingly and
Launceston 1624, but preferred the latter till 1625, Newton (Lan-
cashire) May to Aug. 1625, and Jan. to June 1626, Woodstock
1628 to Jan. 1629, Hindon March to May 1640, and Oct. 1640 till
his death 8 March 1641. 6 Sept. 1604, Grant to Sir Miles Fleetwood in reversion after Sir William Fleetwood, of the office of
Receiver General of the Court of Wards and Liveries. 22 March
1610, Grant to Sir Miles F. of the office of Receiver General of the
Court of Wards. He thus succeeded his father in this lucrative office

in March 1610, and enjoyed it till his death in March 1641, when the office was conferred upon his brother Sir William, (see 1640). March 1610, Notes relative to the value of the manor of Greens-Norton surveyed by Sir Miles F. as under Steward of the honour of Grafton. 16 Feb. 1628, Order of Council for preparing Commissions of Martial Law and of oyer and terminer for co. Northants, addressed to Sir Miles Fleetwood, Sir Guy Palmes, and Sir John Danvers (see Oxford Univ. 1621,) Deputy Lieutenants. 9 July 1625, Grant in accomplishment of the late King's intention to Sir Miles Fleetwood, Receiver of the Court of Wards, of £5000, out of debts due in that Court.

1640.   March 12.   William Lenthall, Recorder.

Sir William Fleetwood Knt.

Sir William Fleetwood of Ardwinkle, Northants, was the 2nd son of Sir William F. and brother to the M.P. 1628. He was incorporated M.A. Oxford 13 March 1633, " as he stood at Cambridge," being then Controller of Woodstock Park. He married twice, his second wife being a Miss Harvey. He was Knighted 20 July 1624, and in May 1642 was, with John Whitton, Comptroller of Works and Surveyor of Woods at Woodstock. He must have succeeded his brother Sir Miles (see 1628) as Receiver of the Court of Wards and Liveries in March 1641, as on 11 Dec. 1643 the House of Commons resolved " That the office of Receiver of the Court of Wards be henceforth sequestered from Sir William Fleetwood." (Commons Journal.) In May 1624 he was described as late High Sheriff of Bucks. He was Cupbearer to James I and Charles I, and resumed his office to the King in 1660. Sir William was evidently a great favourite with James I, who on 23 Dec. 1624, wrote to Thomas Barley of Elmingham, Essex, " To favour Sir W. Fleetwood who intends to become a suitor to his daughter. Testifies to his discretion and good carriage. Recommends him as well fitted by birth and fortune to be a good match for her. Requests a reply." On the same day the King also wrote to Henry Wiseman, " To employ his influence with Thomas Barley to give his daughter in marriage to Sir W. Fleetwood; favours him both for his own and his father's services." He was a Col. in the royal army, a Commr. to surrender Woodstock Manor house 26 April 1646, M.P. for Woodstock March to May 1640, Oct. 1640 till void 5 Jan. 1641, and again 1661 till his death 1674, aged 71. He was assessed at £400 on 6 May 1649, and again assessed at £251 on 1 Sept. 1651. On 23 July 1646, " Col. Charles Fleetwood (see County 1654) informs the Committee for Compounding that Sir William his brother (sic, but should be father) rendered himself to him before 1 May 1646. Dec. 1, Sir William petitions to compound for delinquency. Being a servant in ordinary to His Majesty, attended him at Oxford and elsewhere. With certificate by Geo. Bowle that he is suffering from the dropsy. 14 Jan. 1647, Fine at one-sixth, £720. If it be proved that the estate is charged with £60 a year for Col. Charles Fleetwood's life, and £30 a year for Ann F., then the fine to be £585. 18 June 1649, admitted by Order of Parliament to compound on Oxford Articles. Aug. 1, Fine £510. 6 June 1650, Col. Charles F. having paid ⅓ the fine, writes that he would pay the other ⅓, but cannot go to Norfolk to find the deeds, on which he hopes an abatement for annuities to himself and a sister, being ordered Northwards ; begs delay till his return." On 30 Dec. 1661, Warrant to Sir W. Fleetwood to preserve the game about Woodstock Park, (by procurement of the Duke of Richmond.) He was Ranger there in March 1662, having succ. his uncle Sir Gerrard (see 1625,) in that office, and on 28 July 1665 wrote to Secretary Williamson, " Hopes for his company, as he is so near. Sends him half a buck." By his first wife he had two sons, Sir Miles (see the County 1656,) and Col. William Fleetwood, and by his second wife he had one son the celebrated General Charles Fleetwood, (see the County 1654.)

> 1640.   Oct. 27.   William Lenthall, Recorder. ⎫
>   Hon. William Herbert   ⎭
>
>   Sir William Fleetwood   ⎫
>   Benjamin Mericke   ⎭

This was a Double Return, but on 5 Jan. 1641, the Indenture returning Fleetwood and Mericke was taken off the file, by order of the House.

Benjamin Merrick of Woodstock, was the son of Maurice Meyrick, *alias* Owen, (born in Anglesea, M.A. and Fellow of New Coll. Oxford, Registrar of the Univ. who married a lady of New Woodstock, and d. 1640,) and brother to Sir Wm. Meyrick, M.P. Judge of the Prerogative Court of Canterbury 1641, who died 1669. He compounded with Cromwell's Commrs. for his estate at Woodstock for £35 and died 1675. (M.I. Woodstock.) " He left his dwelling and went to Oxford and resided there, while it was a garrison holden for the King against the Parliamente, and adhered to those forces, and was in Oxford at the time of the surrender." He held a messuage and lands in Woodstock in fee of yearly fee of £7   On 11 Jan. 1650 he was summoned by the Committee for Advance of Money to shew cause why a debt due to him by Harrington Davers should not be sequestered. Jan. 23, He having refused to appear, Order that he be brought up in custody to answer his contempt. Jan. 31, As Merrick has not appeared on summons, order that unless he shew cause next sitting, Davers pay to the Committee £12, balance of the debt of £20. Feb. 1650, Davers petitions that Merrick having omitted from his composition a debt of £20, owing by petitioner as executor to his late father, of which he has paid £8 as an assessment, with £1 bailiff's fees, he has, from good affection, discovered the debt, and begs to compound for it, and to have the allowance to discoverers, and also an order for Merrick to bring in the bond.

Hon. William Herbert of Wilton, Wilts, 5th son of Philip 4th Earl of Pembroke and Montgomery K. G., was born in 1621, matric. Exeter Coll. Oxford, 29 Jan. 1635, aged 13, and was created M.A. 31 Aug. 1653. Although only 19 years of age, he was in Oct. 1640 elected for three constituencies, Woodstock, Downton, and Monmouthshire, when he made his election to represent the last named. He took the Protestatem 1641, had leave of absence from the House in June and July 1641, was absent from the "Call of the House" in June 1642, and "dis abled to sit" 5 Feb. 1644, and died unmarrriad before Nov. 1644.

1640. Dec. 2. Sir Robert Pye Knt.

vice Herbert who preferred, to represent Monmouthshire. Sir Robert Pye was a prominent official personage during the reign of Charles I. He was the second son of William Pye of the Mynde, co. Hereford, and brother to Sir Walter Pye M.P., Attorney General of the Court of Wards, (see *Williams' Parl. Hist. of Wales)*. He was born in 1585, married Mary second dau. and co-heir of John Croker of Batsford, co. Gloucester, and was Knighted 13 July 1621. He was probably at first an officer in the household of the celebrated favourite George Villiers, Duke of Buckingham, through whose influence he obtained several lucrative appointments. 13 March 1617, Grant to Robert Pye of all monies above £3000 yearly arising by the imposition of 3d. in the pound on Merchant Strangers goods. 7 April 1618, Grant to Sir Richard Young and Robert Pye of the office of Clerk of the Letters Patent in Chancery. (They surrendered this office on 27 May 1627.) He became Auditor (or Remembrancer) of the Exchequer in July 1618. On 22 Jan. 1620 Chamberlain wrote to Carleton :—Lady Bingley is gone to Newmarket to solicit against her husband (Sir John's) loss of his place ʿas Remembrancer in the Court of Exchequer) for which he has a life patent, but she will fail, the place being given to Robert Pye, a creature of Buckingham. He was admitted to the Auditorship 24 Jan. 1620. On 21 Aug. 1624 the same gossiping correspondent informed Carleton that " Sir Robt. Pye is talked of as Chancellor of the Exchequer," but he never received that appointment. On 5 Nov. 1615 he was a Commr. for the Prizes brought from Plymouth, and on 18 May 1627 was made a new Commissioner for French Goods and for the sale of such as are perishable and of ships under 100 tons burden. He contributed £1000 towards the recovery of Ireland. Sir Robert purchased from the Untons the manor and estate of Farringdon, Berks, and during the Civil Wars garrisoned his mansion there for the King, when it was stoutly besieged by his eldest son Sir Robert Pye jun. Knt. His loyalty made him a marked man, and on 17 April 1643 the House resolved, " That

Sir Robert Pye and three others be enjoined to give their attendance on this House, and not to depart without leave" (*Commons
Journal*).   On the other hand the King wrote to Francis Lord
Cottington, Chancellor of the Exchequer, on 28 Oct. 1643, as
follows : —You are to sequester the office of Sir Robert Pye the
elder of Writer of the Tallies in the receipt of the Exchequer,
who upon removal of the receipt of the Exchequer to Oxford has
neglected to attend his office, and commit the same to the care
of Robert Long, (see *Williams' Gloucestershire Members*), who has
a grant of the reversion, until Sir Robert Pye shall give satisfaction to us for his contempt. He however held this office of Writer
of the Tallies in the Exchequer, which had been granted him 25
Jan. 17 James I, (1620,) until 30 Jan. 1649, when by " Act of
Parliament the kingly government is taken away." This office,
which was otherwise known as Auditor of the Exchequer, was
resumed by Sir Robert, (at the Restoration,) 25 June 1660.   He
was M.P. for Bath 1624-5, Ludgershall May to Aug, 1625, Westminster 1626, Grampound 1628-9, Woodstock Dec. 1640 till
secluded by Col. Pride's Purge and imprisoned in Dec. 1648, and
for Berks 1654-5, and 1658-9. He died 19 May 1662. His second son
John was made a Baronet 1665, which title expired 1734, while
his eldest son Sir Robert Pye jun. Knt. M.P. for Berks, married
Anne dau. of the celebrated John Hampden, and was an active
Colonel of Horse for the Parliament, but afterwards zealously
aided the Restoration.   His great great grandson Henry James
Pye M.P. for Berks was Poet Laureate 1790-1813.

1653. July. No Members were *appointed* by Cromwell
and his Officers for Woodstock, in Barebone's Parliament.

1654. July. Lieut. Gen. Charles Fleetwood.

One Member only returned for Woodstock in 1654 and
1656.   As to General Fleetwood, see the County 1654.

1656. Aug. Major General William Packer.

Packer was probably of the Berkshire family of that name,
but he cannot be identified. (Quaere the Wm. Packer of Ryegate
in 1642, and one of the Committee for Monmouthshire on 16 Oct.
1643, and an Assistant Commr. app. by Sir Thomas Fanfare for
the sale of the personal estates of Lord Worcester and others in
Ragland Castle).   He was J.P. Herts in June 1654, as Major
Packer.   There are many references to him in the *Calendar of
State Papers*, from which it appears that he was a most active
officer for Parliament.   18 March 1651, Order in Parliament that
£50 be given to Capt. Packer to buy a horse ; the Council of
State to order speedy payment.   He was M.P. for Woodstock
1656-8, and (as Wm. Parker) Hertford Jan. till unseated March
1659.   He was one of the Committee app. by the Council of State
to draft reforms and amendments of the law Jan. 1652, and in
Barebone's Parliament 1653, was placed on several Committees

relating to the army, added to the Hospitals Committee and to the Posts Committee 17 May, app one of the Committee to consider the condition of the several prisoners of war 19 May, and on 31 May he and Lt.-Col. Zanchy (see 1659) were app. with others to be a Committee to consider the state of the Savoy Hospital and Ely House, which were intended to be used as military hospitals or prisons. On 7 July 1653. Declaration that the Council (of State) is satisfied concerning the gifts and abilities of Major William Packer and others to preach the Gospel, and that the public exercise thereof will be of great use in the Church, they being eminent for godliness, and that therefore they may have free use of any pulpits to preach in. On 15 June 1654 the Council sent Col. Scrope and Major Packer to co. Gloucester to appease the business touching tobacco planting, which was causing great local uneasiness. On 4 Jan. 1656 he was added to the Committee concerning collections for the distressed Protestants in Piedmont, and on 6 Feb. following the Council decided to advise a warrant to the Lord Deputy (of Ireland, Charles Fleetwood, see the County 1654,) to depute Major W. Packer to execute in cos. Herts and Oxon all his powers of Major General and Commander in Chief, and Col. Geo. Fleetwood and the said Major W. P. jointly in co. Bucks. This advice was carried out for there are references to Packer acting as Major General of Bucks on 6 March, of the three counties on 21 March, and of Herts on 1 May 1656. Cromwell however soon abolished the almost despotic powers of these Major Generals. On 11 or 21 Feb. 1658 Secretary Thurloe wrote to Ambassador Lockhart as follows:—His Highness has spent this week about his army and made some alterations. He took notice of dissatisfaction amongst his own regiment of horse, and sending for Major Packer and the five Captains, all Anabaptists, found it as he had heard, and dfsmissed them all six from their command. After Oliver's death, the Committee of Safety and for the Nomination of Officers, when the Army gained the upper hand in June 1659, gave Packer the command of a regiment. The Rump however regained its ascendency in the autumn, and on 12 Oct. 1659 discharged Packer and other turbulent officers from all military employment. On 9 Jan. 1660, Col. Packer and others were ordered by the Council of State "to depart the Town," but as they still lingered in London, the Rump on 14 Jan. ordered the Council of State to secure Colonels Lambert, Desborow, Berry, Kelsey, Cobbett, Ashfield, Barrow, Packer, and Major Creed, and any others against whom any orders or warrants have been issued to depart the town to their respective country houses, and who have not obeyed. Packer was some time afterwards apprehended, for on 17 May 1660 the Council of State reported to the House of Commons, " that Col. Wm. Packer was committed and still in custody, which the House approved." Whether he was handed over a prisoner to the new government at the Restoration the same month, or whether he was released and again apprehended, is not clear, but at all events he was in custody on 30 Oct. 1661, when his wife Elizabeth petitioned the King, "for a speedy hearing and release of her husband, for several days confined in the Gatehouse, Westminster, and meanwhile to have access to him, he having several suits of law depending and none to look after him." On 10 Aug. 1662 she again petitions Secretary Nicholas, "to peruse her husband's first petition and mediate for his speedy trial. He has been almost 3 months in close confinement with nothing charged or proved against him; is confident that he has done nothing against His Majesty or the Kingdom's peace since the Act of Grace." A little before this, on 18 May 1662, Secretary Nicholas issued his warrant to the Warden of the Fleet to deliver Colonels Packer and Gladman to the Keeper of the Gatehouse, Westminister, and to the said Keeper of the Gatehouse to receive and keep them close prisoners. The last reference is on 2 Sept. 1662 when a warrant issued to "the Keeper of the King's Bench Prison, to deliver up Packer and Gladman to Capt. Fortescue, and to see that they are put on board the 'Colchester.'" This seems to mean that they were banished the country. After this the curtain drops upon Col. Packer.

1659.   Jan. 12.   Sir Jerome Sankey Knt.

Miles Fleetwood.

As to Miles Fleetwood, see the County 1656. *Wood* states that Hierome Zanchy of All Souls College, "lately made Fellow," was made a Proctor of Oxford Univ. in defiance of all rules 4 April 1649, and says of him :—"This Hierome Zanchy, who was born of a genteel family, was bred in Cambridge, but being more given to manly exercises than logic and philosophy, he was observed by his contemporaries to be a boisterous fellow at cudgelling and foot-ball playing, and indeed more fit in all respects to be a rude soldier than a scholar or man of polite party. In the beginning of the rebellion he threw off his gown, and took up arms for the Parliament, and soon after became a captain, a presbyterian, an independent, a preacher, and I know not what. When the war was ceased, and the King's cause declined, he obtained a fellowship of All Souls College from the committee and visitors, and was the first, or senior of those many, that were by them put into the said college in the place of loyalists ejected by them in 1648 and 1649. But before he had served the least part of his proctorship (about a month only) he returned to his military employment, went in the quality of a commander into Ireland to fight against those that were then called rebels ; and doing good service, in short time was made colonel of a regiment of horse, and as a colonel he had £474 10s per annum for his salary, besides other advantages. In 1651 and 1652 I find him commander in chief of the parliament forces in the county of Tipperary, where, as those of his party said, he did excellent service for the cause, being then a thorough-paced anabaptist. In 1658, being then a knight by the favour of Henry Cromwell, he was, by the endeavours of Colonel Charles Fleetwood, a pitiful Anabaptist, and son in law of Oliver Cromwell, chosen burgess for Woodstock, to serve in Richard's Parliament, that began at Westminster 27 Jan. that year, at which time living much as he had done some time before in the house of the said Fleetwood in Westminster, did often hold forth in conventicles among the anabaptists. It was observed then that he was a dull man, as indeed he was *ab origine*, for by his rebaptization when he went into Ireland, and his herding among the anabaptists, he did improve it to the purpose, otherwise had he continued among the presbyterians or independents, who were accounted a more ingenious sort of people, he might have improved himself perhaps in something of ingenuity. He died in Ireland about the latter end of King Charles II as I have been informed by those that knew him." " 16 Feb. 1650 the delegates of the Univ. decided to make Hierome Zanchy a D.C.L. in the beginning of the next year, but whether it was done, or that he was diplomated it appears not." A newsletter from the Parliamentary headquarters near Colchester 19 June 1648 makes mention of him as follows:—Capt. Zanchie who took Mersea Fort found 2 culverings 2 sacres, and 1 drake in it," but previously to this he had been "mentioned in despatches," for on 18 Jan. 1645 Sir William Brereton wrote from Nantwich to the Committee of both Kingdoms stating that he had " Defeated Lord Byron there. Capt. Zanchie who is a very valiant man and commands my own troop, being without any arms was wounded, but it is hoped not mortally." He afterwards served with distinction in Ireland for several years and from the *Common Journal* it appears that on " 8 April 1652 a letter from Col. Jerome Zankey of 26 of March 1652 from Clonmell, with Articles of agreement between him and the Council of War for the Parliament, and Col. O Dwyre Commander in Chief of the Irish Brigades, of 23 March 1652 were this day read etc. Resolved that a letter be written to be signed by Mr. Speaker taking notice of the good service of Col. J. Z. and giving him the thanks of Parliament.—Bills for settling lands in Ireland £200 a year on him and his heirs." He was " Knighted " by Richard Cromwell 16 Nov. 1658, and was M.P. for cos. Tipperary and Waterford in the Parliament at Westminster 1654-5, and was again so chosen Jan. 1659, but waived his election on 5 March as he elected to serve for Woodstock, for which he sat Jan. to April 1659. As Col. Jerome Sankey he represented Reigate Dec. 1656 to Jan. 1658. On 2 July 1659 " Col. Jerome Zanchy presents to the Committee for Safety and for Nomination of Officers a list of commissioned officers for the forces in Ireland, and makes a short speech." On 16 June 1659 the same Committee app. " Hierome Zanchy to have a horse regiment," and accordingly he was app. Col. of a Horse regiment in Ireland 8 July 1659, and on the royalist outbreak known as Sir George Booth's Cheshire Rising the following month, Zanchy brought over forces from Ireland, and actively aided in quelling the premature rising. "9 Sept. 1659, a letter from Col. J. Z. from Chester 6 Sept., was read. Ordered that a letter of thanks be sent to him and the forces from Ireland for their services in suppressing the rebellion in Cheshire." Soon afterwards he conveyed his troops back to Ireland, and accordingly his name does not appear in the list of officers who gave the Rump so much trouble, until the Restoration brought about a complete change of government. "4 June 1662, Cradley's information to Secretary Nicholas. There are many disaffected persons in Ireland; they boast that they have 20,000 men of whom the heads are Sir Bruce Cockram, Col. Duckinfield, Zanchy, and others."

1660. April. Sir Thomas Spencer Bart.

Edward Atkins.

Sir Thomas Spencer of Yarnton, was the only son of Sir William, whom he succeeded as 3rd Bart., and was therefore grandson of the M.P. 1604. He m. Jane dau. of Sir John Gerrard Bart. of Lamer, Herts, and sat for Woodstock April to Dec. 1660, and 1661 to Jan. 1690. He was app. by the House of Commons an Assessment Commr. for Oxon 2 March 1660, and was High Steward of Woodstock 1661-85. He died suddenly of an apoplexy at Whitfield, Northants, on 6 March 1685, aged 46 or thereabouts, and was buried with his ancestors at Yarnton, under a noble and curious monument of white marble erected to his memory, against the north wall of the south chancel.

Edward Atkins was the younger son of Sir Edward Atkins Knt., Baron of the Exchequer, of Saperton, Gloucestershire, and Cheshunt, Hunts, and was born in 1630, and m. the daughter of — Lucy, of the Strand, brother to Sir Richard Lucy Bart. He ent. Lincolns Inn 19 June 1647, was called to the bar 1653, and became Autumn Reader 1675. On 14 May 1647 he was assessed by the Committee for Advance of Money, but no proceedings were taken thereon. He was M.P. Woodstock April to Dec. 1660, Recorder 1661-2, made a Sergeant at law 7 May 1679, Knighted 26 June 1679, and was a Baron of the Exchequer 22 June 1679-86, and Lord Chief Baron of that Court 11 April 1686 till 18 April 1689, when, refusing to take the oath of allegience to William III, he was, curious to relate, succeeded by his brother Sir Robert Atkyns who differed from him in politics, (see *Williams' Worcestershire Members*). Sir Edward then withdrew to his country seat at Pickenham, Norfolk, and died in London in Oct. 1698, aged 68. His nephew Sir Robert was the Historian of Gloucestershire. Robert Atkins, the Recorder of Oxford in 1574 was of the same family.

1661.   March 21.   Sir Thomas Spencer Bart.
.   Sir William Fleetwood Knt.
1674. March 16.   Hon. Col. Thomas Howard.

vice Fleetwood (see 1640) deceased.   Col. Howard was the 2nd
son of Theophilus 2nd Earl of Suffolk.   He married at the
Hague Walbrook or Walburga Vandevall Kirkhoven, dau. of
John Vandevall lord of Helin-flete and Kirkhoven in Holland,
Chief Forester of Holland and West Friesland, (and had an only
son James who married Charlotte dau. of Charles II,)   The King
to Lord Rutherford 24 Oct. 1661, -- He is to confer the first vacant
Captaincy of Horse on Thomas Howard for faithful services
during the late rebellion.   8 Nov. 1661, Order for a warrant to
pay Wallbrook a wife of Thomas Howard a pension of £500 a year.
29 Nov. 1661, Grant to Wallbrooke wife of Thcmas Howard of a
pension of £400.   He was Col. and Capt. of the King's Company
in the King's regiment of Foot Guards in March 1664, made
Lt,-Col. and Captain of a company in the Holland Regiment (the
Old Buffs) 27 June 1665, and Lt.-Col. of the Earl of Carlisle's
Regiment of Foot 22 Jan. 1673, afterwards disbanded.   On 3
March 1665 John Carlisle wrote from Dover Castle to Williamson
—" Thomas Howard of Suffolk has this day landed," (from
Zealand).   Pass for 12 horses to Ireland for Col. T. H. 10 April 1665
25 April 1667, Reference to the Lord Treasurer on the petition of
Col. Thomas Howard for the stones and materials of Newark
Castle, and a lease of the site of the same.   In *A Seasonable
Argument for a New Parliament,* 1677, he is described as " Thos.
Howard esq. the Lord of Suffolk's brother, £400 per annum pen-
sion."   He sat for Woodstock March 1674 to Jan. 1679, and died
before 1683.

1679.   Feb. 15.   Sir Littleton Osbaldeston Bt.
                    Nicholas Baynton.

The former was the eldest son and heir of John Osbaldeston
of Chadlington, by Joan dau. of Sir Edward Littleton Knt. of
Henley, Salop, (*see Williams' Welsh Judges.*)   He was a demy of
Magdalen Coll. Oxford 1647, until ejected by the Parliamentary
Visitors 1 Aug. 1648, called to the bar at the Inner Temple 4
Nov. 1658, and was created a Baronet 25 June 1664.   He m.
Catherine dau. of Thomas Browker of Sundridge, Kent, sat for
Woodstock Feb. 1679-81, and 1685-7, and died about 1692.   The
title expired with the 5th Bart. in 1749.

His colleague and son-in-law was the 4th and youngest son
of Sir Edward Baynton Knt. of Bromham, Wilts., and matric. St.
John's Coll. Oxford 13 June 1664, aged 15.   He m. Joanna Maria
only dau. of his colleague Sir Littleton Osbaldeston, and was
M.P. Woodstock in three Parliaments Feb. 1679-81, and Chippenham 1689-90.

1679. Aug. 15. The same.
1681. Feb. 3.   Hon. Henry Bertie.   •
                 Nicholas Baynton.

As to Hon. Henry Bertie, see the City of Oxford 1685.

1685. March 11. Hon. Richard Bertie.
                  Sir Littleton Osbaldeston.

Hon. Richard Bertie of Erston, Lincolnshire, was 3rd son of Montagu 2nd Earl of Lindsey, and half-brother to the M.P. 1681. He was elected for Woodstock 1685, was a Captain in the army in 1672, and was app. Captain of an Independent Troop of Horse 18 June 1685, which was incorporated into the Earl of Peterborough's Regiment of Horse, after Sedgemoor, (now the 2nd Dragoon Guards,) but his commission was taken from him for not supporting the Court measures Nov. 1685. He died un-married in Dec. 1685, aged 50. Many of the family represented Oxfordshire and Lincolnshire constituencies, for the Berties had great Parliamentary influence.

1689. Jan. 10. Sir John Doyly Bart.   T.
                 Sir Thomas Littleton Bart.   W.

Sir John was the elder son of John D'Oyly of Chislehamp-ton, (see Oxford 1646,) and was baptised at Stadhampton in 1640, and matric. Wadham Coll. Oxford 15 June 1657. He m. Margaret dau. and co-heir of Sir Richard Cholmeley Knt. of Whitby Abbey, Yorks, was created a Baronet 7 July 1666, app. a Commr. for the regulation of Oxford City 1688, and sat for Woodstock 1689-90. He was High Sheriff of Oxfordshire 1684, and was Captain of the County Troop. Sir John died 13 April 1709, aged 68.

Sir Thomas Littleton was the younger son of Sir Thomas L. of Stoke Milburgh and Wenlock, Salop, whom he succeeded as 3rd Bart (about 13) April 1681. As a younger son he was ap-prenticed to a city merchant. but on the death of his elder brother Edward, he matric. St. Edmund's Hall, Oxford, 21 April 1665 aged 18, and was called to the bar at the Inner Temple 1681. He m. Ann dau. of Benjamin Baun of Westcoate. co. Gloucester. Sir Thomas was a distinguished official. Warrant for a Commis-sion of Prizes to Sir Thomas Littleton and six others 12 June 1689. Warrant for granting the place of Clerk of the Ordnance to Sir T. L. 19 March 1690. He was made First Commissioner of Prizes June 1689, Clerk of the Ordnance March 1690 to May 1696, a Lord of the Treasury May 1696-9, Treasurer of the Navy May 1696 until his death, also Chairman of Ways and Means (probably from Dec. 1695) to July 1698, and Speaker of the House of Commons Dec. 1698 to Nov. 1700. He was Recorder of Woodstock 1695-1709, M.P. for Woodstock 1689-1702, Castle Rising 1702-5, Chichester 1705-8, and Portsmouth Dec. 1708 until his death s.p. 1 Jan. 1710, when the title became extinct.

1690.   Feb. 19.   Sir Thomas Littleton.   W
      Thomas Wheate.   W

  Thomas Wheate of Glympton Park, only son of Thomas W. of that place, by Francis daughter of Sir Robert Jenkinson Knt. of Walcot, (see County 1654,) was created a Baronet 2 May 1696. He m. Anne dau. and co-heir of George Sawbridge of London, was H.S. Oxon 1696, and was app. a J.P. and Assistant of Banbury by the Charter of 16 July 1718.   Sir Thomas was M.P. for Woodstock 1690-5, and 1708-21, and was Storekeeper of the Ordnance March 1708 till his death 25 Aug. 1721.

1695.   Oct. 21.   Hon. James Bertie. · T
      Sir T. Littleton.   W

  Hon. James Bertie was second son of James 1st Earl of Abingdon, and was born 13 March 1673, and m. 5 Jan. 1692 (at the age of 19) the Hon. Elizabeth Willoughby dau. of George Lord Willoughby of Parham.   He sat for Woodstock 1695-1705, and for Middlesex 1710-34, (being also chosen for Westbury 1722, when he preferred Middlesex), and died at Boulogne in France in Oct. 1735.

  1698.   July 23.   The same, re-elected, 4 Jan. 1701, and 27 Nov. 1701.

  1702.   July 18.   Hon James Bertie.   T
        Sir William Glynn Bart. T

  As to Sir W. Glynn, see Oxford University 1698.

  1705.   May 11.   Hon Charles Bertie.   T
        William Cadogan.   W

  Hon Chartes Bertie was the 6th and youngest son of Robert 3rd Earl of Lindsey (being the only son by his third wife, Elizabeth daughter and sole heiress of Thomas Pope, Earl of Downe).   He was M.P. for Woodstack 1705-8, and died unmarried March 1746.   He must not be confused with his uncle Hon. Charles Bertie M.P. Stamford 1689-1711.

  The celebrated soldier William Cadogan was born in 1674, the eldest son of Henry C. barrister at law of Liscarton, co. Meath, who died in Dublin 1714, by Bridget dau. of Sir Hardress Waller. He eminently distinguished himself in the exploits of war under William III and the Duke of Marlborough, and having entered the army 4 March 1694 as Captain in the 19th Foot, from which he was transferred to the 6th Inniskilling Dragoons, and 15th Lancers, became Colonel in the army 25 April 1694, was Quarter Master General of the British Army in Flanders 1701-2, and Col. of the 5th Regiment of Horse 2 March 1703 to 20 Dec. 1712.   He was made Brigadier General 25 Aug. 1704, Major Gen. 1 Jan. 1707, Lieut. Gen. 10 Jan. 1709, and General 12 July 1717, and was Lieutenant of the Tower of London 2 Jan. 1707 to 11 Jan. 1712,

Envoy on a Special Mission to Hanover April 1716, Envoy Extraordinary and Plenipotentiary to the Hague and Brussels Oct. 1707 to Nov. 1710, and was appointed Envoy Extraordinary and Minister Plenipotentiary at the Hague 8 Oct. 1714, and remained there until March 1717, having the rank of Ambassador granted him July 1716. He was also Plenipotentiary at the Congress of Antwerp Sept. 1714 to Nov. 1715, and was M.P. for Woodstock 1705 until he was raised to the Peerage as Baron Cadogan of Reading 30 June 1716. At the general election of 1715 he unsuccessfully contested Reading. Lord Cadogan was Colonel of the Coldstream Guards 15 Oct. 1714-22, made Dep. Lieut. of Berks 30 July 1715, a Knight of the Thistle 22 June 1716, a Privy Councillor 30 March 1717, Dep. Lieut. of the Tower Hamlets, and was created Earl Cadogan 17 April 1718. He was Master of the Robes to the King 1 Aug. 1714 to July 1726, Captain and Governor of the Isle of Wight and Carisbrooke Castle 16 Sept. 1715-26, Commander in Chief of the Forces in Scotland 25 Feb. to 12 May 1716, High Steward of Reading 1716-26, Ambassador Extraordinary to the Hague 6 July 1716, and again Sept. to Nov. 1717, and May 1718 to June 1720. His Lordship was Commander in Chief of the Forces 18 June 1772 to May 1725, and also Master General of the Ordnance 22 June 1722 to May 1725, and Col. of the 1st Regiment of Foot Guards 18 June 1722 until his death 17 July 1726, at the age of 52. Lord Cadogan, who has been styled " the Duke of Marlborough's right hand," was a Lord Justice of England during the King's absence in Hanover 3 June to 28 Dec. 1723. He married Margaretta Cecilia dau. of William Munter, Counsellor of the Court of Holland, but having no son, the Earldom became extinct, but the Barony of Oakley descended by special limitation to his brother Charles Cadogan, whose son was created Earl Cadogan in 1800.

1708.	May 3.	Sir Thomas Wheate Bart.	
		William Cadogan.	
1710.	Oct. 7.	The same.	
1713.	Aug. 27.	Sir T. Wheate.	———
		W. Cadogan.	———
		Sir Thos. Sebright Bt.	———
		Vincent Oakley.	———

Sebright and Oakley petitioned against this return 3 March 1714, and the election was declared void, but on a fresh writ being issued, Wheate and Cadogan were re-elected. Sir Thomas Sanders Sebright 4th Bart. of Bidshut, Herts, was M.P. for Herts 1715 until his death 12 April 1736.

1714.	March 24.	Sir T. Wheate.
		W. Cadogan.

Re-elected, their previous election having been declared void.

1715. Jan. 24. Sir T. Wheate.
         W. Cadogan.
1716. July 2. William Clayton.   W.
vice Cadogan called to the Upper House. This Member was the only son of William Clayton, and was born in 1672, and married Charlotte sister to Lewis Dyves, of the 2nd Horse Guards. (She was Mistress of the Robes to the Queen May 1735 till the Queen's death Nov. 1737.) Mr. Clayton was app. a Clerk in the Treasury 169—, and was Paymaster of the Pensions (? 1714) to March 1718, app. Deputy Auditor of the Exchequer 1716, (to George 2nd Earl of Halifax, who died May 1739,) Auditor General to the Prince of Wales Oct. 1725 to Nov. 1726, and held office as a Lord of the Treasury (£1600 a year) March 1718 to June 1720, and July 1727 to Feb. 1742. He was M.P. for Woodstock June 1716-22, when he was defeated and petitioned, Westminster 1727-41, when unseated, Plympton Earle April 1742-7, and St. Maws 1747 till his death 29 April 1752, aged near 80. He was created Lord Sundon in the Irish Peerage 2 June 1735, and being a staunch sup,orter of Walpole, was one of those ordered to bring in the Excise Bill in 1733. He was the manager of the estates of the great Duke of Marlborough, during his absence, and to this circumstance may be attributed his political advancement.

1717. April 12. Sir Thomas Wheate.
Re-elected after appointment to an office of profit by the Crown.

1718. March 29. William Clayton
Re-elected after appointment as one of the Lords Commissioners of the Treasury.

1721. Oct. 27. Charles Crisp   ———
                    Sir Thomas Wheate   ———
vice Sir T. Wheate (the father) deceased. The son petitioned 10 Nov. 1721, but to no purpose. Charles Crisp of Dornford, H.S. Oxon 1715, sat for Woodstock Oct. 1721-2, when he lost his seat and petitioned in vain. He was the 2nd son of Sir Nicholas Crispe 1st Bart. M.P. of Westerham, Kent, and Hammersmith, (who d. Nov. 1698, and who was the grandson of the celebrated royalist merchant Sir Nicholas Crispe Knt. M.P. who d. 1666,) and succeeded his nephew as 4th Bart. 1 June 1730. He m. 1714 (? 5 May) Anne eldest and only surviving child of his great uncle Sir Thomas Crispe Knt. of London and Dornford, (H.S. Oxon. 1692,) who died 29 July 1714, having by settlement dated 21 April 1714 settled his estates of Dornford and Ludwell upon the young couple, as well as part of his personal estate 5 May 1714.

Sir Charles died 10 July 1740, when the title became extinct, his will being made 16 June 1731, and proved 1 Aug. 1740.

1722.   March 22.   Sir Thomas Wheate   ————

                   Samuel Trotman   — ——

                   Charles Crisp   ——— —

                   William Clayton   ————

Crisp and Clayton petitioned without success.

Sir Thomas Wheate was the elder of the two sons of the M.P. 1690, whom he succeeded as 2nd Bart. 25 Aug. 1721. He m. Mary dau. and co-heir of Thomas Gould of Oak End, Bucks, and sat for Woodstock 1722-7, having been an unsuccessful candidate and petitioner on his father's death in 1721. He d. s.p. May 1746, and was succeeded in the title by his brother Sir George, who was Recorder of Banbury. Their elder sister Frances married Sir Francis Page Knt., Judge of the King's Bench. The title expired with the 6th Bart. in 1816.

Samuel Trotman of Bucknell, who on account of his eccentric conduct was called "the mad Trotman," was the eldest son of Lenthall T. and grandson of Samuel T. who d. 1684. He was connected with the Fiennes family, and his ancestors had settled at Bucknell in 1638. He was born 7 and baptised 9 March 1686 at Bucknell, was called to the bar at the Inner Temple 26 June 1710, and m. 16 Oct. 1712 his cousin Dorothea elder dau. of Samuel Trotman of Syston, who was M.P. for Bath. He was M.P. for Woodstock 1722-34, and d. s. p. 2 Feb. 1748. (M. I. Bucknell.) He was succeeded in the estates by his nephew Samuel Trotman, who was High Sheriff of Oxon 1760.

1727.   Aug. 21.   William de Blandford esq. (*sic.*)   W.

                   Samuel Trotman esq.

William Godolphin, commonly called the Marquis of Blandford, was the elder or only surviving son of Francis 2nd Earl of Godolphin, (see County 1708,) by the Lady Henrietta Churchill eldest dau. of John 1st Duke of Marlborough. This Lady became Duchess of Marlborough by special limitation on her illustrious father's death 16 June 1722, when this Member, previously known as Viscount Rialton, became, by courtesy, the Marquis of Blandford. His Lordship was the first of his House to represent Woodstock. He m. 25 April 1729 Maria Catherine dau. of Peter Yong, a burgomaster of the province of Utrecht, and sister to the Countess of Denbigh. He was a member of Balliol Coll. Oxon, and was created D.C.L. 30 Aug. 1730. Lord Blandford was M.P. for Penryn June 1720-2, and for New Woodstock 1727 until his early death s.p. 24 Aug. 1731.

1732.   Jan. 22.   Hon. John Spencer.   W.

vice his cousin Lord Blandford deceased. This gentleman was the 4th and youngest son of Charles 3rd Earl of Sunderland, a distinguished statesman who was First Lord of the Treasury 1718-21, by Lady Anne Churchill 2nd dau. and co-heir of John 1st Duke of Marlborough. His eldest brother Charles became 2nd Duke of Marlborough on the death of his aunt Henrietta, Duchess of M. in her own right, on 24 Oct. 1738. John Spencer was born 13 May 1708, and m. 14 Feb. 1734 the Lady Georgina Carolina Carteret, 3rd dau. of John 1st Earl Granville K.G. three times Secretary of State. " The Dowager Duchess of Marlborough gave him on this occasion a fine house newly built at Wimbleton." He was described as of Marlborough House, and (though a Whig) voted against the Excise Bill 1733, and the Septennial Act 1734. Mr Spencer was app. Ranger of the Great and Little Park at Windsor Nov. 1744, and sat for Woodstock Jan. 1732 till his death 19 June 1746, aged 38. His son John was created Earl Spencer in 1765.

> 1734. April 24. Hon. John Spencer.
>
> James Dawkins.

James Dawkins of Over Norton, Oxon, 2nd son of Col. Richard D. of Jamaica by his 2nd wife Mrs. Eliz. Masters, matric. Magdalen Coll. Oxford 28 March 1713, aged 16, sat for Woodstock 1734-47, and died unmarried 10 May 1766. He must not be confused with his nephew James Dawkins D.C.L. born in 1723, the celebrated Eastern traveller who discovered the ruins of Palmyra and Baalbec, and was M.P. for Hindon 1754 till his death Nov. 1757.

> 1741. May 4. The same.
>
> 1744. Dec. 5. Hon. John Spencer.
>
> Re-elected after appointment as Ranger of Windsor Great Park.
>
> 1746. July 4. Hon. John Trevor.

vice Spencer deceased. He was the 2nd son of Thomas 1st Lord Trevor, Chief Justice of the Common Pleas 1701-14, and m. 31 May 1731 Elizabeth only dau. of the celebrated writer Sir Richard Steele Knt. M.P. Mr. Trevor was adm. to the Inner Temple in 1691, bar. at law 29 June 1718, Bencher 12 June 1725, Reader 1735, and Treasurer thereof 1738, K.C. 14 May 1730, and was Chief Justice of the Great Sessions for the counties of Carmarthen, Cardigan, and Pembroke for 28 years, Nov. 1724-53, and M.P. for Woodstock from July 1746 until 22 March 1753, when he vacated his Judgeship and his seat in the House on succeeding his brother Thomas in the Peerage as 3rd Baron Trevor. His Lordship, who was a Fellow of the Royal Society, died at Bath 27 Sept. 1764, and was buried in Bromham Church, Beds. His half-brother Richard was Bishop of St. David's 1744-52, and of Durham 1752-71.

216   MEMBERS FOR WOODSTOCK.

1747. June 29.   Viscount Bateman   W.
                 Hon. John Trevor.

John (Bateman) Viscount Bateman in the Peerage of Ireland, was the eldest son of William 1st Viscount Bateman, whom he succeeded ·in the title Dec. 1744. He was seated at Shobdon Court, Herefordshire, and m. 10 July 1748 Elizabeth dau. and co-heir of John Sambroke, and niece of Sir Jeffrey Sambroke Bart. of Gubbins, Herts. Lord Bateman was a well-known personage in his day. The frankness and gaiety of his disposition rendered his society peculiarly agreeable to his Sovereign. His understanding was good, but he loved pleasure of every description more than business. He was an adherent of Henry Fox in 1755, but afterwards supported Lord North. He was Lord Lieutenant and Cus. Rot. of Herefordshire July 1747-1802, a Lord of the Admiralty Dec. 1755 to Nov. 1756, made a Privy Councillor 19 Nov. 1756, and sat for Orford Jan. 1746-7, Woodstock 1747-68, and Leominster 1768-84. He was a Courtier for 35 years, holding the position of Treasurer of the King's Household Nov. 1756 to July 1757, and that of Master of the Buckhounds from July 1757 to June 1782. No other Nobleman ever held the Mastership so long as did Lord Bateman. He died s.p. 2 March 1802, when the title expired with him, having been High Steward of Leominster from Dec. 1759.

1753. March 31.   Anthony Keck.

vice Trevor called to the Upper House. Anthony Keck of Great Tew, Enstone, (quære son of Francis Keck of that place, and brother-in-law to Sir John Dutton 2nd Bart.; see *Williams' Gloucestershire Members*), was M.P. for Woodstock March 1753-67, and a Gentleman of His Majesty's Privy Chamber 1762 until his death 30 May 1767. His wife, who was aunt to the Duke of Hamilton, died 3 June 1755. He must not be confused with Anthony Keck, Serjeant-at-law, who d. 1782.

1754. April 13.   Viscount Bateman.
                Anthony Keck.

1755. Dec. 27.   Viscount Bateman, re-elected after appointment as one of the Lords Commissioners of the Admiralty.

1756. Dec 8.   Viscount Bateman, re-elected after appointment as Treasurer of the Household.

1757. July 7.   Viscount Bateman, re-elected after appointment as Master of the Buck Hounds.

1761. March 27.   Viscount Bateman.
                 Anthony Keck.

1767. June 8.   Lt. Col. Hon William Gordon.   T

vice Keck deceased. This gallant soldier was seated at Fyvie, co. Aberdeen, and was born in 1736, the 2nd son (by his third wife)

of William, 2nd Earl of Aberdeen. He became Lt. Col. 11 Oct.
1762 (on half pay late 105th Foot in 1765), Colonel in the army
on half pay 29 Aug. 1777, Major General 19 Oct. 1781, Lieut. Gen.
12 Oct. 1793, and General 9 Jan. 1798, and was Colonel of the 81st
Highlanders 1778-84, then on half pay till made Col. of the 60th
Foot 3 Oct. 1787, Col. of the 7th Foot 29 Oct. 1788, the 71st Foot
9 April 1789, and of the 21st Foot 6 Aug. 1803 until his death unmarried at Maryculter House, Aberdeen, 25 May 1816, aged 80.
General Gordon was M.P. for Woodstock June 1767-74, and for
Heytesbury 1774-80, and voted against Wilkes in 1769. Like his
colleague he was for many years a courtier, for from April 1775
to 1812, a period of 37 years, he was one of the Grooms of the
Bedchamber to the King, with a salary of £500 a year.

> 1768. March 18. Lord Robert Spencer.   T
>
> Lt. Col. Hon. William Gordon. T

As to Lord Robert Spencer, see Oxford City 1771.

> 1770. April 30. Lord Robert Spencer, re-elected after
appointment as one of the Commissioners for Trade and Plantations.

> 1771. Jan 30. John Skynner K.C.   T

vice Lord R. Spencer, who accepted the Stewardship of the Manor
of East Hendred, county Berks, and was returned for Oxford.

John Skynner was born in 1723, and was the eldest son of
John S. of London and Great Milton, and of the same family as
Matthew Skinner, Serjeant at Law (see Oxford 1734). He was
educated at Westminster School, (King's Scholar at the age of 14),
and being elected to Oxford, matriculated from Ch. Ch. 19
June 1742, aged 18, and graduated B.C.L. 27 Jan. 1751. Having
entered Lincoln's Inn 21 Nov. 1739, he was called to the bar 17
Nov. 1748, invited to the Bench 19 June and sat as a Bencher 28
Nov. 1771. He had an extensive practice on the Oxford circuit,
and was a Commr. of Bankrupts (in 1761 and) until 1768, Attorney
General of the Duchy Court of Lancaster 19 Jan. 1770 to 5 Nov.
1777, (*Patent Rolls*,) app. Recorder of Woodstock 1771, King's
Counsel Jan. 1771, Recorder of Oxford 12 April 1776 to 26 May
1797, M.P. for Woodstock Jan. 1771-7, and Second Justice of
Chester and of the counties of Flint, Denbigh and Montgomery
April 1772-7. He was Knighted 23 Nov. 1777, made a Serjeant
at law 27 Nov. 1777, and raised to the Bench as Lord Chief Baron
of the Exchequer 27 Nov. 1777, which dignified position he filled
with great credit for nearly 9 years, and on retiring from the
Bench was sworn a Privy Councillor 23 March 1787. Chief Baron
Skynner, who was a great friend of the celebrated Sir Elijah
Impey, Chief Justice of India, married 6 March 1778 Martha dau.
of Edward Burn (and his wife Margaret Davie), and dying at
Bath 26 Nov. 1805, aged 82, was buried at Great Milton with his

wife. His only daughter married the Rt. Hon. Richard Ryder
M.P., Home Secretary, brother to the Earl of Harrowby. (See
Williams' Welsh Judges).

1772. April 10. John Skymer, re-elected after being
made a Welsh Judge.

1774. Oct. 6. John Skynner   T.

William Eden   T.

This able statesman was born 3 or 4 April 1744, the 3rd
son of Sir John Eden 3rd Bart. of West Auckland, and co.
Durham, and having passed through Eton, matric. Ch. Ch. Oxford
2 April 1762, aged 17, B.A. 1765, M.A. 2 June 1768, became a
barrister at law of the Middle Temple 14 June 1768, and was
actively employed for over 30 years in the service of his country
both at home and abroad.   He was Recorder of Grantham,
Auditor of Greenwich Hospital 21 March 1771-1814, Under
Secretary of State for the Northern Department Aug. 1772 to
April 1778, a Lord of Trade and Foreign Plantations (£1000 a
year, and quite a sinecure) 15 March 1776 till the Board was
abolished in June 1782, one of the three Joint Commissioners to
treat with the American Colonies for Peace 13 April 1778 to Jan.
1779, Chief Secretary to the Lord Lieutenant for Ireland Oct.
1780 to April 1782, Under Treasurer for Ireland 21 Oct. 1780 to
April 1782, was sworn a Privy Councillor for Ireland 21 Oct.
1780, and was one of the three Joint Vice Treasurers of Ireland
9 April to 19 Dec. 1783. He was M.P. for Woodstock 1774-84,
and for Heytesbury 1784-93, app. Envoy Extraordinary and
Minister Plenipotentiary at Paris 4 Dec. 1785, and was Ambassador Extraordinary and Minister Plenipotentiary at Madrid March
1788 to June 1789, and at the Hague 28 Nov. 1789 to 29 May
1793. He was added to the Privy Council in England 7 April
1783, and was raised to the Irish Peerage as Baron Auckland 18
Nov. 1789, and also created Lord Auckland in the Peerage of
Great Britain 22 May 1793. His Lordship m. 26 Sept. 1776
Eleanor dau. of Rt. Hon. Sir Gilbert Elliot 3rd Bart. M.P., and
sister of Gilbert 1st Earl of Minto, Governor General of India
1807-13. Lord Auckland was Chancellor of Marischal College,
Aberdeen, 1796-1814, Joint Postmaster General 17 Feb. 1798 to
May 1804, and President of the Board of Trade in the Whig
Ministry of "All the Talents" 5 Feb. 1806 to 26 March 1807,
being furthermore made Joint Commissioner to arrange the
differences with the United States 20 Aug. 1806. He died 28
May 1814. One of his brothers, Sir Robert Eden, Governer of
Maryland, was made a Baronet in 1776, while his younger
brsther Frederick Morton Eden, who was also Ambassador to
Spain, was created Lord Henley in 1799.

1776. May 11. William Eden, re-elected after being app.
a Lord of the Board of Trade.

1777. Dec. 1. Viscount Parker. T.

vice Skynner raised to the Judicial Bench. George Parker, commonly called Viscount Parker, of Sherborn Castle, was the elder son of Thomas 3rd Earl of Macclesfield, and grandson of the 1st Earl, who was Lord Chancellor 1718-25. He was born 24 Feb. 1755, educated at Eton, matric. from Exeter Coll. Oxford 2 July 1773, and was created D.C.L. 28 June 1797. Lord Parker m. 25 May 1780 Mary Frances dau. and co-heir of Rev. Thomas Drake D.D. rector of Amersham, Backs, and became a Dep.-Lieut. of Oxfordshire 15 May 1778, Major of the Oxfordshire Militia 25 May 1778, and Lieut.-Col. thereof 10 Dec. 1778, and was a Lord of the Bedchamber to George Prince of Wales 27 Dec. 1780 to April 1791. He was M.P. for Woodstock Dec. 1777-84, and for Minehead 1790 till 29 Feb. 1795 when he succeeded his father as 4th Earl of Macclesfield. He was sworn a Privy Councillor 21 April 1791, and was Comptroller of the King's Household 24 April 1791 to April 1797, High Steward of Henley 1797-1842, a Lord of the Bedchamber to the King April 1797-1804, and Captain of the Yeomen of the Guard for the long period of 24 years, in spite of political changes, from 27 June 1804 to 22 Nov. 1830. His Lordship became Captain of the Watlington Troop of Oxfordshire Cavalry 20 June 1798, was President of the Board of Agriculture March 1816 to April 1818, a Vice Pres. of the Veterinary College in 1800, app. Councillor to the Queen (as Custos Personae) July 1818, and being sworn in Lord Lieutenant and Custos Rotulorum of Oxfordshire 27 March 1817, held that office until his death 20 March 1842, at the advanced age of 87.

1780. Sept. 6. Viscount Parker. T.
William Eden. T.

1783. April 9. William Eden, re-elected after appointment as Vice Treasurer of Ireland.

1784. April 1. Sir H. W. Dashwood Bart. T.
Francis Burton. T.

Francis Burton will be found under Oxford 1790. Sir Henry Watkin Dashwood of Kirklington, was the eldest son of Sir James (see County 1739,) when he succeeded as 3rd Bart 10 Nov. 1779. Born on 30 Aug. 1745, he matric. Bras. Coll. Oxford 16 April 1763, and was created M.A. *honoris causa* 29 April 1766, and D.C.L. 8 July 1773. He m. 17 July 1780 Mary Helen dau. of John Graham of Kinross, N.B., and niece to William Cheyne, Viscount Newhaven. Sir Henry unsuccessfully contested the Wigtown Burghs 1774, but gained the seat on petition 23 March 1775, and sat till 1780. He afterwards represented Woodstock for 35 years, 1784 to 1820. He was app. a Gentleman of the Privy Chamber to the King in 1783, and retained that post for the long period of 44 years, until his death at the age of 83, on 10 June 1828.

1788. July 9.   Francis Burton, re-elected after being made
Second Justice of Chester.

    1790. June 17.   Lord H. J. Spencer.   T.

                  Sir H. W. Dashwood.   T.

The talented Lord Henry John Spencer, whose premature
death cut short a most promising diplomatic career, was born on
20 Dec. 1770, the 2nd son of George 4th Duke of Marlborough,
and from Eton, matric. Ch. Ch. Oxford 14 Nov. 1787, where he
was created M.A. 18 March 1790. He was M.P. Woodstock
1790-5, and was for a short time Secretary of Lord Auckland's
(see 1774,) Embassy to the State General of the United Provinces
of Holland Nov. 1789, till app. Minister Plenipotentiary (*ad
interim*) there 7 April 1790, and he remained in that post till 1793.
He was Minister to Sweden July 1793 to March 1795, and to
Prussia from March 1795 until his death at Berlin of fever on 3
July in the same year, at the early age of 24.

    1795. Oct. 21.   Lord Lavington.   T.

vice Lord H J. Spencer deceased.   Sir Ralph Payne K.B. was the
son of Ralph Payne, Chief Justice and Governor of St. Kitts,
West Indies, where he was born 19 March 1737.   He m. 1 Sept.
1767 Frances Lambertina Christiana Charlotte Harriet Teresa
dau. of Henry Baron Kölbel of Saxony, a General in the Imperial
Service.   Sir Ralph was sometime a Member of the House of
Assembly at St. Kitts, and Chairman thereof.   After coming to
England he was M.P. for Shaftesbury 1768-71, Camelford Nov.
1776-80, Plympton 1780-4, Fowey (in a Double Return) 1790 till
unseated March 1791, and Woodstock Nov. 1795-9.   He voted
against Wilkes in 1769, being then said to be in expectation of
the Captain Generalship of the Leeward Islands   He was made
a Knight of the ·Bath 18 Feb. 1771, and was Captain General,·
Governor in Chief, and Admiral of the Leeward Islands May
1771 to Oct. 1776, and again Jan. 1799 till his death.   Sir Ralph
was one of the four Clerks of the Green Cloth (£1000 a year)
from June 1777 till the Board was abolished by Burke's Reform-
ing Act in June 1782.   He was created a Peer of Ireland as Baron
Lavington 1 Oct. 1795, and sworn a Privy Councillor 30 Oct. 1799.
His Lordship d. s.p. at his seat of government in Antigna 1 Aug.
1807, when the title expired with him.   From a Whig he became
a Tory in 1791.

    1796. May 27.   Lord Lavington   T

                  Sir H. W. Dashwood   T

    1799. Jan. 28.   Charles Moore   T

vice Lord Lavington made Governor of the Leeward Islands.
This gentleman was the 2nd son of the Right Rev. John Moore,
Archbishop of Canterbury 1783-1805, by the sister of Lord
Auckland (see 1774,) and was born at Durham 1771, and matric.

Ch. Ch. Oxford 22 Dec. 1788, aged 17, B.A. 1792, M.A. 1795. He
ent. Lincolns Inn 12 Nov. 1792. In 1800 he and two others
were app. by his father Principal Registrars of the Prerogative
Court of Canterbury, which office he enjoyed until his death in
London 14 Dec. 1826, and he was also in 1813 and 1816
Registrar of the Faculty Office. Mr. Moore who in Jan. 1805
was a Captain in the Loyal Lambeth Volunteers, sat for
Woodstock Jan. 1799-1802, and for Heytesbury Dec. 1802-6, and
again Jan. 1807-12.

1802.	July 6.	Sir H. W. Dashwood	T 91
		Charles Abbot	T 80
		William Camac	W 27

The poll was kept open 2 days, during which 107 voted.
As to Mr. Abbot, see Oxford University 1806.

1806.	Nov. 1	Sir H. W. Dashwood	T 106
		Hon. W. F. E. Eden	W 74
		Arthur Annesley	T 44

The poll only lasted 1 day. Hon. William Frederick
Elliot Eden was born 19 Jan. 1782, the eldest son of William 1st
Lord Auckland, (see 1774,) and having passed through Eton,
matric. Ch. Ch. Oxford 28 Jan. 1801. He was app. Joint
Secretary to the Commissioners to treat with the United States
of America Aug. 1806, and was M.P. for Woodstock 1806-10, and
one of the four Tellers of the Exchequer (a very lucrative
office, executed by deputy,) Sept. 1806 until his mysterious
death unmarried 19 Jan. 1810. On that day, the last on which
he was seen alive, he transacted some business in connection
with his duties as Lieut. Col. of the Westminster Volunteers, but
nothing more was heard about him until his body was discovered
in the Thames off Lambeth Palace on 25 February, five weeks
having elapsed from the time he was missed. The coroner's jury
returned a verdict of " found drowned." He was buried in the
family vault at Beckenham on 27 February.

1807. May 4. The same.

1810. March 10. Hon. George Eden T.

vice his brother Hon. W. F. E. Eden deceased. Born on 25 Aug.
1784, the 2nd but now the eldest surviving son of Lord Auckland
(see 1774,) George Eden went like his brother to Eton, and
matric. Ch. Ch. Oxford 3 May 1802, B.A. 25 Feb. 1806, M.A. 17
Dec. 1808, and a student till 1815. He ent. Lincolns Inn 7 May
1806, bar. at law 13 May 1809, but left the Society in Nov. 1814,
unsuccessfully contested Oxford 1812, but sat for Woodstock
March 1810-12, and again Nov. 1813 to 28 May 1814 when he
succeeded his father as 2nd Lord Auckland. His Lordship was
a Commissioner and Auditor of Greenwich Hospital (in succes-

sion to his father) June 1814-34. Becoming a Whig in politics he remained in opposition until Earl Grey formed his Ministry in 1830. Lord Auckland was then sworn one of the Privy Council 22 Nov. 1830, and the same day appointed Master of the Mint and President of the Board of Trade. He was then First Lord of the Admiralty 28 July to 21 Nov. 1834, and again 22 April to 12 Aug. 1835, when he accepted the responsible position of Governor General of India, which he held till 28 Feb. 1842. His Lordship was made G.C.B. 29 Aug. 1835, and created Earl of Auckland 21 Dec. 1839. He was chosen President of the Senate of University College, London, and for the third time was First Lord of the Admiralty from 7 July 1846 until his death unmarried 1 Jan. 1849, when the Earldom expired. On 14 Jan. 1834 his Lordship received the lucrative appointment of Auditor of the Receipt of the Exchequer, but the office was abolished October following. He was elected President of the Asiatic Society in June 1843.

      1812.   Oct. 5.   Sir H. W. Dashwood   T.

                       William Thornton   T.

The latter was the elder son of Major General William Thornton, 1st Foot Guards, of Brockhall, Northants, who d. 1782, and following in his father's footsteps, became Ensign in the 1st Foot Guards 6 Nov. 1778, Lieut. and Capt. 18 March 1782, and was Captain (and Lt.-Col.) of a company 25 April 1793 to 1804, Adjutant 21 Jan. 1782, (so in 1793,) Third Major of the regiment 16 April 1804-8, and Second Major thereof 15 Sept. 1808 till he retired 29 July 1812. He became Colonel in the Army 3 May 1796, Major Gen. 29 April 1802, and Lieut. Gen. 25 April 1808. Lt.-Gen. Thornton served with the Guards in Flanders, Holland, and Germany 1794-5, and was on the Staff in various parts of England 1805-8. He sat for Woodstock 1812 till Nov. 1813, when he yielded the seat to the Hon. George Eden, but succeeded that gentleman as Member June 1814-18. He died unmarried 18 Nov. 1841, being then the senior Lieut. Gen. (retired).

      1813.   Nov. 10.   Hon. George Eden

vice Thornton, who accepted the Stewardship of the Manor of East Hendred.

      1814.   June 14.   Lt.-Gen. William Thornton.

vice Eden called to the House of Lords.

      1818.   June 17.   Lord Robert Spencer   W.

                       Sir H. W. Dashwood   T.

It is an extraordinary fact that Lord Robert Spencer (as to whom see Oxford 1768,) should have been again returned for Woodstock in 1818, a period of 50 years since he had previously been elected for it in 1768.

1820.   March 7.   John Gladstone   T
                    J. H. Langston   W

James Haughton Langston will be found under Oxford 1826. He was the last of the several Members for Woodstock who also sat for the City of Oxford.

John Gladstone of Liverpool, eldest son of Thomas Gladstones of Leith, corn-merchant, was born at Leith 11 Dec. 1764, and carried on business as a corn-merchant at Liverpool from 1788 until he retired in 1843. He m. (1) 1792 Jane (who d. s.p. 1798) dau. of Joseph M. Hall of Liverpool, and (2) 29 April 1800 Ann dau. of Andrew Robertson, Provost of Dingwall, co. Ross, and Sheriff Substitute of that county. By Royal Licence 10 Feb. 1835 he formally dropped the final letter s. in the spelling of his name. He was M.P. for Lancaster 1818-20, Woodstock 1820-6, Berwick on Tweed 1826 till voided 1827, and was defeated at Queenborough 1830, and Dundee 1837. He was made a Baronet 18 July 1846, and died at Fasque, co. Kincardine 7 Dec. 1851, aged 87 all but 4 days. Sir Thomas was the proprietor of extensive plantations in the West Indies, and it was in the debate to free the slaves there without compensating the owners, that his second son the celebrated William Ewart Gladstone (see Oxford University 1847) made his " Maiden Speech," and distinguished himself by the vigorous manner in which he denounced the proposal.

1826.   June 10.   Marquis of Blandford   T   92
                    Lord Ashley   T   78
                    J. H. Langton   *W*   70
                    R. Mc William   *R*   28

The poll lasted two days. George Spencer Churchill, Marquis of Blandford, was the eldest son of George 5th Duke of Marlborough, (see the County 1790,) and was born 27 Dec. 1793, educated at Eton, and Oxford, and m. (1) 11 or 13 Jan. 1817 his cousin Lady Jane Stewart (who d. 12 Oct. 1844) eldest dau. of George 8th Earl of Galloway, and (2) in Lambeth Palace 10 June 1846 the Hon. Charlotte Augusta Flower 3rd dau. of Jeffrey 4th Viscount Ashbrook. His Lordship was made Dep. Lieut. Oxon 1 Nov. 1815, Captain West Oxford Yeomaury 22 May 1817, Dep. Lieut. Norfolk 16 Feb. 1830, M.P. Chippenham 1818-20, and Woodstock 1826-30, 1832-4, and May 1838 till he succeeded his father as 6th Duke of Marlborough and as a Prince of the Holy Roman Empire 5 March 1840. His Grace who resided at his noble seat Blenheim House, was patron of 11 livings, and High Steward of Oxford and Woodstock. He was created D.C.L. Oxford 15 June 1841, sworn in Lord Lieut. and Cus. Rot. of Oxon 27 April 1842, and was Lieut. Col. Commandant of the Oxfordshire Yeomanry 19 March 1845 until his death at Blenheim Palace 1 July 1857.

His colleague, the well-known philanthropist, Anthony Ashley Cooper, Lord Ashley, was the eldest son of Cropley 6th Earl of Shaftesbury, and was born 28 April 1801, educ. at Harrow, and matric. Ch. Ch. Oxford 27 Oct. 1819, B.A. 17 May 1823, M.A. 21 June 1832, created D.C.L. 16 June 1841. His Lordship m. 9 June 1830 Lady Emily Cowper dau. of Peter 5th Earl Cowper. He was a Commissioner of the Board of Control for the affairs of India Feb. 1828 to Nov. 1830, app. a Commissioner in Lunacy 6 Aug. 1831, and afterwards became Chairman thereof, and was Lord of the Admiralty 22 Dec. 1834 to 18 April 1835, and an Ecclesiastical Commissioner for England 29 Sept. 1841 to 18 Dec. 1847. Lord Ashley was M.P. for Woodstock 1826-30, Dorchester 1830-1, and Dorsetshire 1831 till Feb. 1846, when he vacated his seat on quitting the Conservative party on the question of the repeal of the Corn Laws, and sat as a Liberal for Bath 1847 till he succeeded his father as 7th Earl of Shaftesbury 2 June 1851. He was sworn in Lord Lieut. and Cus. Rot. of Dorset 24 June 1856, and made a Knight of the Garter 21 May 1862. Gifted with a persuasive eloquence, and fitted by birth, talent, and wealth alike, for a prominent position in the political world, Lord Shaftesbury resolutely put all personal ambition aside, and devoted his life to the amelioration of the lot of the suffering poor. This great and good man died 1 Oct. 1885, aged 84.

1828. Feb. 8. Lord Ashley, re-elected after being app. one of Commissioners for the Affairs of India.

1830. July 31.   Marquis of Blandford   T
                  Lord Charles S. Churchill   W

Two brothers. Lord Charles Spencer Churchill was the 2nd son of the 5th Duke of Marlborough (see County 1790,) and was born 3 Dec. 1794, and m. 24 Aug. 1827 Etheldred Catherine 2nd dau. of John Bennet M.P. of Pyt House, Wilts. His Lordship sat for Woodstock 1830-1, and 1835-7 when he was defeated. As Lord Charles Spencer he became Lieut. in the army 9 Sept. 1813, First Lieut. 95th Regt. 9 Dec. 1813, Captain 9 March 1815, Capt. 85th Regt. 2 June 1815, and as Lord C. S. Churchill became Captain 75th Regt. 28 Oct. 1824, Lieut. Col. in the army on half-pay 31 Nov. 1827, but retired from the service before 1836, and died 28 April 1840, aged 45.

1831. May 2.   Lord C. S. Churchill   W   81.
                Viscount Stormont   T   74.
                J. S. Buckingham   W   12.
                Charles Richardson   W   6.

Poll 1 day. Messrs. Buckingham and Richardson also polled 138 householders, but the votes were not counted, as the right of the election before the Reform Act, was in the freemen only.

James Silk Buckingham (1786-1855) was a distinguished traveller, and a clever but somewhat versatile politician. He sat for Sheffield 1832-7.

William David Murray, Viscount Stormont, eldest son of David 3rd Earl of Mansfield, was born in London 21 Feb 1806, educ. at Eton, and matric. Ch. Ch. Oxford 14 April 1823. He m. 8 April 1829 Louisa dau. of Cuthbert Ellison M.P. of Hepburn Hall, Durham, and was M.P. Aldborough (Yorks) 1830-1, Woodstock 1831-2, Norwich 1832-7, and Perthshire 1837 till he succeeded his father as 4th Earl of Mansfield (of the 1792 creation), and as Hereditary Keeper of the Palace of Scone, on 18 Feb. 1840. His Lordship was a Lord of the Treasury Dec. 1834 to April 1835, Lieut. Col. of the Stirlingshire Militia 1828-55, and patron of one living. He succeeded his grandmother Louisa Countess of Mansfield as 3rd Earl of Mansfield (of the 1776 creation) on 11 July 1843, was made a Knight of the Thistle 13 June 1843, Lord Lieut. of co. Clackmannan 1852, Dep. Lieut. co. Perth, and was app. to the post of Her Majesty's High Commissioner to the General Assembly of the Church of Scotland 1852, April 1858, and May 1859. He died "Father of the House of Lords" 2 Aug. 1898, aged 92.

The Reform Act 1832 deprived Woodstock of one of its Members, and from 1837 till 1885 every Member returned for the Borough was a Tory or Conservative.

1832.	Dec. 10.	Marquis of Blandford	T.	
1835.	Jan. 7.	Lord Charles S. Churchill	W.	
1837.	July 25.	Henry Peyton	T.	126
		Lord C. S. Churchill	*W.*	117

243 voted out of 330 registered electors. Henry Peyton was the only son of Sir Henry Peyton M P. of Doddington and Emnett, co. Cambridge, whom he succeeded as 3rd Bart. 24 Feb. 1854, was born in London 30 June 1804, educ. at Harrow, and matric. Ch. Ch. Oxford 29 April 1822. He became Cornet 1st Life Guards 1 Nov. 1824, Lieut. on half-pay 15 Aug. 1826, and was afterwards Captain Oxfordshire Yeomanry. He m. 18 April 1828 Georgiana Elizabeth 3rd dau. of Christopher Bethell-Codrington M.P. of Doddington Park, (see *Williams' Gloucestershire Members,*) and sat for Woodstock 1837 till he vacated his seat in favour of Lord Blandford May 1838. He was made Dep. Lieut. Oxon 1853, and was J.P. Bucks, and patron of Dodington, co. Camb. Sir Henry was an accomplished Whip, and a member of the Four-in-Hand Club. He died at his seat Swift's House, Bicester, 28 Feb. 1866, aged 61.

1838.	May 11.	Marquis of Blandford	T.	160.
		Lord John Churchill	*W.*	155.

vice Peyton who accepted the Stewardship of the Chiltern Hundreds, co. Bucks. The Candidates were Brothers, and the elections of 1837 and 1838 form the only instances in which a Churchill was defeated for an Oxfordshire constituency. Lord Henry John Spencer Churchill was the 4th and youngest son of the 4th Duke of Marlborough. He was born 22 Sept. 1797, became a Captain in the Royal Navy 1826, and died unmarried about 1841.

1840. March 20. Frederick Thesiger. T.

vice Lord Blandford called to the Upper House. Mr Thesiger was one of the most talented of the Members for Woodstock. Born in London on 15 July 1794, the third and youngest son of Charles Thesiger, Collector of Customs in the Island of St. Vincent, and descended from a Dresden family, he entered the Royal Navy as a midshipman on board the 'Cambrian' frigate in 1807, and was present the same year at the bombardment of Copenhagen, (where his uncle Sir Frederic Thesiger, a distinguished naval officer, was Aide de Camp to Lord Nelson.) He however retired from the service on becoming the only surviving son of his father, but on the destruction of the paternal property by the eruption of Mount Souffrier, in St. Vincent's, young Thesiger became a student of Grays Inn 5 Nov. 1813, where he was called to the bar 18 Nov. 1818, and was adm. *ad eundem* to the Inner Temple 21 May 1824. His practise increased so rapidly that in 10 years he "took silk" as a King's Counsel 7 July 1834, and was chosen a Bencher of the Inner Temple 18 Nov. 1834, Reader 1842, and Treasurer 1843. He became the recognised "leader" of the Home circuit, was created D.C.L. Oxon 8 June 1842, and unsuccessfully contested Newark when Sir Thomas Wilde (afterwards Lord Chancellor as Lord Truro) sought re-election on being made Solicitor General in Jan. 1840. He was however returned for Woodstock the following March, and sat till April 1844, when having been app. Solicitor General by Sir Robert Peel, he of course vacated his seat for Woodstock, and Lord Blandford (who was then of age) was returned in his stead, for the Family Borough. Mr. Duffield the Member for Abingdon however accepted the Chiltern Hundreds and Thesiger was returned unopposed for that seat the next month. He was Knighted 23 May 1844, Solicitor General 1844-5, Attorney General June 1845 to July 1846, and again Feb. to Dec. 1852, and M.P. for Abingdon May 1844-52, and for Stamford 1852 to Feb. 1858, when he was app. Lord High Chancellor, and raised to the Peerage as Baron Chelmsford 1 March 1858. His Lordship was added to the Privy Council 26 Feb. 1858, and sat on the Woolsack Feb. 1858 to June 1859, and again July 1866 to Feb. 1868. He m. 9 March 1822 Anna Maria youngest dau. and co-heir of William Tinling of Southampton, and was elected a Fellow of the Royal Society 19 June 1845. His Lordship died in London 5 Oct. 1878. His eldest son the 2nd Lord Chelmsford was in command of the forces that effected the conquest of Zululand in 1879, while the third son the Rt. Hon. Alfred Henry Thesiger Q.C. was Lord Justice of Appeal 1877 till his death in 1880.

1841. June 28. Frederick Thesiger.

1844. April 22. Marquis of Blandford   T

vice Thesiger app. Solicitor General Lebbaeus Charles Humfrey (afterwards a Serjeant at law) issued his address, as a Tory, from the Temple 19 April 1844, as follows :—" My excellent and valued friend Mr. Thesiger has been appointed to the office of Solicitor General, and has, consequently, vacated his seat for your Borough. Has the station which he has been called upon to fill in Her Majesty's councils rendered him less worthy to be your representative? If not, why is he not here? Is it because his seat is wanted for a young Lord just out of his teens ? Let the noble owner of Blenheim answer this question. I come to rescue you from the thraldom which your hard taskmaster would impose upon you." In spite of this spirited address Mr. Humfrey stated his intention of retiring before the show of hands was taken, alleging as a reason that he should lose by about three votes, owing to his having been late in the field. He was afterwards defeated at Northampton 1847, and Lincoln in March 1848.

John Winston Spencer-Churchill, Marquis of Blandford, was the eldest son of George 6th Duke of Marlborough, (see 1826,) and was born 2 June 1822, educ. at Eton, matric. Oriel Coll. Oxford 15 June 1840, and was created D.C.L. 7 June 1853. He was returned for Woodstock at the age of 21 in April 1844, but retired from the House 12 months afterwards. He unsuccessfully fought Middlesex 1852, and again sat for Woodstock 1847 till he succeeded his father as 7th Duke of Marlborough 1 July 1857. He became Dep. Lieut. Oxon 9 May 1842, Lord Lieut. and Cus. Rot. 24 Sept. 1857, Lieut. 1st Oxfordshire Yeomanry 27 March 1843, and Captain thereof 22 April 1847. His Grace was sworn a Privy Councillor 10 July 1866, and held office as Lord Steward of the Household 10 July 1866-7, Lord President of the Council 8 March 1867 to 9 Dec. 1868, and Lord Lieutenant of Ireland 28 Nov. 1876 to 28 April 1880, being also Grand Master of the Order of St. Patrick 12 Dec. 1876 to 28 April 1880. He was a very popular Viceroy. His Grace was elected a Knight of the Garter 23 May 1868, a Governor of the Charterhouse 4 Feb. 1870, and a Trustee of Rugby School, and was High Steward of Woodstock 1857-83. He was found dead on the floor of his bedroom at his town residence 29 Berkeley Square on 5 July 1883, aged 61.

1845. May 1. Viscount Loftus   P

vice Lord Blandford, who accepted the Chiltern Hundreds. John Henry Loftus, Viscount Loftus, was born in London 19 Jan.

1814, the eldest son of John 2nd Marquis of Ely K.P., by Anne Maria eldest dau. of Sir H. W. Dashwood Bart. (see 1784.) He matric. Ch. Ch. Oxford 24 Oct. 1832, and m. 29 Oct. 1844 Jane (who was app. a Lady of the Bedchamber to the Queen 1851,) 4th dau. of James Joseph Hope-Vere of Craigie and Blackwood, N.B., and niece of the 8th Marquis of Tweeddale. His Lordship was defeated at Gloucester 1841, but sat for Woodstock 1 May to 26 Sept. 1845, when he succeeded his father as 3rd Marquis of Ely. He was patron of 2 livings, and died in London 15 July 1857, aged 43.

1845. Dec. 18. Lord Alfred Spencer Churchill P.

vice Lord Loftus called to the Upper House. This Member was the 2nd son of the 6th Duke, and brother of the M.P. 1844. Born 24 April 1824, he became Cornet 4th Light Dragoons 1 July 1842, and Lieut. 83rd Foot 30 Jan. 1846, but retired 1848. He m. 5 Feb. 1857 Hon. Harriet Louisa Hester Gough-Calthorpe 3rd dau. of Frederick 4th Lord Calthorpe, and was app. Captain Oxfordshire Yeomanry Cavalry 1852. Major 1857, and Lieut. Col. thereof 1860 to May 1866. Lord Alfred sat for Woodstock Dec. 1845-7, and 1857-65, and was defeated at Brecon in Oct. 1866. He was J.P. and D.L. Oxon, and J.P. Middlesex, and died in 1893.

1845. July 29. Marquis of Blandford   C.

1852. July 8. ⎫
1857. March 27. ⎬ The same.

1857. July 24. Lord Alfred S. Churchill L.C.

vice his brother Lord Blandford called to the Upper House.

1859. April 29. The same.

1865. July 12. Henry Barnett   C   143.

            Mitchell Henry   L   119.

Mr. Henry was also defeated at Manchester Nov. 1867 and 1868, but sat for co. Galway Feb. 1871-85, and for the Blackfriars division of Glasgow 1885-6, when he was defeated.

Henry Barnett of Glympton Park, was the eldest son of George Henry B. of London, by Elizabeth dau. of Stratford Canning, and only sister to Viscount Stratford de Redcliffe the eminent Ambassador to Turkey. He was born 1815, elected to Eton 1829, matric. Ch. Ch. Oxford 25 Oct. 1832, aged 17, B.A. 1836, M.A. 1847, and m. 1838 Emily Anne dau. of John Stratton of Chesterton. Mr. Barnett was a London banker, J.P. and D.L. Oxon, Chairman of the Economic Life Assurance Co., and a director of the Provincial Bank of Ireland. He sat for Woodstock 1865-74, was Major Oxfordshire Yeomanry till 1866, Lieut. Col. 8 May 1866-78, and Hon. Col. of the regiment 10 July 1878 until his death 5 May 1896, aged 81.

1868.   Nov. 17.   Henry Barnett   C   502
          Hon. G. C. Brodrick L   481

The defeated candidate, the Hon. George Charles Brodrick, was born 5 May 1831, and is the 2nd son of William 7th Viscount Midleton, (Dean of Exeter and Chaplain to the Queen). He was educ. at Eton, matric. Balliol Coll. Oxford 14 March 1850, took a first class in classics 1853, and in law and modern history 1854, B.A. 1854, M.A. 1856, and was created B.C.L. and D.C.L. 1886. He also graduated L.L.B. London Univ. 1858. He entered himself a student of Lincolns Inn 23 Oct. 1856, where he was called to the bar 10 June 1859, and was elected a Fellow of Merton College 1855, and has been Warden since 1881. He is J.P. Oxon, and F.R.G.S., was a member (for Westminster) of the London School Board Nov. 1876-9, and has been a Governor of Eton College since May 1887. He unsucc. cont. co. Monmouth 1880.

1874.   Feb. 4.   Lord Randolph Churchill   C   569
          Hon. G. C. Brodrick   *L*   404

Lord Randolph Henry Spencer-Churchill, the well-known politician, who came into notice as "the Leader of the Fourth Party," while in Opposition 1880-5, was the younger of the two sons of the 7th Duke of Marlborough (see 1844,) and was born 13 Feb. 1849, entered Ch. Ch. Oxon, and matriculated from Merton Coll. Oxford 21 Oct. 1867, B.A. 1871, M.A. 1874. He m. Jan. 1874 Jenny dau. of Leonard Jerome of New York, and became J.P. and D.L. Oxon, Hon. L.L.D. Camb. 1888, was the last Member for Woodstock 1874-85, and sat for South Paddington 1885 till his death 24 Jan. 1895. Lord Randolph became immensely popular as a Conservative Democrat, and wielded great influence in the Party. He was sworn a Privy Councillor 24 June 1885, and was Secretary of State for India June 1885 to Feb. 1886, and Chancellor of the Exchequer and Leader of the House Aug. 1886 till he resigned the following December.

1880.   April 2.   Lord Randolph Churchill   C.   512
          William Hall   *L.*   452
1885.   July 3.   Lord Randolph Churchill   C.   532
          Corrie Grant   *R.*   405

His Lordship was re-elected at this date, after being app. Indian Secretary.

At the Dissolution of Parliament Nov. 1885, the provisions of the Redistribution of Seats Act 1885, came into effect whereby Woodstock was deprived of its remaining Member. The Borough had 317 registered voters in 1832, 336 (of whom 37 were "old freemen") in 1858, 1127 in 1868, and 1884 in 1884. The Mayor was the Returning Officer.

Index to the Members.

Index to the Defeated Candidates.

List of Subscribers.

Sir W. R. Anson Bart., M.P., Warden of All Souls College, Oxford.

Messrs. Asher & Co., Publishers, 13, Bedford Street, Covent Garden, London, W.C.

The Right Honourable Arthur James Balfour, M.P. (First Lord of the Treasury), 10, Downing Street, London, S.W.

W. Henry Barneby Esq,, Longworth House, Hereford.

Col. J. A. Bradney, Talycoed, Monmouth.

Albert Brassey Esq., M.P., Heythrop, Chipping Norton.

The late Right Honourable Sir Joseph William Chitty Knt. (Lord Justice of Appeal), 33, Queen's Gate Gardens, London, S.W. (2 copies).

Mrs. Emily J. Climenson, Shiplake Vicarage, Henley on Thames.

G. E. Cokayne Esq., F.S.A. (Clarenceux King of Arms), College of Arms, London, E.C. (2 copies).

Captain J. G. Cotterell, Garnons, Hereford.

The Right Honourable the Earl of Cranbrook G.C.S.I., Hemsted Park, Cranbrook, Kent.

Thomas M. Davenport Esq., M.A. (Clerk of the Peace), Headington Hall, Oxford.

J. A. Doyle Esq., M.A. Pendarren, Crickhowell, Breconshire. (2 copies).

The Library of Exeter College, Oxford.

Mr Henry Gray, Genealogical Record Office, Goldsmiths' Estate, East Acton, London, W. (6 copies).

J. Eglinton A. Gwynne Esq., F.S.A., Folkington Manor, Polegate, Sussex.

Alexander W. Hall Esq., Barton Abbey, Steeple Aston.

The Right Honourable Lord Hawkesbury F.S.A., Kirkham Abbey, York.

Major R. T. Hermon-Hodge M.P., Wyfold Court, Reading.

The Right Honourable the Earl of Jersey, Middleton Park, Bicester.

Stanley Leighton Esq., F.S.A., M.P., Sweeney Hall, Oswestry.

Sir W. Thomas Lewis Knt. and Bart., The Mardy, Aberdare.

The London Library, St. James's Square, London, S.W. (per C. T. Haghery Wright Esq., Librarian).

W. Dalziel Mackenzie Esq., Fawley Court, Henley-on-Thames.

The Honourable Sir Francis William Maclean Knt. (Chief Justice of the Supreme Court of Judicature of Bengal), Calcutta.

Falconer Madan Esq., M.A., Bodleian Library, Oxford.

Rev. John R. Magrath D.D., (Vice-Chancellor of the University 1894-8), Provost of Queen's College, Oxford.

P. Manning Esq., M.A., F.S.A., New College, Oxford.

The Right Honourable Lord Moreton, Sarsden, Chipping Norton.

G. H. Morrell Esq., M.P. Headington Hill Hall, Oxford. (2 copies).

The late Right Honourable Sir John Robert Mowbray Bart., M.P. ("Father of the House of Commons,") Warennes Wood, Mortimer, R.S.O., Berks.

Messrs. James Parker and Co., Publishers, 27, Broad Street, Oxford. (3 copies).

W. Potts Esq., Banbury.

The Reform Club, Pall Mall, London, S.W. (per Charles W. Vincent Esq., Librarian).

Sir Charles H. S. Rich, Baronet of Shirley, Levyl's Dene, Guildford.

The Right Honourable Lord Saye and Sele, Sunbury House, Reading.

R. F. Scott Esq., M.A., St. John's College, Cambridge.

The Honourable W. F. D. Smith M.P., 3, Grosvenor Place, London, S.W.

Rev. Canon E. Fiennes Trotman, Marsfield Rectory, Chippenham.

The Right Honourable Viscount Valentia, (Comptroller of Her Majesty's Houseld), 62, Pont Street, London, S.W.

R. V. Vassar-Smith Esq., Charlton Park, Cheltenham.

T. M. Joseph Watkin Esq., (Portcullis), College of Arms, London, E.C.

John Weyland Esq., Woodeaton, Oxford.

Henry T. Weyman Esq., Solicitor, Ludlow.

Rev. C. F. Wyatt M.A., Broughton Rectory, Banbury.

Works by the Same Author.

The Parliamentary History of Wales, 1541-1895, price 21/-
Herefordshire Members, 1213-1896, *(out of print)*.
Worcestershire Members, 1213-1897, price 15/-
Gloucestershire Members, 1213-1897, price 15/-
In preparation—The Welsh Judges, 1542-1830, price 5/-

These historical and genealogical studies, which practically form a new Biographical Dictionary for each County of which they treat, open up a previously unexplored branch of Family History, and have met with a most favourable reception. The intention is to give in a clear and concise form as full and exhaustive accounts as possible of the lives and achievements of the Members of Parliament, whose ranks, be it remembered, have ever been supplied from the most learned, the most valiant, and the most eminent of those who have made English History. The Author would esteem it a favour if Gentlemen interested in the matter, would kindly communicate any information in their possession dealing with such Members of their Family as have sat in Parliament, to

W. R. WILLIAMS.

Talybont, Brecknock.